THE MACCORDION FORMAT

An Integrating Mosaic of American Society

William J. Regan

Pandemic Formats
Walnut Creek, California

© 2001 William J. Regan. Printed and bound in the United States of America. All rights reserved. No part of this book may be reproduced or transmitted in any form or by any means, electronic or mechanical, including photocopying, recording, or by an information storage and retrieval system—except by a reviewer who may quote brief passages in a review to be printed in a magazine or newspaper—without permission in writing from the publisher. For information, please contact Pandemic Formats, 703 Woodwren Court, Walnut Creek, CA 94595.

Although the author and publisher have made every effort to ensure the accuracy and completeness of information contained in this book, we assume no responsibility for errors, inaccuracies, omissions, or any inconsistency herein. Any slights of people, places, or organizations are unintentional.

First printing 2001

ISBN 0-9701015-0-3

LCCN 00-133647

ATTENTION CORPORATIONS, UNIVERSITIES, COLLEGES, AND PROFESSIONAL ORGANIZATIONS: Quantity discounts are available on bulk purchases of this book for educational purposes. Special books or book excerpts can also be created to fit specific needs. For information, please contact Pandemic Formats, 703 Woodwren Court, Walnut Creek, CA 94595; ph. 925-930-7419.

THE MACCORDION FORMAT

TABLE OF CONTENTS

Preface vii

Chapter 1 **The General Education Context in Perspective**.. 1

Chapter 2 **What Is Perspective?** 17

Chapter 3 **From Boxes to Formats** 35

Chapter 4 **Early Formats in History** 55

Chapter 5 **Progress in the Search for Basic Models** 73

Chapter 6 **Emerging Formats: The Balky Struggle** 101

Chapter 7 **Building Blocks for Formats** 117

Chapter 8 **Meshing Prescriptive, Proscriptive and Descriptive Models** 141

Chapter 9 **The Metamorphosis of Macro I into the Maccordion Format** 159

Chapter 10 **Energizing the Maccordion Directly** 179

Chapter 11 **Energizing the Maccordion Indirectly** 195

Chapter 12 **The Important and Pervasive Role of Competition** 215

Chapter 13 **Principles for the Maccordion** 235

Chapter 14 **Applying Principles to the Maccordion Format** 253

Chapter 15 **More "Principling" on the Maccordion** 269

Index... 295

List of Diagrams and Figures

Diagram 1	Connections—One World or Many?	85
Diagram 2	Problem-Centered Researching and Decision Making	88
Diagram 3	Integrating Linkages in the Chain of Knowledge	108
Diagram 4	Centering the "Means" to Achievement	109
Diagram 5	Full-Circle Thinking	263
Diagram 6	The Power Matrix	273
Figure 1	The Individualized Human Structure	160
Figure 2	The Institutionalized Superstructure	162-163
Figure 3	The Maccordion Format	174-175
Figure 4	Matching Organizations to Functions and Goals	192-193
Figure 5	Family Household Units Executing Primary and Secondary Functions	198
Figure 6	Business Organizations Executing Primary and Secondary Functions	199

PREFACE

Rationale and Prologue to the Maccordion Format

For twenty-five years of teaching business administration subjects at the University of San Francisco, I had been using a highly simplified but wordy one-page version of Formats as a model of society. (In this book, "formats" stands for *frames of reference for minding action and thought systems*.) Its purposes were to provide students with an overview of our contemporary society and thus provide a better perspective of where the business institution fitted therein, and to encourage discussion into where and how all institutions must necessarily both compete and cooperate at various levels in discharging their distinctive missions.

Upon my retirement in 1990, I began to expand this model and wrote several expository chapters about it, but I didn't have any clear idea of where it could be used. The more I thought about it, the more I came to believe that the holistic model and its components might best be packaged as an introductory general-education textbook for college students. At this level, it could usefully serve as a conceptual model to provide students with a manageable or at least "graspable" overview of their contemporary society—something almost totally lacking in today's college curricula. Comparative models could then be developed to provide contrast for different cultures with alternative dynamics and organizing methodologies.

A Successful Experiment

In the late 1960s, I successfully energized several classes of students with a course-project assignment of creating in three-dimensional form their own models of society. My one-page model of society was the springboard (see Figure 3, Chapter 8). Up to three students were allowed to collaborate on any one model. The energy and excitement this experiment generated were remarkable among the 250 students involved in multiple sections of an introduction to business class. A three-night viewing was staged in the university auditorium and the academic community including students' parents and friends were invited to attend.

Coffee, punch and cookies were served as our guests munched along trying to comprehend the student versions of society.

Many of the student models inspired puzzlement and intrigue as the guests and viewers tried to follow the students' logic in how the various parts of their models functioned and interrelated with other components. Students' imaginations had come alive with wild concoctions depicting the structural elements or institutions, the functional operations and the goal directives of their usually tortured analogies. There were 6-foot-tall floor pieces, wall pieces and many free-standing pieces.

Since this was the late 1960s, there were no less than five full-sized coffins, each with a badly mangled but multi-labeled mannequin depicting the structural, functional and directional pathologies associated with the Vietnam War and the student rebellions of that decade. There were dart-throwing games, miniature baseball, basketball and football fields—even a portable toilet with all parts labeled. There was a large head of President Richard Nixon with his head filled with critical newspaper headlines predicting total gloom and doom.

Not only did students get better acquainted doing a hands-on project like this, they learned something about teamwork, collaboration, execution. Many of their models were shown regionally in a seven-minute coverage provided by a local TV station during its 10:00 P.M. news program. And, of course, the instructors provided surprise awards for superior conceptual skills, craftsmanship, artistry and aptness.

Professional Behavior Requires Overviews

But the major benefit was the implantation of a frame of reference into youthful minds providing potentially useful lifetime benefits for both general-living situations and career applications. The general premise for this assertion is that one's judgment and decision-making ability should be greatly improved when decisions are based on specifics seen in a contextual whole. This is the rationale for extended training in most professional fields, which provides overview perspectives even for those who will be narrow specialists in a restricted field. Proper diagnosis of problems surrounded by frequently ambiguous and camouflaged symptoms requires such overviews.

And the need for better overviews is at least as great for system managers in large organizations. So many long-range plans of large organizations have failed in recent decades that most of such planning today is regarded with great skepticism and might not even be attempted except to satisfy funding requirements. As organizations have grown larger, their many influences have broadened to more and more sectors of society. As the factors that must be accounted for in any strategic plan grew exponentially, it became easier and easier for planners and managers to get lost or overwhelmed in the maze of vague, unproven or ignored assumptions. This permitted their wishful thinking, emphasized by in-house politics and deadlines, to dominate complicated and too frequently cross-purposed proposals. Clearly, better planning will require better foresight than presently exists.

What Is the Right Educational Content?

Aristotle framed the basic dilemma nicely when he wrote the following (*Politics*, 1337 at 33):

> That education should be regulated by law and should be an affair of state is not to be denied, but what should be the character of this public education and how young persons should be educated, are questions which remain to be considered. As things are, there is disagreement about the subjects. For mankind are by no means agreed about the things to be taught, whether we look to virtue or the best life. Neither is it clear whether education is more concerned with intellectual or with moral virtue. The existing practice is perplexing; no one knows on what principle we should proceed—should the useful in life, or should virtue, or should higher knowledge, be the aim of our training; all three opinions have been entertained. Again, about the means there is no agreement; for different persons, starting with different ideas about the nature of virtue, naturally disagree about the practice of it.

The riddle so well articulated by Aristotle still perplexes us. Indeed, most objective assessments of achievement or accomplishment in each of the three educational directions for our collective society would probably receive unsatisfactory grades. While a very small percentage of highly accomplished individuals might rank high in all three dimensions, most of us would be lucky to be judged "fair" in any two.

How can one explain this poor educational performance? Have we spread our educational resources too broadly? Were we too ambitious in trying to educate everybody? Must we settle for "the opportunity to learn" instead of the "right to be educated"? Has modern man lost some of his interest and/or ability to concentrate on learning? Has the amount of basic information and necessary application skills increased faster than his learning capabilities? Has the wide band of diversionary activities available reduced the time available for constructive learning? Has the amount of educational content swamped or confused the traditional organizational orthodoxies and methodologies in education? Perhaps there is some truth in each of the above questions, which when compounded together contributed to our present dilemma.

Of the three levels identified by Aristotle, education for the useful life has clearly dominated in twentieth-century America. Overcoming an institutional bias strongly favoring introductory courses in "higher knowledge" or the traditional liberal arts education, vocational training in many directions grew steadily at most colleges and universities all through the twentieth century. The training for moral virtue fell between the widening institutional cracks of the family, school, church and state. This most basic level is perhaps more important for what good does the overlay of any educational concept have when too many elementary and high-school students lack fundamental training not only in academic subjects but more importantly, social civility. A wake-up call is urgently needed at this level!

In a democracy the answers to Aristotle's questions must come from the consensus among educators, educational administrators, government officials, the students themselves, their parents and the taxpaying public. Any curriculum in any school represents such a consensus built over many decades of continuous planning, improvising and adapting in trial-and-error starts and stops. The consensus for courses offered in the first two collegiate years generally supports the idea of a broad historical and ideological base.

Jumblaya?

Most people, nearly all, do not carry around in their minds any truly comprehensive model of objective society since they received no such training or education. Why should they when the idea was never even presented? What they do have in their heads is a widely varying and fascinating jumble of remembered data about people, places, events, dates, some linear technical procedures from training programs, hopes, ideas, aspirations—many with synaptic connections, many without. The more successful apparently have developed their own mental systems to classify and use central, supportive, tangential and miscellaneous information in appropriate situations.

More than two thousand years after Aristotle's time, philosopher Alfred North Whitehead expressed his exasperation with the state of educational attainment or perhaps rather with educators' inability to synthesize its multiple parts into a unified whole in the following quotation (Whitehead, pp. 528–529):

> There is only one subject matter for education, and that is Life in all its manifestations. Instead of this single unity, we offer children—Algebra, from which nothing follows; Geometry, from which nothing follows; Science, from which nothing follows; History, from which nothing follows; a Couple of Languages, never mastered; and lastly, most dreary of all, Literature, repre-

sented by plays of Shakespeare, with philological notes and short analyses of plot and character to be in substance committed to memory. Can such a list be said to represent Life, as it is known in the midst of living of it? The best that can be said of it is, that it is a rapid table of contents which a deity might run over in his mind while he was thinking of creating a world, and has not yet determined how to put it together.

That we have created such a complex society without better guiding models is awesome and a tremendous tribute to our founding fathers who laid the principled foundation of government including timely feedback from the people who made it all possible. But now the social and physical infrastructures have become so overloaded, our executive, legislative and judicial branches of government so contrived and counterproductive that we need new approaches to continue building on the basic building blocks.

A Sobering International Comparison

Derek Bok, a retired president of Harvard University, recently published a perceptive report in a book titled *The State of the Nation*. While recognizing America's strengths overall, he nevertheless concluded that "over the past few decades, America has moved ahead more slowly than most other leading countries in most areas of activity that matter to a majority of the people" (p. 387). This study, delving deeply into all existing credible sources of international statistics, identified the following areas of deficiency (pp. 406–407):

1. The high cost and limited coverage of America's healthcare system.
2. The inability of many families to provide for adequate care in the event of chronic or long-term illness in old age.
3. The exceptional risks of being victimized by violent crime.
4. The difficulty employees have in establishing any form of organization to represent their interests to employers (such as unions or work councils).
5. The limited safeguards given to workers in case of layoff or unjustified discharge.
6. The relatively high risk of suffering a job-related illness or injury.
7. The failure to meet national goals for vaccinating infants or to do more to provide adequate nutrition to small children, make quality child care or preschool opportunities widely available, or guarantee parental leave following the birth of a baby.
8. The disappointing performance of American students in math and science.

9. The lack of effective job training, vocational education, or school-to-work programs.
10. The excessive burdens of rent borne by many low-income families.
11. The existence of urban neighborhoods marked by high concentrations of poverty, high rates of unemployment, and heavy incidence of crime, drug use, and teenage pregnancy.
12. The small proportion of families rescued from poverty by government programs, including families headed by full-time workers, persons who are disabled, and persons too old to work.
13. America's comparatively modest performance in reducing pollution, and the excessive costs of many of its environmental programs.

Can we do better? Some would look to educational institutions to provide leadership but little has so far been exhibited. Unlike in most other basic institutional areas in society such as health, science, government, business, labor, and law where useful applications to large and small problems are eagerly sought through multiple layers of syntheses and integrations of all received knowledge and techniques, education persists in treating each subject as an independent whole in itself. Twenty-five years after Whitehead's previously mentioned lament was published about education's sterility, little has changed: algebra, geometry, science, history, languages, literature and the rest all continue to be treated as secular fiefdoms to be insulated against dilutive "propaganda" from neighboring disciplines. Lost in this puristic pursuit is the compounding benefits of the hybrid offspring or the leverage gained from the cross-association of relational concepts.

A Bold Blueprint for Future Higher Education

The author has attempted in this volume to lay out the rationale for an in-depth look at conceptual frames of reference as a desirable first step and basic beginning for a college education and for a more insightful and responsible participation thereafter as a citizen, parent and career participant in any contributing organization. This conceptual frame of reference, called the Maccordion Format, will visualize the structural, operational and directional components of our objective, institutionalized society. This frame of reference will incorporate innumerable more specific frames of reference that focus on the widely varying and separate institutionalized activities of modern-day life. The concept of "frames of reference" will be developed in the beginning chapters leading to development of the acronym "formats," which means "frames of reference for minding (or managing) action and thought systems." Later chapters will fuse the countless specific formats existing for nearly every organized individual and group activity into one all-encompassing format to be called the Maccordion Format, an original term derived from a metaphoric comparison.

Unlike Hegel's approach, which attempted to develop a comprehensive system for "all thought" both objective and subjective as differentiations of consciousness, this approach will concentrate on showing only the more obvious connecting relationships between and among all physical units as they both compete and cooperate in the discharge of their distinctive missions. Elements of phenomenology and other philosophical explanations may be applied later if desired.

To begin progress in the direction suggested by Whitehead, two steps are visualized:

1. The Maccordion Format as outlined in this work is suggested for all college freshmen in order to provide a comprehensive intellectual format into which all or most of their past and future objective learning can be related. It identifies the major dimensions of human interrelationships on both cooperative and competitive levels and sheds light on how the various occupational careers satisfy different needs and aspirations of the individual while contributing to the welfare of society. Thus, it can help in orienting students to make better selections on academic majors and career alternatives.

After comprehending the major outlines of the Maccordion Format through various chapter exercises and classroom discussions, students can then turn their attention to the concluding chapters discussing the role and interplay of principles and applying them to improving the ongoing dynamics of institutional and individual behavior in everyday life as reported in the media. With this grounding in both abstract and applied principles, the students will also be better prepared to look for, comprehend and understand the more important concepts in future courses while pursuing their baccalaureate degrees.

2. The Maccordion Format might also be the centerpiece of a required senior course during which each student should be required to review the Maccordion Format and write a one-hundred-page thesis (or at least a fifty-page term paper) about how their major and its component courses fit into the holistic frame of reference. Additionally, they should present their ideas on how modified execution or suggested improvements to specific parts of their majors or careers could improve or benefit society at large. Further exercises on applying principles could also be implemented.

By reviewing the overall format near the conclusion of their baccalaureate education, students would benefit from applying their own thinking to their own majors and gain better appreciation of that elusive integrating or synthesizing benefit that is now almost totally missing in today's college education.

It Ain't "Just Academic"
—It's the Real Maccordion

So much of today's educational content has been presented piecemeal without integrating linkages and without application handles that the phrases "it's only academic" or "it's just academic" have become modern cliches by which many in all fields dismiss or denigrate as irrelevant large chunks of academic learning. The basic concepts in this volume have been united into a comprehensive frame of reference by which to observe, judge and modify as needed the ongoing dynamic interplay of major forces in a complicated society. The concluding chapters on principles are regarded as the major means of comprehending and then engineering desirable change to ensure long-run progress. It is hoped the Maccordion Format and the concepts presented therein will contribute to a better understanding of what makes our society tick.

Purpose: To Stimulate Intellectual Growth

With the necessary fortitude one can master individual concepts ad infinitum in today's educational world and eventually become a competent practitioner of whatever and all without understanding the "why" or the connectedness of significant relationships. But a far more basic satisfaction comes from assembling these countless artifacts into a holistic mosaic that represents a society in its various conditions of well-being. It provides the means or the judgmental capacity to become a more learned diagnostician of society's problems.

And the personal satisfactions gained, although not measurable, are enormous. Fresh insights all through life's journey are the bright lights that keep us searching, keep us alive and young in spirit. As syndicated columnist George Will writes: "The process of learning, for which college is today's most luxurious setting, produces delightful astonishments with a wondrous prodigality. But then, all of life is littered with astonishments for adults blessed with a childlike capacity for amazement" (Will, p. A25).

It is to encourage the search for new insights over a lifetime that the Maccordion Format was conceived. It has the capability for different individuals of variously synergizing and/or cross-pollinating and/or providing significance to the many thousands of disconnected thoughts loosely maintained in our memories and file cabinets. Its potential is to restore a better balance between mind and body. To the extent that the mind has been undernourished or stifled and the body overfed through boredom, the Maccordion Format could serve usefully.

Many years ago at Stanford University when the author was awarded his doctorate of philosophy degree in business administration, he received this perceptive advice from a friendly professor: "Good luck in your career: Now you are finally free to begin your real education." At that point the seeds for the Maccordion Format were planted and its growth was erratic and randomly eclectic. It has been the happiest ride in this lifetime!

REFERENCES

Aristotle, *Politics*, 1337 at 33.

Bok, Derek, *The State of the Nation* (Cambridge, MA: Harvard University Press, 1996). Reprinted by permission of the publisher.

Whitehead, Alfred North, "Aims of Education," *Great Treasury of Western Thought*. Editors: Mortimer J. Adler and Charles Van Doren (New York: R.R. Bowker Company, 1977), pp. 528–529.

Will, George, "A Columnist's Advice to Class of '99" (*San Francisco Chronicle*, June 10, 1999, p. A25).

CHAPTER 1

The General Education Context in Perspective

College and university educators have been wrestling with relatively little success during the course of the twentieth century to find ways to distill the wisdom of history into their four-year educational programs and still leave time for occupational specialization. If the four-year mandated cycle could have been expanded to six, eight or even ten years, the pressure to consolidate so much would have been easier, but they accepted the challenge without attempting to alter the time frame.

Thomas Jefferson had planted well the idea that democracy could only survive if the masses were truly educated and responsibly involved in the running of their country. But, what does being "truly educated and responsibly involved" mean in a country dedicated to preserving individual rights and freedoms? What content mastered or what percentage of ever-increasing knowledge should be comprehended in order to be considered "truly educated"? How should evaluation examinations be administered? These and many similar questions without definitive answers suggest that we haven't even begun to address the question of "education for the masses." If the condition of being "truly educated" is considered a prerequisite to becoming "responsibly involved," shouldn't education receive a far higher priority than now exists?

The rapid industrialization and movement into the cities in the latter half of the nineteenth century provided the impetus for growth in the numbers finishing high school and contemplating the prospect of college. Elementary and secondary enrollment in public schools rose from just under seven million in 1870 to over forty-five million by 1970 with the corresponding percentages of enrolled youth aged 5 to 17 rising from

1.2 percent to 86.9 percent over the same time period (*The World Almanac*, p. 195).

For a variety of reasons, eligible young women began attending colleges and universities in rapidly increasing numbers over the course of the twentieth century thus swelling greatly the total numbers enrolled in those colleges and universities. But general education did not benefit correspondingly because the vast majority of all higher-education students were far more concerned about their personal needs such as occupational specialization, athletics and the mating game than in general education.

Since it was clearly impossible to require even the most gifted students to read any significant portion of the well-regarded classics in the short period of two years, it was necessary to provide abstracts, abridgments and consolidations of whatever the experts could agree on as the most important nucleus. Just reclaiming the lost, partly destroyed, and frequently damaged manuscripts over a 2,500-year period was a major task in itself. Translations from the original languages and subsequent editing and reediting into desirable formats for educational purposes continue today.

A Bridge Too Long?

Trying to make the abstract thoughts of Euripides, Plato, Aristotle and the rest clear to concupiscent youth anxious to live now and get on with their careers was a monumental task doomed to defeat. John Dewey probably sensed this when he advocated in his landmark book on education published in 1916 titled *Democracy and Education* that

> Both practically and philosophically, the key to the present educational situation lies in a gradual reconstruction of school materials and methods so as to utilize various forms of occupation typifying social callings, and to bring out their intellectual and moral content. The problem is not that of making the schools an adjunct to manufacture and commerce, but of utilizing the factors of immediate meaning, more connected with out-of-school experience (pp. 368–369).

Both traditional and innovative educational leaders, anxious to find ways to keep the classics in the foreground of college education but also interested in satisfying those wishing to integrate vocational training into the four-year time span, embraced the idea and thus made John Dewey the titular head of their progressive educational movement. Many combinations of general-education courses were spawned but the great growth was experienced in vocational education. Schools of business, nursing, engineering, architecture, journalism and others were introduced and prospered. It was alleged that the idea of stimulating interest in liberal education by seeing it through the eyes of vocational callings resulted in the runaway growth of vocational training while doing little or nothing to promote liberal education. Education *through* vocational training had in fact become education *for* vocational training.

It should be pointed out, however, that John Dewey's unambiguous position sought unity or harmony in the academic territorial struggle and that he was not a partisan to either liberal or vocational education:

> According to his view [that of John Dewey's], the intellectual view and the practical, the cultural and the vocational, the consummatory and the instrumental—the means of grace and the means of control—are so organically related in any satisfactory community life that nothing but harm can come from tearing them apart in school (Childs, p. 432).

Straying Away from Educational Basics

The previous section suggested that over some 2,500 years the educational bridge or educational wealth to be absorbed became too long or too complicated or too detailed to be readily acquired by increasingly diverted and disinterested youth. Dewey's proposal to restimulate interest by partially vocationalizing the curriculum may have partially succeeded in the short run of the last eighty years but it may also have led us further away from those educational basics our forefathers had emphasized, namely, the elementary three Rs of "readin', 'ritin', and 'rithmetic." These were long considered to be the essentials to understanding and progressing in any field but especially in those that emphasized the systematic growth of knowledge, generally considered to be science in all of its associated parameters.

Indeed, a quick trip to the dictionary world would reveal that in defining science, *Webster's Third New International Dictionary* (p. 2032) provided one of the more comprehensive definitions:

> 3a: accumulated and accepted knowledge that has been systematized and formulated with reference to the discovery of general truths or the operation of general laws: knowledge classified and made available in work, life, or the search for truth: comprehensive, profound, or philosophical knowledge; esp. knowledge obtained and tested through use of the scientific method.

By permission from *Webster's Third New International Dictionary*, Unabridged, 1993, by Merriam-Webster, Incorporated

What could be a more fundamental definition of education and educational goals? And which educational branch of learning has benefitted society most by sticking to its central message? Without question, it's science. The growth of knowledge applied via expanding technology has made the United States the envy of the world. So why not encourage wandering youth back into the central definition of education, the science basics and its derivative fields? Why encourage them to dilute their educations with short-lived vocational "how to's"? Surely, imaginative educators can apply their theatrics and magic to make science appear more attractive to intrigue youth. Hollywood has capitalized on this theme for decades with films such as *Star Wars*.

But over the past seventy-five years, college course curricula have expanded substantially into vocational areas and fostered the growth of many specializations. Indeed, their continued expansion has resulted in a reduction of required science courses in general-education curricula to the point where only a third of colleges and universities require students to take at least one course in the natural sciences. Since most academic administrators received their degrees in non-science fields, there is little support for recognizing the validity of science's claims for academic centrality. Like wandering sheep innocently straying into ever-new pastures blindly seeking a sort of animalistic nirvana, our intellectual leadership has succeeded in cutting all the shepherding cords of restraint to embark on self-serving missions down noncompounding trails.

With science unbelievably relegated to subservient ranking in most universities below the liberal arts and vocational studies, we can now take a look at the jousting between these latter two.

The Arguments for and Against Liberal Education

Liberal education is generally considered to be that found in the best thinking in the subjects of philosophy, history and literature. Its substance assists us in recognizing basic problems, in appreciating distinctions and interrelationships among phenomena and in comprehending or understanding ideas. Its spirit is that of inquiry, of wanting to know for the sake of knowing rather than for its benefits of application, although these will be accepted too. It seeks to answer such universal questions as: What is man? What is the good life? How can man quell or tame his animal nature and emphasize what is good?

No obvious conflict exists between liberal and practical education. They can be complementary as when an expert in educational or business methodology discovers applicable principles in the classics that support his ideas. Or conversely, a classical historian might be able to bring a lesson of history to bear on contemporary problems.

There seem to be no valid arguments against including a generous dose of liberal education into the college curriculum other than that most college-age students are not yet ready or willing to work diligently enough at accepting or understanding it. In its original form, much of it seems convoluted, abstract and irrelevant to the interests of contemporary students. Many instructors have tried mightily over the decades to bridge this gap but with limited success. Many others succeeded in getting watered-down or compromise-content courses accepted as substitutes. But when increasing numbers of students continued to avoid these strongly recommended courses, an angry establishment relabeled them as requirements for graduation, thereby encouraging more evasion.

If the long-range goal of education is to unify the world community in the name of peace and progress, however, then more attention should be paid to identifying and shoring up those principles that unite or harmonize us. Liberal education would seem to offer far more hope in this direction than vocational education.

The Time for Closing the Cultural Gap Is Now

The twenty-first century might well be the crucial testing period for a meeting of the minds between Eastern and Western thought, between Eastern and Western cultures. Either significant progress will be made in this direction or the possibility—even likelihood—of massive destruction and chaos loom large. China has opened its doors wide to Western technology but minimally to Western thought. Russia and Central Europe are struggling along trying to find the handles for increasing economic productivity and a compromise ideology.

The oil-rich countries in the Middle East use their one resource for the wherewithal to shore up their anti-West posturing. The benefits of Western technology are selectively introduced but their general position toward Western thought and ideology remains confused at best.

Clearly, Western technology is being accepted worldwide without much discussion about its impact on the ties that bind or separate us. As the instruments of technology such as transportation and communication systems draw us closer together, it would seem likely that contrary ideological positions would become more important, perhaps ultimately to stifle trade and cause other angry positions to be taken. Regularly we have witnessed technology from the West being used everywhere not only to create powerful weapons of mass destruction but to have those weapons selectively used to "solve" personal problems. This overt reality clearly suggests potentially disastrous covert possibilities.

If we perceive this situation as a threat, there would appear to be at least three major ways to address it: 1) maintain "defensive" military strength; 2) increase attention to educational means of revitalizing liberal education to help defuse the situation; or 3) dismiss the dangers as unrealistic and accept the consequences. We are now in the process of cutting back on military expenditures although there are still some congressional voices recognizing the threat. The higher-education establishment has not improved its potential contribution to the matrix while the general public seems content to permit the country to coast on its Western leadership laurels and dismiss the potential threat.

Advancing technology has a built-in growth momentum far greater than any ascribable to the growth in the understanding of ideological differences that divide us from other cultures. Indeed, our comprehension of other cultures in the short run seems to be supported mainly by the continuing growth of tourism on a pleasure-bent and shallow basis and in the long run by the much slower process of cultural diffusion. At some point in the future this gap may boomerang back on us such that the technology spear that we helped to launch on the world may come back to harpoon us as in persistent terrorist attacks. Fortunately, there is still an indeterminate time left to close the ideological gap. But new tools will be needed and the time remaining, though perhaps indeterminate, may be shrinking relatively because of the rapid growth of technology and weapons of mass destruction.

The Arguments For and Against Vocational Education

The arguments for vocational education are nearsighted but compelling. We are still committed to the idea that every able-bodied person should earn his own living through useful work. The age of specialization has made useful work far more complicated than formerly. It now requires specialized training, lengthier preparations, and more on-the-job training plus midlife training than ever before. Many are now so consumed by the prospect, challenge and rewards of vocational education that they regard liberal education as a waste of time. The pragmatic rewards of successful vocational training may be conspicuous when compared to those achieved through liberal-arts education. And since vocational training promises to provide greater economic benefits, it reinforces the strong hold that materialism has already achieved in our culture.

Perhaps the arguments against the dominant position of vocational education in our culture were best presented by Robert Maynard Hutchins when he wrote the following:

> Vocationalism, scientism, and specialism can at the most assist our people to earn a living and thus maintain the economy of the United States. They cannot contribute to the much more important elements of national strength: trained intelligence, the understanding of the nation's ideals, and devotion to them. Nor can they contribute to the growth of a community in this country. They are divisive rather than unifying forces (Hutchins, pp. 61–62).

A Significant Contribution

The author of the above quotation, Robert Maynard Hutchins, was in 1951 the Chancellor of the University of Chicago and the editor-in-chief of the *Great Books of the Western World*, a movement in which he, Mortimer Adler and other leading intellectuals cooperated in the monumental task of identifying and organizing the format for the collection and publication of those carefully selected books that contributed most to *The Great Conversation* over the preceding 2,500 years. In order to help tie all of the fifty-four volumes together, a two-volume *Syntopicon* was developed with some 202 broad themes ranging from angel and animal to wisdom and world to help guide the reader with special interests into weaving his own mosaic from the best thinking of the Western world.

Realizing that college-age youth were not generally mature enough to appreciate the philosophical wisdom contained therein, the group aimed the educational challenge at the adult population with a ten-year suggested reading program, starting with Plato in volume 7 and ending with Freud in volume 54. There was instant acclaim as reading and discussion groups started all around the country, many of which continue to this day.

Given the strength of symbolism especially in a materialistically dominated culture, one can wonder why a prestigious graduate degree, say the MGB for Master of Great Books, was not promulgated and provided as a goal for those still needing incentive to begin, persevere or finish the great crusade. A timely and provocative question could provide the yearly test for degree seekers and a thirty-page response might be the means by which the top 20 percent or so of applicants earned advanced degrees. A yearly or more frequent publication could reprint the winning essays and thereby contribute to a national debate on significant issues.

Rationale for promoting liberal thought in *The Great Books of the Western World* as opposed to the vocationalism that already was well-entrenched included the following arguments from *The Great Conversation*:

1. The reiteration of slogans, the distortion of the news, the great storm of propaganda that beats on the citizen twenty four hours a day all his life long mean either that democracy must fall prey to the loudest and most persistent propagandists or that the people must save themselves by strengthening their minds so that they can appraise the issues for themselves (p. xiii).

2. Is not the study of occupations the way to hasten the disintegration of such community as still remains, through emphasizing our individuality at the expense of our common humanity (p. 15)?

3. This set of books explodes sociological determinism, because it shows that no age speaks with a single voice. No society so determines intellectual activity that there can be no major intellectual

disagreements in it. The conservative and the radical, the practical man and the theoretician, the idealist and the realist will be found in every society, many of them conducting the same kind of arguments that are carried on today (p. 9).

4. His book [referring to John Dewey's *Democracy and Education*] is a noble, generous effort to solve this *humanization of work dilemma* and other social problems through the educational system. Unfortunately, the methods he proposed would not solve these problems; they would merely destroy the educational system (p. 15).

5. If we are to take the assembly line as the characteristic feature of Western industry, we must regard industrialization as at best a mixed blessing. The monotony, impersonality, and uncreativeness of such work supply strong justification for the movement toward a steady reduction in the hours of labor. But what if the time that is gained for life off the assembly line is wasted, as much of it is today, in pursuits that can only be described as subhuman (p. 22)?

6. Many claims can be made for the American people; but nobody would think of claiming that they can read, write, and figure. Still less would it be maintained that they understand the tradition of the West, the tradition in which they live. The products of American high schools are illiterate; and a degree from a famous college or university is no guarantee that the graduate is in any better case. One of the most remarkable features of American society is that the difference between the "uneducated" and the "educated" is so slight (pp. 44–45).

7. It is impossible to believe that men can long be satisfied with the kind of recreations that now occupy the bulk of their free time. After all, they are men. Man, though an animal, is not all animal. He is rational, and he cannot live by animal gratifications alone; still less by amusements that animals have too much sense to indulge in. A man must use his mind; he must feel that he is doing something that will develop his highest powers and contribute to the development of his fellow men, or he will cease to be a man (p. 53).

8. I do not believe that industrialization and democracy are inherently opposed. But they are in actual practice opposed unless the gap between them is bridged by liberal education for all. That mechanization which tends to reduce a man to a robot also supplies the economic base and the leisure that will enable him to get a liberal education and to become truly a man (p. 23).

And the Divide Remains

Although Hutchins ameliorated his anti-vocationalism stance in the last quotation above by recognizing the complementarity of liberal and vocational education, his posture generally was staunchly pro liberal. And there remains to this day varying amounts of skepticism by each group, campus by campus, as it questions the worthiness of the other. This skepticism can broaden into positive antagonism elsewhere such as at Oxford University in 1996 where a thirty-five-million-dollar donation to establish a new business school was met with a flurry of strong opposition from the traditional educational establishment causing Oxford's parliament to have serious second thoughts about its plans for business education. One don called management studies "a phony academic subject, a shallow contemporary shibboleth promoting a noxious cant" (Micklethwait and Woodridge, p. A14).

Fortunately, some more kindly philosophers have been big enough to offer synthetic analyses of this split and John Dewey's position. One of these was Alfred North Whitehead, an acknowledged philosophic leader of the twentieth century. In the following commentary he offers suggestions that comprehend the whole and at the same time contribute to the current and future dialogue between the East and the West. According to Whitehead (p. 477):

> John Dewey is to be classed among those men who have made philosophic thought relevant to the needs of their own day. In the performance of this function he is to be classed with the ancient stoics, with Augustine, with Aquinas, with Francis Bacon, with Descartes, with Locke, with Auguste Comte.... As a result of their activities the social systems of their times received an impulse of enlightenment, enabling them more fully to achieve such high purposes as were possible.
>
> He has disclosed great ideas relevant to the functioning of the social system. The magnitude of this achievement is to be estimated by reference to the future. For many generations the North American continent will be the living centre of human civilization. Thought and action will derive from it, and refer to it.

Whitehead was prescient. While it is still too early to judge the magnitude of the achievement still in process, observe how many foreign students have already and still continue to come to colleges and universities in the United States, many from those cultures with strong Eastern orientations. Some significant percentage of these have already become leaders in their native countries and have displayed a friendlier or at least more knowledgeable orientation toward the United States thus making the potentials of harmonious dialogue more possible.

Regarding the latent but occasionally visible hostility between the academic groups favoring dominant vocational education, Whitehead wrote the following:

> Nothing is more curious than the self-satisfied dogmatism with which mankind at each period of its history cherishes the delusion of the finality of its existing modes of knowledge. At this moment scientists and skeptics are the leading dogmatists. Advance in detail is admitted: fundamental novelty is barred. This dogmatic common sense is the death of philosophic adventure. The Universe is vast (p. 478).

The Symbiotic Relationship Between General and Special Education

A few thinkers have made perceptive connections between the two diverse but not opposed emphases in education. John Stuart Mill saw them as complementary (p. 527):

> Men are men before they are lawyers, or physicians, or merchants, or manufacturers, and if you make them capable and sensible men, they will make themselves capable and sensible lawyers or physicians. What professional men should carry away with them from an University, is not professional knowledge, but that which should direct the use of their professional knowledge, and bring the light of general culture to illuminate the technicalities of a special pursuit. Men may be competent lawyers without general education to make them philosophic lawyers—who demand, and are capable of apprehending principles, instead of merely cramming their memories with details.

Needed Now: Education to Bridge the Gap

We can now reach a tentative conclusion that liberal education and vocational education are not so much opposed as that each pursues different ends and that the academic time frame is inadequate to do justice to both. Does this mean that the college or university years should be devoted to career preparation only and that the liberal education should come later as proposed by advocates of *The Great Conversation?*

Not at all. It is the thesis of this book that ways can be found to conceptualize our society that will enable students to enhance their appreciation of both liberal and vocational education. It will not immediately or directly enable us to ameliorate our cultural differences with the East but it will provide us with a better understanding of our Western society that will enable us to engage in a more knowledgeable and constructive dialogue whenever Eastern leadership is ready. And the overview it provides can improve one's perspective for vocational education. Unfortunately, it will take a whole book to deliver this concept in an orderly way. We begin by looking at the existing situation for general education at selected colleges in the United States.

Searching for Possible Answers

To review the content of courses taught in various colleges and universities throughout the United States, many recent college catalogs were examined to see how the master formats concept to be presented later might fit into a general-education curriculum. The college most renowned for its staunch adherence to a liberal-arts curriculum is probably St. John's in Annapolis, Maryland. Founded in 1696, St. John's is one of the few colleges in the United States that restricts its offerings to a four-year liberal-arts program based on reading and small seminar discussions of the seminal works of Western civilization. As written in the St. John's College brochure (p. 5), the rationale for liberal education lies in rediscovering

> ... what our ancestors knew: that behind the practical lies theory, that true utility depends on distinguishing means from ends, that economic goods are the means to life but not its sufficient end. In pursuing the useful arts, we have been led back to the liberal arts: the arts of apprehending, understanding, and knowing. It was to teach these higher, and exclusively human, arts that our ancestors founded and endowed the "college of liberal arts".... It is only by discipline in these arts that spiritual, moral, and civil liberties can be achieved and preserved.

Limiting its enrollment to a maximum of four hundred students on both its Annapolis and Santa Fe, New Mexico, campuses, it carries the torch high for liberal education.

While no doubt admiring the courage of St. John's, most other colleges and universities have compromised to include both liberal arts in the first two years and some kinds of preparation for vocational careers in the last two years of their four-year degree programs. *The Swarthmore College Bulletin for 1995–1996* suggests two principles for a liberal education. One is the *principle of depth:* "To make the most of a liberal education, each student must go far enough to grasp systemic connections within a field, to see how fundamental principles combine to make intelligible a range of subordinate principles or phenomena." The *principle of diversity* is needed, the *Bulletin* continues, "to make the most of a liberal education, each student must compare and contrast different methods of inquiry...and so that he can have the experience of making the bright spark of connection leap across wide gaps" (p. 60).

Elaborating further, the *Swarthmore Bulletin* continues: "What we are proposing is a curriculum that leans rather sharply toward specialized diversity and away from uniform generality.... Our emphasis is on serious encounters with special topics and problems at a comparatively high level of competence, and on student programs that reflect individual constellations of diversified interests."

Extensive Education Before Intensive

Most college and university catalogs that were reviewed agreed generally on the broad or "extensive" emphasis and requirements in the first two years and the narrower or "intensive" requirements in the junior and senior years. Little was discovered about the desirability of a fourth-year synthesizing course attempting to recap or integrate the major concepts covered in the preceding three years. The idea is discussed here and there but since we don't have any ready-made integrating tools, the reigning philosophy is to let the students synthesize for themselves if they care to. Analysis has long served as the cutting edge of progress and early became the obsession of academicians. And after all, they rationalized, experience is the best teacher for showing how anything is put together.

Nowhere was found an introductory course attempting to model or holistically present society as it is or was or could be. No single course was focused on the notion of attempting to integrate or conceptualize into a coherent whole the necessary components of either a simple or complex society. The more ambitious attempts to provide basic depth and breadth in the early collegiate years combined several courses into a sequential series. The 1995–1996 Colgate University Catalog (p. 35) requires four courses in sequence to satisfy its general-education requirements. GNED 101, Roots of Western Civilization, and GNED 102, Modern Experience in the West, comprise the required courses in tier I. In Tier II, students may select a course from a list of approved courses focusing on a single non-Western country or area culture. The third-tier required course may be taken in the third or fourth year after completing the preceding three courses. Students may select one team-taught course from an approved list to explore some problems of contemporary society from a perspective not limited to methods of a single discipline. Thus, it appears that a broad historical sweep provides the context to appraise contemporary social problems.

And Out in the West...

The 1993–1994 Pitzer College Catalog requires a minimum four-course introductory exploration of social issues and cultures. Individually designed, "each program will bring together the perspectives of at least two disciplines and will explore both another culture and a particular social issue" (p. 10). This plan attempts to combine interdisciplinary perspectives and intercultural understandings while focusing on social and ethical issues.

The 1995–1997 General Catalog for the University of California at Los Angeles identifies 111 different bachelor of arts and bachelor of science degrees plus nineteen other special programs that can be taken jointly with an approved major. Its general education requirements included one course in math or statistics or an introductory course in computers, two courses from different departments in the physical or biological sciences, three courses from the social sciences, and three courses from humanities with a wide selection from the arts, culture and civilization, literature, and philosophy and religion.

Stanford University had been well regarded for its introductory courses in Western civilization until they came under heavy criticism in the 1980s. After much discussion and compromise, the new program outlined in the 1995–1996 Bulletin contains no mention of Western civilization as such. The concept of distribution requirements for students entering after 1991 consists of "…eleven courses certified for this purpose in nine areas with three sequential courses in the Program in Cultures, Ideas and Values and one course in each of eight other subject areas that together embrace all areas of the Undergraduate Curriculum. One of those must also be certified as concentrating on Gender Studies." These requirements "…are also intended to introduce students to the major social, historical, cultural, and intellectual forces that shape the contemporary world" (p. 29).

If indeed we are interested in all those forces shaping the contemporary world, might it not be advisable to start with a model or format of that contemporary world that was so shaped?

Simplifying the Model of Talcott Parsons

Of course, the idea of holistic models to portray the essential functionality of interacting social systems within a society has occurred to earlier cultural anthropologists, sociologists and other synthesizing social scientists. Foremost and latest among these was Talcott Parsons. In the 1940s he developed a structural-functional concept to simplify the modeling of the organizational complexities of a society. Trained in economics and sociology, he came to believe that both economic and sociological theory should be conceived as standing within some kind of theoretical matrix.

Parson's approach was based on a four-function paradigm positing that every social system must confront and solve the following four sets of organizational requirements: adaptation, goal attainment, integration and latent pattern maintenance. Three main levels were distinguished in each functional sector: primary-technical or direct interactional, managerial or formal organizational and institutional or super managerial.

Society itself was viewed as the system at the highest level, which served to link the various institutions together. The result was a three-dimensional model of developed societies where differentiation must be seen in both horizontal and vertical relationships. Complicating easy comprehension of this model is the dynamic that social systems tend to become more complexly organized and specialized over time in such variegated ways that the four-function system can only partly portray. In addition, Parson's model does not emphasize enough the role of goal setting and achievement in providing direction for the structure-function interaction.

Desperately needed, but still unrecognized, at the beginning of one's college education, is the explication of a more simplistic model, comprehensive enough, and yet far more easily understood than Parson's more abstract, comprehensive and inclusive model.

If You Don't Know Where You're Going…

It is probably not surprising to find little or no use of modeling to convey basic thought structures since communication has traditionally relied on sequential thoughts expressed in words, sentences and paragraphs, chapters and books. Even the language of music uses sequential symbolism. Perhaps the conductor's score of a musical composition showing all of the parts for various instruments or voices comes closest to a conceptual model for a leadership role.

That one picture is worth a thousand words seems to apply more to cartoons and comics than to visualizing aggregated complexities. Graphs, engineering blueprints, maps and diagrams all have their acknowledged usefulness. Students have constructed United Nations models ever since that organization was founded in San Francisco in 1946. Many varieties of celestial globes depict the heavenly bodies in various ways to enable easier comprehension. No doubt there are other applications of visual models being used to show relationships of interdependent parts in both static and dynamic modes.

Consider, for example, how useful the ordinary terrestrial globe is. By depicting the whole surface of the earth in ordered latitudes and longitudes, we can easily find any particular location and at the same time retain the perspective of the whole in relation to the particular. Note, for example, the attention paid to getting from place to place by traveling the shortest distances in miles or by spending the least time. Road maps provide both distances in miles and average travel times between major locations thus making transportation more efficient for all who use the information. It is this way of seeing the specific in relation to its whole that is important. Without a comprehensive view of the whole, individual decisions and operations made in partial or total isolation from the entire contextual configuration can and frequently are incomplete, inaccurate, inefficient, ineffective or in some way counterproductive to the intent desired.

The Blind Leading the Blind

When this occurs, it becomes easier to get lost in social space as contrasted with finding one's way in physical space. Without holistic models to help provide guidance, the unintended consequences of most legislation either destroy or variously limit their beneficial intents. Not only must architects, engineers and builders use detailed blueprint plans and specifications for every building construction undertaken, we now enforce environmental impact studies to assure that proposed new construction blends harmoniously or least annoyingly into its local setting. No such tools exist to aid planning in legislating social improvements. We must rely on the "wisdom" or experience of our elected officials, few of whom have any idea of a holistic model to guide them.

The advent of spreadsheets in computer usage gave rise to another kind of simulated model in which many variations of "what if" scenarios can be played out incorporating many different assumptions. They can become excessively complicated, however, as computer capacity to handle data has become practically inexhaustible. Of course, it is easier to depict and comprehend space and spatial dimensions in a model than it is to arrange words in a visual order other than sequentially. Indeed, the word models to be described shortly are very clumsy aggregations of classifications juxtapositioned sequentially. But they do represent a start, a beginning. Perhaps the advent of interactive television and virtual reality programming will be able to develop holographic three-dimensional models far superior to my earlier classroom experiment that are easier to comprehend and manipulate.

Throughout this examination of introductory courses for general education, frequent use of the word "perspective" was found. Since this is what formats and modeling are trying to provide, let's next examine its derivation and meanings.

REFERENCES

Childs, John, "The Educational Philosophy of John Dewey," in *The Philosophy of John Dewey*, volume I of The Library of Living Philosophers. Editor: Paul Arthur Schilpp (Menasha, Wisconsin: George Banta Publishing Company, 1939).

Dewey, John, *Democracy and Education* (New York: The Macmillan Company, 1916).

Hutchins, Robert Maynard, *The Great Conversation* (Chicago: The Encyclopaedia Britannica, 1951).

Mill, John Stuart, "Inaugural Address at St. Andrews," in *Great Treasury of Western Thought*, Editors: Mortimer J. Adler and Charles Van Doren (New York and London: R.R. Bowker Company, 1977).

Micklethwait, John and Adrian Woolridge, "Oxford Dons vs. Management Gurus," *The Wall Street Journal*, November 8, 1996, p. A14.

Webster's Third New International Dictionary (Springfield, Massachusetts: G. and C. Merriam Company, 1981).

Whitehead, Alfred North, "John Dewey and His Influence," in *The Philosophy of John Dewey*, volume I of The Library of Living Philosophers. Editor: Paul Arthur Schilpp (Menasha, Wisconsin: George Banta Publishing Company, 1939).

The World Almanac (New York: Newspaper Enterprise Association, 1986).

CHAPTER 2
What Is Perspective?

Two of the major purposes of general education are to provide that historical overview of history that will enable us not only to extend the "civilizing process" generally but also help us both individually and collectively avoid or at least anticipate and thereby lessen the destructive impact of natural and behavioral catastrophes that occurred in the past. Because this panoramic view is so highly regarded in providing a general context within which specialized functions are organized and activated, it is important to examine the term "perspective" carefully. Not that we seem to have benefitted so much from past experience or reflection but the potential for doing so is still there when we are ready.

Consultation with several dictionaries suggests that it is

1. ...a method of representing solid objects on a plane surface, as they would appear to an observer's eye when viewed from a given point (*Van Nostrand's Scientific Encyclopedia*, p. 1734).
2. Any of various techniques for representing three-dimensional objects and depth relationships on a two dimensional surface (*American Heritage Illustrated Encyclopedic Dictionary*, p.1126).
3. The relation or proportion in which the parts of a subject are viewed by the mind: the aspect of a matter or object of thought, as perceived from a particular mental "point of view"; and "in epistemology, the perspective predicament, the limited though real viewpoint of the individual; the plight of being confined to the experience of only part of actuality" (*Oxford English Dictionary*, pp. 606–607).
4. The relationship of aspects of a subject to each other and to a whole: *a perspective of history: a need to view the problem in the proper perspective* (*American Heritage Dictionary of the English Language*, p. 1352).

From the Latin *perspicere*, perspective meant literally to see through or into. The term was used extensively by such as Aristotle, Chaucer, Bacon, Shakespeare and many others. Creation of the first celestial globe has been credited to astronomers of ancient Mesopotamia, Egypt and Greece. The first terrestrial globe was invented by a Greek astronomer in the second century B.C. The first modern globe was constructed in 1492 by a German, Martin Benhaim. Large wall maps have long served usefully to help us conceptualize the spatial relationships of the oceans, continents and countries therein.

While the concept of perspective has long been available and was frequently used by thinkers and writers of all descriptions, its direct and most useful applications remained in scientific fields. Perceptive writers understood the meaning of the term perspective but were limited to sequential words, phrases, sentences and paragraphs to provide it through contrast, comparison and other syllogistic techniques.

Contemporary Adaptations of Perspective

Artists in the recent past have capitalized on the "particular point of view" dimension in which a picture or figure is constructed so as to produce some fantastic effect such as appearing distorted or convoluted except from one particular point of view. Picasso, Salvador Dali, Alexander Calder and others started new schools of painting with this technique. The concept of perspective has been applied to sound as well with an apparent spatial distribution in perceived sound now greatly modified by electronic enhancement. Seemingly endless combinations and special emphases of melody, harmony, rhythm and timbre continue to capture the imaginations of youth and others seeking refreshing musical sound. Many future adaptations of perspective await us with the further development of its various dimensions in aerial, isometric, linear, parallel, oblique and conical modifications.

Perspective in Daily Life

A kind of perspective is sought almost automatically in many ways in the daily living cycle as a sort of reflex or balancing action such as stretching after a long period of confinement or being cooped up in one position. Dogs and cats do it after hours of sleeping. It provides healthy reactions to the continuous activities of daily life that without such relief often lead to either excessive boredom on the job or stressful tension produced by excessive strain. It provides a balancing readiness for the next challenge whether it be in the decision-making arena that comes from thought or whether it be a round of activity on the sporting front or simply organizing oneself for efficiency on a simple shopping tour. Being ready for the next event is a primary organizing device for effectiveness in the dance of life.

Without analyzing why, we instinctively seek out the activity, place or company that is the near opposite of our previous focus. If we live in the busy city, we enjoy picnics in the more peaceful country. If we're country folk, we enjoy occasional romps into the faster-paced city. If we live in mountainous country, we enjoy going to the oceanside and vice versa. If we're cooped up in an office all day, we may use humor to counter the deadly seriousness during working hours and before seeking balancing perspective through that relaxing early-evening cocktail, by exercising strenuously at the local gym, by taking a college-extension evening course or simply by engaging in a drag-out poker game with the old gang. When we get tired of eating pasta dishes, we switch to meat or fish or foul or become vegetarians for a time. Certain sporting activities provide sharp contrast to normal living such as golfing, swimming, skiing, scuba diving, fishing and many others all of which become proportionally more attractive as the work or other daily routine becomes more boring or otherwise overextended.

Perhaps a distinction should be made about the character or quality of diverting contrast sought in our nearly unconscious efforts to lead the good life. These changes of pace or venue may range from positively constructive venting or ameliorating patterns to negatively damaging and destructive practices. All mentioned above when indulged in moderately are perceived to be on the constructive side. Excessive reaction to on-the-job stress may induce some more emotionally unstable people into seeking balancing relief through such activities as excessive consumption of alcoholic beverages, reckless driving, excessive gambling, promiscuous sex, illegal drug consumption or trafficking, even fraud and assorted other crimes.

Most such changes of pace and activity occur on the physical plane and in the present. Television, the theater or the reading of history books or fiction can transport us to another time and place and thereby put some beneficial space and time between then and now. Music can take us into other worlds where contemporary problems may be temporarily forgotten. And finally, there is sleep, beautiful blissful sleep, where we can dismiss today and be bugged only by our ever-present unconscious in the form of dreams.

Thinking and Living "Inside the Box"

It is with the relationship of perspective to the individual mindset, however, that we are most concerned in this volume. Each of us is born into a particular subset of cultural traditions and definitions and we develop our early frames of reference from the concepts and ideas presented to us and in many cases "trained into us" from our immediate families, the family-selected or family-inherited church and the neighborhood schools we attend. Each of these institutions works to the extent of its current capabilities to bestow and/or imprint its value systems on the youth under its care. Most would agree that "current capabilities" are not what they were several generations ago and that today's youth has a far different and broader collection of mindsets. The former disciplined, training-oriented and generally more highly structured environment has been replaced by variously modified programs designed to cope with the emerging realities of advancing technology, population growth, and faster change in new directions than these institutions can comfortably manage.

At first, we conform more or less willingly to whatever course in "introduction to life" we receive because of the love extended and/or the sanctions imposed, and then gradually over the years we learn to understand more about behaving within this framework and also within the legal prescriptions that society has ordained for us. Thus, imperceptibly, our little "box" of reality grows larger with the added years. Most of us are content to think and live by the central norms and conventions that we inherited and learned with perhaps minor adjustments later to accommodate marriage and career. It is with this set of "normal" expectations that we pass judgment on the passing parade of events in our lives.

But wait! What we perceived as normal or conforming to our expectations continues to change, albeit more slowly as we advance into the upper levels of the life cycle. For the great majority, the views or perspectives we held as firmly sacrosanct when teenagers gradually evolve into more accommodating views in middle age and into broader postures still as senior citizens. Various combinations of peer pressure, experiential history and adaptive flexibility unite to alter our original endowments. The process, however, is highly variable among individuals and imperceptible overall to most of us. Thus, we may appear to project firmly held views on this or that even though our perceptions of the matter have changed and we no longer believe in our former positions so strongly. In order to be perceived by others as reasonably consistent, however, we become adept at changing our positions so gradually or so cleverly that in many cases we even fool ourselves. And so, for a lifetime, we try to maintain a face-saving consistency by judging life's events from perspectives originally obtained from living "within the box," our original mindset positions. Our actual positions do change variously over time, however, and often more than others perceive in our reactions or behavior.

To show this attitudinal change in perspective, compare the posture held by most youth in regard to gardening or to cultivating plants and flowers to that held by many if not most older people. The process is far too tedious and the rewards far too slow in developing to intrigue youth. Over the years, however, some combination of processes works on some of us to increase interest in what we originally disdained and to decrease interest in that to which we were initially attracted. Reflect on the attraction that the thrilling rides and daring-do at amusement parks have for youth while most older people smile indulgently and prefer just to watch.

Thinking and Living "Outside the Box"

Not all thought and behavior take place inside the box of traditionally received reality with which each of us is initially primed. Indeed, in a country so enriched by continued immigration and the resultant wealth of differing views of reality, much if not most of our thinking and behavior after we leave the family home must take place "outside the box" we inherited and developed in early life. Since we must increasingly interact with others possessing widely varying sets of perceived reality based on their ethnic roots, religious beliefs, traditional customs and mores, we must learn to adapt by searching for common ground and by finding behavioral patterns that respect the rights of others while also serving mutual ends sought. Thus, we have become variously agile "jack-in-the-box" or perhaps "jack-out-of-the-box" athletes and many may have jumped so far as to never return to their original boxes.

This can be done passively such as when tourists visit foreign countries and observe their differing ways of meeting life's challenges with the resources available to them. So great is our curiosity to do this that commercial tourism has become one of the largest industries in most receptive countries. Or consider the great attraction of science fiction, space-age stories, the theater and movies that regularly provide us with adventure and excitement beyond our everyday experience. Somewhat more active proselytizing may take us outside our original boxes when we join groups such as political parties or evangelizing religions or missionary sales teams that adopt expansionist activities to gain new members or to increase their sales. In these cases we may attempt to persuade others to adopt our causes or join our crusades.

This attempt to get others to think and act like us or like those in our box, to get others to drop comfortable "inside their box" mindsets and join our causes can get quite uncomfortable for those being pursued, depending on the vigor of the persuasion used. An example of this is when rabid supporters of a political cause or candidate use your friendship excessively as leverage to gain your support. Or if the minister of your church uses his pulpit to argue for an unpopular cause. Or when a gay son in a straight family insists on bringing his partner home for social events against the preferences of some members of his family.

This imposition of one set of values on others occurs among organizations also even up to situations in which our federal government insists that continuing good trade relations with other countries depends on their adoption of certain human rights, ethical standards or nuclear proliferation guidelines. The United States has coupled its trade position with a number of these desirable but questionable initiatives in dealing with other countries. But when these countries balk at such restrictions as a challenge to their sovereignty, we have little choice but to back down. And in a bit of clever one-upmanship, they have correctly pointed out that families in their cultures are far more cohesive and protective of their children than we in the United States. Some Muslim countries in southeast Asia, especially Iran and Iraq, have felt so pressured to adopt Western living patterns that religious and other fiercely nationalist leaders succeeded in gaining political control that they use to maintain their cultures with a minimum of Western influence or interference.

This Shrinking World

Given the tensions and frictions caused by increasingly interdependent nations in a technologically dominated age, it is imperative we find ways to bridge the barriers between East and West. It will be necessary to find ways to improve the quality of communication along with the advances in its technology.

Since all thinkers and writers to the present have relied on narrative discourse to communicate their ideas, educators in charge of general education have had no choice but to use the materials available. Perhaps their frequent use of the very term "perspective" suggests an increasing need or desire to present more compactly the hills and valleys of contrasting ideologies and methodologies. If so, it is hoped that the present volume, clumsy and awkward though it is, will constitute a jump-start in the direction of word modeling or concept formatting to make that "bright spark of connection cross wide gaps."

Why Perspective Is Needed Now

Better perspective has always been sought but has become more important than ever and not just for better integration among the nation states alluded to above. A growing number of disaffected countries now have nuclear capability and what some perceive as unstable leadership. This may be identified as the major problem "outside the box." But the challenges "inside the box" may be even more insidious and dangerous although not so obvious. Several trends have gained considerable momentum over the preceding centuries and decades and now require better perspective to see them in contexts clearly enough to combat the dangers they present. Among them the following are dominant:

1. The compounding of knowledge in the last five hundred years or so.
2. The accelerating rates of technological and social change that produce increasing confusion in individual and group value systems.

3. The rising but hidden costs of education. Let us look at each.

The Compounding of Knowledge

Knowledge is generally considered to be justified or justifiable true beliefs. While a considerable part of one's personal knowledge may be intuitively accepted faith or beliefs, the vast growth in knowledge in the recent past has been derived from science and technology where facts may be verified by reproducible experiments. Until the advent of the modern scientific revolution, the mental inventory of most people must have been composed mainly of nonverifiable and intuitively accepted ideas as suggested mainly by the persuasive and/or authoritative leaders representing the activities of religion, government and commerce.

Factual knowledge had grown so abundant by the 1700s that Diderot in France and then leaders in the Scottish Enlightenment period deemed it necessary to compile the first encyclopedias. The first edition of the three-volume *Encyclopaedia Britannica* was not fully assembled and published until 1771.

The proliferation of special-interest encyclopedias has grown since then to cover so many specific fields that in 1986 Libraries Unlimited published a 570-page *Guide to Subject Encyclopedias and Dictionaries*. In the introduction its editor, Bohdan S. Wynar, wrote:

> This book offers a representative selection of subject dictionaries that will be useful in the reference and information process of libraries of all types.... Most of the material was carefully selected from *American Reference Books Annual (ARBA)* which in the past seventeen years has reviewed over 28,000 titles, including about 3,500 subject dictionaries and encyclopedias.

More than four hundred professors, librarians and educational administrators contributed reviews of each listing to the volume, which includes such titles as:

Encyclopedia of American Agricultural History (467 pages)
Encyclopedia of Electric Circuits (760 pages)
Harvard Encyclopedia of American Ethnic Groups (1076 pages)
Kirk-Othmer Encyclopedia of Chemical Technology (25 volumes)
Encyclopedia of Electrochemistry of the Elements (15 volumes)
The Modern Encyclopedia of Russian and Soviet History (50 volumes)
New Encyclopedia of Sports (543 pages)
The Illustrated Encyclopedia of Aviation (20 volumes)
The International Wildlife Encyclopedia (20 volumes)

Clearly, factual knowledge has compounded at some astronomical rate and in doing so has correspondingly limited our perspectives of the whole domain and the interrelationships of each component therein.

Many technologies have expanded and continue to break off into subset branches requiring encyclopedic treatment to cover just the subset area. As research in all its forms continues, we can be assured that the growth of verifiable knowledge will continue to accelerate. And, if current trends continue, most of us will be compelled to become ever-narrower specialists vocationally and probably avocationally as well.

Hero to the Rescue: The Mighty Textbook

Educators, confronted with the tradition-bound time frame and degree structure for a college education, have packaged and repackaged the increasing flood of published data. Ever more sophisticated textbooks in every field have become the handles by which students carry their preparations into the future.

Granting that the textbook approach to synthesizing knowledge has more or less attuned tens of millions for successful careers and that it has served brilliantly in doing so, we must still inquire as to whether it will continue to do so. The growth in material for textbook coverage continues to accelerate forcing ever more frequent textbook revisions. Where revised editions formerly replaced their predecessors only every generation or so, they now succeed each other every three to four years. Over time, therefore, we provide ever more coverage in depth and less in breadth thus giving credence to the observation that today's expert is one who knows more and more (depth) about less and less (breadth).

As the specialized technical composition of most college textbook titles has continued to narrow just to cover their newer but essential components, the more descriptive and historical background covering the evolution of that specialty has shrunken. Such specialists are losing the former educational "breadth" of their specialty. As a consequence of this continuing focus, we have lost touch not only with the historical general education breadth but also now the former breadth of our specialties. At some point in this continuing process, useful perspective may totally disappear.

While many retired professors are prone to criticize some of these textbooks for their perceived overemphasis here and neglect there, they represent admirable compilations and syntheses of vast collections of data, ideas, experiences and anecdotes. Indeed, without them, students would have been forced back into reading great works in their original or abridged form and the task of career preparation would have been assumed by pre- and post-graduate technical schools or perhaps taken over by the various organizational entities themselves.

Fortunately, computer networking in interactive modes will help here and feverishly competitive activity is now underway to provide an alternative to the textbook. Experiments at all levels of education are now searching for ways to integrate the computer and its Internet capabilities to the benefit of education. Most students at all levels enthusiastically embrace the computer and its potentials. After all, the computer involves action and the use of more senses than only listening, which has always been the "donnybrook" of most classroom teachers in the lower grades. Since most youth were introduced to the computer via games and other heroic simulations, they embrace its action-orientation in a positive fashion.

Within the next generation, this alternative will enable any student at any time to call up whatever information is needed for learning purposes. However, we still need not only better classroom integrating formats and models than sequential courses in interdisciplinary studies, we also need better knowledge-filtering mechanisms so that the old computer concept of GIGO (garbage in/garbage out) doesn't drown us. At the present time there is a huge and growing amount of distracting and diversionary material designed to entice youth in wayward directions.

The Acceleration of Social and Technological Change

The market system has succeeded in raining down on its beneficiaries an astonishing standard of living. The interplay of the vastly increased knowledge base, plentiful capital, venturesome entrepreneurs, willing labor and abundant natural resources all harnessed by an abiding work ethic and sense of progress combined to produce an explosion of goods and services to "improve" our scale of living. The majority of us in the United States and industrialized world have ridden this vehicle skillfully and benefitted correspondingly. Now it has grown into a mammoth steamroller that is threatening to flatten the institutional base on which our abundance was built. As the cult of materialism has taken over, more and more of us aspire to ever greater affluence and willingly do whatever we think it takes to achieve it. Other values have suffered in their execution if not in avowed rhetoric.

In the post–World War II era in the United States more working mothers have contributed to growth of the suburban home and two-car garage. But in too many cases the family's children were left without sufficient care and guidance to maintain their parents' momentum in capturing more of the "goods" life. As youthful alienation and resistance mounted, discipline in the schools eroded. Not only did the quality of education decline markedly but a whole raft of wayward trends descended on an unsuspecting public. Child neglect and abuse have contributed substantially to growing social problems involving alcohol and drug abuse, homelessness, irresponsible parenting, AIDS, random violence, growing theft, rape and other assorted antisocial acts.

Most of our basic institutions are operating under severe stress and failing to maintain healthy national profiles in the services they provide.

With notable exceptions, these include the institutionalized units of government, education, religion and especially the nuclear family as we have idealized it. The confluence of ongoing social and technological changes has disrupted the unity, harmony, and bases of economic support for the family. To the extent that the nuclear and extended family provide these supporting elements, social problems might at least be contained. But home-life conditions are worsening. A recent U.S. Census Bureau report shows that the percentage of married couples with children living in single households declined from 40.3 percent in 1970 to 25.5 percent in 1995 (McLeod, p. A15). This can only result in further decline in the nurturing conditions for youth.

Schools have become massified and depersonalized to such an extent that too many individual children have lost the incentive to take their studies seriously. There are simply no other good substitute objectives for young children. They must take their studies seriously or they will seek to escape in wayward activities that too often lead to deteriorating values and poor performances later in marriage, family life and career.

A Time for "Tough Love"

A return to stronger discipline and training emphasis in elementary schools is needed but may not be enough. Youth needs better rationale or incentives for continuing to focus on studies that frequently appear irrelevant or purposeless. Worse, the word "boring" seems to summarize a majority of students' attitudes toward their studies. Why are they bored? Is it because they fail to appreciate the meaning and significance connecting their studies to real-life situations? Isn't it the challenge of educators to bridge this gap with connections that students can understand? Attention to models and formats should be combined with smaller classes, computer technology, tightened discipline, fun projects and especially more dedicated teaching to help maintain student attention and interest in subject matter. Many combinations of these elements are possible for flexible and innovative applications but the prevailing mentality produced by bureaucratic malaise and teacher burnout stifles their implementation.

To be fair, both groups of administrators and teachers have been stretched to the breaking point by the vastly increased demands of orderly housekeeping, record-keeping maintenance and especially disciplinary procedures for its increasingly neglected and therefore belligerent, rebellious and confrontational youth. And as a consequence of deteriorating educational results, society sees no compelling reason to increase teachers' salaries above minimal levels.

It is clear that the school's ability to accept or absorb the increasing overflow problems from broken-family arrangements and uncontrollable immigration has been overextended under the current educational setups. It is possible, however, that under radically revised educational programming, a substantial improvement could be made to reduce existing and future social problems.

The Dangers Inherent in Just Coasting Along

In a competitive and predatory world the maintenance of a healthy balance among basic values is the soundest long-run strategy for progressive survival with improving conditions. Technological leadership capable of diversion into weapons development may be a strong deterrent against potential aggressors from outside. The growth of individualism and materialism spilling over into hedonism, however, may eat away at the other core values sufficiently to bring about enough moral decay to cause internal collapse before external challenge.

A number of recent books by concerned authors and analysts warn us of the dire possibilities. The titles alone suggest their alarming content:

- *The United States of Incompetence,* by Art Carey, 1991.
- *America at Century's End,* by Alan Wolfe (editor), 1991.
- *The New Individualists: The Generation After the Organization Man,* by Paul Leinberger and Bruce Tucker, 1991.
- *Money, Murder and the American Dream: Wilding from Wall St. to Main St.,* by Charles Derber, 1992.
- *The De-valuing of America: the Fight for American Culture and Our Children,* by William J. Bennett, 1992.
- *Dumbing Down: Essays on the Strip-Mining of American Culture,* by Katherine Washburn and John Thornton, 1996.
- *Slouching Towards Gomorrah,* by Robert Bork, 1996.
- *Life Without Father,* by David Popenoe, 1996.

The Rising Costs of Education-Assisted Social Problems

Unfortunately as a nation, we will probably be able to continue supporting the present education budget into the foreseeable future at the same expenditure levels plus costs of yearly inflation as we have in the past. This will continue to hide the scandalous true costs of our national educational catastrophe, which should include actual federal, state and local government costs for education at all levels plus the very large public and private costs in policing, monitoring and financially supporting the whole range of social problems caused by the maladjusted who were permitted to drop out of our poorly designed nurturing and educational lifeline networks for children.

It could be argued that the basic or core problem is breakup of the traditional family unit and its nurturing capabilities for youth. But the family unit has been breaking up all through the latter half of this century and no clear pattern for social stability or community has emerged. How and with whom people choose to live is probably not a government-controllable item in a democracy as free and affluent as that of the United States. Given the state of new-combination families, single-parent families, abandoned children and other sorry aspects of the modern American family, it is unrealistic to expect any dramatic short-run improvement in the nurturing capabilities of families so stressed out. One emerging remedy is the growth of well-managed daycare centers into which the more affluent and caring parents can deposit their offspring. But the curative emphasis should be on prevention rather than remedy.

It is the thesis of this work that the better perspective provided by a formats model will help to clarify contemporary problems. To whatever extent this proves true, problems, such as educational reform among others, may be better perceived and acted on. It is hoped deeper insight provided by modeling the whole society will show us more clearly just where major imbalances and deficiencies exist and where remedial corrections and preventive restructurings might better be made. The growing specialization on all occupational fronts combined with a "live now before it's too late" materialistic bent coupled with increasingly hedonistic indulgences make it harder than ever to see the big picture forest because of all the local and alluring trees surrounding us.

The Failure of Short-Term Educational "Fixes"

From educational "statesmen" to "educationist tinkerers," many influential change engineers have been allowed to experiment with educational curricula but with varying and generally ineffective results. None has succeeded in a major way in reversing our educational deterioration. Although increased financing would help, it alone would be inadequate. Needed are basic ideas comprehending the entire social, technological and moral structures in ways designed to facilitate integration and synthesis. Well-intentioned "fixings" here and there are insufficient.

One such approach supporting the hypothesis of this volume is that proposed by the wide-ranging and brilliant biologist Edward O. Wilson. In his recent book titled *Consilience: The Unity of Knowledge*, Wilson writes (p. 8):

> Consilience is the key to unification. I prefer this word over "coherence" because its rarity has preserved its precision, whereas coherence has several possible meanings, only one of which is

consilience. William Whewell, in his 1840 synthesis *The Philosophy of the Inductive Sciences*, was the first to speak of consilience, literally a "jumping together" of knowledge by the linkage of facts and fact-based theory across the disciplines to create a common groundwork of explanation. He said, "The Consilience of Inductions takes place when an Induction, obtained from one class of facts, coincides with an Induction, obtained from another different class. This Consilience is a test of the truth of the Theory in which it occurs.

Wilson makes the following major points in his evaluation of higher education and its future prospects:

1. The greatest enterprise of the mind has always been and always will be the attempted linkage of the sciences and humanities. The ongoing fragmentation of knowledge and resulting chaos in philosophy are not reflections of the real world but artifacts of scholarship (p.8).
2. Disciplinary boundaries within the natural sciences are disappearing, to be replaced by shifting hybrid domains in which consilience is implicit. These domains reach across many levels of complexity, from chemical physics and physical chemistry to molecular genetics, chemical ecology, and ecological genetics. None of the new specialties is considered more than a focus of research. Each is an industry of fresh ideas and advancing technology.

   Given that human action comprises events of physical causation, why should the social sciences and humanities be impervious to consilience with the natural sciences (pp. 10–11)?
3. The unification agenda does not sit well with a few professional philosophers. The subject I address they consider their own, to be expressed in their language, their framework of formal thought. They will draw this indictment: *conflation, simplism, ontological reductionism, scientism,* and other sins made official by the hissing suffix (p. 11).
4. In his 1941 classic *Man on His Nature*, the British neuro-biologist Charles Sherrington spoke of the brain as an enchanted loom, perpetually weaving a picture of the external world, tearing down and reweaving, inventing other worlds, creating a miniature universe. The communal mind of literate societies—world culture—is an immensely larger loom. Through science it has gained the power to map external reality far beyond the reach of a single mind, and through the arts the means to construct narratives, images, and rhythms immeasurably more diverse than the products of any solitary genius. The loom is the same for both enterprises—for science and for the arts, and there is a general explanation of its origin and

nature and thence of the human condition, proceeding from the deep history of genetic evolution to modern culture. Consilience of causal explanation is the means by which the single mind can travel most swiftly and surely from one part of the communal mind to the other (p. 12).

5. In education the search for consilience is the way to renew the crumbling structure of the liberal arts. During the past thirty years the ideal of the unity of learning which the Renaissance and Enlightenment bequeathed us, has been largely abandoned. With rare exceptions American universities and colleges have dissolved their curriculum into a slurry of minor disciplines and specialized courses. While the average number of undergraduate courses per institution doubled, the percentage of mandated courses in general education dropped by more than half.... The trend cannot be reversed by force-feeding students with some-of-this and some-of-that across the branches of learning. Win or lose, true reform will aim at the consilience of science with the social sciences and humanities in scholarship and teaching. Every college student should be able to answer the following question: What is the relation between science and the humanities, and how is it important for human welfare (pp. 12–13)?

6. There was another, humbler reason for the lack of interest in the big picture. Scientists simply didn't have the requisite intellectual energy. The vast majority of scientists have never been more than journeymen prospectors. This is even more the case today. They are professionally focused; their education does not orient them to the wide contours of the world. They acquire the training they need to travel to the frontier and make discoveries of their own, and as fast as possible, because life at the growing edge is expensive and chancy. The most productive scientists, installed in million-dollar laboratories, have no time to think about the big picture and see little profit in it (pp. 38–39).

7. Professional scholars in general have little choice but to dice up research expertise and research agendas among themselves. To be a successful scholar means spending a career on membrane biophysics, the Romantic poets, early American history, or some other such constricted area of formal study (p. 39).

8. Fragmentation of expertise was further mirrored in the twentieth century by modernism in the arts, including architecture. The work of the masters—Braque, Picasso, Stravinsky, Eliot, Joyce, Martha Graham, Gropius, Frank Lloyd Wright, and their peers—was so novel and discursive as to thwart generic classification, except for this: The modernists tried to achieve the new and provocative at any cost.

What Is Perspective • 31

They identified the constraining bonds of tradition and self-consciously broke them. Many rejected realism in expression in order to explore the unconscious. Freud, as much a literary stylist as a scientist, inspired them and can be justifiably included in their ranks (pp. 39–40).

9. *Culture is created by the comunal mind, and each mind in turn is the product of the genetically structured human brain. Genes and culture are therefore inseverably linked. But the linkage is flexible, to a degree still mostly unmeasured. The linkage is also tortuous: Genes prescribe epigenetic rules, which are the neural pathways and regularities in cognitive development by which the individual mind assembles itself. The mind grows from birth to death in absorbing parts of the existing culture available to it, with selections guided through epigenetic rules inherited by the individual brain* (p. 127).

10. The brain constantly searches for meaning, for connections between objects and qualities that cross-cut the senses and provide information about external existence. We penetrate that world through the constraining portals of the epigenetic rules…. In order to grasp the human condition, both the genes and culture must be understood, not separately in the traditional manner of science and the humanities, but together, in recognition of the realities of human evolution (p. 163).

11. There is also progress in the social sciences, but it is much slower, and not at all animated by the same information flow and optimistic spirit (as in medical science). Cooperation is sluggish at best, even genuine discoveries are often obscured by bitter ideological disputes. For the most part, anthropologists, economists, sociologists, and political scientists fail to understand and encourage one another (p. 182).

12. Everyone knows that the social sciences are hyper complex. They are inherently far more difficult than physics and chemistry, and as a result they, not physics and chemistry, should be called the hard sciences. They just seem easier, because we can talk with other human beings but not with photons, gluons, and sulfide radicals. Consequently, too many social-science textbooks are a scandal of banality (p. 183).

But Slow Down, Mister!

Despite the many insightful statements (taken out of context) both above and throughout his work, Wilson's ideas received a vote of no confidence from a respectable source. Well titled as "Biosocial Speculations: The Gene Is Jumping," the reviewer recognizes Wilson's outstanding career achievements and the concept of the book as being "remarkable for its scope and ambition" (p. 15) but adds "Mr. Wilson hopes beyond hope that the next century will see a much broader consilience, one that will knit the social sciences, and perhaps even the humanities, firmly into the natural sciences..." (p. 16). After identifying a few stumbling blocks to achieving this potential, the reviewer concludes that "this book is a mishmash," "less than the sum of its parts" and "not an auspicious beginning for the programme of consilience" (p.16).

Of course it is a book reviewer's job to analyze and judge the strengths, weaknesses and potentials of books assigned for review. Unfortunately, the reviewer assumed that Wilson's book on consilience was "...his blueprint for how such a great unification of human endeavor might come about" (p. 16). One might just as easily assume that Wilson had no thoughts about detailing a blueprint but rather was merely trying to generate a spark of interest in the consilience idea, to encourage others of like interests to reach out and cross borders to help break the academic gridlock.

This volume also is not a "blueprint" but mainly a foray into uniting some major disparate elements in the social sciences and humanities into a more comprehensible whole. Wilson's vision is far more sweeping by thinking to merge the physical sciences with the social sciences, humanities and liberal arts in general. That such an all-inclusive concept should be promoted by a physical scientist is remarkable in that most contributions to knowledge from science stem from the reductionist focus, which consists mainly of the breaking apart of nature into its constituent elements through the use of layers and layers of analysis on even more analysis. Synthesis or consilience works in the opposite direction and in the academic world has grown conspicuously short in supply. An interesting exception might be in the practical world of technological product adaptation where the enticing presence of profit incentives creates a strong motivation to adapt new knowledge to create and assemble new products. Perhaps the incentives to encouraging consilience in the social sciences and humanities needs corrective attention.

The Dawn of a New Academic Era?

In addition to the stir created by E. O. Wilson's illuminating discourse on consilience, there is some evidence that we are on the right track as other social scientists are struggling with the same need for better perspective. *The Chronicle of Higher Education* reported in its April 5, 1996, issue (p. A8) that a Portuguese foundation under the leadership of a sociology professor from the State University of New York at Binghamton has sponsored a three-year study "...to consider ways in which the traditional social-study disciplines, especially the boundaries between them, might be reconceptualized." An interim report published by the Stanford University Press in 1996 suggested more interdisciplinary interaction with professors holding joint appointments in two departments. The coming stage two calls for "more deliberation."

And still another hopeful venture into interdisciplinary potentials has been initiated at Duke University through a twenty-million-dollar grant given by alumna and trustee Melinda French Gates (wife of Bill) to encourage up to eighty carefully selected young students "to pursue their intellectual curiosity across disciplinary boundaries. According to William Chafe, dean of Trinity College at Duke, "a lot of universities function like silos, each silo with its separate disciplines. We want to build bridges between those silos" (Arenson, Karen W., p. A27). The program, which began in the fall of 1999, will try to meld or synthesize diverse student interests into more unified wholes. This is something Melinda Gates found lacking at Duke where she double majored in economics and computer science while also taking a heavy dose of art and literature courses—and all before earning her MBA degree in a fifth year.

"And a Little Child Shall Lead Them"

A sobering insight recently surfaced in the author's mind when an innocent incident with a very cute granddaughter took place. It occurred around a Christmas tree at a preholiday gathering when this seven-year-old spontaneously arranged spur-of-the-moment gifts before each of the adults present. As we "oooh'd" and "ahhh'd" appreciatively and thanked her for her generosity, her grandmother launched into a lecture on how it was better to give than receive gifts. Her little face frowned over the language and thoughts and she asked, "Why?" but then responded brightly after placing her hand over her heart: "Maybe I *know* what you mean, Grandma, because I *feel* so warm inside."

This play of events and language triggered the thought that perhaps we've again placed the cart before the horse by attending so much to formal education in terms of knowledge and the manipulation of words and numbers while at the same time neglecting that other wellspring of insight, feelings and the senses. Surely to continue generating the needed higher levels of brotherly love, international harmony and world peace, we will need to encourage all facets of understanding and compassion. There is ample evidence that simply knowing what should be done is frequently insufficient as means to accomplishing complex ends sought. The knowing must be accompanied by the right balance of motivation, concern and generosity of spirit. To meet this challenge, all institutions have major roles to play and must become reorganized and reinvigorated to contribute better. As one of those major institutions, education must work to find a better balance between general or liberal education and its current focus, vocational education or training. While admittedly "light" on the role of the senses and feelings in contributing to restoration of the balances needed, it is hoped that the formats concept presented in this book, combining more liberal thought with vocational applications, may be a step in the right direction.

REFERENCES

American Heritage Dictionary of the English Language, 3rd Edition (New York: Houghton-Mifflin, 1992).

American Heritage Illustrated Encyclopedia Dictionary (Boston: Houghton-Mifflin, 1987).

ARAB Guide to Subject Encyclopedias and Dictionaries. Editor: Bohdan S. Wynar (Littleton, Colorado: Libraries Unlimited, 1986).

Arenson, Karen W., ""Gateses Give Duke $20 Million to Nurture Geniuses," *San Francisco Examiner*, September 13, 1998, p. A27.

"Biological Speculations: The Gene Is Jumping," *The Economist*, July 11, 1998, pp. 15–16.

"Footnotes," *The Chronicle of Higher Education*, April 15, 1996, p. A8.

McLeod, Ramon G., "2-Parent Families at Record Low—25% of Homes," *San Francisco Chronicle*, November 27, 1996, pp. A1, A15.

Oxford English Dictionary, 2nd Edition, volume XI (Oxford: Clarendon Press, 1989).

Van Nostrand's Scientific Encyclopedia, 5th Edition (London: Reinhold Company, 1976).

Wilson, Edward O., *Consilience: The Unity of Knowledge* (New York: Alfred A. Knopf, 1998). Copyright © 1998 by Edward O. Wilson. Reprinted by permission of Alfred A. Knopf, a division of Random House, Inc.

CHAPTER 3
From Boxes to Formats

In the previous chapter reference was made to how we learn to think and behave when guided by precepts bestowed on us in early life mainly by our parents, church and school. These "inside the box" reality benchmarks established the early basic foundation on which our continued growth after leaving home added still more concepts while modifying some of the earlier precepts to develop our ongoing individualized "outside the box" way of looking at the world. It is with this combination of "inside the box" *and* "outside the box" perceptions of reality that we respond to the challenges and opportunities of daily life. However, more analysis is needed to understand just how we come to grips with the specific problems and/or opportunities we face. The concept suggested for this experience is formats.

Formats in this book is an acronym for *frames of reference for minding action and thought systems.* Many alternative terms could be substituted for that most inclusive verb form "minding," depending on one's specific focus or general orientation. Managing, mastering, monitoring, mixing, matching, merging, meshing, mediating, mounting and moving are a few options that have positive connotations. Maneuvering and manipulating are terms suggesting duplicitous thinking in the use of frames of reference. The term "minding" was selected because it suggests becoming more "mindful" or attentive in applying usefully the wide range of available thought through the application of frames of reference to different situations, a skill we hope to advance in this work. The mind, of course, refers to the totality of conscious and unconscious thought, perception, feeling, will, memory and imagination available to humankind.

It takes only a little thought to appreciate the importance of such frames. Take, for instance, the necessity of knowing the rules of baseball or bridge to understanding and playing those games. Of knowing the tax codes to understanding and calculating our taxes or of having learned the social conventions for understanding and relating acceptably in society. Where would we be without such frames to provide orientation for our thoughts and behavior?

One can turn enjoyably to the confused world of *Alice's Adventures in Wonderland* and *Through the Looking Glass* (p. 172) for delightful scenarios of a topsy-turvy world without customarily useful frames of reference:

"I don't understand you," said Alice. "It's dreadfully confusing!"

"That's the effect of living backwards," the Queen said kindly: "It always makes one a little giddy at first—"

"Living backwards!" Alice repeated in great astonishment. "I never heard of such a thing!"

"—but there's one great advantage in it, that one's memory works both ways."

"I'm sure *mine* only works one way," Alice remarked. "I can't remember things before they happen."

What kind of world is this Wonderland where Alice had to adjust herself to a life without predictable conventions or laws of nature? Or at least to adjust to totally different laws? How confusing in Looking-Glass Land to be governed by laws to which she was unaccustomed. To learn, for example, to walk away from a place to reach it or to run fast to remain in place. In addition to being young and adaptable, Alice must have been quite intelligent to have accepted so many paradoxical and/or quixotic directions and rebuffs.

What Are Frames of Reference?

Although used unconsciously no doubt by many philosophers, historians and other literati before the time of Sir Isaac Newton (1643–1727), the great English physicist and mathematician, it was his insights that most directly originated the objective frame of reference. His laws of gravitation and motion (with earlier help from Galileo and others) led to the visualization of systems of graduated lines symbolically connected within larger structures and which function to describe various position points relative to the larger body.

On a large scale, consider the solar system or the global latitude and longitude coordinates to delineate points on earth. On a personal scale, observe the second and minute hands of your wrist watch circling around and overtaking the hour hand. Both large- and small-scale frames of reference contain a series of graduated lines or points symbolically connected to the larger body or frame. With rudimentary understanding of these frames of reference, we can visualize where Capetown or Chicago are relative to our city or quietly gauge the time remaining in a boring lecture. Putting the two frames together (space and time), we can estimate the time needed to fly from our city to Capetown or Chicago.

Frames of reference provide the boundaries within which we learn what behavior is normal, expected, punished or rewarded. They may have quantifiable capabilities such as a set of coordinate axes in terms of which static positions or dynamic movement may be specified such as in physics, mathematics, economics or geography. Or the frame of reference may be more qualitative or descriptive in nature such as a set of ideas with ordered values in terms of which other ideas are interpreted or compared and assigned meaning as in music or philosophy.

Perhaps the verb or noun use of the word "frame" is suggestive. As a verb it means to construct an object by putting together its various parts. As a noun it stands for anything composed of parts fitted and joined together such as the frame of a house. The word "reference" denotes that matrix of interlocking ideas or set of relationships that altogether provides relational significance for any particular fact or value within its context.

Thus the geographic frame of reference for the state of California would be a western state of the United States of America on the North American continent bordered on the north by the state of Oregon, on the east by the state of Nevada, on the south by the state of Arizona and country of Mexico, and on the west by the Pacific Ocean. It lies between 32 degrees and 42 degrees north latitudes and 115 degrees and 125 degrees west longitudes.

The Computer Format

The term formats has achieved considerable visibility in recent decades with the fantastic explosion of computer technology. The "old" typewriters provided relatively few hardware variables and the major challenge was to learn the keyboard arrangement and develop finger dexterity. The format or typing setup was rather simplistic and mechanically achieved with margin releases, spacing levers and a few other "tabs." Today all is powered by electricity and one must spend weeks or months to learn just the basics of word and number processing for general documents, databases and spreadsheets. The term "formatting" has come to embrace all tasks that affect the appearance of a document. Our use of the term "formats" has a much broader application in that it refers to those multiple frames of reference used to provide contexts for understanding situations before initiating subsequent behavior patterns.

Personal Frames of Reference

Individuals have innumerable small personal frames with which to make sense out of daily events and to guide their specific behaviors. They have family, friendship, occupational, avocational, recreational, leisure, educational, ideological, religious, political, investment, retirement and consumer frames with multiple subframes within each, all of which help them organize alternatives within relatively narrow limits. They have frames of reference that guide their clothing selections, tooth-brushing habits, friend selection, exercise patterns and eating habits. They shift from one frame to another with ease and within each can be quite comfortable. Self-interest is the guiding principle in choosing among alternatives within each frame of reference. It is based on the intensity of felt needs at any particular time in any particular situation. Influencing these frames in countless ways are the precepts and concepts usually with value connotations that we have accepted in earlier life.

For instance, consider the orientation exercise most of us would go through on arriving late to a baseball game. Almost automatically and intuitively we seek to establish a meaningful frame of reference so that we can share the rhythms of victory or defeat for our favorite team. In order, we want to learn what inning it is, what the score is and who's pitching. For more insight we need to know the standings of all teams in the league, the number of remaining games on the schedule, individual player's batting averages, pitching records and indeed, the whole mountain of baseball trivia on which we seem to thrive.

Or consider the sequential questions used by an investor analyzing yesterday's changes in stock prices: How did my stocks do? How did the averages do? How have the averages done in this year-to-date as compared to my stocks? How well might I have done in alternative investments? What should I do to improve my position? Should I buy that new investment service? Should I change brokers?

Another example is the taken-for-granted but complicated matching process when dining out in a restaurant and the waiter places a menu on the table. The diners then must match their preferences with what is listed on the menu. The restaurant's offerings are traceable (among other diverse factors) to the manager's choices based on his or her frame of food preferences and interpretation of local competitive dynamics. That is, what can most easily be offered at attractive prices that will best differentiate this restaurant from others in the area and perhaps best induce repeat patronage. The diners must appraise the selections, reflect back on recent dining experiences from their "eating out" frames of reference, identify those two or three most tempting dishes based on the allure of the language used to compare the entree against its price, decide which of the several dishes will most satisfy whatever felt hunger needs are most demanding in his or her current state of physical being, and all before nonchalantly telling the waiter "the poached salmon, please." This simple matching process neglects to consider many of the human imponderables such as the psychological needs the diner might be tempted to satisfy such as the need for a new gustatory adventure, the safety need to watch fat or calorie intake or the need to impress a special companion.

The game's results, the investor's financial decisions and the chosen dinner can be important to the individual. The game's strategy, the goals of the investor and the satisfaction of the diner are important too. But the context or relevant frame of reference is crucial for basic comprehension and understanding. All baseball team managers, investment managers, restaurant operators and frequent restaurant diners are full of knowledge about the specifics and the history of their domains. But a few specialists somehow put it all together better. Is it luck? Or might those few have better or more complete or better integrated frames of reference, which enable them to achieve better-than-average to superior results? Financial analysts, sportswriters, restaurant critics and gourmet analysts probe endlessly to learn the secrets of their success. Do they simply know more details of their callings or do they have a better way to look at those details? Usually the quest ends in blind admiration: They're just some kind of "genius!"

Sharing Common Frames of Reference

When self-interest must be blended with the interests and goals of others we often find that our individual frames do not exactly match. We may be misunderstood. Or we may misinterpret the meaning or actions of others. Then we must reflect, reconsider, question the possible frames of those who confuse us. "Where is this person coming from?" is a common reaction. "Can he be trusted?" "Maybe I'll have to get to know her better before we agree on a deal." At other times the confusion may be in our own minds between two or more conflicting frames of reference and we beg off on taking a position with such lame comments as, "Give me some time; I'll have to sleep on it."

Individuals relate to others in families and small groups. Families and small groups relate to other families and small groups. Small groups relate to larger groups and so on. When self-interest must be integrated into family groups and larger groups, we often find that individual frames of reference become less useful, occasionally ambiguous, sometimes confusing. And we have little training and few guidelines in how to conceptualize group and larger social frames of reference. Even at the parenting level, we are mostly amateurs in training our children to learn how to accommodate others.

In the Beginning...

Imagine the challenge a child has in adapting to its ever-enlarging social world. Born with the desires only to satisfy one's basic necessities by winning the attention of its mother, the child must successively learn to enlarge that small, original format to include the father and other family members, playmates, schoolmates, teachers, teammates, working colleagues, as well as for many a married spouse and one's own children and grandchildren. It is during this progressive interaction with new personal relationships that the full range of human behavioral expression gradually evolves.

Those early childhood behaviors that elicited favorable responses tend to be retained and repetitively used in similar situations; those behaviors that were received neutrally or with outright rejection tend to be discarded. The warm and friendly smile, the pouting look, the wide-eyed look, the sullen look, the serious look, the questioning look, the wink, the frown, the affirmative or negative tilt of the head, the arched eyebrow, the contrived smile, the dimpled smile—all of these and indeed selections from the full range of body language get built into our personalities along the highway of life as we more or less unconsciously program ourselves in response to the perceived feedback from relationships along the way. How very important, then, to receive in those early formative years the genuine love and affection that can initiate a positive receptivity and response to others. Most mothers understand this intuitively and give their offspring a loving sendoff. Increasing stress in many contemporary forms, however, distract some mothers (and fathers) from bestowing their full endowment of love on their children.

Most of this relating is on the face-to-face behavioral level and can't be ignored except at one's personal expense. One relates to others more or less according to patterns established in one's early training and subsequently developed ability and interest in accommodating the wide swings in emphasis coming from people with very different backgrounds, including those with both much larger and much smaller frames than one's own. Some mysterious combination of intelligence, intuition and disposition guides our willingness to refocus our own frames of reference to those of others.

Beyond this interactive strictly behavioral world, one can enter the realm of the imagination and mind and expand one's frames of reference in countless directions forward or backward in time and with varying degrees of accuracy to total fantasy. From recalling the smallest personal incident to contemplating international political dynamics requires daily flexing of one's many formats. Integrating all of one's frames of reference into a comprehensive whole with a minimum of inconsistency becomes a life-long challenge. The relationships and combinations are nearly endless.

Organizational Frames of Reference

The same is true of most larger complex organizations such as business corporations, educational and religious institutions or government units. People relate to other people, to their jobs, to organizational objectives, to the work rules that guide them in daily activities. But they don't always do so in consistent or in timely patterns. Quite often their minds and attention wander to elsewhere and their behavior appears errant to organizational ends desired.

Each organization seeks to optimize its objectives within its operating jurisdiction and does so with varying results. If successful, the organization benefits and its employees and all others associated also benefit. If something goes wrong in any particular business, receivership and bankruptcy procedures are well established and frequently followed. Government units in trouble can rely on such well-known practices as cutting expenses, raising taxes and/or borrowing money. Religious and charitable organizations in trouble can shrink selected components of their missions, hire expert fund-raising specialists, invent phantom heresies or intensify their pleadings for special causes. Specific organizational frames of reference thus serve specific purposes well. It is between individual organizational behavior and performance and the collective social behavior and performance that linking-pin connections are inadequate.

Too Many Ideas to Associate

In both cases—that of the individual relating to surrounding spheres of interest and the organization relating to individuals as employees, customers, clients, or competitors on the one hand, and to the whole spectrum of other organizations on the other—there are simply too many associations to make for easy communication and understanding. Since the middle of the eighteenth century, "...the concept of the association of ideas has increasingly been seen as the most basic, the most fecund, and the most pervasive explanatory principle in the human, and to a lesser extent, the biological sciences." (Young, p.111).

The principle of association relies on two basic notions: 1) Complex mental images are compiled from simple elements derived ultimately from personal sensations, and 2) similarity, contrast and repeated behaviors in time and space provide the raw material from which the complex associations, thoughts and constructs are compounded.

The rapid growth of technology in recent decades has vastly increased the amount of knowledge available, the range of impressions possible, the number of theories and speculations generated, the character and quality of feelings experienced. Given this exponential expansion in the potential units of association or in the possibilities of commingling in different combinations the growing supply of facts, theories, feelings, prejudices, assumptions and other mental images, it was inevitable that confusion, ambiguity and misunderstanding would also grow.

Needed Now: Better Organization of Thought

This defect or limitation in the associationist tradition of explaining human behavior has been acknowledged. It provided no basis for the classification of larger elements, of aggregates or composites analogous to the physicist's table of fundamental particles or the chemist's table of elements. In short, it offered no classification systems or suitable frames of reference within which to organize the growing flood of observations, data and experiences obtainable both directly and indirectly from an increasingly dynamic and expanding worldwide communications network.

The result is that impression and interpretation feedback from one objective context may supply a thousand different subjective interpretations when many people selectively assemble what they choose into their own personal formats. Needed is a range of standardized frames of reference telescoping variously into larger ones such that excessive distortions and especially major errors in perception are minimized. This is the major focus for formats, or *frames of reference for minding action and thought systems*. The hope is that by improving the frames of reference for individuals-at-large and for managers at all levels of all organizations, strategic planning and directional efforts will be able to produce better results that we all can share.

Frames of reference that do exist are generally limited to one field such as baseball, investing, engineering, medicine, law, economics, or cooking and plumbing. Cross-field or general-purpose frames of reference between any two or more fields are not yet developed. These cross-field frames don't exist for at least two reasons. In the first place, working schedules and complexities in most operations are so demanding that little time is available for the necessary thought. And second, the conceptualization of useful social formats is poorly developed and not widely shared. Education treats the idea of frames of reference only indirectly. The consequences are many but several are especially significant.

The "Robotizing" of Workers in Large Organizations

In one major industry after another, the drive to achieve economies of scale and to become the biggest and the best resulted in huge organizations of manpower, capital equipment and specialized jobs and work arrangements. Necessarily this meant that the work area and responsibilities of each worker were lessened as specialization increased. The reduction or simplification of larger more complex contexts to simpler ones ostensibly to increase operating efficiency may do so in the shorter run but ultimately leads to worker alienation and the reduction of volunteerism and teamwork—all of which promote individualism and opportunistic self-interest. Workers who are not fully engaged in the complexities at hand must use their idle capacities otherwise, first in benign ways but ultimately to punish their organizations for not challenging them or for not sharing with them the significance of their work. This is mainly an illustration of the counteraction between the principle of division of labor and the principle of integration where specialized function requires increasing coordinated relationships, which in turn requires the positive cooperation of the workers.

According to one prescient observer (Thomas, pp. 170–171), this ongoing process has resulted in near chaos:

> We are ignorant about how we work, about where we fit in, and most of all about the enormous, imponderable system of life in which we are embedded as working parts.... We are *dumb*. This is, in a certain sense, a health problem after all. For as long as we are bewildered by the mystery of ourselves, and confused by the strangeness of our uncomfortable connection to all the rest of life, and dumbfounded by the inscrutability of our own minds, we cannot be said to be healthy animals in today's world. We need to know more.... We need science, more and better science, not for its technology, not for leisure, not even for health or longevity, but for the hope of wisdom which our kind of culture must acquire for its survival.

Limited managerial appreciation of the need for worker fulfillment on the job has led to various expressions of job enlargement or enrichment. Much more needs to be done. The step suggested here is an intellectual one. It leads to progressively more holistic or encompassing frames of reference whereby workers are challenged to see more clearly where their jobs and their products fit into the larger scheme of things.

The "Robotizing" of Students in Education

Textbook writers on all topics have provided us with their organizations of the contents in each field. Quite often it has an historical orientation and nearly always it is largely descriptive of what has been, is, and might be. The need for better organizing or conceptualizing models has often been expressed, but few concerted efforts have been made to inspire interest in this direction. Thus, we continue to drown in an ocean of increasing facts, hypotheses, conjectures, opinions and the rest while doing little to impose new or better organization and conceptual frames on the whole. Indeed, a whole new genre of unconnected facts was created in the 1980s with the intriguing name of "trivia." Presumably connectedness to a frame of reference would elevate a fact to more than trivial significance.

One of the more salutary improvements may have been initiated by college students who rebelled at having to master basic textbook content beyond eight- to nine-hundred pages. Some publishers required textbook writers to shrink their works to five- to seven-hundred pages, thus squeezing out less relevant ideas and perhaps encouraging a few writers to become more conceptual, more holistic, more model-oriented.

Like workers who rebel when they lose sight of the purpose or significance of their jobs and their products, students lose interest in memorizing facts and ideas when the grand organizing design is not clear and compelling. Since specialization is here to stay, better integration of ideas becomes an important means to restore purpose to workers and students. This does not necessarily mean a return to greater educational emphasis on the liberal arts as is so often proclaimed as the answer to man's myopia. Rather, it is a call for the reconceptualization of all thought into modules and designs that average people can assimilate, personalize and thereby gain meaning in their lives.

From the Simple to the Complex in Formatting

It is always possible that the study of formats or frames of reference may be too abstract at advanced levels for students at all levels to comprehend, assimilate or use effectively. Indeed, most of us get lost at some point along the complexity-of-abstract-thought trail. For example, on the concrete level, most of us have progressed from riding a tricycle or bicycle to driving an automobile without too much difficulty. At the automobile stage we are assisted by more technology feedback in the form of dashboard instruments that tell us our current speed, miles traveled, and engine revolutions per minute. In addition, we have such aids as headlights, turn-signal lights, rear-view mirrors and a horn to assist us. The more complicated the operation, the more help we need.

Driving a truck or qualifying as an engineer in charge of a train requires more preparation, training and more technical assistance. To fly an airplane or captain a large ocean-going vessel requires more training still and experience in using the facilitating technical instrumentation. Astronauts are selected for space probes on both physical and mental superiority. In addition to handling the provided hardware effectively, they require more abstract knowledge in understanding and manipulating the various software programming that guides the hardware. Gradually as the physical task becomes more complicated we must qualify also by being able to comprehend and shift intellectual gears or frames of reference appropriately. Both physical-space instrumentation and intellectual-concept manipulation must be satisfactorily integrated.

The leaders of large organizations substitute movements in economic, social and intellectual space for movements in physical space. Their instrumentation is format manipulation, accounting and financial ratio feedback, quotas established and achieved, efficiency or effectiveness in operation. They move organizational effort through political, economic, social and intellectual space with the emphasis more on synchronizing abstract frames of reference than on synchronizing physical movement through monitoring feedback gauges. To lead us, the great and growing power of interactive and multidimensional communications technology will no doubt become more important in blipping us into the future.

The mastery of mathematics requires both intuitive and analytic reasoning and for this reason proves too difficult for many at the calculus and higher levels. But even if true, the study of formats, like the study of higher math, should be made available to those who can handle it and benefit from it.

Converting Dilemmas to Manageable Problems

The dehumanizing of workers in most occupations and students in education was not the only consequence of our growing scale of operations and interdependence. The problems inherent in these changes have become more elusive, more difficult or in the current vernacular, "problematic." When a problem clearly resides within a well-defined frame of reference, the good problem-solver can quickly remedy the situation. For instance, the manager of a baseball team can replace any player not performing up to expectations. But as our problems have become more interwoven or interdependent among overlapping jurisdictions, the solutions are not so clearcut. The baseball commissioner charged with managing the twelve teams in a league, for instance, faces a more difficult challenge than the team manager in identifying the appropriate frame of reference in which to see the league's problem. How much more difficult to solve problems when the frame of reference is nebulous or ambiguous or missing altogether! Unless the parameters of the frame of reference are known, it is not even possible to locate the problem accurately in its setting.

It has become a cliché to state that a problem well defined is half solved. This suggests that the problem should be clearly located in its proper context such that surrounding coordinates can indicate in what directions and with what magnitudes corrections can be applied. Without the proper frame or format, any problem becomes a dilemma. Dilemmas can't be solved except by accident. The growing worldly interdependence in social, political and economic liaisons has created more dilemmas, which will require better frames of reference to convert them to manageable problems. Most of our persistent larger "problems" are dilemmas for which analytic frames are too narrow: war, nuclear armament, nuclear-waste disposal, affirmative action, sexual harassment, crime, inflation, poverty, distribution of wealth, unemployment.

A Preliminary Sweep of the Social Science Horizon

In order to gain some perspective on the models of society that were in vogue in earlier days when problems were more directly and more quickly solved, the author conducted an informal search through a wide range of basic anthropology, sociology, human ecology, political economy and economic literature mainly from the twentieth century to find how society was viewed and how it operated. It was hoped that such a model or models might be helpful in providing more comprehensive frames for putting some of society's contemporary dilemmas into better focus and thus reducing them to manageable problems. It was a long and generally disappointing search but a few such models (or near models) will be presented for background purposes.

More recently, another sociologist has complained about the lack of scholarly attention devoted to the organization of thought comprehending larger realities (MacCannell, p. 3):

> Now, it seems to me that sociology will not progress much beyond its current glut of unrelated findings and ideas until we begin to develop methods of approaching the total design of society and models that link the findings of the subfields together in a single framework.

Theoretically, this linking of findings in subfields together could begin at either end of the spectrum. That is, two adjacent fields could be linked into one composite model. Or a more comprehensive model could attempt to link all of society together into one grand design and specialists in specific fields could then work backward from this common frame. It is the purpose of this book to present a general and comprehensive model of contemporary society that could be useful to all. But first, let's see what some of the earlier organizing schemes looked like.

Some Early Organizing Concepts

1. There are two things in which all well-being consists: one of them is the choice of a right end and aim of action, and the other the discovery of the actions which are means towards it; for the means and the end may agree or disagree (Aristotle, p. 536).

    This is probably the most profound statement of organizational design found. It is the keystone of all that follows in this book.

2. Through the channels of its standards, codes, and policies; of its ideals, tastes, and faiths; of its creeds, "isms", and investigations, the mental life of society flows in an ever-changing distribution. One generation is absorbed in political concerns, another in business affairs. At one time society is religious, at another time creative and artistic, at yet another time scientific. Always, however, a tendency towards the establishment of a normal equilibrium may be observed (Giddings, p. 147).

Early sociologists like Giddings occasionally rhapsodized about the grand sweep of events around a balancing equilibrium.

3. Once all things were phases of a single destiny: the church, the state, the family, the school were means to the same end; the rights and duties of the individual in society, the rules of morality, the themes of art, and the techniques of science were all of them ways of revealing the adumbrating, of applying the laws laid down in the divine constitution of the universe. In the modern world, institutions are more or less independent, each serving its own proximate purpose, and our culture is really a collection of separate interests sovereign within its own realm (Lippman, p. 112).

Walter Lippman was a noted American author and journalist who was disturbed by the apparent deflections of institutional behavior from a perceived unified direction.

4. It is impossible to get a comprehension of any complex societal structure without taking it to pieces, somewhat as one takes down an automobile. The mind cannot understand either the whole or the interrelation of the parts without the employment of that expedient. Yet it is not always realized that when analysis is done, results are dead, unreal, and misleading unless the investigator or student frees himself from his categories and, enlightened but not hampered or bound by what analysis has taught him, reassembles the parts and rises to a view of the intricately interlocking action of all the factors. Neat piles of springs, bolts, wheels, and other parts, lying about on the floor, are not an automobile. Similarly with a society; it is not composed of sets of institutions that have been analyzed out and separately examined; it is the whole of them acting together. If we take society and societal life down into its components, we must put them together again, and try to see them in their involved interactions; thus only shall we form a real conception of them.... There is no way to portray at once the whole intricacy of society and societal life. But if the mind remains alert to the shortcomings of all analysis and classification, the conceptions of society as a living whole, ought to break over it as the various sets of its institutions are passed in review (Sumner and Keller, p. 87).

Mores gather, then, about interests, and develop where the interests are salient, into institutions. Aligned with the social forces, and of course resulting from their action, are what we might call the hunger-interest, the love-interest, the gratification- interest, and the fear-interest: the interests involving the self-maintenance, self-perpetuation, and self-gratification of society, and its relations with the supernatural. About these basic, permanent, and engrossing interests the mores have formed in their characteristic way and on them the taboo has exercised its distinctive function. The result has been the development of massive institutions or blocks of institutions, corresponding to three of the four interests, and of a numerous but far less integrated galaxy of minor institutions in the case of one of them—the gratification-interest. These are:

I. The institutions of societal self-maintenance, including the industrial organization, property, war for plunder, and the regulative organization—all corresponding to the hunger-or-preservationinterest;

II. Those of societal self-perpetuation, including marriage and the family—corresponding to the love-interest;

III. Those of societal self-gratification, including more or less unrelated societal forms, such as practices of ostentation in dress, ornament, social etiquette, war for glory, and other particulars, and forms of pleasure-seeking, such as games,gambling, the use of stimulants and narcotics, dancing, play-acting, and the fine arts—corresponding to the gratification interest;

IV. Those of religion in the broadest sense, including animism, daimonis, and their derivatives—corresponding to the fear-interest.

All of these institutions interpenetrate, as do the interests that summoned them into being. Property, for instance, goes back in no small degree to vanity; marriage is not by any means to be connected solely with sex and love; gambling does not find its sole motive in pleasure-seeking; dancing is often religious in nature; and religious practices are not unresponsive altogether to the hunger-interest or to that of sex. Each of these interests produces consequences on the domain of the others which are often, indeed, foreign to its own satisfaction. These cross-relations will reveal themselves as we go on… In no case of evolution is there a possibility of drawing hard and fast distinctions. Categories run into one another across zones of transition, and no such zones are clean-cut but all are blurred (Sumner and Keller, pp. 88–90).

Sociology as a social science attempting to describe the general structure of society and to identify the basic influences affecting that structure gradually emerged as a recognizable discipline somewhere after the middle of the nineteenth century. Only after decades of assembling enough component parts were attempts made to integrate them into more cohesive wholes. The work of Sumner and Keller was a milestone in this direction.

5. Nevertheless, even today it is not generally recognized how numerous and diverse are the elements common to all known cultures. The following is a partial list of items, arranged in alphabetical order to emphasize their variety, which occur, so far as the author's knowledge goes, in every culture known to history or ethnography: age-grading, athletic sports, bodily adornment, calendar, cleanliness training, community organization, cooking, cooperative labor, cosmology, courtship, dancing, decorative art, divination, division of labor, dream interpretation, education, eschatology, etiquette, faith healing, family, feasting, fire making, folklore, food taboos, funeral rites, games, gestures, gift giving, government, greetings, hair styles, hospitality, housing, hygiene, incest taboos, inheritance rules, joking, kin-groups, kinship nomenclature, language, law, luck superstitions, magic, marriage, mealtimes, medicine, modesty concerning natural functions, mourning, music, mythology, numerals, obstetrics, penal sanctions, personal names, population policy, postnatal care, pregnancy usages, puberty customs, religious ritual, residence rules, sexual restrictions, soul concepts, status differentiation, surgery, tool making, trade, visiting, weaning, and weather control (Murdock, p. 124).

The true universals of culture, then, are not identities in habit, in definable behavior. They are similarities in classification, not in content. They represent categories of historically and behaviorally diverse elements which nevertheless have so much in common that competent observers feel compelled to classify them together (Murdock, p. 125).

Many cultural habits, however, instead of gratifying basic drives directly, serve only to facilitate their eventual satisfaction. Cultures contain an immense number of so-called "instrumental responses" which of themselves reduce no basic drives but merely pave the way for other acts which have rewarding results. Instrumental acts acquire in time of course, the support of learned or derived drives, but they are seldom innately rewarding in themselves. Making a spear or a pot, for instance, gratifies no basic impulse, although at some future time the result may serve to lessen the interval or the expended effort between the onset of the hunger drive and its reduction (Murdock, p. 132).

Anthropologist Murdock's listing of cultural common denominators shows how diverse human behavior has become and therefore, how difficult it is to develop satisfactory classification schemes.

6. Human ecology attempts to describe the factors that influence the location, size, and physical organization of the community. It distinguishes community from society, and accepts an organic interpretation

of the dynamics of community (an aggregate of individuals, groups or institutions) as a series of interdependent , *natural areas* one within the other, each area controlled by a center of dominance, and varying in its characteristics (physical and the correlated social) according to the distance from the center of dominance. Competition is the driving force, both for determining relative positions, and for changes in spatial relations over time, when equilibrium or balance, is disturbed. Changes take place through the locomotive powers of man (mobility being the means of survival and readjustment), through *invasion* and *succession*. This change is evidenced in *concentration*, *segregation* and *centralization* (Llewellyn and Hawthorn, pp. 470–471).

From plant ecology were taken certain concepts which have remained central to the human ecological approach.

1. *Community* as an aggregate of individuals spatially located.
2. *Competition* as one of the fundamental conditions of their need to obtain sustenance, and cooperation as one of the means of mutually adjusting to this common need. This *competitive-cooperation* for the basic physical resources has been summed up by ecologists in the word *symbiosis*.
3. All of the sub-social or basic physical adjustments made by individuals to each other on a non-thoughtful level are called *biotic*.
4. The series of relations and mutual adjustments of individuals to each other in the acquisition and distribution of sustenance is the "web-of-life."
5. The role played by each individual in the acquisition and distribution of sustenance determines his *niche* in the *division of labor* or function.
6. This community of individuals achieves an *equilibrium* with the environment, wherein needs are adjusted to natural resources.
7. When this equilibrium between community and environment is upset, and when new factors enter in to disturb the status quo, then a state of disequilibrium, or unbalance, involves new processes of adjustment and reassertion (Llewellyn and Hawthorn, pp. 471–472).

The recognition of human ecology as a branch of general ecology emerged as a separate academic subject even later than sociology. It too, however, has made useful contributions to the generalizations about the human social structure as the above quotations attest.

7. A society is a group of human beings sharing a self-sufficient system of action which is capable of existing longer than the life-span of an individual, the group being recruited at least in part by the sexual

reproduction of the members. The functional prerequisites for a society:
   a. Provision for adequate relationship to the environment and for sexual recruitment.
   b. Role differentiation and role assignment.
   c. Communication.
   d. Shared cognitive orientations.
   e. A shared, articulated set of goals.
   f. The normative regulation of means.
   g. The regulation of affective expression.
   h. Socialization.
   i. The effective control of disruptive forms of behavior (Aberle et al, pp. 100–110).

   This is another listing of the social prerequisites that an on-going society must recognize. Some of the terms are different but most of the functions were included in previous listings.

8. In the dynamic substratum we cannot separate economic forces and political forces and cultural forces as though they operated in detachment, nor can we speak of technological forces and geographical forces and biological forces and all the rest. There are emergent means that we call technological and there are emergent forms that we distinguish as economic or political. But these are, as such, undynamic; impotent outside the conjuncture. The dynamic conjuncture is the complex of means, conditions, and values. They meet and focus in what I have termed the "dynamic assessment," that is the judgment that carries a decision to act. Such a judgment is the prime mover in social change, it is a fusion of emotion and desire and opinion and imagination that discharges itself in action as it masters means and accommodates itself to conditions (MacIver, p. 139).

   This is a favorite quotation and one which lends itself to graphic portrayal. Create a graphic model using MacIver's key concepts.

9. The crisis of our times is not a crisis simply in economics, politics, or thought, nor is it merely a crisis in all three conjointly. It is a crisis in which economic, political, and ideological problems each compounded by the other two, must be resolved by nations opposed in their political doctrines. Not only can no one set of problems be discussed independently of the other, but also no positive program of action can be limited and self-contained enough to escape suspicion as a possible device to advance interests, or to seize power, or to solidify preconceptions (McKeon, pp. 233–260).

This quotation illustrates well how a problem between large complex entities becomes extremely difficult to work out.

10. Man has the same basic problems to face on this earth, no matter in what age or in what region he lives. First of all, there has always been the pressing problem of sustenance and shelter, necessitating *economic* patterns. The fundamental fact of bisexuality and the helplessness of the human infant have forever demanded some form of the *family*. The great and ominous confusion of the universe must be studied, and, if possible, controlled, notably through the development of the culture pattern known as *religion*. Despite the fact that men are social beings, ever found in groups, they need some organized system of rules under a *government*. Basic to the creation and development of culture is some form of *language* for the interchange of ideas. Man is a busy descendent from the anthropoids, and like all animals of that stock must busy himself at nonpurposeful pursuits. Here we find the basis for *recreation* and the *arts*. Finally, there must be dependable knowledge and the concretion of this knowledge in tools and techniques to manage the physical, organic, and cultural environment (Merrill and Eldredge, p. 84).

By the mid-twentieth century general summaries such as the one above appeared more frequently in basic sociology and cultural anthropology textbooks.

11. Man is unique: he is the only living species that has a culture. By *culture*, we mean an extrasomatic, temporal continuum of things and events dependent on symboling. Specifically and concretely, culture consists of tools, implements, utensils, clothing, ornaments, customs, institutions, beliefs, rituals, games, works of art, language, etc. All people in all times and places have possessed culture; no other species has or has had culture… (White, p. 3).

…We may divide the components of culture into four categories: ideological, sociological, sentimental or attitudinal, and technological (White, p. 6).

We see, then, that everything comprising *culture* has been made possible by and is dependent on the symbolic faculty: the knowledge, lore, and beliefs of man: his social systems; his institutions, political and economic; his rituals, paraphernalia, and forms of art: his traditional attitudes and sentiments: his codes of ethics and etiquette; and finally his technology (White, p.8).

Man needs food and materials of many kinds for clothing, utensils, ornaments, etc.: these must be obtained, of course, from the external world. But man has inner psychic, social, and "spiritual" needs that can be fed and nourished without drawing on the external world at all. Man needs courage, comfort, consolation, confidence, companionship, a feeling of consequence in the scheme of things that life is worthwhile; and some assurance of success. It is the business of culture to serve these needs of the "spirit" as well as the needs of the body (White, p. 9).

It is fairly obvious that the social organization of a people is not only dependent on their technology but is determined to a great extent, if not wholly, by it, both in form and content. As a matter of fact, a social system might well be defined as the way in which a society makes use of its particular technology in the various life-sustaining processes: subsistence, protection from the elements, defense from enemies, combating disease, etc. The activities of hunting, fishing, gathering, farming, tending herds and flocks, mining, and all the processes by means of which raw materials are transferred and made ready for human consumption are not merely technological processes; they are social processes as well. And as social processes they are functions of their respective technological processes; as the latter change, so will the former. The processes of combating disease, "controlling" the weather, providing protection against the elements and defense against enemies are likewise social processes. Social systems have, therefore, like technological systems, subsistence, health, protection, and defense coordinates. Of these, the subsistence function is the most important because all others are dependent on it. Thus, hunting, herding, gathering, fishing, farming, mining, manufacturing, and transportation will influence, each in its own way, and in proportion to its magnitude, the form and content of a social system (White, pp. 19–20).

Thus we may say, in summary of our discussion of the interrelationship of technological, social, philosophic, and sentimental sectors of culture, that technology is the basis on which the cultural system as a whole rests. Secondly, it is the technology of a culture that determines in a general way the form and content of social systems, philosophies, and sentiments. In the system that is culture, technology is the independent variable, the other sectors the dependent variables... (White, pp. 26–27).

These concepts by Leslie White were the most comprehensive description of culture found. Most of the foregoing quotations were variously successful attempts to identify the different sectors making up our societal composition. But even if all the sectors are identified, the parts do not comprise the whole. Missing is an integrating dynamic to differentiate among the parts and then to coordinate and unify the operational togetherness of the composite "going or doing or being system." To contribute to that elusive integrating dynamic is the mission of this work.

REFERENCES

Aberle, D. F. et al, "The Functional Prerequisites of a Society," *Ethics*, volume LX, number 2, January 1950. Reprinted with permission of the University of Chicago Press.

Aristotle, *Politics*, 7:13, as reproduced in *The Works of Aristotle, Volume II*, from *Great Books of the Western World*. Editor in Chief: Robert Maynard Hutchins, volume 9 (Chicago: Encyclopaedia Britannica, 1952).

Carroll, Lewis, *Alice's Adventures in Wonderland and Through the Looking Glass* (Signet Classics, 1960).

Giddings, Franklin Henry, *The Principles of Sociology* (New York: The Macmillan Company, 1921).

Lippman, Walter, *A Preface to Morals* (New York: The Macmillan Company, 1929). Reprinted with the permission of Scribner, a Division of Simon & Schuster.

Llewellyn, Emma C. and Audrey Hawthorn, "Human Ecology," in *Twentieth Century Sociology*. Editors: Georges Gurvitch and Wilbert E. Moore (New York: Philosophical Library, 1945).

MacCannell, Dean, *The Tourist: A New Theory of the Leisure Class* (New York: Schocken Books, 1976).

MacIver, Robert M., "History and Social Causation," in *The Tasks of Economic History*. Papers presented at 3rd Annual Meeting of the Economic History Association, Princeton, New Jersey, September 3-4, 1943. A supplemental issue of *The Journal of Economic History*, pp. 135–145 at 139, December 1943. Reprinted with permission of Cambridge University Press.

McKeon, Richard, "Philosophy and the Diversity of Cultures" (*Ethics*, volume LX, July 1950). Reprinted with permission of The University of Chicago Press.

Merrill, Francis E. and H. Wentworth Eldredge, *Culture and Society* (New York: Prentice Hall, 1952).

Murdock, George Peter, "The Common Denominator of Cultures," *The Science of Man in the World Crisis*. Editor: Ralph Linton (New York: Columbia University Press, 1945). Reprinted by permission of the publisher.

Sumner, William Graham and Albert Galloway Keller, *The Science of Society*, volume I (New Haven: Yale University Press, 1927).

Thomas, Lewis, "Biomedical Science and Human Health: The Long-Range Prospect," *Daedalus* 106 (3) Summer 1977. Reprinted by permission of *Daedalus*, Journal of the American Academy of Arts and Sciences, from the issue entitled "Discoveries and Interpretations: Studies in Contemporary Scholarship."

White, Leslie A., *The Evolution of Culture* (New York: McGraw-Hill, 1959).

Young, Robert M., "Association of Ideas," in *Dictionary of the History of Ideas*. Editor-in-chief: Philip P. Weiner, volume 1 (New York: Charles Scribner's Sons, 1973, p. 111).

CHAPTER 4

Early Formats in History

Before attempting to set forth the general system model or format, which is the centerpiece of this work, it was felt worthwhile to spend some time combing through recorded history to gain some sense of how early thinking developed elementary formats and how they were adapted to serve man's need for understanding.

From Points of Reference to Frames of Reference

It is in the nature of man's greatest asset—his restless and inquiring mind—to seek explanations for the unknown. When relatively little was known for certain, he simply embraced the most plausible or powerful theory or explanation from a credible source, tested its credibility for as long as patience lasted, and then enshrined those that seemed to have enduring positive value. It became a valuable point of reference to be called on again and again when our earlier ancestors wanted an explanation. When many theories, mythical or not, existed to explain life's contingencies, many points of reference altogether formed a matrix or frame of reference.

Because relatively little was generally known and especially verifiable until the so-called "scientific method" became central to intellectual endeavors, the range of acceptable answers to life's persistent questions was enormous. Because so much was based on the subjective imaginations of gifted leaders in early communities, the variety and richness of explanations far exceeded that of most fields dependent on provable cause and effect relationships. Thus, elaborate matrices linking many explanatory points of reference together could have been developed by those gifted leaders. That many explanations were patently contradictory placed burdens on both deliverers and receivers of the messages. The deliverers had to enshroud their messages with persuasive packaging for credibility and the recipients had to differentiate among the widely varying alternative explanations. This persuasive packaging ranged wildly from zany dances and body torture to self-hypnotism and gobbledygook communication with the gods. It was a form of disguised early entertainment coupled with advice that most took seriously.

From Cave Pictographs to Early Language

From the Natufian culture of cave dwellers in the valley of the Wadi en Natuf in Israel in 10,500 to 8,500 B.C. and thereafter, we have only sketchy information. Before these times and back some two hundred thousand years to when man is alleged to have become a distinct species, we must rely on scientific analyses of uncovered burial remains.

Excepting cave pictographs perhaps, man's recording of major events began about 3500 B.C. according to the latest significant findings. The earliest cemetery found at Ur in what is now Iraq released artifacts that provided some sketchy information historians and archaeologists have used to trace the Sumerian culture back to about 3100 B.C. An additional four hundred years was added to account for earlier graves found in that cemetery.

Early Egyptian culture has been traced back to about 3300 B.C. Indeed, we may in the future be able to deduce fragments of history back another two hundred thousand years or so based on the Kings Lists, which were recorded around 2000 B.C. when Suzerain scribes felt the need to sort through and organize what must have been a confusing mess of historical data (Woolley, p. 27). These Kings Lists identify kings prior to the reign of Hammurabi who assumed his kingship about 1940 B.C. at the end of the First Dynasty of Babylon. Unfortunately, their historical data were destroyed and we must await further deductions from possible future discoveries.

From Cuneiform to the Alphabet

Apparently the Suzerains had early invented their cuneiform script after developing "…an agglutinative language somewhat resembling ancient Turkish (Turanian) in its formation though not in its etymology" (Woolley, p. 6). Cuneiform was the oldest form of analytic script and as such was a transitional stage between ideograph and pure phonetic writing based on an alphabet. With the ability to speak and communicate in writing, the explanations for natural phenomena occurring in their environments must have expanded rapidly.

Archaeologist Leonard Woolley's analysis of early Sumerian artifacts led him to conclude: "So far as we know, the fourth millennium before Christ saw Sumerian art at its zenith. By the First Dynasty of Ur if there is any change it is in the nature of a decadence, and from later ages we have nothing to parallel the treasures of the prehistoric tombs" (Woolley, p. 44). This impression of a relatively highly developed art was based on embellishments and refinements found in their architecture, jewelry, weaponry and metallurgy. To have reached this impressive stage of development by 3500 B.C. suggests that many centuries of evolutionary progress must have preceded it, perhaps back another six or seven thousand years or more when it is estimated that settled agriculture began to replace nomadic gathering, hunting and fishing.

During this prehistoric period scholars have speculated about early communication by horns, trumpets, reed flutes and the tom-tom drum since many such have been found among buried artifacts. But their sounds were not recorded and therefore no record exists to piece together earlier man's thought processes.

Once the concept of a script was developed and found to be useful, however, its applications grew and many adaptations were overlaid on the original to suit the needs and whimsies of neighboring tribes in their attempts to customize the great ideas that they had recently stolen or borrowed. According to one source (*The New Encyclopaedia Britannica*, p. 64), the northern Semites living in Egypt in the seventeenth century B.C. adapted hieroglyphic characters to develop the earliest purely consonant alphabet and added two letters to designate vowels "…used with the glottal catch."

The Use of Vowels to Make Speech Smoother

Several centuries later about 1000 B.C. the direct ancestor of all modern European alphabets was developed in Greece. By adding several new letters, modifying or dropping several others, and converting the Semitic consonants alef, lie, yod, ayin and waw to the Greek letters alpha, epsilon, iota, omicron and upsilon (the English vowels of a, e, i, o and u, respectively), the Greek alphabet was made more accurate and understandable for both written and verbal communication (*The New Encyclopaedia Britannica*, p. 456). The few vowel and symbol sounds of a, e, i, o and u (and occasionally y and w) connecting the much more common consonant symbols and sounds produced smoother sound without occluding, diverting or obstructing the flow of air from the lungs.

Before the fifth century B.C. the Greek alphabet could be divided into two principal and similar branches, the Ionic (Eastern) and the Chaldean (Western). The Chaldean alphabet probably gave rise to the Etruscan alphabet of Italy around the eighth century B.C. and hence indirectly to the other Italic alphabets, including the Latin alphabet. In 403 B.C. Athens officially adopted the Ionic alphabet and its use spread rapidly thereafter as the classic Greek alphabet with twenty-four letters, seven of which were vowels. Its symbols consisted of capital letters, most suitable for monuments and inscriptions. A cursive and minuscule running script was developed thereafter for easier writing (*The New Encyclopaedia Britannica*, p. 456). Until 500 B.C. the Greek language was always written from right to left like its Semitic forebears but changed thereafter from left to right.

Original Uses of the New Languages

Most of the literary forms of the modern Western world were invented or at least formalized by the ancient Greeks. The epic meant a long verse narrative using a wide array of characters and events. Other forms included elegiac and lyric poetry, drama, the pastoral, history chronologies, oratory and philosophy.

As epic poems, the *Iliad* and *Odyssey* usually attributed to Homer dominated the Greek mind. These oldest known literary sources were written in the ninth or eighth centuries B.C. and described the siege of Troy and the Greeks in the Trojan War and the wanderings of Odysseus during the ten years after the fall of Troy. They were originally sung by wandering minstrels rather than read and were the outcome of centuries of oral tradition.

The epics of Hesiod (possibly eighth or seventh century B.C.), have been called didactic or pedantic as they were intended to instruct. His *Theogeny* was a genealogy of the gods and his *Works and Days* was a combination of homily, agricultural treatise and almanac.

Elegiac poetry developed from the end of the eighth century B.C. The name had nothing to do with the laments or praises for the dead but rather with the Greek word for flute. Flute songs is what they were, composed for different occasions: amatory, martial, family events. Unlike epics, they allowed scope for the individual viewpoint and feelings. Usually composed in stanza form as odes, sonnets or hymns, they were better adapted to vocal communication by song. Since written messages were dependent on the learned scribes and organized postal delivery systems were nonexistent, the minstrel form of communication dominated for centuries.

From Language to Myth and Magic

Speculation about the evolution of human development must include the assumption that the growth of myths expanded rapidly with the early advent of spoken and much later written communication. Myth is generally considered to be traditional stories of unknown authorship to explain some phenomenon of nature. They usually involved the exploits of gods and heroes in preliterate societies. Magic is generally considered to be producing results through mysterious and scary forces or unexplained powers. Magic involved the practice of using charms, spells or mind-boggling rituals to invoke supernatural intervention or to produce supernatural effects.

Variations of magic seeking negative effects have come to be known as necromancy, sorcery or witchcraft in which the devil or evil spirits were invoked for harmful or sinister purposes. Both myth and magic flourished in primitive societies and helped to answer some of the more persistent questions involving the vast mysteries of life that surrounded them and were so powerful, so unpredictable and yet so pervasive.

Why were myth and magic so important in early societies? Then as now, meaning requires that we develop whole or comprehensive explanations within our frames of reference whether verifiable or not, conclusive or not. Meaning refers to the why and how of events transpiring within a context. With no computers and internets, no television, newspapers, religions or libraries full of detail and explanation, early man was totally dependent on credible myth for understanding.

Quite likely, individuals before language and thought transfer generated their own personal mythologies for understanding and guidance. Language and conversation made possible the sharing of mythic patterns, which enlarged each community's store or inventory of such and contributed to the enrichment of that community's shared culture. Culture refers to the sum total of the beliefs, behaviors and ways of living built up by a group of human beings and transmitted from one generation to the next. Although the Sumerian and Egyptian communities were relatively well developed in their art and craft by 3000 B.C., they were essentially simple agriculturally dominated societies with relatively little trading among neighboring groups. Nevertheless, they both had long-established and rich traditions of gods and heroes to explain the mysteries they encountered.

The Vast World of Mythology

There is an immense literature describing and interpreting what we have been able to reconstruct from our knowledge of the past. It is so huge and diverse that it is difficult to summarize. Many brilliant scholars, such as Joseph Campbell, spent entire careers investigating and seeking enlightenment about its various dimensions. Indeed, the term mythology had no boundaries as its explanations covered all or nearly all of life's activities. As he observed:

> Throughout the inhabited world, in all times and under every circumstance, the myths of man have flourished; and they have been the living inspiration of whatever else may have appeared out of the activities of the human body and mind. It would not be too much to say that myth is the secret opening through which the inexhaustible energies of the cosmos pour into human cultural manifestation (Campbell, p. 3).

Myths describe imaginative stories and traditions about the nature, history and future of life on earth and beyond, about our gods, man, other animals and their societies. They concern both fundamental issues and peculiar quirks associated with various earthly conditions.

As one source summarized (*Mythology, An Illustrated Encyclopedia*, p. 10):

> Many myths have a dream-like quality. Strange distorted figures move through them, monsters and hybrid beings. Animals walk and talk like men and animals intermarry, change shape and possess magical powers. Women are impregnated and children born in physically impossible ways. There are sinister and disturbing motifs of parricide, fratricide, cannibalism, castration, incest, rape and murder, which often are not condemned.

Other themes are alluded to in these summaries, such as the following (*Mythology, An Illustrated Encyclopedia*, pp. 9–12):

- the many myths of origin: the dark and watery chaos that first existed, with no light, no sun, moon and stars;
- the cosmic egg, creation from the dismembered body of a god or a monster;
- the separation of earth and sky, which were originally joined together;
- the bringing of order from chaos;
- the making of man from the ground, clay or mud, or his emergence from the ground;
- man's immense catastrophe in the past, often a great flood, after which the world was restored anew;
- various predictions of when and how the world will be destroyed;
- how myths provide a charter of authorization for and sanction kinship rules and marriage customs, the authority of kings and chiefs, the subordination of women, the techniques of hunting, husbandry, art and war;
- how fire, work, old age, disease, death and every other manifestation of life came into being.

Mythology in Early Recorded History

The Sumerian religion was polytheistic and its gods were innumerable. Each city had its own particular god of that city: At Babylon it was Marduk; at Larsa, Shamash; at Ur, Nannar. All the gods originally had their functions: Enki of Eridu was lord of the waters and the god of wisdom who invented handicrafts and the art of writing, Enlil the lord of rain and wind, Nabu of vegetation, Nargal of the plague, Shamash the Sun-god of justice, Ishtar the goddess of love (Woolley, p. 121).

Daily sacrifices were made to the many gods mainly out of fear and with the intention for the god to intervene positively on behalf of the petitioner. Mingling with the medicine men and the priesthood were the magicians whose job it was to conjure away evil and the soothsayers who gave warning of its approach and told how it might be avoided. The people were very superstitious and every kind of accident or chance event had its meaning for good or bad. Books of omens were compiled for consultation on future guidance.

The predynastic Egyptians (before 3400 B.C.) believed their whole environment of sea, earth, air and sky overflowed with spirits, some of whom were involved in carrying out the designs of nature, and others who concentrated on helping or hindering or doing both to man on earth. All the events of nature were attributed to these spirits. It was hoped for by some but believed by many that the continued friendship of the good spirits could be appeased and the hostility of the evil spirits averted by gifts and inducements of many varieties.

The Rise of Animal Worship

For most of their history, the people of ancient Egypt revered only the sacred animal. Zoolatry, or animal worship, did not originate until the Twenty-Sixth Dynasty (664–525 B.C.). Each tribe or separate group had its own protective deities who were incarnated as animals, birds, reptiles or simple fetishes such as rams, bulls, hippopotamuses, cats, hawks, crocodiles and snakes. These animal deities gradually became endowed with human characteristics. At one time there were more than a thousand. Our uses of such terms as talisman, charm and amulet can be traced back to original superstitions in which particular objects were regarded as sacrosanct.

The identities of deities gradually merged to form composite gods, such as Osiris-Ra and Amen-Ra in whom two distinct natures and sets of attributes were joined. Osisris was the great Egyptian deity and personification of all physical and moral good. Ra was the sun god. Amen or Amon was the god of life and reproduction or literally the hidden one who merged with the energy of the sun god. Much creative syncretism was required over the centuries to merge or unite various gods and their characteristics into ever fewer on the road from polytheism to monotheism.

The Greeks Take Over

The Sumerian and Egyptian mythologies evolved as their needs changed until the rise of the Greek influence beginning around 1000 B.C. and the Roman influence thereafter. The period from 462 to 429 B.C. is known as the Age of Pericles. Pericles lived from 495 to 429 B.C. and it was during his years as a leader and statesman in Athens that great intellectual and artistic achievements were accomplished. One scholar (Hampden-Turner, p. 16) describes this period as follows:

> It witnessed the height of the Athenian empire, the establishment of democracy, the centralization of the Delian League in Athens, the *Oresteia* of Aeschylus, the poetry of Pindar, the sculpture of Myron, the philosophy of Anaxagoras, the building of the Parthenon, *Antigone* by Sophocles, Phidias's statue of Athena Parthenos, the Thirty Years Peace, *Medea* by Euripides, the medicine of Hippocrates, the history of Herodotus, and the first production of *Oedipus Rex*.

The richly descriptive Greek mythology accounted for the genesis of the cosmos, the succession of divine rulers, the origin of human woes and the origins of sacrificial practices. Myths were preserved in archaeological remains, Greek literature, poems, Homeric hymns, fragments of epic poems on the Trojan War, and in writings by the tragedians, scholars and poets of the Hellenistic Age (323–30 B.C.) and in writers of the time of the Roman Empire.

According to Hesiod's *Theogeny* (eighth century B.C.), describing the origin or genealogy of the gods, the world was produced by the coming into existence of four divine beings, Chaos (Space), Gaea (Earth), Tartarus (the Abyss) and Eros (love), followed later by the separation of Uranus (the Sky) from Gaea when he was mutilated by his son Cronus. Cronus was then violently overthrown by his son Zeus, who was thought to be the current chief of the gods. An alternative account of the Orphics relates that the primal god, Phanes, emerged from a cosmic egg, married Night and begat heaven and earth. Other well-known myths include the story of the Argonauts who led by Jason sailed into the Black Sea in search of the Golden Fleece; Heracles or Hercules and his labors; Theseus who killed the monster with the body of a man and the head of a bull (the Minotaur); Oedipus who unwittingly killed his father and married his mother; and many other tales. Some of these stories are still celebrated in opera and music today.

The Romans' Turn

Unlike the imaginative and romantic Greeks, early Romans honored limited and more functional-type gods. According to one account (*Mythology, An Illustrated Encyclopedia*, p. 136), a third-century B.C. historian, Fabius Pictor, wrote that specific gods were appealed to for each of the work activities on the farm: Vervactor for the first ploughing, Redarator for the second, Insitor for the sowing, Oberator for the top dressing and for follow-up functions, Messor (harvester), Convector (gatherer), Conditor (storer) and Promitor (producer).

Other spiritual powers were connected with rites of passage, marriage, birth but all were in origin somewhat colorless, and sexless without personality, without offspring. Nevertheless, there is evidence that elaborate lists of liturgical formulas were developed to address each deity (*Encyclopaedia Britannica,* p. 556). Through such developments, the daily activities of each member of a community, whether free or bonded, were prescribed. An elaborate priesthood developed to regulate the codes of ceremonial conduct.

As the generations rolled on, the Romans gradually encountered more contact with Greek communities of southern Italy and Greece itself. The Romans readily embraced the more colorful and artfully endowed deities of the Grecian lore. An early import was the cult of Apollo, which grew rapidly in importance as the Romans had no equivalent. With the Greek cults also came Greek art, statues of Greek deities and Greek mythology. Since Greek cities had divine connections and gods who protected their citizens, the competitive Romans became more receptive to generating their own higher connections. The Greek or Trojan legends were acceptable but there also was a tendency to adopt various highly artificial stories concerning the foundation of Rome.

Early Cultural Diffusion

Thus, the tale of Romulus and Remus, sons of Mars and descendants of Aeneas of Troy were born of a Vestal Virgin and exposed to die in a basket on the river Tiber. Instead, the basket was washed up on a bank where a fig tree grew and a she-wolf saved them, cared for them until a shepherd named Faustulus rescued them and took them to his wife for rearing. When they grew up, they founded a new city that was to become Rome. Later they quarreled and Romulus killed Remus and became the ruler of the city.

The Romans freely adopted the Greek gods modifying their associated myths to serve their own purposes. Zeus, Greek god of the sky and father of gods and men, became Jupiter; Hera became Juno, consort of Jupiter, goddess of motherhood and women; Aries became Apollo, god of light, intellect, the arts, healing and prophecy; Aphrodite to Venus; Hermes to Mercury; Poseidon to Neptune; Kronos to Saturn; Eros to Cupid; Dionysus to Liber; and so on. All of this adoption and adaptation of Greek deities took place during the period roughly from 500 B.C. at the earliest to about 200 B.C. It came at a time when Plato, Aristotle and other Greek philosophers questioned serious belief in traditional mythology but the great majority of Romans were unimpressed and made the transfers anyway. Belief systems have a life of their own.

The Move From Event to Context

Enough has been presented by now to show how the invention of language sparked the development and spread of explanations to account for, explain, or protect against all of life's experiences and contingencies. No single event could take place without that event being placed in a larger context and one in which the individual might seek help from a friendly god. The predatory character of man and nature required that the individual and his associates protect themselves both physically and psychologically against both predictable and unpredictable future challenges. Then as now, an inordinate amount of time, effort and money was spent to curb the predatory conditions of man and nature.

Our review has been limited to a small part of the world from whence Western civilization sprang. But even in that geographically small area surrounding the Mediterranean note the wide range of differing explanations and interpretations of the major events of birth, life and death. Equally diverse and imaginative rationale were invented to explain similar events in other areas around the world, in the South Pacific, South America, Africa, Asia, Northern Europe and the Americas.

For instance, an informative brochure distributed by *American Hawaii Cruises* as recently as 1999 still romances its passengers with the following mythology:

> Ancient Hawaiian chants sing that Maui, the second island child of Wakea and Papa, was a demi-god and half-human mythological sorcerer revered throughout Polynesia. He was a prankster on a grand scale and used guile and humor to perform amazing feats. Legends tell us that he served mankind by fishing up the islands of Hawaii from the ocean floor and acquired the use of fire from a tricky mud hen. He also lifted the sky so humans could walk upright. On the summit of the great mountain *Haleakala* (House of the Sun), he slowed down the sun god with a lasso of braided rope from his sister's hair, thus securing more daylight hours to fish and dry tapa cloth" (from a brochure titled "The Valley Island Maui" placed in each cabin aboard the SS *Independence* on docking at Maui).

Although still being circulated, what stopped the growth of mythological explanations for man's adventures and misadventures? Had we exhausted all possible combinations of metaphysical imagery? Hardly. Practical leadership simply began using different formats.

A Parallel Development in Leadership Direction

Paralleling the development of mythology to explain man's adventures in a mystifying universe was the growth of more practically inspired initiatives designed to control his behavior on a day-by-day basis. This was the province of the tribal leaders, chieftains, or kings who were either chosen to provide clan direction, inherited it, or who assumed it after a conquering battle. The merging of two or more clans or neighboring groups meant that the dominant leadership had the difficult task of integrating different customs, work roles and expectations. This could not have been easily or quickly done, then or now. Note how little effect Russian rule in Central Europe had in changing fifty years of basic and accumulated patterns of behavior in the latter half of the twentieth century A.D. Strong enforcers usually applied coercive tactics to enforce central planning's dictates but fifty years later most of the old patterns re-emerged with smoldering hatreds and centuries-old prejudices bursting into flames.

The first recognizable formation of a written body of laws so far discovered goes back to the kingly reign in Babylon of Hammurabi in 1792 to 1750 B.C. Excavated in 1901 and now residing in the French Louvre is a 7-foot stela or stone pillar, which remains the major source of information about the Code of Hammurabi. Altogether, there were 282 laws or prescriptions written in Akadian cuneiform script, which attempted to establish and/or maintain order among the three classes of citizens living thereunder.

Hammurabi in Action

A leading reference source (*Encyclopedia Americana*, p. 751) states that the laws were grouped by subject and broad categories:

(1–5) Offenses against the administration of justice, such as false accusation;

(6–25) Offenses against property such as theft, robbery, and harboring fugitive slaves;

(26–k) Land and houses—regulations governing tenure, rent, lease, damage;

(L–126) Trade and commerce—loans, debt, deposit;

(127–194) Marriage, family, property-rights of family members regarding status and property legitimization and adoption, inheritance, sexual offenses;

(195–214) Assaults;

(215–240) Regulations concerning professional men—physicians, barbers, builders, boatbuilders, boatmen;

(241–267) Laws concerning agriculture—the hire of oxen, agricultural workers, and shepherds, and misuse of implements and supplies;

(268–267) Wage and fee rates—for animals, workmen, artisans, boats;

(278–282) Laws regulating the sale of slaves.

Although there is some disagreement and various interpretations of many of the provisions of Hammurabi's Code, it is surprising to find such a comprehensive code so well articulated by the eighteenth century B.C. Other legal prescriptions of a piece-meal nature preceding Hammurabi's have been found with estimated dates back to about 2400 B.C.

We can only speculate about the possibilities of still earlier unwritten codes of conduct originating with the various rulers of kingdoms, tribes and communities. These must have existed and been passed along rather carefully to succeeding generations if any semblance of order and progress was to be achieved. Since the 7-foot stele was found in Susa, a ruined city in what is now western Iran, it was believed to be taken there as booty by an Elamite king of the twelfth century B.C.

Predatory strikes by restless neighboring tribes appear to have been nearly continuous throughout all these centuries as no visible or perceived "balance of power" concept had been achieved. Emerging from permanently wandering groups into partly nomadic and temporarily settled tribes, there was much opportunistic movement around the entire Mediterranean area.

The Time Was Getting Ripe for Something Major

No clear picture of even the major events has been assembled from discovered historical fragments between the time of Hammurabi to the tenth or eighth centuries B.C. However, one of the major events of all time has been reconstructed by biblical scholars interpreting possible scenarios mainly from two of the five books of the *Pentateuch: Genesis* and *The Exodus*. *The Pentateuch* was comprised of the first five books of the Old Testament or bible known in Hebrew as the humash or the torah. They are also referred to as the five books of Moses or "the law of Moses."

It was during the thirteenth or possibly twelfth century B.C. that one of these semi-nomadic tribes encamped around the Canaanite cities adopted the Hebrew language of Canaan and in addition differentiated itself from the other Canaanites by rejecting the worship of multiple gods to profess recognition of just one God. Moving into the Goshen district of Egypt, the followers of the so-called Patriarch (Abraham, Isaac and Jacob), encountered the legendary Ten Plagues, the miraculous crossing of the Red Sea and the Revelation on Mount Sinai. The central figure in this reconstruction of events was Moses. He became the great liberator, leader, lawgiver, man of God and "father of the prophets" who would piece together the biblical prophecies, another charismatic function. Thus, the Exodus became the cornerstone of Jewish history, religion and nationhood.

Since no objective or external evidence is available to prove that Moses lived or experienced what he recounted, some scholars believed that some of the concepts advanced in the Ten Commandments were too advanced for the Mosaic era and that they might better be associated with the later seventh century B.C. Nevertheless, few deny the genius of the organization and brevity of the Ten Commandments.

The Most Enduring Frame of Reference

Simply stated, "The Ten Commandments are the most terse, inclusive, and celebrated abridgement of a code of ethical conduct in all of mankind's tradition" (*Encyclopedia Americana,* p. 469 quoting Charles E. Sheedy, C.S.C., University of Notre Dame).

An abridged text of the Ten Commandments in *Exodus* follows (*Encyclopedia Americana,* p. 470):

1. I am the Lord your God, who brought you out of the land of Egypt, out of the house of bondage. You shall have no other gods before me (vs. 2a, 3).
2. You shall not make for yourself a graven image (vs. 4). You shall not bow down to them or serve them (vs. 5a).
3. You shall not take the name of the Lord your God in vain (vs. 7).
4. Remember the Sabbath day, to keep it holy (vs. 8).
5. Honor your father and mother (vs. 12a).
6. You shall not kill (vs. 13).
7. You shall not commit adultery (vs. 14).
8. You shall not steal (vs. 19).
9. You shall not bear false witness against your neighbor (vs. 16).
10. You shall not covet (vs. 17a).

These injunctions were allegedly spoken by God from the top of Mount Sinai and addressed to the children of Israel seven weeks after the exodus from Egypt. Subsequently, they were inscribed by God on the two stone tables of the Covenant and handed to Moses to be placed in the temple built by Solomon (*Encyclopedia of Judaism,* p. 697). "The exact date of the Exodus is not indicated in the *Pentateuch,* but many scholars, basing themselves on external evidence, place the event as occurring approximately in 1280 B.C.E." (*Encyclopedia of Judaism,* p. 249).

So powerful was the impact of these commandments as delivered by God from Mt. Sinai that they have endured for some three thousand years and been accepted by succeeding Christian sects with little modification. Altogether, they have provided the most powerful and pervasive single frame of reference guiding human behavior yet recorded.

Enter the Big Three: Socrates, Plato and Aristotle

Socrates wrote nothing but spent much time with young men of promise during his lifetime in Athens from c. 470 B.C. to 399 B.C. He directed their thought toward analyses of the character and conduct of human life: "to know thyself." Because he was a prominent figure and persisted in what was then considered questionable behavior for many years, he was indicted in 399 B.C. for "impiety," "corruption of the young," "neglect of the gods whom the city worships and the practice of religious novelties." Found guilty, he was sentenced to death. Declining an opportunity to escape, he drank the fatal hemlock.

His method of operation was to engage in friendly but serious dialogue questioning not only the young men in the local gymnasia of the time but also the politicians, poets and artisans in the marketplace and the streets about their various callings and their ideas of right and wrong. He is grouped with Plato and Aristotle because it was his persistent and penetrating questioning that greatly influenced Plato directly and Aristotle indirectly through Plato.

Plato (b. 428/427 B.C. d. 348/347 B.C.) was born into a distinguished Athenian family and nurtured political ambitions until he became persuaded that a life in politics was no place for a man of conscience. Greatly influenced by his mentor, Plato reconstructed the life and thought of Socrates in several of his well-received dialogues. His dramatic dialogue, *Protagoras*, sets forth the main principles of the Socratic morality. In the *Euthyphio*, *Apology* and *Crito* dialogues, Plato deals with the behavior of Socrates before, during and after his trial. Plato succeeded in establishing Socrates, who was martyred in his time for unconventional ideas, as the important "hinge" figure between the previous fanciful explanations and the newer rational and more philosophical thinking.

Plato After Socrates

After Socrates' death, Plato spent several years traveling in Greece, Egypt, Italy and Sicily. About 387 B.C. he founded the Academy in Athens as an institute for the systematic pursuit of philosophical and scientific research. He presided over the Academy for the rest of his life and considered it to be his chief accomplishment. But he underestimated the power of the written word and the enormous influence of his seminal thinking.

Several valuable frames of reference were suggested in his works that provide guidance today. For instance, in the ethical scheme of *The Republic*, three lives are distinguished: those of the philosopher, of the votary (or devoted follower) of enjoyment, and the man of action. The end of the first, he wrote, is wisdom; of the second, the gratification of appetite; and of the third, practical distinction. According to Plato, these reflect the three elements or active principles within a man: 1) considered rational judgment of good; 2) a multitude of claimant and conflicting appetites for particular gratifications; and 3) a factor of spirited higher ideal emotion manifested as resentment against infringements both by others and our own appetites.

The Cardinal Virtues

The same three distinctions reappear in the structure of society; there are 1) the statesmen; 2) the general civilian population who provide for material needs; and 3) the executive force of army and police. These three orders are thus respectively the judgmental, appetitive and spiritual elements. The four cardinal virtues are therefore wisdom, the excellence of the thinking part; courage, that of the spirited part (loyalty to the rule of life laid down by judgment); temperance, that of the appetitive part (acquiescence of the nonrational elements to the plan of life prescribed by judgment); and justice, (the state in which each of the elements is vigorously executing its own function and, in loyal contentment, confining itself within its limits). Such a society is a true aristocracy or rule of the best.

Plato saw successive deviations from aristocracy (rule of the wisest) as: timocracy (the benign military state); oligarchy (the state dominated by a few persons); plutocracy, (the state run by merchant princes); democracy (the state run by the inexpert); and worst of all, tyranny (the state subjected to an irresponsible or criminal will).

Plato's *Republic* is an example of synthetic thinking. Beginning with a simple question about justice, he slowly and progressively brings additional topics into focus: first ethics; then politics; then educational theory; then theory of knowledge; and then metaphysics. Throughout he was seeking an overall unity or synthesis or format. This synthetic impulse operates by seeking to comprehend the whole, to place all major pieces into a comprehensible pattern. In this way he was enormously influential in the thinking and writings through the centuries of such great figures as St. Thomas Aquinas, Benedict de Spinoza, G.W.F. Hegel and Alfred North Whitehead, among others.

Aristotle After Plato

Aristotle (384–322 B.C.) was a student at Plato's Academy for twenty years during which he engaged in many dialogues and from which he formed a strong Socratic-Plato orientation. His approach was different, however, as he emphasized a more analytic or critical emphasis by concentrating on a single concept or part by breaking it into its constituent components for greater clarity and precision. His conception of systematic knowledge was rationalistic aiming at deductive organization. He felt that the scientist must look for basic materials, structure, causal agencies and directive goals or functions. These concepts he saw as answers to the essential questions: Out of what? What is it? From where? And for the sake of what? These have been called the material, formal, efficient and final causes, respectively. This methodology served admirably for discovering existent order in many fields of inquiry, whether in classifying animal species or mapping constitutions of city-states.

Uniting Eclecticism With Analytic Rigor

Aristotle's goal-oriented or teleological approach sees man striving toward one ultimate end, which he identifies as happiness. Since the good or goal is defined as what all men aim at, the normative is not invoked transcendentally. Rather it is systematically grounded in the needs, goal seeking and possible outcomes of human social interaction. No doubt many other writers have also discovered in hindsight that Aristotle's thinking preempted theirs and that his theories and conceptualizing laid the groundwork for many fields of inquiry such as in logic and the theory of science, physics, biology, psychology, metaphysics, ethics, politics, rhetoric and esthetics. Many of these disciplines are indebted to Aristotle for their subsequent development.

Aristotle's *Politics* has served as a foundation for the whole Western tradition. It had a central influence from the thirteenth to fifteenth century, notably in the political thought of Thomas Aquinas and subsequent Christian political thinkers who used his analytical platforms to extend their own thinking. In his *Politics* there is the concept of a natural order of human institutions, the conceptualization of an ideal order, and the classification and analysis of existent sociopolitical structures and their behavior to execute practical programs. His ideal order was similar to Plato's with an aristocracy emphasizing the quality of men and apportioning the authority of rule according to merit. His classification of constitutions was twofold: 1) a dichotomy between genuine forms dedicated to the common interest and perverted forms considered exploitive on behalf of the ruling party; and 2) a numerical classification of rulers into one or few or many. The dual classification yields kingship, aristocracy and polity (rule by numerous substantial citizens) as genuine forms and tyranny, oligarchy and democracy as perversions on behalf of the monarch, the wealthy and the poor respectively.

The Great Socrates-Plato-Aristotle Immersion

We can only stand in awe when reflecting on the depth and breadth of the intellectual contributions of Socrates-Plato-Aristotle to civilization's progress. Even though Socrates wrote nothing and many of Aristotle's works were lost and had to be reconstructed over many centuries, their total contributions were simply mind boggling. Only in science and technology have we today forged well beyond their reach. As Alfred North Whitehead is alleged to have said, "Everything written since is a mere footnote to their thoughts."

The great conceptualizing in the glory days of Athens effectively stunted the growth and influence of mythology in the following centuries and gradually substituted more rational thought to explain natural phenomena. Since then writers from all disciplines have added their prescripts and postscripts to the SPA platforms to the point in each field where the amount of material to be assimilated is simply overwhelming. Our educational systems have adapted by eliminating more and more of general education and permitting more and more specialization. We now turn out specialized doctors of philosophy with minimal knowledge in other fields of inquiry. Few truly educated generalists remain.

And so the challenge to provide a relatively simple yet holistic model of society remains. The potential leverage of its usefulness has increased dramatically but remains unmeasurable. The Ten Commandments can stand as the all-time model for ethical conduct. The grand conceptual ideas from Socrates, Plato and Aristotle can be elaborated on field by field. But the need to put it all together, to frame it for better comprehension, remains.

REFERENCES

Campbell, Joseph, *The Hero With a Thousand Faces* (Princeton, New Jersey: Princeton University Press, The Bollingen Series XVII, 1973). Reprinted by permission of Princeton University Press.

Encyclopedia Americana, volume 13 (Danbury, Connecticut: Grolier, 1992).

Encyclopedia Americana, volume 26, International Edition (Danbury, Connecticut: Grolier, 1992).

Encyclopaedia Britannica, volume 19, 1969.

Encyclopedia of Judaism (New York: Macmillan Publishing Company, 1989).

The New Encyclopaedia Britannica, Volume 26, Macromedia, 15th Edition (Chicago, Illinois: Encyclopaedia Britannica, Inc.,1985).

Hampden-Turner, Charles, *Maps of the Mind* (New York: Collier Books, 1981).

Mythology, An Illustrated Encyclopedia. Editor: Richard Cavendish (New York: Rizzoli International Publications, 1980).

Woolley, C. Leonard, *The Sumerian* (New York and London: W. W. Norton and Company, 1965). Adapted with permission of Oxford University Press, Inc.

CHAPTER 5

Progress in the Search for Basic Models

The search for basic models by which to comprehend complex situations must begin with a brief analysis of the phrase "typological classifications." They have played an enormous role in enabling man to develop thus far.

After the invention of the alphabet, man started recording his thoughts. The daily challenges in ancient times still occupy much of our attention today: how to cope with the vagaries of nature, how to assure a more comfortable continuity to our scales and styles of living, no matter at what level they have existed then or now.

Faced with frequent challenges to their very survival, primitive tribes had to rank the devils or events they feared most and then develop sets of gods or antidotes to help them combat the terrors of the unknown demons. In some such manner as this was first employed the idea of typological classification. And ever since man has searched mightily to create a less threatening or more useful or otherwise satisfying order out of the perplexing confusion bordering on chaos that surrounded him.

Early Greek philosophers, artisans and writers began classifying body parts (Herodotus), applying number relationships to music theory, acoustics, geometry and astronomy (Pythagoreans) and then came the giant intellectual Aristotle in 384 B.C. to establish organizational and conceptual bases in both science and philosophy still in use today. Aristotle provided the following correlated concepts we have been building on ever since *(Encyclopaedia Britannica,* p. 73):

"Subject and predicate" in grammar and logic;

"Form" (information, transform) and "matter" as expressing the two correlative aspects of something that has acquired something else that is possibly essential to it;

"Energy" as the active power inherent in a thing;

"Potential" for what is latent but can be released;

"Substance" and "essence";

"Quantity" and "quality";

"Accidental," "relation," "cause," "genus," and "species."

Altogether, his many original contributions represented a quantum leap in providing a more comprehensive and solid foundation for the incremental improvements that have followed ever since.

The Spread of Classification Technology

Taxonomy is the theory and practice of classifying organisms. More than a million species of plants have already been described and classified, and estimates on the number of still undescribed living species range up to ten million (*Encyclopedia Americana*, p. 324). Linnaeus in the eighteenth century developed the basic classification that, with additions, is still in use today (*Academic American Encyclopedia*, p. 359). The current sequence from broadest to smallest category follows this linearity: kingdom, subkingdom, phylum, sub-phylum, class, subclass, superorder, infraorder, family, subfamily, tribe, genus, subgenus, species, subspecies (*Van Nostrand's Scientific Encyclopedia*, p. 2761). It includes all organisms that can interbreed and produce fertile offspring in nature.

Observing the success of physical scientists in establishing useful order in differentiating among natural objects, scholars in the emerging social sciences where widely varying human behavior is dominant began creating and using classification systems too. How else to perceive order or make sense out of the ever-changing, heterogeneous, and unpredictable variations in this world? According to one authority from the science world, "taxonomy...is the theoretical study of classifications, including its bases, principles, procedures, and rules (Simpson, p. 11). Generalizing from definitions such as this, social scientists accepted more general descriptions such as the following: "A typology is a multidimensional classification. Classification can be defined as the grouping of entities on the basis of similarity" (*Encyclopedia of Sociology*, p. 2188).

Major Limitations and Benefits of Classification Systems

Derived from observation, typological classification or grouping is one in which the basic categories are inductively arrived at rather than formally deduced. Empirically derived typologies are generally static and are sometimes criticized for being too stiff, inflexible or unchangeable. Other difficulties with typologies include their being basically descriptive rather than explanatory or predictive. To be useful in most situations, they can't also be exhaustive or cover all cases. Nor can they be mutually exclusive because of the many definitions ascribed to most words. Given their qualitative nature, we must continue to search for appropriate balance between excessive parsimony on one side and excessive detail on the other.

A major problem in applying typological classifications lies in not recognizing that differences of degree may be as important or essential as differences in kind. Quantitative typology construction has important contributions to make in this regard beyond numerical taxonomy, cluster analysis or pattern recognition.

The benefits of useful typologies include their brevity, which aids focus and analysis, and enables analysts to bring simplicity and order out of complexity and confusion. The blending of quantitative typology constructs referred to above with qualitative classifications could improve the explanatory and predictive value of classification analysis. Besides lessening the problem of excessive stereotyping, it might also contribute some heuristic value in that it may point to previously overlooked or ignored relationships among the phenomena under observation. High-school and college students for decades have honed their short-term memories over untold thousands of classifications just to pass tests. Not often enough have they had to apply those memorized classifications to problematic situations.

Hybridized Classification Schemes

Especially useful for many purposes is the creation of a theoretical or "ideal model" with selected characteristics or specifications against which the usually wide variations or units within a type or category may be compared. Another variation from Max Weber's "ideal type" is the assembled or constructed type: "a purposive, planned selection, abstraction, combination, and (sometimes) accentuation of a set of criteria with empirical referents that serves as a basis for comparison of empirical cases" (McKinney, p. 3).

This concept has become widely adopted in the establishment of "standards" for minimum compliance in many operational fields where measurement is desired. Note the pervasiveness of the idea in the following applications: standard of living, standard cost, standard conditions, standard measurements in time, gauge, money, temperature, pressure.

Other variations from hierarchically ordered classification systems have proved immensely valuable as "thinking tools." One such is that of

Gorg Wilhelm Friedrich Hegel's dialectical frame of reference in which he proposed that the progress of history and ideas moved from thesis to antithesis and thence to a higher and richer synthesis. Hegel applied this concept in detail to religion, politics, logic, esthetics, history and ethics. He believed that reality could only be understood as a totality and not from the summation of individual unconnected phenomena from nature. At the abstract level he contrasted pure "being" as the thesis against "nothingness" as the antithesis. However, since the holistic truth must contain both being and nothingness, the interaction dynamic between them creates a "becoming" or synthesis. Karl Marx rejected Hegel's emphasis on spirit and substituted economic factors in his gospel of dialectical materialism.

Either This or That

This dialectical continuum model for rationalizing opposites and/or including everything has been effectively applied in many practical situations. It suggests a connection between "type" and "gestalt" since both derive from study of apparently natural "wholes" as primary units of observation.

Gestalt psychology originated as such in the twentieth century as another opponent to the atomistic orientation of studying parts in isolation from the whole. The word "Gestalt" is used in modern German to mean the way a thing has been put together or assembled. Gestalt theory suggests that the whole of anything is greater than its parts and that the attributes of the whole of something are not deducible from analysis of its parts in isolation. Perhaps in time we may see the emergence of an organizing concept in which both parts *and* their whole are mutually useful or complementary in solving problems.

Conceptual dichotomies have frequently proven useful in dramatizing differences among phenomena. Among the more familiar are Nietzsche's affective *Dionysian* contrasted to his rational *Apollonian*. This conceptual contrast has been almost as influential in the intellectual history of the social sciences as German philosopher Ferdinand Tonnies' division of types of social structure into *Gemeinschaft* (community emphasizing tradition, sentiment and family) as contrasted to *Gesellschaft* (larger society dominated by more calculated conduct traceable to legal and economic interdependencies).

Other useful and widely used formulations contrasting two or more opposite types are introvert/extrovert, primary/secondary, subjective/objective, theory/practice, absolute/relative, formal/informal, normal/abnormal, static/dynamic, order/disorder, specificity/diffuseness, universal/particular.

The development, elaboration and refinement of ever more detailed typological classifications continue unabated, perhaps even accelerating given the explosion of media channels and messages directed to us. Fortunately, there are many familiar classification systems available for "on the spot" application in daily life that are useful with only minor alterations. Additionally, useful classification systems can be constructed freely on any topic at any time. They serve as valuable frames of reference for the immediate tasks at hand.

Bridging From Inductive Classifications to Basic Deductive Tools

As the Middle Ages phased out between 1300 and 1500 A.D., most prior thinking had been empirically based or inductive in nature. That is, reasoning that moved from specific observations to general conclusions or from particular facts to accepted generalizations. An early illustration of brilliant inductive reasoning was that provided by Archimedes, a Greek mathematician and inventor in the third century B.C., who was formally credited with the discovery of the lever and of specific gravity. Given the challenge of determining whether or not a filigreed gold crown given to the King of Syracuse was pure gold or adulterated with silver, Archimedes struggled for days to find an answer. He knew the weight of gold per volume but couldn't melt down the irregular shaped crown to separate out any other metals. Allegedly the answer came to him in a flash of insight one day while he was taking a bath. He had noticed and wondered to himself why the water rose around him as he lowered himself into it. Of course! A solid object displaces water of a volume equal to its own. He could therefore measure the volume of water displaced by the crown alone.

As the age of the Renaissance developed after 1500 A.D., however, the introduction of several key elements provided a basis for the future growth of more deductive lines of thought. Even though the origin of the basic idea that something equals something else may be as old as thinking man, the equality sign was not introduced until 1557 A.D. Pythagoras who lived in the sixth century B.C. was the founder of the Pythagorian Principle concerning properties of triangles. The ancient Egyptian pyramids must have been planned by sophisticated engineers who intuitively understood the principles of leverage and balance. And there was evidence that the equilibrium concept was applied, perhaps indirectly, in Babylonian times over dividing inheritances and making trades. Nevertheless, it took an English physician and mathematician, Robert Recorde in 1557 A.D. in an algebra textbook titled *The Whetstone of Witte* to initiate use of the = symbol. His colorful language was emphatic: *"I will sette as I doe often in woorke use, a paire of paralleles, of Gemowe* [twin] *lines of one lengthe, thus: = = = =, because noe .2. thynges can be moare equalle"* (The VNR Concise Encyclopedia of Mathematics, p. 81).

The symbols of plus (+) and minus (−) had been introduced a bit earlier, probably originating in the commercial language of the Middle Ages: "In Germany, and perhaps in other countries, the Latin words *plus* and *minus* were used by merchants to mark an excess or deficiency in weight or measure, the amount of which was appended in figures" (The Oxford English Dictionary, p. 830).

The Curtain Opens Slowly to the Deductive Future

These elementary symbols sufficed to help manage the relatively simple transactional needs of people until the latter decades of the Middle Ages. But they were inadequate for the emergent needs of the Renaissance when people began breaking away from the constraints of the past and challenge their inherited belief systems.

As masterfully described by Peter L. Bernstein (p. 3), the Renaissance "…was a time when much of the world was to be discovered and its resources exploited. It was a time of religious turmoil, nascent capitalism, and a vigorous approach to science and the future." He makes these points:

1. The revolutionary idea that defines the boundary between modern times and the past is the mastery of risk: the notion that the future is more than a whim of the gods and that men and women are not passive before nature. Until human beings discovered a way across that boundary, the future was a mirror of the past or the murky domain of oracles and soothsayers who held a monopoly over knowledge of anticipated events (p. 1).

2. By defining a rational process of risk-taking, these [innovative thinkers] provided the missing ingredient that has propelled science and enterprise into the world of speed, power, instant communication, and sophisticated finance that marks our own age. Their discoveries about the nature of risk, and the art and science of choice, lie at the core of our modern market economy that nations around the world are hastening to join. Given all its problems and pitfalls, the free economy, with choice at its center, has brought humanity unparalleled access to the good things of life (p. 2).

3. The ability to define what may happen in the future and to choose among alternatives lies at the heart of contemporary societies. Risk management guides us over a vast range of decision-making, from

allocating wealth to safeguarding public health, from waging war to planning a family, from paying insurance premiums to wearing a seatbelt, from planting corn to marketing cornflakes (p. 2).

Realize that this quantum conceptual leap into the future has only come to be appreciated in the past few decades. With many discoveries, their potentials and applications may remain hidden to most for long periods, even centuries. How could a sixteenth-century physician named Girolamo Cardano who was a gambling addict know that his daily gambling and careful record keeping with dice would pave the way for developing the statistical principles of probability? He wrote his *Liber de Ludo Aleae* (Book on Games of Chance) as a young man and then rewrote it years later.

Elaborating on its significance, Bernstein writes:

> Cardano begins *Liber de Ludo Aleae* in an experimental mode but ends with the theoretical concept of combinations. Above its original insights into the role of probability in games of chance, and beyond the mathematical power that Cardano brought to bear on the problems he wanted to solve, *Liber de Ludo Aleae* is the first known effort to put measurement at the service of risk (pp. 53–54).

> But the real hero of the story, then, is not Cardano but the times in which he lived. The opportunity to discover what he discovered had existed for thousands of years. And the Hindu-Arabic numbering system had arrived in Europe at least three hundred years before Cardano wrote *Liber de Ludo Aleae*. The missing ingredients were the freedom of thought, the passion for experimentation, and the desire to control the future that were unleashed during the Renaissance (p. 54).

And so began several centuries of massaging probability concepts with significant contributions from such illustrious names as Galileo, Blaise Pascal, Pierre de Fermat, Chevalier de Mere, John Graunt, Daniel and Jacob Bernoulli, Abraham de Moivre, Thomas Bayes, Marquis Pierre Simon de Laplace, Carl Friedrick Gauss, Francis Galton, Lambert Adolphe Jacques Quetelet, Von Neumann, Frank Knight, Kenneth Arrow, Harry Markowitz and many others.

The Ever-Bearing Format

Altogether, their tortuous turnings and zigzaggings along the quantitative routes "... have transformed the perception of risk from chance of loss into opportunity for gain, from *Fate* and *Original Design* to sophisticated, probability-based forecasts of the future, and from helplessness to choice" (Bernstein, p. 337). All branches of pure mathematics blossomed thereafter: arithmetic, algebra, geometry, trigonometry, calculus and applications therefrom extended to endless varieties of magnitudes, forms and dynamics, all with relationships deducible from others known or hypothesized. These applications of quantitative expression in all the various sciences were funneled into the practical world of machines, manufacturing and building, into insurance, accounting, forecasting, even weather predicting. Indeed, the latest scientific concepts derived from the quantitative sciences are eagerly sought for immediate technological implementation by most aggressively competitive organizations. Their applications compounded over several centuries have been the dominant contributor to improving standards of living. The ability to infer by deduction through insightful use of quantitative symbols has so far proven greatly superior to results obtained from reasoning in the opposite inductive way or from the specific to the general.

When considered in the context of formats, the positive impact of measuring and acting on perceived risk based on probability experience from the past was and probably will remain unmatchable. No other pre-existing or newly introduced frame of reference for managing action and thought has had nearly its impact on the collective welfare of participating societies. Compared to the regressive and/or change-inhibiting formats existing before the Renaissance, this breakthrough may prove unmatchable in both man's history and future. It deserves a memorable name.

The Ever-Bearing Format Is Hereby Nominated!

Briefly put, the ever-bearing format oriented thinking man's plans ahead into the future. It initiated risk-taking enterprising ventures, which reaped the rewards of the accelerating changes wrought by steadily advancing technology and organization. The word "rewards," however, hides a two-edged sword as not all change so engineered is necessarily beneficial. There are many negative side-effects spun off from the new and radically realigned living arrangements that advancing technology makes possible. These frictions show up in increased social problems within the traditional structures of family, education, religion, health and city life in general. Still needed is that inductively based comprehensive format which can provide the overview perspective to enable quicker social adaptation to the quickening thrust of technological change.

And Now What?

Hurrah for the winner of the first race in the Marathon of Formats Development, the deductively based ever-bearing format and its many derivative offspring! But what about the still undeveloped and lagging inductively based collective models? Much more needs to be done and could be if their development received adequate attention. Probably the potential rewards emanating from such models cannot now be appreciated just as the hugely beneficial consequences of the ever-bearing format were not foreseen for centuries. Please bear with us for still more stage setting before the star performer in this production is presented, the Maccordion Format, an inductively derived model purporting to present our collective society, faults and all. Perhaps there is a two-step dance here in which "progress" from the deductively based models must be matched by "insight" from advancing induction-based models to facilitate faster social adaptation to achieve better overall balance among society's increasingly complex and interdependent structures.

The Slow Development of Comprehensive Models

For reasons not yet fully understood, the inductive development of holistic models that attempt to unite and explain the more significant elements of a functioning society have not been developed nor does there seem to be much interest in doing so. Perhaps there was little reason to do so until the last hundred years or so when advancing technology exploded and made us all so specialized and interdependent.

Increasingly over the centuries, scholars came to rely more on analysis rather than synthesis as their dominant thinking mode. That is, they tended to focus more and more on discrete and more isolated data and more specific phenomena to which they could apply quantitative techniques. This tendency annoyed some outstanding scholars such as Joseph A. Schumpeter (p. 3) who insisted that "the social process is really one indivisible whole. Out of its great stream the classifying hand of the investigator artificially extracts economic facts."

Schumpeter (1893–1950) had been educated in Europe in an atmosphere of methodological pluralism from which he came to believe that economics should be a part of a broad-based social science network encompassing not only economics and sociology but especially history with its social, political and cultural bases.

Sociologist Talcott Parsons (1902–1979) who was friendly with Schumpeter and had studied economics as well as sociology may have accomplished the most in a modeling direction in the second half of the twentieth century with his multi-leveled social structure in which he recognized societal values as the most general and abstract normative conceptions of the ideal society from the viewpoint of most participants in the society (Parsons, pp. 30–79).

At the next level of his controlling hierarchy he placed institutional patterns such as the rules of kinship obligations, the rights and obligations regarding property and the various patterns of authority. Below institutional patterns he recognized the specialized collectivities such as families, firms, schools, churches and political parties. His fourth level consisted of the various roles of the individual occupants within their special collectivities as they performed their assigned functions to make contributions to collective goal attainment.

When any lower level's behavior became inconsistent with that of a higher level, the other levels would ordinarily exert corrective pressure on the deviating level. Parsons then argued that for a social structure to persist over time, four functions must be performed: adaptation, goal attainment, integration and pattern-maintenance or tension management. He showed that societies tend to differentiate functionally to produce institutions specializing in each of these functions. The economic or business institution is most adaptive, the polity or political institution specialized in goal attainment, the stratification system is integrative while education and religion seek pattern maintenance.

Parsons acknowledged that his model was indebted to Weber, Durkheim and other leading theorists before him. Despite this huge contribution to the modeling of society, his model was criticized for being incapable of dealing adequately with change even though he had explicitly incorporated the concepts of "adaptive upgrading, inclusion and value generalization" into his model. Perhaps also, it was not concrete enough to be easily visualizable or usable.

Kenneth Menzies in writing about Talcott Parsons (p. 573), stated that "his self-image was that of a theoretical synthesizer of social science in general and sociology in particular. Seeing sociocultural forces as the dominant ones shaping human activity, he [Parsons] assigned sociology the role of integrating the analyses of psychology, politics and economics into a science of human action." In the approximately 150 years of sociology as an academic discipline, nobody else has come close to shaping a model as comprehensive as that of Talcott Parsons.

Just Smell the Flowers!

Another sociologist believes that Parson's general theory has had little effect on social science in general other than in sociology (Dahrendorf, p. 785). This same reviewer then suggested that "in the absence of a synthesis, it is desirable to let a hundred flowers bloom." True, of course, but this attitude tends to deprecate the value of an all-encompassing model capable of allowing beginning students as well as academics and operating professionals in all fields to visualize the whole in order to understand better what their lifetimes of frenzied gyrations are about. Just smell or look at the flowers but keep hustling!

More sanguine, however, is the opinion of another leading sociologist, Edward Shils, when he writes (p. 801) that "despite their aspirations to be systematic, no sociologist has yet been able to synthesize all this knowledge." Elaborating, Shils continues (p. 808):

> Nevertheless, it remains a genuine intellectual deficiency that the results of sociological investigations are not clearly and precisely cumulative and that they do not contribute in a definite manner to an explicit general theory which is open to corrections and revision as research goes on, and as it is undertaken in more societies and for longer and remoter historical periods.

Of the social sciences only economics has been able to develop cumulative and sequential views of the economy because of the specificity and compoundability of the dollars and units of production that it deals with. None of the other major social sciences are the beneficiaries of such conditions as they must deal more with the unpredictably wide swings of human behavior for which there are less precise units of measurement. Indeed, economists have perhaps overemphasized the behavior of "rational man" in their efforts to legitimize their calculable findings.

The Intellectual Cleavage Between the Past and Present

The great and growing emphasis on the use of equilibrium models and quantitative measures wherever and whenever possible in the practical arts has no doubt greatly increased the short-run efficiency and effectiveness in those delivery systems. At the same time it is difficult to make a persuasive case that much has been lost in the great decline in historical interest and perspective. It can be argued that this decline has contributed to an unappreciated change in collective value systems in a materialistic-hedonistic direction. The change is so gradual, however, as to be undetectable to those born into the "modern era" while intergenerational parents and grandparents can only "cluck cluck" in disbelief and helplessness.

Since education no longer emphasizes comprehensive or holistic understanding in favor of memory and mechanics, the cleavage may deepen until and unless a major directional program change can be introduced. A better balance is needed in education to unite the benefits of both analysis and synthesis, to integrate the wisdom of the past with the present and emerging technology. Both the statics of the present as treated in equilibrium models and the dynamics of the past as shown in historical descriptions and functionalist models need to be integrated into the educational patterns of the future. It is hoped that the Maccordion Format may make a contribution to this end.

The Academic Focus on Specialization

In most of the social sciences, most academicians seem to emphasize specialties within their disciplines rather than reaching out to integrate their findings into larger macro models. This orientation may be partly due to their deeply felt needs to secure the publication of articles about their research results for promotion in rank at their various colleges, universities and research organizations. Because the readers of most professional journals are quite knowledgeable in their specific fields, they tend to seek out new information or application potentials that may help them in their careers. These readers are not especially interested in how the latest findings embroider the edges or expand the frames of their disciplines. Incoming new editors of the various professional journals are usually accomplished specialists in their own fields and accept editorial mandates to stay focused on those specialties and not allow their journals to be perceived as "growing fuzzy" with fringy contributions.

As a consequence, state of the discipline or field updates are special events that are neglected more often than not by the leading professional journals. This leaves it to the encyclopedia press to organize the state of the art or science summaries, which they execute quite well, but do so in a chronological and sequential manner rather than in a more integrating conceptual way.

One major consequence and arguably a major drawback of this academic orientation focusing far more on the analyses and not the syntheses of the latest research findings field by field is that beginning and intermediate students may not receive the most inspiring or thoughtful instruction about the parameters of their subjects or how one field integrates or competes with others. Some college majors offer an "introduction to" course but relatively few offer a senior capstone course attempting to summarize or integrate the various dimensions of the major into a synthesized whole or unify that major subject into their larger social- or physical-science realms.

There is no way yet devised to measure student disaffection with the approach now in vogue as no alternatives exist. And leading professors and college administrators have long claimed that the best teaching comes from those active and successful in specialized research and publication. There is no challenging the truth that analysis has been the cutting edge of technological progress and should remain so. But eventually the specialization it generates will blind most of us to the point of rebellion due to the shortsightedness of it all.

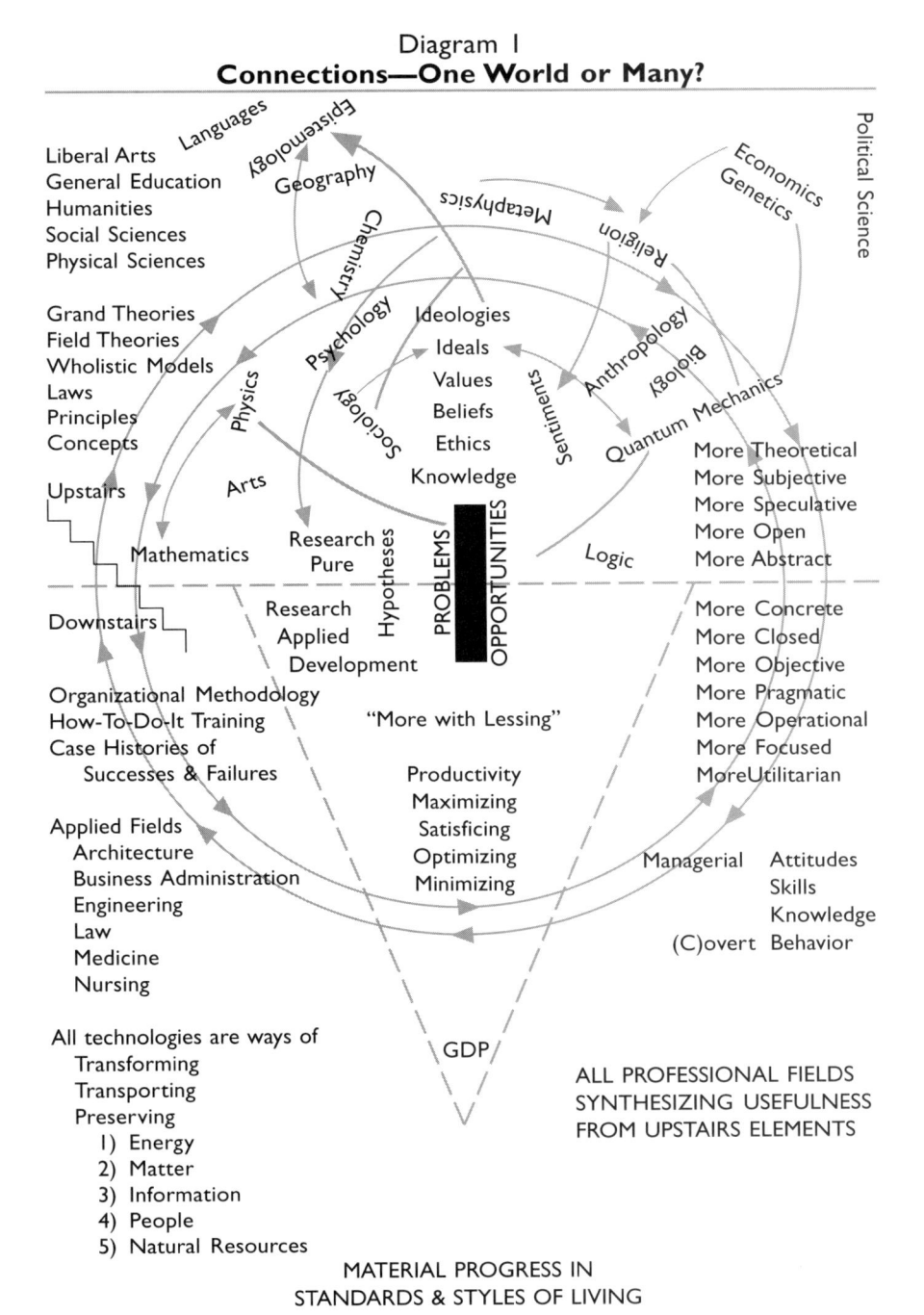

Diagram 1
Connections—One World or Many?

Liberal Arts
General Education
Humanities
Social Sciences
Physical Sciences

Grand Theories
Field Theories
Wholistic Models
Laws
Principles
Concepts

Upstairs

Mathematics

Downstairs

Organizational Methodology
How-To-Do-It Training
Case Histories of
    Successes & Failures

Applied Fields
  Architecture
  Business Administration
  Engineering
  Law
  Medicine
  Nursing

All technologies are ways of
  Transforming
  Transporting
  Preserving
  1) Energy
  2) Matter
  3) Information
  4) People
  5) Natural Resources

Languages
Epistemology
Geography
Chemistry
Metaphysics
Psychology
Physics
Sociology
Arts
Anthropology
Biology
Religion
Economics
Genetics
Quantum Mechanics
Logic
Political Science

Ideologies
Ideals
Values
Beliefs
Ethics
Knowledge

Research
Pure

Research
Applied
Development

Hypotheses

PROBLEMS   OPPORTUNITIES

Sentiments

"More with Lessing"

Productivity
Maximizing
Satisficing
Optimizing
Minimizing

GDP

More Theoretical
More Subjective
More Speculative
More Open
More Abstract

More Concrete
More Closed
More Objective
More Pragmatic
More Operational
More Focused
More Utilitarian

Managerial   Attitudes
                   Skills
                   Knowledge
(C)overt   Behavior

ALL PROFESSIONAL FIELDS
SYNTHESIZING USEFULNESS
FROM UPSTAIRS ELEMENTS

MATERIAL PROGRESS IN
STANDARDS & STYLES OF LIVING

The Upstairs-Downstairs Syndrome

To gain a different kind of perspective on the benefits of conceptualizing holistic models, it might be helpful to examine diagrams 1 and 2. Diagram 1 is entitled Connections—One World or Many? The entire scheme is intended to convey the following ideas:

1. That the entire range and depth of accumulated human knowledge about the universe or everything contained in all the encyclopedias and dictionaries can be ordered or classified under the headings shown.

2. That the educational institutions charged with classifying and passing on the heritage of received and verified information to the next generations have largely organized their efforts to serve the more practical or utilitarian interests in society. Thus the broken horizontal line in the middle is meant to suggest rather a strong or clear differentiation between liberal-arts education and professional or vocational training at the college level.

3. That the upper half of Diagram 1 is referred to as "upstairs" and the lower half as "downstairs." In the upstairs level there is a swirling melange of floating and tipsy terms covering some (but not all) of the important academic disciplines. They are arranged in hodgepodge order to suggest that while each in itself may have an ordered hierarchy of fact, theory, principles and speculation, there may be little perceived connection between or among the gyrating elements. For instance, the connections between art and biology and epistemology are tenuous at best even though each in itself may have a well-ordered content to be learned. The downstairs level is meant to suggest a much more highly ordered arrangement of academic disciplines leading to occupational activity.

The central dividing line is meant to convey the idea that potentially useful knowledge or relationships may be discovered upstairs and float down or be pulled down to augment the existing application potentials in those applied fields, which altogether over time more directly contribute to rising gross domestic product (GDP) and improving scales and styles of living.

1. That the "black box" in the middle symbolizes a problem or set of problems about which much activity in all areas of institutional life seems to center. The term "opportunity" is paired with problem because the solution to any problem opens up new possibilities for progress or improving conditions. The idea of research and identifying hypotheses for pure research is placed in the upstairs half while applied research and development is placed downstairs below the line.

2. That practitioners and teachers of practitioners in the applied fields downstairs work to assemble coherent bodies of knowledge and application techniques by searching through and researching beyond the relevant upstairs fields most directly related to their subjects.
3. That most college curricula are organized to emphasize some combination of general education, liberal arts, social and physical sciences and/or the humanities at least in the first two years of college and many recommend a full four years before beginning professional education for careers. The great saltation or increase in general knowledge has not expanded the sacrosanct four-year period nor has it encouraged much in the way of integrating or modeling knowledge.

   For those who can't afford high cost of college tuition, those more anxious "to get going" with their careers and those who grow impatient with the apparent disconnectedness or irrelevance of the liberal-art subjects, compromises exist in which abbreviated or truncated versions of general-education subjects are offered in the first two years. Most community colleges and many private training schools offer vocational training without the general-education preparation. Community colleges also offer general-education programs fully transferable and often superior to those provided in four-year institutions.
4. That the outer circles enclosing the upstairs and downstairs are intended to suggest systemic feedback or that information flows both ways with each part of the education and knowledge syndrome influencing the other and contributing to the growth of knowledge in the upper sphere and to improved efficiency of technology in serving the applied fields in the lower sphere.

   Diagram 1 is intended to provide a simplistic but holistic orientation for those already in college or about to enter. A related concept is presented in Diagram 2.

Problem-Centered Researching and Decision Making

Diagram 2 presents another simple picture modeling the connection between research for new knowledge or relationships in the upper half and that "decision-making and/or direction taking" in the lower half that is important for operating organizations. Again, the linking connection at the center is that old devil, "problem."

In its dictionary sense, "problem" literally means anything thrown forward, hence "a question raised or to be raised for inquiry, consideration, discussion, decision, or solution." A large part of its generalized (and misleading) meaning stems from its common use in education where it usually stands for an incomplete proposition or study assignment to be

88 • The Maccordion Format

Diagram 2
Problem-Centered Researching and Decision Making

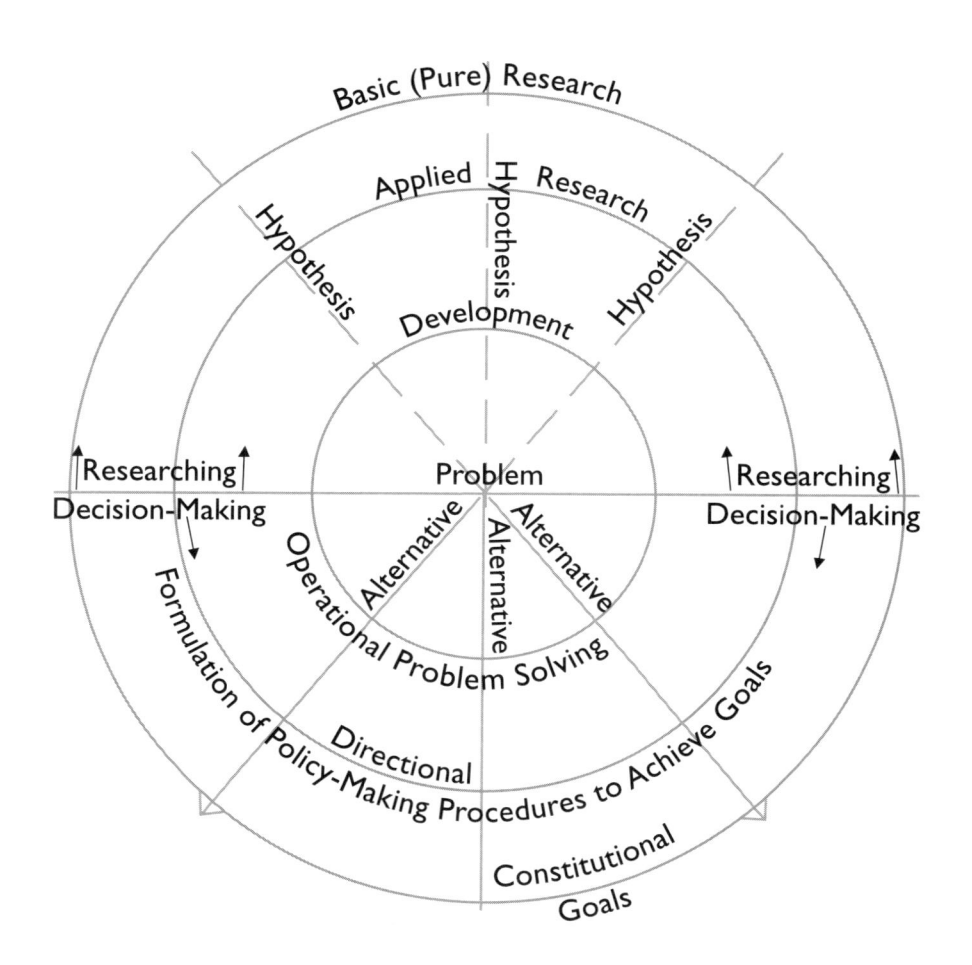

Basic (Pure) Research
Applied Research
Hypothesis
Hypothesis
Hypothesis
Hypothesis Development

↑Researching↑
Decision-Making

Problem

↑Researching↑
Decision-Making

Alternative
Alternative
Alternative
Operational Problem Solving
Formulation of Policy-Making Procedures to Achieve Goals
Directional
Constitutional Goals

solved or developed for homework. But problems are for real and extend beyond education to become the focal point in all or nearly all of life's endeavors. Indeed, finding and defining *the* problem in its frequently camouflaged context surrounded by ambiguous and overlapping symptoms is often more difficult and valuable than simply finding a solution.

In seriousness, problems may range from occasional "hiccoughs" in any system to destroying convulsions. By type, there are problems of logical consistency, fact and value. Some may be quantified, some only classified, and some dismissed through implicit value-judgment solutions. Operationally, problems may be of a technical, trouble shooting, fact finding, counseling or planning nature. They may range in clarity from being concrete and obvious to abstract and obscure. In order of urgency, solutions to a problem may be required immediately, in the near or distant future or postponable. Not all problems have solutions and some may demand more than the individual or organization can deliver.

Hypotheses are shown in Diagram 2 as issuing upward from the problem through levels of development, applied research and basic research to the frontiers of knowledge in any field. Alternative hypotheses to solving the problem or question are considered, evaluated and ranked carefully before embarking on any extended investigation.

Decision-making alternatives are shown pointing downward through operational, directional and constitutional levels of organizational-goal aspirations. These also are carefully considered and ranked before implementation. The purpose of Diagram 2 is to show the utility of simple models that relate apparently different and unrelated concepts. Diagrams 1 and 2 are simple models, but they integrate diverse concepts usefully. Now there is yet another inductively based model that needs recognition.

The Mission of Alvin Toffler

Less academic than others who tried to develop models, Toffler represents more the hungry reporter in search of meaning in his synthesis of that huge jungle of accumulated historical fact and interpretive fancy. He makes no attempt to provide an inclusionary model for instructional or research purposes. Rather, he desperately wants to use the past to focus better on operational alternatives for use now and in the future. He has the zeal of an intellectually driven chief executive who wants to capitalize on the lessons of the past to accelerate progress with that insightful implementation of the most workable solutions to contemporary and emerging problems.

Toffler projects the air of a missionary in promoting models (*Previews and Premises*, p. 187): "To shape the emergent future, we will need powerful new intellectual tools—new theories of change and causation capable of explaining the new social and political complexity; new categories and classification systems; and new models to help us interrelate the disparate, discordant data that now threatens to drown us in meaninglessness."

About models in general, he was quoted as follows in the same source above (p. 190):

> All of us, and here I mean all human beings, not just writers or futurists—all of us also create models of reality. When confronted with a mass of data, the human mind creates a model—in fact, multiple models—which help us to order and manipulate, that is, make sense of the data. Most writers do not make their models explicit and may even be unaware of the models they are applying. But there is no escape from the need for modeling reality.

Note that he used the phrase "multiple models" and did not argue specifically for any one model. Thus situational models, specific task models, studying models, frames of reference of all sorts to more inclusionary general models to whatever model provides the best view of the situation are needed to help visualize the totality of that situation and its prospective consequences. He is arguing for a more explicit or objective recognition of models he suggests are implicit in many if not most important works. He is quoted (p. 190) as saying, "I think you can actually identify implicit models in the work of many authors—Balzac and Zola, for example, come to mind—not to mention the work of social thinkers, whether Adam Smith, Freud, or Marx."

Toffler's Model in the Third Wave

Toffler's model identifies the major groups of elements that all civilizations have in common and which he labels the techno-sphere, socio-sphere, info-sphere, bio-sphere and power-sphere all integrated by that "super-ideology" or cultural rationale that every civilization uses to justify itself and explain its place in history. Each of these spheres is variously affected by the principles of standardization, specialization, synchronization, concentration, maximization, and centralization. With the skill of a talented science-fiction writer, he colorfully illustrates how each of these activated principles influences the existing conditions and emerging trends in each of his spheres.

This completes our examination of the dominant inductively based models attempting to show the broad outlines of an interactive society. Far more prevalent is the widespread use of equilibrium based models wherever possible throughout society. Before identifying a few of these, however, the question of model types should be examined briefly.

About Models

Models are miniaturized versions of more complex realities. They may be physical or ideational. They are convenient ways of representing the salient features of an operating system or a complex whole in order to facilitate either synthesis or analysis. Physically we are acquainted with model bridges, buildings, dams, cars and airplanes. Ideationally, we know about capitalistic or free-market models as compared to more centralized budget-directed models imposed by dictatorial governments. And, of course, within these large networks there are many systems, a term that has been richly endowed with such modifiers as open or closed, living or non-living, concrete or abstract. There are supra systems and subsystems that are variously local, combined, laterally dispersed, joint upwardly dispersed, downwardly dispersed and outwardly dispersed. They may be cohesive or noncohesive, integrated or segregated, critical or parasitic.

Indeed, the word "system" may have broader connotations than the word "model" as its dictionary definitions are more complete and less ambiguous: "a complex unity formed of many often diverse parts subject to a common plan or serving a common purpose," or "an aggregation or assemblage of objects joined in regular interaction or interdependence" (*Webster's Third New International Dictionary*, p. 2322). Clearly this is the popular term by which organizational managers and network thinkers link together the myriad of combinations to achieve results desired from one unified operating complex. Nevertheless, we will stick with the term "models" as it suggests visual portrayals more than the word "systems," and may be more suitable as a framework for multiple systems.

A useful classification of models includes those that have been termed proto mathematical, mathematical and speculative. Proto mathematical models are mathematical in form but not in content as in psychologist William James' formulation that

$$\text{Self-Esteem} = \text{Success/Pretensions}$$

Another would be one used in consumer economics, which suggests that for any purchasable commodity in a retail store,

$$\text{Value} = \text{Satisfactions Delivered} \times \text{Time of Consumption Utility/Price}$$

Mathematical models may be fully mathematical both in form and content. They may be either analytic (pure math) or empirical (applied math). Speculative models are those that deliberately attempt to direct attention to what must be learned to test the hypotheses involved.

Widely used in the humanities and social sciences where people's behavior can't easily be quantified, speculative models may be metaphoric or analogous to conceptualize relationships whose specifications are unknown or they may be cast as stage models or on a presumably larger scale, developmental models. Examples of stage models include Rostov's *Stages of Economic Growth* (1960) or the author's own "Stages of Retail Development" (Regan, 1964). Toffler's *The Third Wave* alluded to earlier might be an illustration of a more comprehensive developmental model incorporating speculation about possible future states from data derived from the present and past. Most sciences and technology-based organizations use the mathematical and protomathematical type models. Business organizations and government use all three types but emphasize use of more specific equilibrium models when capable of quantitative fulfillment.

Business Use of Equilibrium Models

In accounting the entire double-entry system centers around the idea that

$$\text{Assets} = \text{Liabilities} + \text{Proprietorship}$$

that,

$$\text{Debits} = \text{Credits}$$

and that assets are increased by debits and decreased by credits, while liabilities are decreased by debits and increased by credits.

$$\text{Gross Income} - \text{Expenses} = \text{Net Profit or Loss}$$

$$\text{Capital} - \text{Revenue Surplus} = \text{Equity}$$

Many other business functions have also resorted to the use of quantitative formulae when possible to simplify their operations. In purchasing, the optimum order quantity or economic order quantity (EOQ) = 2 AB/I where A is the annual usage in dollars, B is the cost of issuing a purchase order in dollars and I is the cost of carrying inventory as a decimal percentage of inventory value. In insurance terminology,

$$\text{Premium Income} = \text{Investment Income} - \text{Benefits,}$$
$$\text{Commissions and Taxes} - \text{Net Gain From Operations}$$

$$\text{Premiums} = \text{Expected Losses} + \text{Loadings}$$

$$\text{Loadings} = \text{Commissions, Administrative Expenses,}$$
$$\text{Taxes and Profit Goal}$$

Almost the entire production side of business is conceptualized in formulae amenable to quantitative manipulation.

In economics, gross domestic product (GDP) equals price level times the output of goods and services.

Marginal Cost = Marginal Revenue

Net Domestic Product = Gross Domestic Product – Capital Consumed

National Income = Net Domestic Product – Indirect Business Taxes – Subsidies

Personal Income = Domestic Income – Social Insurance Contributions, Corporate Income Tax and Undistributed Corporate Profit = Transfer Payments

Supply = Demand

Tautologies in Action

The organizing idea in these equations is based on the tautological nature of mathematics: An effect or outcome can be expressed as a function of the variables that define the system.

$$E = f(x, y)$$

where E, the measure of effectiveness, is a function of the controllable variables x, and the uncontrollable and sometimes unidentified variables, y. The equilibria being achieved are the points of balance resulting from counteracting forces, usually expressed in dollars or other quantifiable units. Other kinds of equilibrium are recognized in physics. Stable equilibrium, as in the case of a stone pyramid, differs from unstable equilibrium as when a ball is balanced on a baseball bat. The pyramid will remain in its position if disturbed by small forces, the ball will not. Then there are static equilibrium, thermal equilibrium and thermodynamic equilibrium.

Much of all organizational systems-management in all fields is based on equilibrium formulae. Daily maintenance in most functioning systems attempts to sustain prescribed normal ranges that previous experience proved most efficient or otherwise desirable. When problems arise as when any subsystem reveals feedback either above or below acceptable ranges, practitioners must usually correct a state of disequilibrium. The great value in quantifying relationships in equilibrium models lies in being able to compare operating results over many periods and thus being able to prove with factual evidence that certain input combinations produce better results than others. Not all operating systems are equally capable of being so quantified, however. Especially as the human element increases, managerial judgments become more subjective and the scales of operation or analysis move from micro systems to more complex macro multi-systems. The equilibrium balance retains its central pivoting position but becomes more hidden or obscured by the mountains of paperwork, bureaucracy and complexity, thus providing an opportunity for functionalist models to enter and become useful.

Functionalist Models

After purely equilibrium models, the next most widely used format is that of the so-called equilibrium functionalists. According to one sociologist, "Following W. B. Cannon's *Wisdom of the Body*, Parsons and other equilibrium functionalists conceive of human society as a normative order which is not only stable but intrinsically harmonious" (Mack, p. 390).

The normative order referred to is the preferred or perhaps idealized state of balance among the major structural and functional components. Given agreement on results desired or ends to be achieved, analysts can alter various components of structure and function at will to determine which new combination produces the best results in terms of the results desired. Or as Tumin has put it: "...a functionalist approach permits the investigator to take certain ends or interests or system-states as given, and to analyze the consequences—supportive and destructive—of any given set of practices for those ends, interests or system-states" (Tumin, p. 390).

It thus appears that there are three major elements to be examined in the functionalist model: structure, function, and goals. Most scholars assume general agreement on goals or otherwise have agreed to dismiss them from close analysis. As a result they confine most of their attention to structure and function. But unless goals are expressly addressed and clearly identified within appropriate time spans, the direction that function takes in acting on structure can often be aimless or purposeless. It therefore appears necessary to recognize goals as an independent concept as is done in the shorter "means-ends" configuration in which "means" lumps together both structure and function.

Differentiating Between Structure and Function

The concept "structure" suggests that something exists and consists of identifiable parts arranged in functional relationships, that is, the parts work together as a whole. The concept "function" (or process) suggests that a structure under the play of external forces and through its own energy undergoes action or acts so that change affects it. By functions, therefore, structures are broken down and built up, and all structures may be conceived as having existence in terms of some functions or processes.

Together, the concepts "structure" and "function" may be seen as exhibiting the static and dynamic aspects of phenomena. In some cases the static aspect may appear more significant while in others the dynamic aspect may seem decisive or more important. Actually, they should be viewed together, each as a manifestation of the other. Structure, however enduring or apparently unchangeable, exists in terms of function (or process), and the latter, no matter how slowly or rapidly it operates, always moves through structure. Structure and function are correlative, not opposing phenomena.

Or, as anthropologist Leslie A. White has differentiated between structure and function (p. 58):

> Structure and function are, of course, closely related; they are merely complementary aspects, static and dynamic, of a single phenomenon. The word "organization" embraces both of these aspects, although it emphasizes structure perhaps more than function. But since we cannot fully understand a formal arrangement of parts without knowing how they are related to each other functionally, the term organization may be taken to include both. Organization is a network of things and the relationships obtaining among them. Social organization is the subclass of organization that is concerned with living beings in particular; in short, it is simply a network of relations between living material bodies.

And further, White observed that "the basic problems of all science are those of structure and function, of differentiation and integration" (Ibid., p. 60).

A Triumvirate of Goals

As shown in Diagram 2, goals may be long-run, intermediate or short-run in duration. They may be constitutional, directional or operational in nature. Constitutional or organizationally mandated goals are those usually specified in originating charters. They are usually very broad and rarely changed. On the individual level they refer to cultural values often sustained and passed on by successive generations of families. They provide basic orientation mindsets or frames of reference or models to which youth unconsciously adapt and are highly resistant to change.

Directional refers to generally unmeasurable and more general objectives that guide the entire structure-function design in the intended direction. As social vectors, they represent direction without magnitude such as choosing among major alternative vocational pursuits or choosing among various hobbies.

Operational refers to specific, local, and most importantly, measurable objectives. When well-defined, in suitable time frames and measurable, they facilitate progress along those chosen directional paths that were originally selected because they were felt to be compatible with the basic values or constitutional goals of the individual or organization.

It has become imperative that social goals be rethought. For centuries physical survival itself and then physical survival at various comfort levels sufficed. But now physical survival is in jeopardy and an increasing percentage of people in all cultures are not happy with material comfort even at sumptuous levels. New combinations must be found between work and leisure, hedonism and spartanism, materialism and immaterialism or more pluralistic idealism. The "ends, interests and system-states" have for too long been taken for granted.

Triangulating Among Components of the Triumvirate

When the ends or targets of any activity are clear, it becomes possible to coordinate the means, the structure and function, to serve those ends. In navigation or surveying, accurate measurements of distance and direction may be made by the application of trigonometry when any two of three numerical dimensions are known. In a similar triangulation way, but with the use of words and ideas instead of numbers, arrangements of elements may be identified for a third concept when any two of the other tripartite concepts are fixed or assumed fixed for purposes of analysis. Examples of this technique will be demonstrated in later sections.

Business Use of Functionalist Models

Marketing is the major activity in business that uses functionalist models, although not explicitly or consciously. Pure equilibrium models are used wherever possible for marketing activities where operating efficiency is sought: inventory control, optimum reordering points, pricing, break-even analysis, marketing research, forecasting, distribution activities, cost accounting.

Much of marketing planning and activity, however, is based on unpredictable consumer behavior, unknown market conditions and competitive reactions and is difficult to quantify. Even here, however, quantitative attempts are made to predict the future. Bayesian inference (named for early nineteenth century mathematician Thomas Bayes) is an important method for combining subjectively assessed probabilities with objective data that enables one to make probabilistic estimates to provide measurable operational feedback.

Given the "softness" of much marketing data, marketing executives must often devise and execute plans to undertake risks on new product/service offerings without the ability to use finely tuned formulas closely. It is part of collective marketing's challenge to help the materialistic future emerge by catering to the latent velleities of consumers in whatever product/service areas a company is willing to gamble its venture capital. Progress in the "right" direction means establishing a market niche that consumers will support and then working to broaden that product's demand and increase sales and profits.

Collectively in the world marketplace, marketing's impact is powerful and pervasive, if unmeasurable and widely suspect. With the combined aid of sales promotion, advertising and public relations, marketing provides much of the common denominator symbolizing in the western world. "All the world's a stage," wrote Shakespeare (*As You Like It*, p. 239) "and all the men and women merely players...." Modern marketing communications magic defines and redefines meaning for most of the artifacts used in the seven ages Shakespeare described.

The Commercial Product as Language

It was Karl Marx who first anticipated the symbolic or fetishistic dimensions of the manufactured product with its potential to organize meaning beyond practical usefulness. He wrote: "Value...converts every product into a social hieroglyphic....We try to decipher the hieroglyphic, to get behind the secret of our own social product; for to stamp an object of utility as a value is just as much a social product as language" (Marx, p. 74).

In making this prediction happen far beyond Marx's dream, marketing contributed much beyond economic calculations to the social fabric of the world. In accomplishing this, it became a most important institution in providing thrust for improving standards of living and direction for styles of living in all industrialized countries.

Computer programs that model human thinking (artificial intelligence) have become an important stimulus to the development of useful frames of reference in marketing research. It is this research that probes into the growing flood of demographic data about consumers in all markets that helps to identify the aspirational leanings of the never-satisfied public and provides the direction and incentives for business institutions to give them what they want. As these models become more sophisticated, their capacity to read our minds will grow. According to one pioneer in this field (Yarnell, p. 24):

> A frame is an abstract knowledge structure that humans use to process information, guide attention and perception, recall information, and solve problems...if behavior is patterned, it is rule-governed, though the rules may be difficult to describe, or even ascertain. If the behavior is rule-governed, then there is an algorithm, grammar, or mechanism capable of generating the behavior. There is no doubt that the work in artificial intelligence, especially that involving the elucidation of the concept of frame, has deepened our understanding of human thought and behavior....

Government Use of Functionalist Models

The biggest user of the structure-function-goal or functionalist model is government, and government at all levels. It is the job of legislators to assess the body politic, identify areas of structural and/or functional weakness and to strengthen them in light of what are perceived to be the collectively held desires and goals of its citizenry. Because measures of these desires and goals taken through public polls are frequently capable of polarized interpretations, the positions, preferences and judgments of the elected officials become important. And when debating each issue before it, the full spectrum of ideological, political and social positions must be thrashed out by legislators and the press while behind the scenes vested interests work quietly but influentially.

It is this process of extended deliberation, during which the full play of special interests must also be heard, that makes government efforts seem sluggish or less responsive when compared to action in the private sector. Business has earned a general reputation for quicker delivery systems mainly by emphasizing equilibrium models. Obviously, if the functionalist models used by government were capable of easier quantification, quicker and less controversial results might be expected. Unlike in business, there is no profit motive to encourage development of operational objectives with measurable results.

REFERENCES

Academic American Encyclopedia, volume 12 (Danbury, Connecticut: Grolier, 1995).

Bernstein, Peter L., *Against the Gods: The Remarkable Story of Risk* (New York: John Wiley and Sons, 1996). Adapted with permission of John Wiley & Sons, Inc.

Dahrendorf, Ralf, "Social Science," in *The Social Science Encyclopedia*. Editors: Adam Kuper and Jessica Kuper (London: Routledge and Kegan Paul, 1985).

Encyclopedia Americana, International Edition, volume 26 (Danbury, Connecticut: Grolier, 1992).

Encyclopaedia Britannica, Macropaedia, volume 14 (Chicago: Encyclopaedia Britannica, 1985).

Encyclopedia of Sociology, volume 4. Editors: Edgar F. Borgatta and Marie L. Borgatta (New York: Macmillan Publishing Company, 1992).

Mack, Raymond W., "Components of Social Conflict," (*Social Forces*, Spring 1965, p. 390).

Marx, Karl, *Capital*, volume I (Moscow: Progress Publishers, 1965).

McKinney, John C., *Constructive Typology and Social Theory* (New York: Appleton, Century, Crofts, 1966).

Menzies, Kenneth, "Parsons, Talcott," in *The Social Science Encyclopedia*. Editors: Adam Kuper and Jessica Kuper (London: Routledge and Kegan Paul, 1985).

The Oxford English Dictionary, 2nd Edition (Oxford, England: Oxford University Press, 1989).

Parsons, Talcott, "An Outline of the Social System," in *Theories of Society*, volume I. Editors: Talcott Parsons, Edward Shils, Kaspar D. Naegele, Jesse R. Pitts (New York: The Free Press of Glencoe, 1961). Reprinted with the permission of The Free Press, a Division of Simon Schuster, Inc.

Regan, William J., "Stages of Retail Development," in *Theory In Marketing*. Editors: Reavis Cox, Wroe Alderson, Stanley Shapiro (Homewood, Illinois: Richard D. Irwin, 1964).

Rostow, W. W., *The Stages of Economic Growth, A Non-Communist Manifesto* (New York: Cambridge University Press, 1960).

Schumpeter, Joseph A., *The Theory of Economic Development: An Inquiry into Profits, Capital, Credit, Interest and the Business Cycle*. Translator: R. Opie (Cambridge: Harvard University Press, 1934).

Shakespeare, William, "As You Like It," in *The Complete Works of Shakespeare* (New York: Avenal Books, MCMLXXV).

Shils, Edward, "Sociology," in *The Social Science Encyclopedia*. Editors: Adam Kuper and Jessica Kuper (London: Routledge and Kegan Paul, 1985).

Simpson, George C., *Principles of Animal Taxonomy* (New York: Columbia University Press, 1980). Reprinted by permission of the publisher.

Toffler, Alvin, *The Third Wave* (New York: William Morrow and Company, 1980).

Toffler, Alvin, *Previews and Premises* (New York: William Morrow and Company, 1983).

Tumin, Melvin, "The Functionalist Approach to Social Problems," in *Social Forces*, Spring 1965.

Van Nostrand's Scientific Encyclopedia, volume II, 16th Edition (New York: Van Nostrand Reinhold Company, 1988).

The VNR Concise Encyclopedia of Mathematics. Editors: W. Gellert, H. Kustner, M. Hellwick, H. Kaster (New York: Van Nostram Reinhold Company, 1977).

Webster's Third New International Dictionary (Springfield, Massachusetts: Merriam-Webster, Incorporated, 1959). By permission from *Webster's Third New International Dictionary*, 1959, by Merriam-Webster, Incorporated.

White, Leslie A., *The Evolution of Culture* (New York: McGraw-Hill Book Company, 1959).

Yarnell, Steven M., "Artificial Intelligence's 'Frame' Concept: A New Tool for Marketing Researchers" (*Marketing News*, Section I, May 25, 1984).

CHAPTER 6

Emerging Formats: The Balky Struggle

Previous chapters speculated about the development of frames of reference for the earliest recorded events from about 3500 B.C. until Greco-Roman times and the arrival of Christianity. Neglected among other topics was any mention of the calendar and the keeping of time itself on hourly, daily, weekly, monthly and yearly bases. All were valuable because chronology has been the single most important ordering and sequencing device yet invented. By providing timelines over the centuries, we now have some five thousand years of ever-more-detailed accounts of man's thinking and behaving. These records enable us to compound our leap-frogging in all directions and continue to build on our predecessors' achievements. Only thinking man has this capability.

The Ambiguous Calendar

Because there was no simple or unambiguous way to divide time into convenient units, man has floundered over the centuries with many calendar variations. The magic of night and day and the distinctive seasonal changes were enough for early tribal organization of time. They survived on a fortuitous basis but still needed to plan ahead. The moon was the celestial body that most intrigued them and early astronomers calculated that the moon passed through its various phases in about twenty-nine and one-half days. In many cultures for centuries time was estimated in "so many moons ago." Twelve lunar cycles, therefore, takes about 354 days, eight hours and forty-eight minutes. The earth completes its orbit around the sun in 365 days, five hours, forty-eight minutes and forty-six seconds to comprise the solar year. The discrepancy between the lunar and solar years has caused no end of confusion over the centuries and prompted many unsuccessful attempts to reconcile the difference.

The Pythagoreans around 500 B.C. had developed some earth-centered ideas with the sun and planets circling around the earth. It wasn't until the 1500s that the Polish astronomer Nicolaus Copernicus developed his theory of the sun-centered universe with the earth and planets revolving about a point in space near the sun, another master frame of reference.

Other early astronomers led in the building of fascinating structures such as that at Stonehenge in Wiltshire, England, possibly about 2000 B.C. to determine the summer and winter solstices and also to keep track of twenty-nine- and thirty-day positions for twenty-nine- and thirty-day lunar months (*Encyclopaedia Britannica, Macropaedia*, p. 418). More than six hundred similar kinds of carefully built structures or early calendars have been discovered elsewhere in Britain, Brittany and elsewhere in Europe and the Americas.

The Calendar as the "Second" Most Encompassing Frame of Reference

Most cultures through history usually centered their calendar numbering around their most important events or gods. Thus, the Roman era, the Olympiads of Greece and the Muslim era which dates from the Hegira or from 622 A.D. when Mohammed fled from Mecca. The era would usually start at a fixed point in history and the years preceding or following were numbered from that point.

The Christian era, according to the *Encyclopedia Americana* (p. 189), was first proposed in 582 A.D. by a monk named Denys le Petit, but it did not come into general use in the West for several centuries thereafter. From his research into the life of Jesus Christ, Denys calculated the birth of Christ at December 25 of the Roman year 753. Chronologists, however, moved the beginning of the Christian era to Saturday, January 1, 0001 A.D.

The Julian calendar was named after Julius Caesar who drastically revised the Roman Republican calendar in 46 B.C. after excessive political maneuvering had gotten it hopelessly confused. The Julian calendar was widely used thereafter throughout western Europe for some 1600 years until advent of the Gregorian calendar.

In 1592 Pope Gregory XIII eliminated ten days to correct for the accumulation of surplus time and ordained that thereafter the years ending in hundreds should not be leap years unless they were divisible by four hundred (*The Columbia Encyclopedia*, pp. 421–422). Thus, the present calendar is called Gregorian even though it is only a slight modification of the Julian calendar. This reform was quickly accepted in the Catholic countries of Europe but the more Protestant Britain held out until 1752 at which time the English calendar was eleven days different from that of continental Europe.

Except for the Muslim-dominated countries, most of the rest of the world now use the Gregorian calendar although some maintain two or more calendars for specific purposes. Given man's propensity to take a self-centered view of his universe, it is easy to understand the reluctance of political rulers outside of the West to adopt a calendar with an alien god as its central fixed point of reference. The entire calendar frame of reference would thereafter highlight the religious celebrations of a strange god and other holidays of a foreign culture. Alice in Wonderland might still be amused or at least befuddled and disoriented by a trip through countries with different calendars. That is, until she reasoned that the calendar was subservient to the era and the significant event that it represents. A movement has been started to neutralize the religious connotations associated with usage of B.C. and A.D. converting the "before Christ" and *"anno Domini"* to B.C.E., before the common era and C.E., the common era.

The Restructuring of the Months

The early Roman Republican calendar appears to have consisted of only ten months named Martius, Aprilis, Maius, Junius, Quintilis, Sextilis, September, October, November and December. Note that the last six names correspond to the Latin words for the numbers five through ten. Altogether they comprised 304 days, well short of the actual number in a solar year. According to the *Encyclopaedia Britannica* (p. 154), the Roman ruler Numa Pompilius is credited with adding January at the beginning and February at the end of the calendar to create the twelve-month year. In 452 B.C., February was moved between January and March.

In reconstructing the calendar in 46 B.C., Julius Caesar, on the advice of his leading astronomers of the time headed by Sosigenes, added ninety days to the calendar, changed the length of most months, and added two days to January and Sextilis. Later Quintilis was renamed August in honor of Augustus Caesar and Sextilis was changed to July in honor of Julius Caesar. To manage the troublesome fraction of time not accounted for, February was twenty-eight days long except that on every fourth year a day was inserted between the twenty-third and twenty-fourth of the month, a confusion that the Gregorian calendar modified to its present status of a twenty-ninth day in so-called leap years.

Naming of the Months and Days

To show the influence of early times, the derivation of the names of the months and days might be interesting. The word "month" itself is derived from the Anglo-Saxon word for moon, and inferentially its lunar cycle. January was derived from the god Janus, a deity represented with two faces looking opposite ways, perhaps back toward the previous year and ahead to the coming year? February was an afterthought month named for a great Roman feast of purification that was held on the fifteenth of the month of expiation. March, the original first month of the calendar year, was named for the great god of war in Roman mythology, Mars. It shows the early primacy attached to combat and conquering. April, from the Latin *aprilis,* speculatively means second month, latter or successor after March, the original first month.

May was derived from the goddess of growth or increase, Maia. June came from the Latin Junius, often associated with the Roman goddess of marriage, Juno, wife of Jupiter and queen of the gods. July was named after Julius Caesar who was born in July. August comes from the Roman emperor Augustus Caesar, a grandnephew of Julius and the first emperor of Rome from 27 B.C. to 14 A.D. September, October, November and December came from the Latin words for seven, eight, nine and ten, representing the positions on the early Roman calendar Julius Caesar had changed.

The days of the week show similar mythological and/or time-calculating connections. Sunday, the first day of the week, came from the Anglo-Saxon word for day of the sun. Monday, like month, came from the word for moon. Tuesday recognized the day of Tiw, the northern Mars, or god of war. Wednesday was Woden's day or the name of the principal god of northern mythology. Thursday was Thor's day, the second principal god of ancient Scandinavians, the god of thunder and son of Woden. Friday was the day sacred to Frigga or Freya, wife of Wodan and the Teutonic goddess of heaven presiding over marriage and the home. Saturday was Saturn's day and in ancient Roman times, the festival of Saturn.

Each day was defined to consist of twenty-four hours. The earth is divided into twenty-four time zones, each of which is about 15 degrees of longitude wide and corresponds to one hour of time. Standard time is based on Greenwich Mean Time. Greenwich is a location in England that was formerly the site of an astronomical observatory. Greenwich time is the mean solar time of the prime meridian located there and from which the other meridians are distanced.

Population Growth and the Explosion of Ideas in the Past Two Thousand Years

To gain some perspective of the great and accelerating changes wrought by man's continuing attempts to conquer nature over the calendar frames described above, consider population growth (*The World Almanac and Book of Facts*, 1996, p. 553). The population was estimated as follows:

A.D. 0001	200 million
1650	500 million
1850	1 billion
1930	2 billion
1975	4 billion
1995	5.73 billion

Along with this astonishing growth in population was an equally astonishing growth in the number of ideas, thoughts, concepts, theories and connecting linkages in the arenas of knowledge and speculation. So vast has become the domain of recorded thought that its total is nearly incalculable. The quantity if not the quality of memorable thought recorded in writing has compounded at some accelerating rate, especially since the invention of the printing press by Johann Gutenberg in 1455.

Nearly all well-regarded writing focused on single topics or at most perhaps a series of related topics. Very few consciously attempted to conceptualize comprehensive frames of reference as such. Nevertheless, a large number of exciting concepts were developed that have usefully served as points of reference over the centuries. For illustrative purposes a few of these points of reference will be presented in the next chapter. But first it seems relevant to describe the emergence of two relatively new organizing tools designed to facilitate access to and/or comprehension of the many great ideas accumulated through history.

Topical Road Maps

The first major attempt to find a way to organize the huge accumulated mass of knowledge was initiated in *The Syntopicon*, volumes 2 and 3 of *The Great Ideas of the Western World*, published in 1952. This is a fifty-four-volume collection of writings deemed most significant by an impressive editorial board. The second major effort to provide a road map for better access to this vast treasure is *The Propaedia*, volume 30 of the thirty-two-volume set comprising the fifteenth edition of the *Encyclopaedia Britannica*, first published in 1971.

It had become apparent to a few encyclopedia editors sometime before 1911 that the systems of continuing to arrange the content of the huge and swelling numbers of articles on single subjects alphabetically (Another master format!) resulted in ever more difficulty for researchers to assemble all relevant material for a thorough study of any one topic. Consequently, the editors of the eleventh edition of the *Encyclopaedia Britannica* constructed a "Classified Table of Contents" to ease the awkwardness of its previous editions. Some twenty-four major categories were developed from Anthropology and Ethnology to Sports, Pastimes and Miscellaneous to assist readers in locating their areas of interest. Thus was started a continuing attempt to organize the growing mass of intellectual fact, theory and other ideas considered worthy enough to be included. It was to be followed in 1971 by a more aggressive approach to organize the great mass of published works.

The Syntopicon to the Great Books of the Western World

A major breakthrough in the organization of the most worthy written material since the invention of the alphabet occurred in 1952 with the inclusion of the two-volume *The Syntopicon* to facilitate more direct access to specific ideas in the 443 works published in the fifty-four volumes of *The Great Books of the Western World*. Additionally, the seventy-seven books of the *Bible* were included, raising the total number of books to 520. To assist further, some 2,603 titles by 1,181 authors were listed under "Additional Readings."

The Syntopicon was an aptly coined word suggesting a synthesis of topical coverage. Volume 1 includes chapters 1 to 50, covering alphabetical topics from Angel and Animal to Logic and Love. Volume 2 includes chapters 51 through 102, covering topics from Man to World. The 102 topical terms were carefully selected from over seven hundred terms to best capture or organize the central or basic thoughts of the *Great Ideas*. They front an additional three thousand subtopics, averaging some thirty to a chapter.

To assist readers in developing a fuller depth and continuity on any topic, an "Inventory of Terms" was developed. It comprises 1,800 terms including the basic 102 great ideas. It helps to serve as a table of contents for *The Syntopicon* by enabling readers to find particular subjects from among the three thousand subtopics.

Objectives of *The Syntopicon*

As stated in the Preface to *The Syntopicon* (p. xi), "the aim of this 'syntopical reading' was to discover the unity and continuity of western thought in the discussion of common themes and problems from one end of the tradition to the other." None of the works was presented in digest form; the reader must integrate multiple ideas but may do so with the help of *The Syntopicon,* which "tries to show the many strands of this conversation between the greatest minds of western civilization on the themes which have concerned men in every epoch, and which cover the whole range of man's speculative inquiries and practical interests" (p. xii).

Another aim of the editors of *The Great Books of the Western World* was to position this enormous work as a third basic format centering on *ideas* behind the dictionary in the sphere of *language* itself and the encyclopedia in the sphere of *fact*. The extent of its success in this aim probably lies in the cumulative usage it has attracted since its publication in 1952. Certainly the potential of its aspiration remains whenever man is inclined to develop a more constructive orientation to his world but which temporarily at least seems to be increasingly caught up in occupational specialization, sensationalized trivia or "pop culture."

One of the most important human linking pins between the innovative *Syntopicon* published in 1952 and the enterprising fifteenth edition of the *Encyclopaedia Britannica* first published in 1971 was Mortimer Jerome Adler. Teaching law at the University of Chicago from 1930, he teamed up with Robert Maynard Hutchins to lead in the creation and publication of *The Great Books of the Western World*. He then served as chairman of the Board of Editors for the *Encyclopaedia Britannica* from 1974 to 1995. For being an inspirational and dedicated leader in these innovative endeavors, he has earned the gratitude of all intellectual followers.

The New Propaedia to the Fifteenth Edition of *The New Encyclopaedia Britannica*

Fully aware that more steps should be made to complement that great alphabetical organizing format because of the continuing explosion of knowledge, *The Propaedia* was developed as an alternative to *The Syntopicon* and as an improvement to the eleventh edition of *The Encyclopaedia Britannica* first published in 1911.

The organizing concept in volume 30, *The Propaedia*, as explained by Mortimer J. Adler (p. 6), lies in a metaphor called a circle of learning, which suggests that "a circle is a figure in which no point on the circumference is a beginning, none is a middle, none is an end. It is also a figure in which one can go from any point, in either direction, around the circumference; in addition one can go across the circle from any point to any other; or by any number of transecting lines, starting from a given point, one can go to any number of other points on the circumference, near or far."

The Circle of Learning

The twenty-four major categories from the 1911 consolidation were reduced to ten for the 1974 "Outline of Knowledge":

Part One	Matter and Energy
Part Two	The Earth
Part Three	Life on Earth
Part Four	Human Life

Part Five	Human Society
Part Six	Art
Part Seven	Technology
Part Eight	Religion
Part Nine	The History of Mankind
Part Ten	The Branches of Knowledge

Each of the major categories was broken down into subheadings. A series of compartmentized circles was then used to show possible relationships among all ten components of the *Outline of Knowledge*. The first pair simply divided a circle into 10 compartments and then suggested that they could cycle like a merry-go-round. The second pair illustrated below in Diagram 3 showed a small circle within a larger compartmentized circle with numbered knowledge components such as the following:

Diagram 3
Integrating Linkages in the Chain of Knowledge

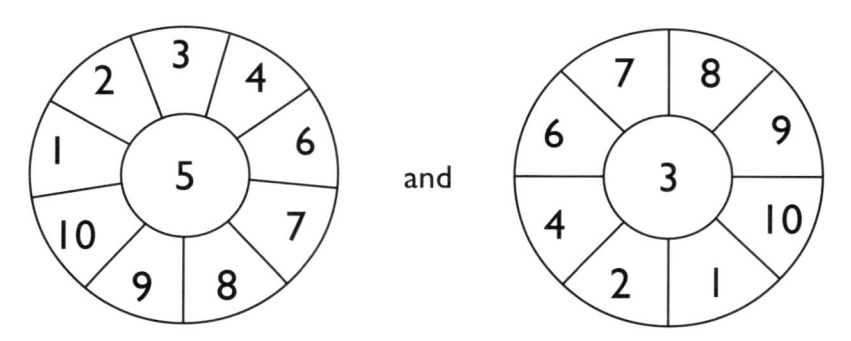

The third and larger diagram shows Part Ten, the Branches of Knowledge, as the center hub of the *Outline of Knowledge* wheel. Part Ten is centered to suggest a study into the *means* (or the nature, methods, problems and history) of the various branches of learning, the actual content or results of which are set forth in Parts One through Nine.

Other Features of *The Propaedia*

To quote from *The Propaedia* (p. 7):

1. It serves as a Table of Contents for the long articles in the Macropaedia and also for the tens of thousands of shorter articles in the Micropaedia.
2. Each of the 10 parts of the Outline and the several Divisions of each of those parts is prefaced by a brief summary of the topics covered.
3. The Divisions of each Part are followed by a number of Sections in which each of the topics covered is outlined.

4. At the end of each sectional outline, there is a list of suggested readings, first in the *Macropaedia*, second in the *Micropaedia*, which is followed by a list of the biographical articles that are relevant to the subjects covered in the outline of that section.
5. In the topical outline of each Section, cross-references are made, when relevant, to other Sections in the *Propaedia* on which related subjects are treated.

Diagram 4
Centering the "Means" to Achievement

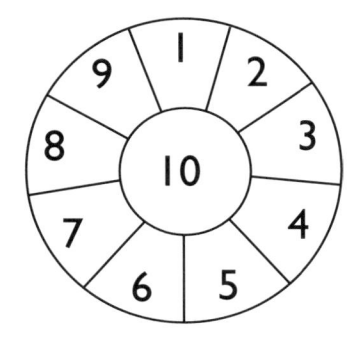

Altogether, the fifteenth edition of *The Encyclopaedia Britannica* attempted to incorporate much of the same organizational methodology of *The Syntopicon*. Since the articles for each section were named, outlined, commissioned, written and edited after the *Outline of Knowledge* was constructed, the planners of this fifteenth edition have a right to be proud of their "Table of Intents" as compared to all previous editions' "Table of Contents." Just the organizational logistics of this accomplishment are awesome. More than 220 individuals comprised the membership of the editors, staff, advisory committees and contributors to the *Outline of Knowledge* while over four thousand other knowledgeable individuals from many countries in the world were the authors of *Propaedia* essays.

It is highly encouraging to see and be able to use these monumental efforts that have created new organizational formats that simplify learning from all the insightful thinking that has preceded us. The continuing development of innovative formats as educational tools to provide frames of reference to master historical and contemporary action and thought systems should be sustained and nurtured.

The Use of Models in *The Syntopicon*

From the standpoint of formats as used in this study, the major one used in *The Syntopicon* layout would appear to be the use of dialectical comparisons. Among the 102 selected general topics, the following nine were actually paired topics: custom and convention, good and evil, life and death, memory and imagination, necessity and contingency, pleasure and pain, same and other, sign and symbol, universal and particular virtue and vice, war and peace. Most of these lend themselves to the linear continuum kind of separation that makes dialectical analysis useful. Note that not all of the above paired topics have oppositional characteristics.

The editors of *The Syntopicon*, however, were more concerned about dialectical impartiality or balance or not appearing to favor any one position or set of positions over any others. "Dialectical objectivity" is the phrase used (*The Syntopicon*, p. 1260) "...as the ideal of the encyclopedist" to present neutrally all sides of every issue. Thus, the paired topics identified above were chosen more for convenience rather than as formats for learning or understanding. Nevertheless, in doing so perhaps some unconscious contribution was made in the direction of advancing the use of formats.

Some Early Premonitions of Formats to Come

Excepting perhaps a few of the great Greek philosophers, not many of the outstanding thinkers and writers from the past attempted to develop holistic models of society. Then, as now, most focused their attention on single topics and analyzed them into further subdivisions. Altogether, the composite effect of their insightful efforts produced many individual beacons of light or points of reference. Occasional synthesizers would come along periodically and link two or more concepts together for a "new" concept. Perhaps, however, this compounding or linking process has been far more successful in the practical or material world with its associated market rewards than in the intellectual world where market recognition has not yet been ignited except in the politically sensational and fictional sectors.

In the remaining pages of this chapter, a few selected quotations will be sequenced from the more recent past that bear on the creation, utility and limitations of linked or associated thoughts, which in this work have been labeled "frames of reference." Little commentary is needed as the thoughts tend to flow into each other naturally.

A quotation from Benjamin Spinoza provides a general starting point:

Benjamin Spinoza (1632–1677)

This is the end I aim at: to acquire knowledge of the union of mind with the whole of nature.... To do this it is necessary first to understand as much of nature as suffices for acquiring such knowledge, and second to form a society of the kind which permits as many as possible to acquire such knowledge. Third, attention must be paid to moral philosophy.... Fourthly, because health is no small means to achieving this end, the whole of medicine must be worked out. And fifthly...because it is possible to gain more free time and convenience in life, mechanics is in no way to be despised (p. 11).

P. D. Ouspensky (1878–1947)
Philosophy is based on speculation, on logic, on thought, on the synthesis of what we do not know. Philosophy must include within its confines the whole content of science, religion and art. But where can such a philosophy be found? All that we know in our times by the name of philosophy is not philosophy, but merely "critical literature" or the expression of personal opinion, mainly with the aim of overthrowing and destroying other personal opinions (p. 25).

Immanuel Kant (1724–1804)
Synthesis in general...is the mere result of the power of imagination, a blind but indispensable function of the soul, without which we should have no knowledge whatever, but of which we are scarcely ever conscious (*Critique of Pure Reason*, translated by N. Kemp Smith, A 78B 103).

David Hume (1711–1776)
...Notwithstanding the empire of the imagination, there is a secret tie or union among particular ideas, which causes the mind to conjoin them more frequently together, and makes the one, on its appearance, introduce the other.... These principles of association are reduced to three, *viz. Resemblance;* ...*Contiguity;*...*Causation;*...as it is by means of thought only that any thing operates on our passions, and as these are the only ties of our thought, they are really to us the cement of the universe, and all the operations of the mind must, in a great measure, depend on them (p. 661).

John Locke (1632–1704)
... Ideas that in themselves are not at all of kin, come to be so united in some Mens Minds, that 'tis very hard to separate them, they always keep in company, and the one no sooner at any time comes into the Understanding but its Associate appears with it; and if they are more than two which are thus united, the whole gang always inseparable shew themselves together...to this, perhaps, might be justly attributed most of the Sympathies and Antipathies observable in Men, which work as strongly, and produce as regular Effects as if they were Natural and are therefore called so... (pp. SS5, 7).

Nelson Goodman (1906–1998)
Briefly, then, truth of statements and rightness of descriptions, representations, exemplifications, expressions—of design, drawing, diction, rhythm—is primarily a matter of fit: fit to what is referred to in one way or another, or to other renderings, or to modes and manners of organization. The differences between fitting a version to a world, a world to a version, and a version together or to other versions fade when the role of versions in making the worlds they fit is recognized. And knowing or understanding is seen as ranging beyond the acquiring of true beliefs to the discovering and devising of fit of all sorts (p. 138).

John Dewey (1859–1952)
To assume that anything can be known in isolation from its connections with other things is to identify knowing with merely having some object before perception or in feeling, and is thus to lose the key to the traits that distinguish an object as known.... The more connections and interactions we ascertain, the more we *know* the object in question (p. 213).

Richard Rorty (b. 1931)
It is pictures rather than propositions, metaphors rather than statements, which determine most of our philosophical convictions. The picture which holds traditional philosophy captive is that of the mind as a great mirror, containing various representations—some accurate, some not—and capable of being studied by pure, non-empirical methods. Without the notion of the mind as mirror, the notion of knowledge as accuracy of representation would not have suggested itself. Without this latter notion, the strategy common to Descartes and Kant—getting more accurate representations by inspecting, repairing, and polishing the mirror, so to speak—would not have made sense. Without this strategy in mind, recent claims that philosophy could consist of "conceptual analysis" or "phenomenological analysis" or "explication of meanings" or examination of "the logic of our language" or of "the structure of the constituting activity of consciousness" would not have made sense (p. 12).

Willard V.O. Quine (b. 1908)
The totality of our so-called knowledge or beliefs, from the most casual matters of geography and history to the profoundest laws of atomic physics or even of pure mathematics and logic, is a man-made fabric, which impinges on experience only along the edges. Or, to change the figure, total science is like a field of force whose boundary conditions are experience. A conflict with experience at the periphery occasions readjustments in the inte-

rior of the field. Truth values have to be redistributed over some of our statements. Re-evaluation of some statements entails re-evaluation of others, because of their logical interconnections—the logical laws being in turn simply certain further statements of the system, certain further elements in the field. Having re-evaluated one statement we must re-evaluate some others, which may be statements logically connected with the first or may be statements of logical connections themselves. But the total field is so under determined by its boundary conditions, experience, that there is much latitude of choice as to what statements to re-evaluate in the light of any single contrary experience. No particular experiences are linked with any particular statements in the interior of the field except indirectly through considerations of equilibrium affecting the field as a whole (p. 43).

Virginia Held (b. 1929)
Frequently in the past various descriptive or normative models have been put forward as appropriate for describing or judging the whole of a society composed of legal and political and economic and personal and other components. But these models have been derived from consideration or study of some part of a society and then extended, purportedly to take in the whole. For instance, a model of an egoistic society may be constructed by assuming that the self-interested pursuits of much of economic life characterize all social activity. How faulty such a view is can be seen by considering the behavior of a parent sacrificing much for the sake of a child; such behavior simply makes no sense on the egoistic economic model…we should accept the suitability of partial views for partial contexts. We should try to improve the normative thinking we do, and the practice of morality we engage in, in the special domains in which we concentrate our efforts. The efforts of some people should be devoted to seeing these parts in relation to one another, but we should not think that morality demands us all to do so all the time. Too often the attempt to devise moral theories and systems that can encompass all problems leads to so much vagueness, unclarity, grandiosity, and indeterminacy in applying them that these theories and systems are actually applied to almost nothing (p. 4).

G.W.F. Hegel (1770–1831)
Each of the parts of philosophy is a philosophical whole, a circle rounded and complete in itself. In each of these parts, however, the philosophical Idea is found in a particular specificity or medium. The individual circle, since it is internally a totality,

bursts through the limits imposed by its special medium, and gives rise to a wider circle. The whole thus resembles a circle of circles. The Idea appears in each single circle, but, at the same time, the whole Idea is constituted by the system of these peculiar phases, and each is a necessary member of the organization (p. 15).

David Lewis (b. 1941)

Human Supervenience is named in honour of the great denier of necessary connections. It is the doctrine that all there is to the world is a vast mosaic of local matters of particular fact, just one little thing after another....We have geometry: a system of external relations of spatio-temporal distance between points. Maybe points of space-time itself, maybe point-sized bits of matter or aether or fields, maybe both. And at these points we have local qualities: perfectly natural intrinsic properties which need nothing bigger than a point at which to be instantiated. For short: we have an arrangement of qualities. And that is all. There is no difference without difference in the arrangement of qualities. All else supervenes on that (p. ix).

Auguste Comte (1798–1857)

Here then is the great, the only lacuna that must be filled if we are to complete formation of positive philosophy. The human mind has created celestial and terrestrial physics, mechanics and chemistry, vegetables and animal physics, we might say, but we have still to complete the system of the observational sciences with *social physics* (p. 27).

REFERENCES

The Columbia Encyclopedia, Editors: Barbara A. Charnow and George A. Vallasi (New York: Columbia University Press, 1993). By permission of the publisher.

Encyclopedia Americana, International Edition, volume 5 (Danbury, Connecticut: Grolier, 1995).

Encyclopaedia Britannica, Micropaedia, volume 10, 15th Edition (Chicago: Encyclopaedia Britannica, 1995).

Encyclopaedia Britannica, Macropaedia, volume 15, 15th Edition (Chicago: Encyclopaedia Britannica, 1995).

The Great Ideas: A Syntopicon, in *Great Books of the Western World*. Editor-in-chief: Mortimer J. Adler (Chicago: Encyclopaedia Britannica, 1952). Reprinted with permission from *Great Books of the Western World*, 1952, 1990, Encyclopaedia Britannica, Inc.

The New Encyclopaedia Britannica, Propaedia, volume 30, 15th Edition (Chicago: Encyclopaedia Britannica, 1971). Reprinted with permission of the publisher.

Riesman, David A., *Sociological Economics* (New York: Barnes and Noble Books, 1976).

The World Almanac and Book of Facts (Mahwah, New Jersey: World Almanac Books, 1996).

A *Dictionary of Philosophical Quotations*. Editors: A. J. Ayer and Jane O'Grady (Cambridge, Massachusettes: Basil Blackwell, 1994). **Note:** The following quotations were selected from the immediately preceding source. A full citation will be given as shown in this source followed by its page in A *Dictionary of Philosophical Quotations*.

Comte, Auguste, *The Course in Positive Philosophy*. Translator: M. Clarke, p. 27.
Page number in A *Dictionary of Philosophical Quotations*: p. 94.

Dewey, John, *The Later Works, 1925–1953*, 4. Editor: Jo Ann Boydston, p. 213.
Page Number in A *Dictionary*: p. 116.

Goodman Nelson, *Ways of Worldmaking*, p. 138.
Page Number in A *Dictionary*: p. 154.

Hegel, G.W.F., *Encyclopedia*. Translator: W. Wallace, 15, Amended.
Page Number in A *Dictionary*: p. 172.

Held, Virginia, *Rights and Goods: Justifying Social Action*, p. 4.
Page Number in A *Dictionary*: pp. 180–181

Hume, David, A *Treatise of Human Nature* (Abstract), p. 661.
Page Number in A *Dictionary*: p. 200.

Kant, Immanuel, *Critique of Pure Reason*. Translator: N. Kemp Smith, A 78B 103.
Page Number in A *Dictionary*: p.220.

Lewis, David, *Philosophical Papers, II*, p. ix.
Page Number in A *Dictionary*: p. 255.

Locke, John, B, *An Essay Concerning Human Understanding, Book 2*, Chapter 33 SS5, 7.
Page Number in A *Dictionary*: p. 263.

Ouspensky, P. D., *A New Model of the Universe*, p. 25.
Page Number in A *Dictionary*: p. 331.

Quine, Willard V. O., *From a Logical Point of View*, p. 43.
Page Number in A *Dictionary*: p. 363.

Rorty, Richard, *Philosophy and the Mirror of Nature*, p. 12.
Page Number in A *Dictionary*: p. 378.

Spinoza, Benedict, *The Emendation of the Intellect*. Translator: E. Curley, *CollectedWorks, I*, p. 11.
Page Number in A *Dictionary*: p. 429.

CHAPTER 7

Building Blocks for Formats

In the previous chapter some attention was devoted to sequencing selected quotations taken from the writings of philosophers and scientists over the past several hundred years. These quotations were selected because each contributed some insight into how man consciously and unconsciously organized formats for help in coping with life's challenges or they discussed the roles of imagination, synthesis or intuition in generating implicit if not explicit frames of reference. One even rejected the utility of so-called master systems or comprehensive models.

Perhaps it should be pointed out that science has still not discovered just how the mind organizes or unifies its still mysterious components into coherent formats with which we can feel comfortable in "acting rationally." Psychologists call this "the binding problem" and a major part of the mind-body dilemma for which there yet are no satisfying intellectual answers.

The Coming of the Scientific Age

It was found that most useful commentary was recorded in the past four to five hundred years or so. The advent of the scientific age brought about a quantum increase in discussions about the objective, visible, tangible and quite often measurable characteristics of physical objects. Still important but increasingly less so as the objective side of reality gained dominance was the earlier focus on the subjective more introspective side of reality dealing with concepts of the soul, truth, spirit, free will, virtue and sin.

The basic building blocks selected for quotation in this chapter represent just a very few of the great ideas that could be presented. They have been loosely organized under a few general headings. A major criterion for inclusion here was a perceived fecundity or provocation in the statement's ability to generate additional or deeper thought along the same or different lines. The focus was on identifying a few noteworthy statements from the past that challenged previously held concepts or that seemed to be better balanced or in Nelson Goodman's previous quotation somehow "fit" the emerging and increasingly complex reality that continuing study and research in all fields make available.

By no means does omission or inclusion hereafter suggest anything about the relative significance of these contributions. The point of this exercise is twofold: 1) to highlight just a few beacons of light from the past that still guide us today, and 2) to encourage interested readers to use the great tools already cited to gain some greater depth and appreciation of their various contributions and perhaps see more clearly how the lessons of history and the great ideas have relevance today. This additional investigation will help to put a richer contextual frame of reference around the quotation(s) studied. (Most of the following quotations can be found in *A Dictionary of Philosophical Quotations.*)

Early Greek Philosophers

Socrates (c. 470–399 B.C.)
The first philosophers met together and dedicated in the temple of Apollo the first fruits of their wisdom, the famous inscriptions "know thyself" and "nothing too much" (Plato, *Protagoras*).

Plato (c. 428–347 B.C.)
Socrates: The ideal society we have just described can never grow into a reality or see the light of day, and there will be no end to the troubles of states, or indeed of humanity itself, till philosophers become kings in this world, or till those we now call kings and rulers really and truly become philosophers *(Republic).*

The absurdity of this will become evident if we stop using all these names together—pleasant, painful, good and evil—and since they have turned out to be only two, call them by only two names—first of all good and evil, and only at a different stage pleasure and pain.... So, like an expert in weighing, put the pleasures together and the pains together, set both the near and distant in the balance, and say which is the greater quantity. In weighting pleasures against pleasures, one must always choose the greater and the more; in weighing pains against pains, the smaller and the less: whereas in weighing pleasures against pains, if the pleasures exceed the pains, whether the distant, the near or vice versa, one must take the course which brings those pleasures; but if the pains outweigh the pleasures, avoid it *(Protagoras).*

Aristotle (384–322 B.C.)
The origin of action—its efficient, not its final cause—is choice, and that of choice is desire and reasoning with a view to an end. This is why choice cannot exist either without thought and intellect or without a moral state; for good action and its opposite cannot exist without a combination of intellect and character. Intellect itself, however, moves nothing, but only the intellect which aims at an end and is practical (*Nichomachean Ethics*).

The weaker are always anxious for justice and equality. The strong pay no heed to either (*Politics*).

But how is it that thought is sometimes followed by action, sometimes not; sometimes by movement, sometimes not? What happens seems parallel to the case of thinking and inferring about the immovable objects. There the end is the truth seen (for, when one thinks the two propositions, one thinks and puts together the conclusion), but here the conclusion drawn from two propositions becomes an action (*De Motu*).

On Government and Law

Cicero (106–43 B.C.)
The good of the people is the chief law (*De Legibus*).

Thomas Hobbes (1588–1679)
For by art is created that great LEVIATHAN called a *Commonwealth* or *State*, in Latin *Civitas*, which is but an artificial man; though of greater stature and strength than the natural, for whose protection and defense it was intended; and in which the *sovereignty* is an artificial *soul*, as giving life and motion to the whole body; the *magistrates*, and other officers of judicature and execution, artificial *joints*; *reward* and *punishment*, by which fastened to the seat of sovereignty every joint and member is moved to perform its duty, are the nerves, that do the same in the body natural... (*Leviathan, English Works*).

Benedict Spinoza (1632–1677)
The ultimate aim of Government is not to rule or restrain by fear, not to exact obedience, but on the contrary, to free every man from fear, that he may live in all possible security; in other words to strengthen his natural right to exist and work without injury to himself and others. The object of government is not to change men from rational beings into puppets, but to enable them to develop their minds, and bodies in security, and to employ their reason unshackled.... The true aim of Government is liberty (*Tractatus Theologico-Politicus*).

Giambattista Vico (1668–1744)
Legislation considers man as he is, in order to create of him good practices in human society; as, from violence, avarice and ambition, which are the three vices prevalent throughout the whole of mankind, it creates the army, commerce and the court, and thus the strength, wealth and wisdom of states; and from these three great vices, which would certainly destroy the human species on earth, it creates civil happiness. This axiom proves that divine providence exists and that it is a divine legislative mind which, from the passions of men concerned only for their own personal advantage, in pursuit of which they would live as wild beasts in solitude, has created the civil orders through which they may live in a human society (*The Third New Science*).

Jean-Jacques Rousseau (1712–1778)
There is only one law which by its nature requires unanimous assent. This is the social pact: for the civil association is the most voluntary act in the world; every man having been born free and master of himself, no one else may under any pretext whatever subject him without his consent. To assert that the son of a slave is born a slave is to assert that he is not born a man. If, then, there are opposing voices at the time when the social pact is made, this opposition does not invalidate the contract; it merely excludes the dissentients; they are foreigners among the citizens. After the state is instituted, residence implies consent: to inhabit the territory is to submit to the sovereign (*The Social Contract*).

Karl Marx (1818–1883)
Right can never be higher than the economic structure of society and the cultural development conditioned by it. In a higher phase of communist society, when the enslaving subjugation of individuals to the division of labour and thereby the opposition between intellectual and physical labour have disappeared; when labour is no longer just a means to life but has itself become the primary need of life; when the all-round development of individuals has also increased their productive powers and all the springs of co-operative wealth flow more abundantly—only then can society wholly cross the narrow horizon of bourgeois right and inscribe on its banner: *from each according to his abilities, to each according to his needs (Critique of the Gotha Program)!*

On Models and Systems

Adam Smith (1723–1790)
By preferring the support of domestic to that of foreign industry, he [the owner of capital] intends only his own security; and by

directing that industry in such a manner as its produce may be of greatest value, he intends only his own gain, and he is in this, as in many other cases, led by an invisible hand to promote that of the society more effectively than when he really intends to promote it. I have never known much good done by those who affected to trade for the public good (*The Wealth of Nations, Everyman Edition*).

Karl Marx (1818–1883)
The bourgeoisie, wherever it has got the upper hand, has put an end to all feudal, patriarchal, idyllic relations. It has pitilessly torn asunder the motley feudal ties that bound man to his "natural superiors," and has left remaining no other nexus between man and man than naked self-interest, than callous "cash payment." It has drowned the most heavenly ecstasies of religious fervor of chivalrous enthusiasm, of philistine sentimentalism, in the icy water of egotistical calculation. It has resolved personal wealth into exchange value, and in place of the single unconscionable freedom—Free Trade. In one word, for exploitation, veiled by religious and political illusions, it has substituted naked, shameless, direct, brutal exploitation… (*Manifesto of the Communist Party*).

Max Weber (1864–1900)
An ideal type is formed by the one-sided accentuation of one or more points of view and by the synthesis of a great many diffuse, discrete, more or less present and occasionally absent concrete individual phenomena, which are arranged according to those one-sidedly emphasized viewpoints into a unified analytical construct. It is a utopia (*Sociological Perspectives*).

Friedrich Nietzsche (1844–1900)
We have arranged for ourselves a world in which we can live—by positing bodies, lines, planes, causes and effects, motion and rest, form and content; without these articles of faith nobody now could endure life. But that does not prove them. Life is no argument. The conditions of life might include error (*The Gay Science*).

Rudolf Carnap (1891–1970)
Science is a system of statements based on direct experience, and controlled by experimental verification. Verification in science is not, however, of single statements but of the entire system or a sub-system of such statements (*The Unity of Science*).

On Morality and Justice

Thomas Hobbes (1588–1679)
To this war of every man, against every man, this also is consequent; that nothing can be unjust. The notions of right and wrong, justice and injustice have there no place. Where there is no common power, there is no law: where no law, no injustice. Force and fraud, are in war the two cardinal virtues. Justice, and injustice, are none of the faculties neither of the body, nor mind. If they were they might be in a man that were alone in the world, as well as his senses, and passions. They are qualities, that relate to men in society, not in solitude. It is consequent also to the same condition, that there be no propriety, no dominion, no *mine and thine* distinct; but only that to be every man's, that he can get; and for so long, as he can keep it (*Leviathan, English Works*).

Immanuel Kant (1724–1804)
Finally, there is an imperative which commands a certain conduct immediately, without having as its condition any other purpose to be attained by it. This imperative is categorical. It concerns not the matter of the action or its intended result, but its form and the principle of which it is itself a result; and what is essentially good in it consists in the mental disposition, let the consequence be that it may. This imperative may be called that of morality (*Fundamental Principles of the Metaphysic of Morals*).

Jean-Jacques Rousseau (1712–1778)
Distributive justice would still be opposed to the strict equality of the state of nature, even if it were practicable in civil society, and as all members of the state owe it services proportionate to their talents and their strength, the citizens in turn ought to be honoured and favoured in proportion to their services (*Second Discourse*).

Alasdair MacIntyre (b. 1929)
A crucial turning point in that earlier history occurred when men and women of good will turned aside from the task of shoring up the Roman *imperium* and ceased to identify the continuation of civility and moral community with the maintenance of that *imperium*. What they set themselves to achieve instead—often not recognizing what they were doing—was the construction of new forms of community within which the moral life could be sustained so that both morality and civility might survive the coming ages of barbarism and darkness. If my account of our moral condition is correct, we ought also to be able to conclude that for some time now we too have reached the

turning point. What matters at this stage is the construction of local forms of community within which civility and the intellectual and moral life can be sustained through the new dark ages which are already on us. And if the tradition of the virtues was able to survive the horrors of the last dark ages, we are not entirely without hope. This time, however, the barbarians are not waiting beyond the frontiers; they have already been governing us for quite some time *(After Virtue)*.

Ted Honderich (b. 1933)
The Principle of Equality...is that our principal end must be to make well-off those who are badly off, by way of certain policies: increasing means to well-being and transferring means from the better-off which will not affect their well-being; transferring means from the better-off which will affect their well-being, those at the higher levels to be affected first, and observing a certain limit; reducing the necessity of inequalities *(Violence for Equality: Inquiries in Political Philosophy)*.

On Truth and Logic

Soren Kierkegaard (1813–1855)
If subjectivity is the truth, the conceptual account of truth must include an expression of the antithesis to objectivity, a mark of the fork in the road where the way swings off; that expression will serve at the same time to indicate the tension of the subjective inwardness. Here is such a definition of truth: the truth is an objective uncertainty held fast in an appropriation process of the most passionate inwardness, the highest truth attainable for an existing individual *(Concluding Unscientific Postscript)*.

Friedrich Nietzsche (1844–1900)
What then is truth? A mobile army of metaphors, metonyms, and anthropomorphisms—in short, a sum of human relations, which have been enhanced, transposed, and embellished poetically and rhetorically, and which after long use seem firm, canonical, and obligatory to a people: truths are illusions about which one has forgotten that this is what they are; metaphors which are worn out and without sensuous power; coins which have lost their pictures and now matter only as metal, no longer as coins *(The Portable Nietzsche)*.

Gottlob Frege (1848–1925)
I hope I may claim in the present work to have made it possible that the laws of arithmetic are analytic judgements and consequently a priori. Arithmetic thus becomes simply a development of logic, and every proposition of arithmetic a law of logic, albeit

a derivative one. To apply arithmetic in the physical sciences is to bring logic to bear on observed facts; calculation becomes deduction (*The Foundations of Arithmetic*).

Paul Feyerabend (1924–1994)
It is clear, then, that the idea of a fixed method, or of a fixed theory of rationality, rests on too naive a view of man and his social surroundings. To those who look at the rich material provided by history, and who are not intent on impoverishing it in order to please their lower instincts, their craving for intellectual security in the form of clarity, precision, "objectivity," "truth," it will become clear that there is only one principle that can be defended under *all* stages of human development. It is the principle: *anything goes* (*Against Method*).

Michel Foucault (1926–1984)
…Truth isn't outside power, or lacking in power: contrary to a myth whose history and functions would repay further study, truth isn't the reward of free spirits, the child of protracted solitude, nor the privilege of those who have succeeded in liberating themselves. Truth is a thing of this world: it is produced only by virtue of multiple forms of constraint. And it induces regular effects of power. Each society has its regime of truth, its "general politics" of truth: that is, the types of discourse which it accepts and makes function as true; the mechanisms and instances which enable one to distinguish true and false statements, the means by which each is sanctioned; the techniques and procedures corded value in the acquisition of truth: the status of those who are charged with saying what counts as true (*Power/Knowledge*).

On Being and Reality

Rene Descartes (1596–1650)
Thought: this alone is inseparable from me. I am, I exist—that is certain. But for how long? For as long as I am thinking. For it could be that were I totally to cease from thinking, I should totally cease to exist. I am, then, in the strict sense only a thing that thinks; that is, I am a mind, or intelligence, or intellect, or reason words whose meaning I have been ignorant of until now. But for all that I am a thing which is real and which truly exists. But what kind of thing? As I have just said—a thinking thing (*Second Meditation II*).

Friedrich Nietzsche (1844–1900)
How should explanation be at all possible when we make everything into an image, *our* image! …Cause and effect: such a duality

probably never occurs—in reality there lies before us a continuum out of which we isolate a couple of pieces...(*The Gay Science*).

I also maintain the phenomenality of the *inner* world: everything of which we become *conscious* is, through and through, merely arranged, simplified, schematized, interpreted. The actual situation behind inner perception, the causal uniting between thoughts, feelings, desires, and between subject and object, is absolutely concealed from us, and is perhaps pure fancy. This "apparent inner world" is manipulated with just the same forms and procedures as "the external world." We never hit on "facts" (*Nachlass*).

Over one man *necessity* stands in the shape of his passions, over another as the habit of hearing and obeying, over a third as a logical conscience, over a fourth as caprice and a mischievous pleasure in escapades. These four will, however, seek the *freedom* of their will precisely where each of them is most firmly fettered: it is as if the silkworm sought the freedom of its will in spinning. How does this happen? Evidently because each considers himself most free where his *feeling of living* is greatest (*The Wanderer and His Shadow*).

Martin Heidegger (1897–1976)
Only by the anticipation of death is every accidental and "provisional" possibility driven out. Only Being-free for death gives Dasein (the human being) its goal outright and pushes existence into its finitude. Once one has grasped the finitude of one's existence, it snatches one back from the endless multiplicity of possibilities which offer themselves as closest to one—those of comfortableness, shirking, and taking things lightly—and brings Dasein into the simplicity of its fate. This is how we designate Dasein's primordial historizing, which lies in authentic resoluteness and in which Dasein *hands* itself *down* to itself, free for death, in a possibility which it has inherited and yet has chosen (*Being and Time*).

On Science and Technology
Auguste Comte (1798–1857)
Since Bacon, all good intellects have agreed that there is no real knowledge save that which rests on observed facts. In our present advanced age, this principle is evidently incontestible. But...if on the one hand every theory must be based on observation, on the other it is equally true that facts cannot be observed without the guidance of some theory. If in contemplating phenomena we had no principles to which to attach them, not only would we

John Stuart Mill (1806–1873)
...The most scientific proceeding can be no more than an improved form of that which was primitively pursued by the human understanding, while undirected by science. When mankind first formed the idea of studying phenomena according to a stricter and surer method than that which they had in the first instance adopted, they did not, conformably to the well-meant but impracticable precept of Descartes, set out from the supposition that nothing had been already ascertained.... The first scientific inquirers assumed [various] known truths, and set out from them to discover others...it is impossible to frame any scientific method of induction, or test of the correctness of inductions unless on the hypothesis that some inductions deserving of relevance have been already made *(A System of Logic)*.

P. D. Ouspensky (1878–1947)
The whole of our positive science physics, chemistry and biology is based on hypotheses contradictory to Kant's propositions...positivist philosophy appears to consider Kant's view erroneous and assumes that scientific experience acquaints us with the very substance of things, with the true causes of our sensations, or, if it does not yet do that, it may succeed in doing so later. "Positivists" believe in the very thing the possibility of which Kant denied, namely in the comprehension of the true essence of things through the study of phenomena *(Tertium Organum)*.

Martin Heidegger (1889–1976)
The epoch of completed metaphysics stands before its beginning.... The basic form of appearance in which the will to will arranges and calculates itself in the unhistorical element of the world of completed metaphysics can be stringently called "technology." This name includes all areas of beings which equip the whole of beings: objectified nature, the business of culture, manufactured politics, and the gloss of ideals overlying everything. Thus "technology" does not signify here the separate area of the production and equipment of machines.... The name "technology" is understood here in such an essential way that its meaning coincides with the term "completed metaphysics" *(The End of Philosophy)*.

Anthony Kenny (b. 1931)
It is characteristic of our age to endeavor to replace virtues by technology. That is to say, wherever possible we strive to use

methods of physical or social engineering to achieve goals which our ancestors thought attainable only by the training of character. Thus, we try so far as possible to make contraception take the place of chastity, and anaesthetics to take the place of fortitude; we replace resignation by insurance policies and munificence by the Welfare state. It would be idle romanticism to deny that such techniques and institutions are often less painful and more efficient methods of achieving the goods and preventing the evils which unaided virtue once sought to achieve and avoid. But it would be an equal and opposite folly to hope that the take-over of virtue by technology may one day be complete... (The Anatomy of the Soul).

On Power and Will

St. Thomas Aquinas (c. 1225–1274)
Since conscience is the dictate of reason, the application of theory to practice, the inquiry, *whether a will that disobeys an erroneous conscience is right*, is the same as, *whether a man is obliged to follow a mistaken conscience*. Now because the object of an act of will is that which is proposed by the conscience, if the will chooses to do what the conscience considers to be wrong, then the will goes out to it in the guise of evil. Hence it should be said that every act of will against conscience, whether the conscience be correct or mistaken, it is always bad (Summa Theologiae).

Nicolo Machiavelli (1469–1527)
Thus it is well to seem merciful, faithful, humane, sincere, religious, and also to be so; but you must have the mind so disposed that when it is needful to be otherwise you may be able to change to the opposite qualities. And it must be understood that a prince, and especially a new prince, cannot observe all those things which are considered good in men, being often obliged, in order to maintain the state, to act against faith, against charity, against humanity, and against religion (The Prince).

David Hume (1711–1776)
...By the *will*, I mean nothing *but the internal impression we feel and are conscious of, when we knowingly give rise to any new motion of our body, or new perception of our mind* (A Treatise of Human Nature).

Jean-Jacques Rousseau (1712–1778)
Finally, since each man gives himself to all, he gives himself to no one; and since there is no associate over whom he does not gain the same rights as others gain over him, each man recovers the equivalent of everything he loses, and in the bargain he acquires more power to preserve what he has. If, then, we eliminate

from the social pact everything that is not essential to it, we find it comes down to this: "Each one of us puts into the community his person and all his powers under the supreme direction of the general will; and as a body, we incorporate every member as an indivisible part of the whole" *(The Social Contract)*.

Friedrich Nietzsche (1884–1900)
[Anything which] is a living and not a dying body…will have to be an incarnate will to power, it will strive to grow, spread, seize, become predominant not from any morality or immorality but because it is *living* and because life simply is will to power…. "Exploitation"…belongs to the *essence* of what lives, as a basic organic function; it is a consequence of the will to power, which is after all the will of life *(Beyond Good and Evil)*.

On Creativity, Imagination and Intuition

Immanuel Kant (1724–1804)
Without sensibility no object would be given to us, without understanding no object would be thought. Thoughts without content are empty, intuitions without concepts are blind…. The understanding can intuit nothing, the senses can think nothing. Only through their union can knowledge arise *(Critique of Pure Reason)*.

Friedrich Nietzsche (1844–1900)
What is originality? To *see* something that has no name as yet and hence cannot be mentioned although it stares us all in the face. The way men usually are, it takes a name to make something visible for them *(The Gay Science)*.

Alfred North Whitehead (1861–1947)
Opposed elements stand to each other in mutual requirement. In their unity, they inhibit or contrast. God and the World stand to each other in this opposed requirement. God is the infinite ground of all mentality, the unity of vision seeking physical multiplicity. The World is the multiplicity of finites, actualities seeking a perfected unity. Neither God, nor the World, reaches static completion. Both are in the grip of the ultimately metaphysical ground, the creative advance into novelty. Either of them, God and the World, is the instrument of novelty for the other *(Process and Reality)*.

Theodor Adorno (1903–1969)
Properly written texts are like spiders' webs: tight, concentric, transparent, well-spun and firm. They draw into themselves all the creatures of the air. Metaphors flitting hastily through them

become their nourishing prey. Subject matter comes winging toward them. The soundness of a conception can be judged by whether it causes one quotation to summon another. Where thought has opened up one cell of reality, it should, without violence by the subject, penetrate the next. It proves its relation to the object as soon as other objects crystallize around it. In the light that it casts on its chosen substance, others begin to glow (*Mimima Moralia*).

Daniel C. Dennett (b. 1942)
Only some of the portions of the physical universe have the property of being designed to resist their own dissolution, to wage a local campaign against the inexorable trend of the Second Law of Thermodynamics. And only some of these portions have the further property of being caused to have reliable expectations about what will happen next, and hence to have the capacity to control things, including themselves. And only some of these have the further capacity of significant self-improvement (through learning). And fewer still have the open ended capacity (requiring a language of self-description) for "radical self-evaluation." These portions of the world are thus loci of self-control, of talent, of decision making. They have projects, interests, and values they create in the course of their own self-evaluation and self-definition. How much less like a domino could a portion of the physical world be? (*Elbow Room: The Varieties of Free Will Worth Wanting*).

On Perception and Art
Gottfried Wilhelm Leibnitz (1646–1716)
I take as an illustration a block of veined marble rather than a wholly uniform block of blank tablets, that is to say what is called *tabula rasa*...if there were veins in the stone which marked out the figure of Hercules, this stone would be more determined thereto, and Hercules would be in some manner innate in it, although labour would be needed to uncover these veins.... It is in this way that ideas and truths are innate in us, like natural inclinations and dispositions, natural habits or potentialities... (*New Essays on Human Understanding, Philosophical Writings*).

Friedrich Nietzsche (1844–1900)
The word "Dionysian" means: an urge to unity, a reaching out beyond personality, the everyday, society, reality, across the abyss of transitoriness: a passionate-painful overflowing into darker, fuller, more floating states.... The word "Apollinian" means: the urge to perfect self-sufficiency, to the typical "individual" to all

that simplifies, distinguishes, makes strong, clear, unambiguous typical: freedom under law. The further development of art is as necessarily tied to these two natural artistic powers as the further development of man is to that between the sexes. Plenitude of power and moderation *(The Will to Power)*.

Clive Bell (1881–1964)
What quality is shared by all objects that provoke our aesthetic emotions? What quality is common to Sta. Sophia and the windows at Chartres, Mexican sculpture, a Persian bow, Chinese carpets, Giotto's frescoes at Padua, and the masterpieces of Poussin, Piero della Francesca, and Cezanne? Only one answer seems possible—significant form. In each, lines and colours combined in a particular way, certain forms and relations of forms, stir our aesthetic emotions. These relations and combinations of lines and colours, these aesthetically moving forms, I call "Significant Form" and "Significant Form" is the one quality common to all works of visual art *(Art)*.

Herbert Marcuse (1898–1979)
We can tentatively define "aesthetic form" as the result of the transformation of a given content (actual or historical, personal or social fact) into a self-contained whole: a poem, play, novel, etc. The work is thus "taken out" of the constant process of reality and assumes a significance and truth of its own. The aesthetic transformation is achieved through a reshaping of language, perception, and understanding so that they reveal the essence of reality in its appearance: the repressed potentialities of man and nature. The work of art thus re-presents reality while accusing it *(The Aesthetic Dimension)*.

Nelson Goodman (1906–1998)
Emotion and feeling…function cognitively in aesthetic and in much other experience. We do not discern stylistic affinities and differences, for example, by "rational analysis" but by sensations, perceptions, feelings, emotions, sharpened in practice like the eye of a gemologist or the fingers of an inspector of machined parts. Far from wanting to desensitize aesthetic experience, I want to sensitize cognition. In art—and I think in science too—emotion and cognition are interdependent: feeling without understanding is blind, and understanding without feeling is empty *(Of Mind and Other Matters)*.

On Laws and Principles
Jeremy Bentham (1748–1832)
Nature has placed mankind under the governance of two sovereign masters, *pain* and *pleasure*. It is for them alone to point out

what we ought to do, as well as to determine what we shall do. On the one hand the standard of right and wrong, on the other the chain of causes and effects, are fastened to their throne. They govern us in all we do, in all we say, in all we think: every effort we can make to throw off our subjection will serve but to demonstrate and confirm it. In words a man may pretend to abjure their empire: but in reality he will remain subject to it all the while. The *principle of utility* recognizes this subjection, and assumes it for the foundation of that system, the object of which is to rear the fabric of felicity by the hands of reason and of law. Systems which attempt to question it deal in sounds instead of sense, in caprice instead of reason, in darkness instead of light (*An Introduction to the Principles of Morals and Legislation, Collected Works*).

So far as depends on wealth—of two persons having unequal fortunes, he who has most wealth must by a legislator be regarded as having most happiness. But the quantity of happiness will not go on increasing in anything near the same proportion as the quantity of wealth.... The effect of wealth in the production of happiness goes on diminishing, as the quantity by which the wealth of one man exceeds that of another goes on increasing: in other words, the quantity of happiness produced by a particle of wealth (each particle being of the same magnitude) will be less and less at every particle; the second will produce less than the first, the third less than the second, and so on (*Works, III*).

Soren Kierkegaard (1813–1855)
It's quite true what philosophy says, that life must be understood backwards. But one then forgets the other principle, that it must be lived forwards. A principle which, the more one thinks it through, precisely leads to the conclusion that life in time can never properly be understood, just because no moment can acquire the complete stillness needed to orient oneself backwards (*Soren Kierkegaard's Papirer*).

P. H. Nowell-Smith (b. 1914)
What sort of principles a man adopts will, in the end, depend on his vision of the Good life, his conception of the sort of world that he desires, so far as it rests with him to create. Indeed his moral principles just *are* this conception. The conception can be altered: perhaps he meets someone whose character, conduct, or arguments reveal to him new virtues that he has never even contemplated; or he may do something uncharacteristic and against his principles without choosing to do it and, in doing it, discover how good it is. Moral values, like other values, are sometimes discovered accidentally. But the one thing he cannot do is to *try*

to alter this conception that all his choices are made. And the fact that he cannot choose to alter this conception neither shields him from blame nor disqualifies him from admiration (*Ethics*).

Bernard Williams (b. 1929)
There are indeed areas in which the "inculcation of principles" is an appropriate phrase for the business of moral education: truth-telling, for example, and the sphere of justice. But more broadly, as Aristotle perceived, we are concerned with something not so aptly called the inculcation of principles, but rather the education of the emotions (*Problems of the Self*).

John R. Commons (1862–1945)
The transaction is two or more wills giving, taking, persuading, coercing, defrauding, commanding, obeying, competing, governing, in a world of scarcity, mechanism and rules of conduct. The court deals with the will-in-action. Like the modern physicist or chemist, its ultimate unit is not an atom but an electron, always in motion—not an individual but two or more individuals in action. It never catches them except in motion. Their motion is a transaction. A transaction occurs at a point of time. But transactions flow one into another over a period time, and this flow is a process. The courts have fully developed the notion of this process in the concept of a "going concern," which they have taken over from the customs of business, and which is none other than a technological process of production and consumption of physical things and a business process of buying and selling, borrowing and lending, commanding and obeying, according to shop rules or working rules or laws of the land. The physical process may be named a "going plant," the business process a "going business," and the two constitute a "going concern" made up of action and reaction with nature's forces and transactions between human beings according to accepted rules (*John R. Commons, Legal Foundations of Capitalism*).

On Consequences, Ends and Goals

Thomas Hobbes (1588–1679)
...He that will do anything for his pleasure, must engage himself to suffer all the pains annexed to it; and these pains, are the natural punishments of those actions, which are the beginning of more harm than good. And hereby it comes to pass that intemperance is naturally punished with diseases; rashness with mischances; injustice with the violence of enemies: pride with ruin; cowardice, with oppression; negligent government of princes, with rebellion; and rebellion, with slaughter (*Leviathan, English Works*).

J. G. Fichte (1844–1900)
What sort of philosophy one chooses depends, therefore, on what sort of man one is; for a philosophical system is not a dead piece of furniture that we can reject or accept as we wish; it is rather a thing animated by the soul of the person who holds it. A person indolent by nature or dulled and distorted by mental servitude, learned luxury, and vanity will never raise himself to the level of idealism *(Science of Knowledge)*.

Friedrich Nietzsche (1844–1900)
People are accustomed to consider the goal (purposes, vocations, etc.) as the *driving force*, in keeping with a very ancient error; but it is merely the *directing force*—one has mistaken the helmsman for the steam. And not even always the helmsman, the directing force *(The Gay Science)*.

Max Weber (1864–1920)
...The *summum bonum* of this [modern capitalist] ethic, the earning of more and more money, combined with the strict avoidance of all spontaneous enjoyment of life...is thought of so purely as an end in itself, that from the point of view of the happiness of, or utility to, the single individual, it appears entirely transcendental and absolutely irrational. Man is dominated by the making of money, by acquisition as the ultimate purpose of his life. Economic acquisition is no longer subordinated to man as the means for the satisfaction of his material needs. This reversal of what we should call the natural relationship, so irrational from a naive point of view, is evidently as definitely a leading principle of capitalism as it is foreign to all peoples not under capitalist influence *(The Protestant Ethic and the Spirit of Capitalism)*.

Nicholas Rescher (b. 1928)
While ideals are, in a way, mere fictions, they nevertheless direct and canalize our thought and action. To be sure, an ideal is not a goal we can expect to attain. But it serves to set a direction in which we can strive. Ideals are irrealities, but they are irrealities that condition the nature of the real through their influence on human thought and action *(Ethical Idealism: An Inquiry into the Nature and Function of Ideals)*.

On Education and Learning

Marcus Fabius Quintilianus Quintilian (35–95 A.D.)
Narrow-necked vessels reject a great deal of any liquid that is poured over them, but are filled up with whatever is gradually poured into them. Likewise, it is for us to ascertain how much the minds of boys can receive at any one time. What is too much

for their minds to grasp will not enter at all, because their minds are not sufficiently expanded to accept it (*Institutio Oratoria*).

John Locke (1632–1704)
Let us then suppose the Mind to be, as we say, white Paper, void of all Characters, without any *Ideas*; How comes it to be furnished? Whence comes it by that vast store, which the busy and boundless Fancy of Man has painted on it , with an almost endless variety? Whence has it all the materials of Reason and Knowledge? To this I answer, in one word, From *Experience*: In that, all our Knowledge is founded; and from that it ultimately derives it self. Our Observation employ'd either about *external, sensible Objects; or about the internal Operations of our Minds, perceived and reflected on by our selves, is that, which supplies our Understandings with all the materials of thinking* (An Essay Concerning Human Understanding).

Mary Wollstonecraft (1759–1797)
A kind of mysterious instinct is *supposed* to reside in the soul, that instantaneously discerns truth, without the tedious labour of ratiocination. This instinct, for I know not what other name to give it, has been termed *common sense*, and more frequently *sensibility*: and, by a kind of *indefeasible* right, it has been *supposed*, for rights of this kind are not easily proved, to reign paramount over the other faculties of the mind, and to be an authority from which there is no appeal.... It is to this instinct, without doubt, that you [Burke] allude, when you talk of the "moral constitution of the heart".... Sacred be the feelings of the heart! concentred in a glowing flame, they become the sun of life; and, without his invigorating impregnation, reason would probably lie in helpless inactivity, and never bring forth her only legitimate offspring—virtue. But to prove that virtue is really an acquisition of the individual, and not the blind impulse of unerring instinct, the bastard vice has often been begotten by the same father.

In what respect are we superior to the brute creation, if intellect is not allowed to be the guide of passion? Brutes hope and fear, love and hate; but, without a capacity to improve, a power of turning these passions to good or evil, they neither acquire virtue nor wisdom.—Why? Because the Creator has not given them reason (*A Vindication of the Rights of Men, Works*).

John Dewey (1859–1952)
Most everyone has had occasion to look back on his school days and wonder what has become of the knowledge he was supposed

to have amassed during his years of schooling, and why it is that the technical skills he acquired have to be learned over again in changed form in order to stand him in good stead. Indeed, he is lucky who does not find that in order to make progress, in order to go ahead intellectually, he does not have to unlearn much of what he learned in school.... One trouble is that the subject matter in question was learned in isolation; it was put, as it were, in a water-tight compartment. When the question is asked, then, what has become of it, where has it gone to, the right answer is that it is still there in the special compartment in which it was originally stored away. If exactly the same conditions recurred as those under which it was acquired, it would also recur and be available. But it was segregated when it was acquired and hence is so disconnected from the rest of experience that it is not available under the actual conditions of life. It is contrary to the laws of experience that learning of this kind, no matter how thoroughly ingrained at the time, should give genuine preparation (*Experience and Education*).

Amatai Etzioni (b. 1929)
...The author does not expect that the prevailing neoclassical paragidm will be abandoned; indeed, much of what it has contributed might well be integrated into a more encompassing paradigm. At the same time, it seems only prudent that some fraction of the effort dedicated to constructing theories, to guiding research and improving understanding of the personal and social realm, especially of choice and economic behavior, should be invested in attempting to advance new paradigms, paradigms that might synthesize the work of neoclassicists and other social scientists, and that once in a while such paradigms should be granted a fair hearing (*The Moral Dimension, Toward a New Economics*).

On Anticipating the Future
Robert Rubin
The division between the haves and have nots, developing countries, [raises] issues that won't automatically be met by markets and by openness to change. If we don't meet the challenges that these issues pose, I think it is conceivable that we [will] have a backlash against market-based systems, against technological development, against openness to trade, and a movement back toward a more statist economic system, which I think will result in a far less successful global economy (*Voices of Authority*).

Stephen L. Carter
One of my fears, as we go into the new century, is whether our rate of technological change is outstripping our ability as a society to hold moral and ethical deliberations about it. Should we clone humans or not? Everybody's got a commission—there's something like seven commissions. While they're all studying, the science is zipping along. The answer to difficult moral questions is not determined by national commissions or public-opinion surveys. It's determined by individual people who have been raised and trained in such a way that they can exercise moral judgment (*Stephen L. Carter, Voices of Authority*).

Edward O. Wilson
In the 21st century, we are going to pass through a bottleneck. The land required to maintain one American's standard of living, on average, is 12 acres; the amount required to sustain the current standard of living of someone in one of the developing countries, where 80 percent of the world's population lives, is one acre. Now here's the problem: The whole world wants to live like Americans. Thus we have the aftershock following the population explosion: not only too many people, but people attempting legitimately, understandably, to increase the quality of their lives. It's been estimated that to bring the whole world up to America's standard of living would require two more planet Earths. The results, politically, economically, and environmentally, of the rush to achieve that impossibility in the next century will be our greatest problem (*Voices of Authority*).

Ray Funkhouser
Starting in the 1920's, America has developed a uniquely marketing-based culture…. Until the advent of American marketing culture, all human societies involved values that constrained choice and individual appetites in the interest of social harmony…The erosive effect of American media on our more traditional values is well understood by those facing the onslaught…Given the state of American morals, manners, values, education and waist-lines after 70-odd years of indoctrination by commercial mass media, one can sympathize with the nations trying to resist the campaign to train their children to be American-style consumers (*The Economist*).

REFERENCES

A *Dictionary of Philosophical Quotations*. Editors: A. J. Ayer and Jane O'Grady (Cambridge, MA: Basil Blackwell, 1994). **Note:** Where indicated, most of the above quotations were selected from the immediately preceding source. A full citation will be given as shown in this source followed by its page in A *Dictionary of Philosophical Quotations*.

Adorno, Theodor, *Minima Moralia*. Translator: E.F.N. Jephcott, p. 87.
   Page number in A *Dictionary*: 4.

Aquinas, St. Thomas, *Summa Theologiae*, I, Pt. la, qu.19, a.5.
   Page number in A *Dictionary*: 12–13.

Aristotle, *Nichomachean Ethics*, 1139a.
   Page number in A *Dictionary*: 16.

Aristotle, *Politics*, 1318.
   Page number in A *Dictionary*: 18.

Aristotle, *De Motu*, 701a.
   Page number in A *Dictionary*: 21.

Bell, Clive, *Art*, p. 8
   Page number in A *Dictionary*: 43.

Bentham, Jeremy, *An Introduction to the Principles of Morals and Legislation, Collected Works*), p. 321.
   Page number in A *Dictionary*: 46.

Bentham, Jeremy, "Pannomial Fragments," *Works, III*, p. 228.
   Page number in A *Dictionary*: 48.

Carnap, Rudolf, *The Unity of Science*. Translator: M. Black, p. 42.
   Page number in A *Dictionary*: 83.

Carter, Stephen L., "Voices of Authority," *Civilization: The Magazine of the Library of Congress*, August/September 1999, 72.

Cicero, *De Legibus*, III, 3.8. Translator: C.W. Keyes (Loeb Edition), p. 467.
   Page number in A *Dictionary*: 89.

Comte, Auguste, *The Essential Comte*. Editor: S. Andreski; translator: M. Clarke, p. 21.
   Page number in A *Dictionary*: 97.

Descartes, Rene, II, *Second Meditation*, p. 18.
   Page number in A *Dictionary*: 112.

Dennett, Daniel C., *Elbow Room: The Varieties of Free Will Worth Wanting*, p. 199.
   Page number in A *Dictionary*: 104–105.

Dewey, John, *Experience and Education*, III.
   This quotation is not found in A *Dictionary*.

Etzioni, Amatai, *The Moral Dimension, Towards a New Economics* (New York: The Free Press, Division of Simon & Schuster, Inc., 1988).
   This quotation is not found in A *Dictionary*.

Feyerabend, Paul, *Against Method*, p. 27.
   Page number in A *Dictionary*: p. 132.

Fichte, J. G., *Science of Knowledge*. Translators: P. Heath and J. Lachs, p. 16.
Page number in *A Dictionary*: p. 133.

Foucault, Michel, *Power/Knowledge*. Translators: C. Gordon, L. Marshall, J. Mepham, and K. Soper, p. 131.
Page number in *A Dictionary*: p. 141.

Frege, Gottlob, *The Foundations of Arithmetic*. Translator: J. L. Austin, p. 99.
Page number in *A Dictionary*: p. 144.

Funkhouser, Ray, Letter to the Editor, *The Economist*, October 3, 1998, p. 8.

Goodman, Nelson, *Of Mind and Other Matters*, p. 7.
Page number in *A Dictionary*: p. 155.

Heidegger, Martin, *Being and Time*. Translators: John Macquarrie and Edward Robinson, p. 384.
Page number in *A Dictionary*: p. 175.

Heidgger, Martin, *The End of Philosophy*. Translators: E. Kadloubovsky and P.D. Ouspensky, p. 8.
Page number in *A Dictionary*: pp. 178–179.

Hobbes, Thomas, *Leviathan, English Works*, 3, p. ix.
Page number in *A Dictionary*: p. 183.

Hobbes, Thomas, *Leviathan, English Works*, 3, p. 113.
Page number in *A Dictionary*: p. 184

Hobbes, Thomas, *Leviathan, English Works*, 3, p. 357.
Page number in *A Dictionary*: p. 185.

Honderich, Ted, *Violence for Equality: Inquiries in Political Philosophy*, p. 54.
Page number in *A Dictionary*: p. 189.

Hume, David, *A Treatise of Human Nature*, p. 399.
Page number in *A Dictionary*: p. 197.

Kant, Immanuel, *Fundamental Principles of the Metaphysic of Morals*. Translator: T. K. Abbott, p. 33.
Page number in *A Dictionary*: pp. 228–229.

Kant, Immanuel, *Critique of Pure Reason*. Translator: N. Kemp Smith, A 51B 75.
Page number in *A Dictionary*: pp. 219–220.

Kenny, Anthony, *The Anatomy of the Soul*, p. 26.
Page number in *A Dictionary*: p. 232.

Kierkegaard, Soren, *Concluding Unscientific Postscript*. Translators: D. F. Swenson and W. Lowrie, p. 182.
Page number in *A Dictionary*: p.233.

Kierkegaard, Soren, *Soren Kierkegaard's Papirer*. Editor: N. Thulstrup; translator: A. Hannay, IV, p. 61.
Page number in *A Dictionary*: p. 235.

Liebnitz, Gottfried Wilhelm, *New Essays on Human Understanding*, *Philosophical Writings*, p. 153.
Page number in *A Dictionary*: p. 248.

Locke, John, *An Essay Concerning Human Understanding*, Book 2, Chapter 1, 52.
Page number in *A Dictionary*: p. 259.

Machiavelli, Nicolo, *Summa Theologiae*, I, Pt. la, qu. 19, a.5.
Page number in *A Dictionary*: p.274.

MacIntyre, Alasdair, *After Virtue*, p. 244.
Page number in *A Dictionary*: p. 276.

Marx, Karl, "Critique of the Gotha Program" *Marx Engels Werke*, 19:21. Translator: A. Wood.
Page number in *A Dictionary*: pp. 292–293.

Marx, Karl, *Manifesto of the Communist Party*, 6: 486.
Page number in *A Dictionary*: pp. 287–288.

Mill, John Stuart, *A System of Logic, Collected Works*, VII, p. 318.
Page number in *A Dictionary*: p. 306.

Nietzsche, Friedrich, *The Gay Science*. Translator: Walter Kaufmann, s. 121.
Page number in *The Dictionary*: p. 317.

Nietzsche, Friedrich, *The Portable Nietzsche*. Translator: Walter Kaufmann, p. 46.
Page number in *The Dictionary*: pp. 317–318.

Nietzsche, Friedrich, *The Gay Science*. Translator: Walter Kaufmann, s.112.
Page number in *The Dictionary*: p. 318.

Nietzsche, Friedrich, *Nachlass*. Editor: K. Schlechta; translator: A. Danto, p. 673.
Page number in *The Dictionary*: p. 319.

Nietzsche, Friedrich, *The Wanderer and his Shadow*. Translator: R. J. Hollingdale, s. 9.
Page number in *The Dictionary*: p. 323.

Nietzsche, Friedrich, *Beyond Good and Evil*. Translator: Walter Kaufmann, s. 259.
Page number in *The Dictionary*: p. 320.

Nietzsche, Friedrich, *The Gay Science*. Translator: Walter Kaufmann, s. 261.
Page number in *The Dictionary*: p. 322.

Nietzsche, Friedrich, *The Will to Power*. Translator: Walter Kaufmann, s. 1050.
Page number in *The Dictionary*: p. 325.

Nietzsche, Friedrich, *The Gay Science*. Translator: Walter Kaufmann, s. 360.
Page number in *The Dictionary*: p. 320.

Nowell-Smith, P. H., *Ethics*, p. 313.
Page number in *The Dictionary*: p. 327.

Ouspensky, P. D., *Tertium Organum*. Translators: E. Kadloubovsky and P. D. Ouspensky, p. 8.
Page number in *The Dictionary*: p. 331.

Plato, *Republic*. Translator: H.D.P. Lee, 473C10.
Page number in *The Dictionary*: p. 343.

Plato, *Protagoras*, 358 C.
Page number in *The Dictionary*: p. 344.

Quintilian, Marcus Fabius Quintilianus, *Institutio Oratoria*, I, 2.
This quotation is not found in *The Dictionary*.

Rescher, Nicholas, *Ethical Idealism: An Inquiry into the Nature and Function of Ideals*, p. 133.
Page number in *The Dictionary*: p. 376.

Rousseau, Jean-Jacques, *The Social Contract*. Translator: Maruice Cranston, p. 152.
Page number in *The Dictionary*: p. 383.

Rousseau, Jean-Jacques, *Second Discourse*. Translator: Maurice Cranston, p. 48.
Page number in *The Dictionary*: p. 384.

Rousseau, Jean-Jacques, *The Social Contract*. Translator: Maurice Cranston, p. 61.
Page number in *The Dictionary*: pp. 383–384.

Rubin, Robert, "Voices of Authority" *Civilization: The Magazine of the Library of Congress*, Washington, D.C., August/September 1999, p. 72.

Smith, Adam, *The Wealth of Nations*, Everyman Edition, p. 400.
Page number in *The Dictionary*: pp. 427–428.

Spinoza, Benedict, *Tractatus Theologico-Politicus*, Chapter 20, III, p. 241.
Page number in *The Dictionary*: p. 432.

Vico, Giambattista, *The Third New Science*. Translator: Leon Pompa, p. 161.
Page number in *The Dictionary*: p. 446.

Weber, Max, "The Ideal Type" *Sociological Perspectives* Editors: K. Thompson and J. Tunstall, p. 63.
Page number in *The Dictionary*: pp. 450–451.

Weber, Max, *The Protestant Ethic and the Spirit of Capitalism*. Translator: T. Parsons, p. 181.
Page number in *The Dictionary*: p. 451.

Whitehead, Alfred North, *Process and Reality*, p. 244.
Page number in *The Dictionary*: p. 454.

Williams, Bernard, "Morality and the Emotions," *Problems of the Self*, p. 225.
Page number in *The Dictionary*: p. 461.

Wilson, Edward O., "Voices of Authority," (*Civilization: The Magazine of the Library of Congress*), August/September 1999, p. 67.

Wollstonecraft, Mary, *A Vindication of the Rights of Men*, *Works*, Editors: J. Todd and M. Butler, V, p. 30.
Page number in *The Dictionary*: pp. 475–476.

CHAPTER 8

Meshing Prescriptive, Proscriptive and Descriptive Formats

Format in this book means *frames of reference for minding action and thought systems*. Prescriptive refers to a laying down of rules or directions in a normative sense as "the way things ought to be." Proscriptive refers to prohibited behavior such as to proscribe or prohibit smoking in public. Descriptive refers to factual, empirical relationships of things as they are or have been. It is the intent hereafter to show generally how the prescriptions of our founding fathers and the proscriptions invoked since then have worked out descriptively in the two-hundred-plus years of this country's existence.

Objective and Subjective Frames of Reference

Man's perception of the reality he lives and works in is his basic orientation, the frame within which he senses all that he senses, knows all that he knows, does all that he does. It is 100 percent of his past, present and future. It is a totalizing idea adding up to all that he perceived and assumes into one grand scenario. It is his playing field representing the range and depth of his awareness and imagination. It is his basic living arena within which all thought, values, imagination and behavior interplay.

It is composed of two major parts. The subjective part refers to his personal private world where fact and fantasy interplay along with such important variables as one's values and beliefs, ideals and aspirations, needs and wants, all guided or moderated by one's assimilated knowledge, attitudes and skills. This personal subjective side perceives many different worlds and magnifies, shrinks and otherwise distorts particular elements at will.

The other major part of a person's largest format may be differentiated as mainly objective. It consists of all received and stored data that are correct or can be verified from sources external to the individual. Because most of us also honestly receive, store and occasionally try to use some erroneous data, not all of the information retained in the objective side of our memory banks is accurate. This would vary among individuals depending on the degrees of scrutiny and rigor by which each defines and accepts as true the information chosen to be retained.

Of course, each individual mixes some blend of subjective impression and objective facts in the assessment of most situations. Call it "strained reality," "fanciful maneuvering" or "wishful thinking," most of us are at least tempted to engage in such antics, especially when we intensely desire any preconceived outcome.

The thrust of this book is to provide a master format of the major outlines of this society as based on objective criteria. This format does not pretend to provide a complete model by which both objective benchmarks and subjective motivations are integrated and/or netted out into predictable behavior patterns. But first we should take a look at the prescriptive format the founding fathers provided in our basic documents.

The Brilliant Prescriptive (But Proscriptive) Format

In establishing this society our founding fathers did not set forth a descriptive model or detailed blueprint of how their new creation should operate. Instead, in the Bill of Rights they focused on a prescriptive model designed to establish and maintain conditions of freedom. The first eleven Articles were ratified before 1800 and dealt with such matters as freedoms of religion, speech, the press, the right to bear arms, the prohibition against quartering troops in private homes except during wartime, the prohibition against unreasonable searches and seizures, the rights to speedy and public trial by peers and not to be tried twice for the same offense, the right to due process of the law, the right to receive just compensation for property taken for public use, the rights to be confronted in court by one's accuser and to have legal counsel.

It was believed that more individuals in a free society could achieve their goals or at least pursue their ideas of happiness better when directed by a leadership periodically endorsed by its constituencies. This endorsement was removed in the case of the judiciary. Individual citizens could have maximum freedom to conform or be different as long as they didn't abridge the rights of others. And a tripartite system of government branches was established to check and balance any power excesses that might develop.

For more than two hundred years this prescriptive format endorsing a proscriptive government posture overall has worked conspicuously well in contrast to other forms of government organization tried elsewhere. A substantial body of legislative and judge-made law now surrounds each new executive-office initiative and all three governing branches operate somewhat frenetically but also symbiotically with each other in the presumed best long-run interests of the people. The original format was not frozen in concrete as an additional fifteen amendments have been added to the Bill of Rights since 1800 and others are slowly working their way into possible formal recognition.

Greatly elaborated, expanded and differentiated over time, the resulting body of law, interpretation and opinion have served as the basic frame of reference to guide the formalistic aspects of our institutionalized hierarchy. Before attempting to set forth a comprehensive descriptive model or format showing how the prescriptive model has actually operated for the whole society, it might be well to ask what more specific formats guided other major institutions such as business, religion and education.

Don't Ask Dumb Questions

Anticipating the possibility that some help might be available for the asking from our national leaders, a questionnaire was mailed in 1986 to the chief executive officer of every fifth listing in the Forbes 500 listing of the largest corporations as taken from the April 28, 1986, issue of *Forbes* magazine. The same questionnaire was mailed to each governor of the fifty states, to all senators in the U.S. Senate, to one hundred members of the U.S. House of Representatives, to one hundred college and university presidents, to twenty-five mayors of large U.S. cities, to twenty-five leaders of religious groups and to selected others all of which had addresses in *The World Almanac of 1986*.

The inquiry referred to the world globe as the valuable model that orients us in physical space on earth and by analogy asked for descriptions of models used to help orient them in the social, political, religious or economic arenas of their particular jurisdictions. It was hoped that educators might suggest the educational code, lawyers the legal frame, ministers the bible and so forth, and then "reach out" to describe larger frames by which they saw the entire society. No such luck!

This Questionnaire Was a Total Failure

No questionnaire ever produced such dismal results! Not one response addressed itself to the questions asked. Even though the sequential questions were asked in a way designed to intrigue the respondents into "getting intellectually involved," nobody fell for the persuasion used. Indeed, few even saw it. Responses received were mainly dismissals from subordinates charged with screening out irrelevant, unimportant or perhaps unanswerable requests. Either the addressees were "out of town" on important missions and unavailable to respond to anything not considered urgent or "too busy at this critical time." A number of annual reports, copies of speeches made and miscellaneous reports accompanied a few rejection letters. Most simply did not respond at all. No doubt most at these high levels of responsibility were so busy with the perceived pressures of daily operations that they were pleased to be able to dismiss such a fatuous questionnaire from one of those loonies in academia.

Just Looking "Visionary" Will Do

To acknowledge that the line of questioning was irrelevant or useless would have been the logical thing to do. But still, how could leaders in all of our major institutions lead without some vision of the society in which their organizations participated? Without some model of the larger society, how could they presume to develop or even approve any long-range strategic plans for their organizations or their constituencies? How could they know when existing strategic plans were outmoded or obsolete without a comprehensive model of the society to serve as a backdrop against the dynamics of their current plan? None of these leaders had learned much about comprehensive formats in their schooling because it wasn't taught then or even today. But one could easily assume that at least a few had generated their own visions and would be pleased to share them with an academic loner on the prowl for empirical evidence. Wrong again! And so it's back to the academic drawing boards for plausible explanations and further detailing in pursuit of the elusive descriptive format.

The Business Format

The publication in 1776 of Adam Smith's *Wealth of Nations* provided a most timely and persuasive rationale for the writers of the U.S. Constitution to ignore all previous dogma on how mercantile systems, commerce or business was to be permitted to operate.

Supply and demand in the marketplace was to be regulated by the invisible hand of competition in contrast to the visible hand of central government as wielded by the incumbent power elite. The use of this concept fitted beautifully into the precepts articulated in the Bill of Rights. Just keep competition alive and meaningful and let it harness self-interest to serve the public good. A policy of regulation by exception could then be followed to minimize distortions against the public interest.

Thus it developed that the institution of business was expected to operate within the national legal format and also within the intellectual format of the market system with its supply and demand parameters. There was no conflict, just a natural harmony joining individual means to achieve both individual goals and social goals while maintaining freedom for all.

Certain other formats, both more specific and more general, also came into view and demanded recognition. Local and statewide laws sometimes were more liberal or restrictive than national law depending on local conditions. Industry-wide conventions and traditions gradually developed and required servicing. International trade required its practitioners to conform to two or more sets of national laws, traditions and trade practices. Since it is in the nature of self-interest and competition to stretch the letter and spirit of law, tradition and trade practice, it follows that more elaborated formats will become necessary as international trade increases. Indeed, the informal internationalizing of formats has already begun with hundreds of thousands of youth taking college degrees in foreign countries. The identification of cultural common and uncommon denominators and workable trade procedures will be one of the major focuses of the twenty-first century.

In Pursuit of Profit

It is axiomatic that the top management of the large corporations needs broad overviews of the entire economy/society and its interrelationships with the other major sectors of the larger society. These broad overviews are basic to developing the strategic plans and operations necessary to earn the monetary profit that competitively superior positioning requires. Highly sophisticated management-consulting groups and specialized "think tanks" provide advice and prepare special statistical data on a regular basis.

These panoramic (eagle's eye views) may be contrasted to the more specific or technical (beaver's-eye views) that first-level management needs for operational efficiency at the production and service levels. Middle-management levels need enough understanding both of the technical mechanics at operational levels and top management's strategic plan so as to integrate the two for optimum performance. These two-way (gopher's-eye views) require middle managers to understand the grand plan so as to better execute the specific operations for integrational connectedness. This three-tiered management structure remains valid today even though the numbers in middle management have been shrunken drastically by computer programming and robotics plus offshore manufacturing have to some extent altered the roles of first-level management.

The Religious Format

Framers of the Constitution had more than three thousand years of recorded history to guide them when they addressed the question of the place of religion in the new order. More recently, the Religious Wars of 1562 to 1598 in France between the Protestants and the Catholics for freedom of worship and the right of establishment had resulted in a successful conclusion for the Protestants in the Edict of Nantes. But the subsequent revocation in 1685 of that edict by Cardinal Richlieu and King Louis XIV not only greatly weakened the French economy but sustained at hatred levels centuries-old religious rivalries.

Indeed, from 1620 with the landing of the Mayflower in Plymouth Harbor, the New World was to provide religious sanctuary for one group after another seeking religious freedom. Apprehensions were real that religious freedom might be abridged at any time by a new government.

To accommodate these fears, the architects of our governing structure fell back on an exclusionary tactic. They had not prescribed a methodology for commerce and trade choosing to let competition in the marketplace be the chief regulator. The concept of freedom could just as easily be ascribed to religion, freedom to worship as one chose. The government's main job would be to monitor that precious freedom that all previous governments had circumscribed and to maintain strict separation of church and state. Thus, the First Amendment begins with this clause: "Congress shall make no law respecting an establishment of religion, or prohibiting the free exercise thereof." The state constitutions followed through consistently, usually with more detail.

The Role of Religion

Although specific religions may deal with practical matters such as codes of interpersonal conduct and modes of worship, they are also major channels to interpret the supernatural or metaphysical. The religious response varies widely but is a universal one. Most people at some point in their lives grapple with the meaning of life and the hereafter.

It is possible that the influence of religion generally is less than in previous centuries for a number of reasons. Once the predominant explainer of all phenomena, the explosive rise of the measuring sciences reduced the role of myth, fables and assertions to unprovable matters. The great spread of popular education concentrating on the known or verifiable fund of common knowledge further reduced the role of religious interpretation. The separation of church, state and public education worked to minimize the influence of religious persuasion in those realms. But even if the religious influence is less, it is still mighty as conditions in some Southeast Asian countries attest. Basic precepts of religious thought reinforce law with persuasive rationale for supporting constructive interpersonal behavior and rejecting harmful behavior.

The Management of Religious Institutions

The large organized religions today have developed complex international hierarchies of management with all of the problems inherent in such bureaucracies. The three-level managerial structure discussed for business organizations also applies to religious organizations but with a few differences. The top religious leadership needs more than a panoramic eagle's-eye view of contemporary world society. Since much of our legal structure and day-to-day behavioral patterns have been molded by ethical prescriptions derived from religious thinking, top-level religious leaders are expected to offer us insightful judgment of the future. Perhaps advancing technology and political interpretation identify most of the emerging visions, but religious leadership is respected for its longer-range views on social justice and human rights.

First-level managements in the hands of local clerics are beset not only by practical matters such as bill paying and revenue generation, but also must practice complex individual and social psychology with their memberships. Perhaps more than first-level business managers, they work for effectiveness more than efficiency. Middle-level managers of religious organizations, like their business counterparts, are fully extended in trying to execute top management's strategic aspirations through supporting first-level management's ministerial operations. Together with the political, business, education and assorted affluent and influential leadership of very major community, they form the prestigious local social establishment.

The Educational Format

The U.S. Constitution does not mention education. The 10th Amendment gives the states any powers the Constitution does not prohibit or specifically grant to the federal government.

Every state except Hawaii has transferred some of its control over public education to local school districts. Most states have an elected or appointed board of education and an elected or appointed superintendent or commissioner of education. They also have departments of education with various educational agencies. The board of education sets state educational policies and the state superintendent who heads the department of education sees that they are carried out.

States variously require children to attend school until they are between fourteen and eighteen years of age, but parents decide whether the schools attended will be public or private. The United States Supreme Court has held that public funds may not be used for direct support of private parochial schools. But the Court also rules that they may receive textbook and transportation aid to and from school. About 7.5 percent of gross domestic product is spent on education. Levels include early childhood, elementary, secondary, higher, and continuing education.

Growing dissatisfaction with the results of public education generally has resulted in growing federal interest based on its powers to provide for the "general welfare of the United States." The so-called "voucher system" is one possibility designed to increase competition among schools, public and private. The administration of education is extremely important but beyond our central concern of formats in education. More relevant in the present context are formats for learning and formats for teaching and research.

How Learners Learn

Huge literatures have been developed explaining how people of all ages learn. Generally, they may be categorized into three groups: 1) behavior modification or stimulus-response; 2) cognitive or problem-solving shading into discovery, and problem-finding; and 3) humanistic theories based on the importance of emotional components in learning. When motivation to learn is high, learning achievements can be impressive as often happens with older people going back to school or with young immigrants from opportunity-poor countries. Younger people with frames of reference oriented to physical action, outside diversions and short-run excitement require more structured environments and probably more personalized attention, incentives and effective parental reinforcement than is currently provided.

Capacity to learn and understand may be another dimension in learning achievement. People with large capacities may simply have needs to exercise their mental faculties to a higher or more satisfying level. After underutilizing these capacities for a time, they may simply develop a physical itch or need to exercise that potential.

Informal learning outside of school situations has always been important and still is. Today's more complicated work demands, however, require more technical training. The mass media, particularly television and the rapidly growing Internet, are influential in providing broad content time absorbers with pop-art entertainment and information in both trivial and substantial pursuits. Meanwhile the lure of displacing the boring present via drugs is ever more available and increasingly indulged in by students in both elementary- and high-school levels.

The Casual Alignment of Youthful Interests to Careers

To the extent that the tropistic principle that man bends in the direction of his nourishment is true, then we can hypothesize that people develop highest interest in those areas they believe will reward them with the satisfactions they seek. How do they identify these areas? Doting parents are usually the first to note special tendencies or abilities in their children and provide encouragement. Competition among siblings or in school settings is often influential in identifying areas of ability or providing high-achievement feedback that starts youngsters on a career track. Youth also unconsciously selects role models to emulate from family, church, school and neighborhood. Nevertheless, perhaps a majority of youth remains generally undirected in career paths through high school or even college and allow availabilities on the job market to determine their career interests when they are ready to go to work.

The Myopia in Assembly-Line Production and Education

Beginning with the master-apprenticeship system of learning, man seems to have emphasized the mastery of specific tasks on a serial basis. After years of experience learning the different operations of his trade, the artisan becomes a master craftsman and he trains his apprentices in the same system he followed. This format may well have been and perhaps even today may be the best methodology in making relatively simple physical things from start to finish. A person can see the finished product and to a large extent appreciate the care, dedication and skill that each component required. Not so with today's complicated assembly of sophisticated products where assembly-line specialist teams focus on the delivery of one component or the detailed processing of one phase.

In most academic fields today the same pattern is followed. The student takes college courses in one facet of the subject after another and in his last semester is lucky if he has even one course pretending to help him integrate all the parts into one conceptual whole. The individual courses en route are loaded with the micro chips of analytical minutiae and the assumption is that if a student can handle the analytical challenge, the synthetic comprehension of all the parts working together will be either automatic or not important enough to worry about.

The Role for a Comprehensive Descriptive Integrating Model

More than this, in today's and tomorrow's increasingly interdependent world, people must learn how complex systems operate and interrelate with their confusing mixtures of things, ideas and workers all synchronized into elaborate input networks. How can students possibly understand the operational togetherness of complex wholes without far more emphasis on the integrational problems and potentials of holistic models? The old question of whether students learn better from the specific to the general or vice versa needs reexamination and probably specific tailoring for each academic area. The hypothesis behind this study suggests that teaching content generally has been slanted too heavily toward specifics without enough attention to the integration of those specifics into the contexts they serve.

Overall, it is likely that a vast majority of students at all education levels have become diploma- or degree-oriented rather than process- or content-oriented. It is generally known what diploma or degree requirements are needed for various jobs or careers and it is assumed that possession of the requisite diploma or degree will automatically qualify one for jobs or careers in the content area studied. Higher grades than average are a strong plus factor for serious achievers but even here persistent "grade inflation" has eroded this motivator. And for many in grade school through high school when horizons are most limited, the process seems endless and only those with strong faith in their parents/teachers persist. The waywardness of others is documented in the insufficiently publicized records of student rebellion.

How Teachers Teach

Formats for teachers vary widely being most prescribed in grade school and least prescribed during college and later. Curriculum content is standardized within a relatively narrow range and achievement tests are keyed to the content covered. The teacher's area of freedom lies mainly in methods used to generate student interest in the content to be covered.

The content in many applied fields may be taught from each of the following levels and teachers usually stratify themselves by spending most of their teaching time on the level they find most comfortable:

1. Comprehensive frames of reference (or formats, general theories).
2. Elaboration of principles, useful generalizations, specific theories.
3. Discussion of how-to-do-it techniques, operational formulae and guidelines.
4. Anecdotal descriptions of past, current successes and failures of techniques used.

All courses should probably include a well-considered balance of all levels. Students also tend to be more interested in the level that most satisfies their curiosities and/or abilities. Most are probably interested in the "how to" or applied techniques of performance level with a goodly portion of anecdotal material thrown in on how various techniques worked in various recent applications. Fewer are interested in the organizing principles, theories or concepts and least in the broader frames of reference.

Content for courses in the liberal arts and social sciences also suffers from the lack of comprehensive frames of reference. Without a generally accepted holistic context within which to develop their course content, teachers in these areas frequently rely on the traditional historical continuum or chronology replete with its datelines, major events, places and personages. Surprisingly, the relationship of content to comprehensive context occurs to few.

It is the teacher's job in each field to stay abreast of the latest findings and synthesize useful ideas into the most potent content possible for transmission to learners. In the attempts to synthesize research and latest findings into the most potent contents to be delivered, it is asserted that student interest in any subject matter can be greatly stimulated by pointing out the interconnectedness of new intellectual findings to various fields, either adjacent or contrasting. In support of the thesis that we have greatly overemphasized differentiation at the expense of integration, one scholar wrote:

> This entire book is a plea for the revision of social science, religion and philosophy to stress connectedness, coherence, relationship, organicism and wholeness, as against fragmenting, reductive and compartmentalizing forces of the prevailing orthodoxies (Hampden-Turner, p. 8).

How Professors Research

Another side of education at the college-university level involves research, the finding and authenticating of new knowledge. The basic prescribed format here is the scientific method: 1) define both the problem and its troublesome or baffling context clearly; 2) develop a falsifiable hypothesis; 3) explicate and execute a sound test of the hypothesis; and 4) confirm, reject or qualify the hypothesis and make recommendations for further research based on the findings. When verifiable, new bits of knowledge become facts, add to the existing fund of knowledge and increase the base available for further research.

Factual truth sought is what is coherent in a comprehensive thought system or what conforms to our experience and sensory perceptions or pragmatically, what works. For the faithful, truth may be that asserted by a charismatic leader or by revelation. Note that this prescription known as the scientific method evolved naturally from scholarly effort and has proven to be the key that continues to energize scientific and technological progress. Note also the comments quoted in previous chapters about the ephemeral nature of some truths accepted at the time as eternal!

The Belabored Proscriptive Format

Now that we have briefly examined the prescriptive formats our present society inherited from historical precedents and the prescient thinking by the authors of our basic government documents, just what proscriptive or negative sanctions accompanied the explicit prescriptive format?

The first set of proscribed or prohibited behaviors recognized either directly or indirectly by our founders can be traced to the *Ten*

Commandments and directives against the sins of killing, stealing, lying and committing adultery. A large derivative set of proscriptive injunctions or recommended behaviors followed. A second set of "no-no's" was derived from collective agreement on perceptions of wrong-doing perpetrated on the citizens of those European countries from which our leaders and their flocks had fled.

A rereading of the paragraphs on specifics in the Bill of Rights will show that there was a far greater emphasis on proscribing and limiting the role of government than in elaborating on its prescriptive recommendations. Thus, it becomes clear that we have developed a general governing format based on predominantly proscribed behavior rather than prescribed behavior. Little attention was originally devoted to how any function of the people should be carried out so long as the all-important human freedoms were maintained. Notice also that discussions of the major institutions of business, religion and education showed that no or minimal government control should be exercised on the free functioning of operators in each of the three fields. Only recently has the federal government intervened substantially in the operations of another major institutionalized area, that of healthcare where no original prescribed or proscribed government behavior was mandated.

Proscribed Meddling Contributes to a Confusing Medley

The most important prescriptive model of freedoms to be maintained was established in Colonial times and now, over two-hundred-plus years later, we have greater difficulty in seeing this model as clearly as our forefathers did because of all the proscriptive interdiction and legal prohibitory instruments adopted in trying to keep the original prescriptions working as they were originally intended. Another way of expressing this idea is to note that as people in their multiple roles do not voluntarily conform to prescriptive norms, more law and other controlling sanctions are needed and vice versa. Even though regarded as burdensome to unhealthy by many, each restriction and law was only added after much consideration and debate to fix a situation considered intolerable at the time. Much of this 'meddling' was acted on by government agencies and legislators to rectify practices perceived as unfair under its mandate to maintain an orderly but also equitable environment. Of course, the initiation of government interest was usually traceable to law suits generated by competitive interests crying "foul" over some perceived invasion of their territories or rights.

In the twenty-plus decades since the Constitution was written, the conditions of living and competing and cooperating in the United States have changed considerably. From a predominantly agricultural, decentralized, moralistic, unspecialized and nonlitigious environment, we have moved by degrees toward being a more urbanized, centralized, specialized, amoral, opportunistic and litigious society. It has been the growth and combination of the latter three of these changing characteristics that has swollen the country's courtrooms with an increasing flood of frivolous lawsuits. Between 1980 and 1994, the number of civil cases commenced in U.S. District Courts rose over 18 percent (*Statistical Abstract of the United States*, p. 213). Perhaps worse for the future, the number of juvenile arrests for "aggravated assault" more than tripled between 1970 and 1993 rising from 20,914 to 68,873 (*Statistical Abstract of the United States*, p. 206).

The Payoffs From Lobbying

In seeking personal advantage over these years and among these changing conditions, the individual, acting in both self-interest and group interest for employers and clients has greatly altered the original prescriptive model. Altogether, through legislation, the legal system and aided by the courts, they have variously squeezed and stretched and shrunk the original Constitutional intent into almost unrecognizable patterns. The original basic structure is still there but invisibly buried under multiple restrictions, exceptions, exemptions and modifying qualifications in all directions. In nearly every field the legal and administrative regulatory contexts are overwhelming: every branch of medicine, insurance, real estate, communication and transportation, taxes, pollution control, education, trade, government, religion, business and construction. Only professional athletics has been spared and some think that its time for regulation by government has arrived.

Some variable blend of legitimate pressure groups including many variously disguised but well-funded all compete for the attention and favors of government officials. The original prescriptive intent has become so proscribed and murky that even scholars on constitutional law get lost in its mazes of red tape and snarled trappings. One such, Gerhard Casper, a former president of Stanford University, was reported to carry a well-worn copy of the U.S. Constitution in his jacket pocket for reference when needed (*San Francisco Chronicle*, p. 3).

From the Spirit to the Letter of the Law to ...Armageddon Again?

Managers and citizens at all levels no longer seek operational guidance from the spirit of the original prescriptive model. Instead, they rely on their interpretations of legalistic codes and judicial decisions field by field or else hire expert managers and lawyers to advise them on what specific behavior is best under differing circumstances. In the aggregate and over two hundred years later, the results are profound. In many fields the country is now leaning into the future figuratively with heads in the sand, defensively positioned to minimize losses no matter what. We are not leaning into the future as our founders did: boldly peering ahead, courageously and confidently acting on the conviction and confidence that right will win. What is right or fair is not as clear now, as judges and juries have discovered.

On the international level, perhaps things are better, at least from the perspective of the United States. Having achieved leadership levels in world politics and business competitiveness, American spokesmen may be better able to articulate persuasively basic American values to confused populations elsewhere sick of their own governments. At least for now the Cold War with the USSR is over and many former communist countries are launching experiments with the Western market system. On the domestic front we are not yet totally lost but we are definitely floundering in oceans of political tradeoffs and red tape that nearly hide the original prescriptive principles behind clouds of proscriptive smoke. Many of us have forgotten or now take for granted the magic in those basic principles. And we do so at the risk of losing our collective balance.

While most enjoyed the increasing affluence since World War II, several social trends have combined to raise serious questions about the direction of future civility. A noted journalist, George Will, has summarized these trends "The Tyranny of Nonchalance—Whatever" (Will, p. A19):

> There is a certain troubling lack of refinement in Dennis Rodman's America, a lack linked to three linked ideas: distinguishing between liberty and license is incipient fascism; manners are servants of hypocrisy; concern for appearances and respectability is a craven treason against self-expression, hence not respectable.

More graphically in the same source, Will (p. A19) pictures this: "… coarse and slatternly society" with "…boom boxes borne through crowded streets by young men wearing pornographic T-shirts and baseball caps backward; young women using language that formerly caused stevedores to blush." All this, he concludes, "… in a land where plenitude inflames the sense of entitlement to more of almost everything, but less of manners and taste, with their intimations of authority and hierarchy."

Clearly, a free society as heterogeneous as that of the United States and with the capacity to express itself and experiment freely in any direction has a multitude of choices. Not all citizens, and especially energetic youth with various combinations of rebellion and idealism, may choose to follow the normally accepted behavior patterns unless they are strictly enforced. An affluent society generously leans toward being permissive until the negative consequences of the wayward behaviors become obvious to a majority. By the time late sanctions are imposed, an institutionalized group of dissidents feel wronged and quickly get organized to combat the new sanctions. Social ferment and turmoil have been a continuous characteristic of the American growth pattern. So far it has been managed without catastrophic results but the potential for a destructive scenario in the "Bad As I Wanna Be" direction is evidently possible.

The Emergent Descriptive Format

Having elaborated sufficiently on the original prescriptive format and subsequently evolved proscriptive modifications, the remaining chapters will attempt to present basic elements of the descriptive format that so far have eluded us. The descriptive model to be presented attempts to comprehend the basic structure of the original prescriptive model and subsequent proscriptive "enablements" into one wordy but "visualizable" whole with clear outlines.

Presumably the more we can visualize the overall design and operation of a descriptive model, the more we can fine tune it for the efficiency and effectiveness or other qualities we seek. Not to have such a model to guide us means in effect that we are steering the nation blindly and/or impressionistically on a trial-and-error basis. Even worse, many of the erroneous trial balloons launched become more or less permanently attached to our operational structures providing shelter for supporting selfish vested interests. Thus do additional overhead costs, confusion and distraction encumber our operating systems.

Completing the Functional Requisites

Enough has been written on a superficial level to demonstrate that specific identifiable formats may be found for each of our society's major institutional entities: government, business, religion and education. Most basic of the necessary functions is the role of government in providing an orderly environment for the effective execution of all a society's basic needs. Within that dependable environment, business is needed for the production and distribution of necessary goods and services. Religion must be provided to handle spiritual needs. Education must be available for the transmission of the knowledge necessary to sustain the status quo. These are dominant institutions but there are other major organizations engaged in executing other necessary functions for the general welfare also. What are they?

The purpose here is to identify in general all of the major functions or activities that a healthy society needs for continuity and growth and then to place them in a larger context. This larger context will be the master descriptive model or format purporting to show in general how the major institutions have developed to serve society over the two-hundred-plus years of the country's formal existence. It grew out of the prescriptive model based on maximizing the individual freedoms established by our founding leadership. Now what are the other basic activities that must be performed regularly for any society's continuity and progress? Care must be taken in developing such a list to identify master or major activities only, those under which countless subsidiary activities can be subsumed. Otherwise, the list would become too long and cumbersome.

For a beginning, the following may provide a first approximation:

1. Procreating and nurturing
2. Providing community and fellowship
3. Socializing and acculturating
4. Producing, distributing and consuming goods and services
5. Providing orderly and equitable environment or governing
6. Communicating and informing
7. Transporting
8. Recreating and playing
9. Teaching and learning
10. Servicing health needs
11. Participating in religious and ceremonious rites
12. Discovering new knowledge and techniques
13. Providing welfare and philanthropic aid
14. Creating and preserving works of art

And the Last May Be First

There is no particular logic to ranking society's needed activities in this way. Procreating, providing community and socializing are listed first only because they are so obvious. Others are equally important and any one at some time or under some set of assumptions may assume a top priority. All have been identified with a gerund form to suggest action, and "inging" as it were. Not all are of the same order. Transporting and communicating are essentially facilitating functions enabling higher levels of involvement in the other functions. Perhaps the circular representation such as suggested in *The Propaedia* and discussed earlier would make a better ordering device and eliminate the ranking problem.

These are the basic functions that a modern society must get performed in expeditious fashion. Not all functions need to be performed in a primitive society. A stagnant society need not discover new knowledge or techniques. It could coast on its inheritance. Providing philanthropic aid may also not be necessary. Indeed, its institutionalization in the United

States may be an American innovation or extension of the concept of *noblesse oblige*. Creating and especially preserving works of art (and/or artifacts) may also not be absolutely necessary, though it seems necessary that man must express himself.

Thus, even a highly primitive society would need to perform the first ten or eleven functions for group survival. The latter three may be regarded as institutionalized activities of more developed countries.

The Greatest Mesh in the World

It is through the day-by-day execution of all these master functions and their many subfunctions that a society's necessary collective and individual conditions for survival and progress are secured. In sociologist Parsons' classification (Parsons, pp. 60–79), these were pattern maintenance of basic values, integration of all subunits into the larger system, adaptation to the environment, and goal achievement. In carrying out their basic missions all organizations contribute to the achievement of these requisites and ultimately, to the goal-achievement aspirations of the society. Most business organizations, perhaps, contribute directly to the goal-attainment need as pertains to raising standards of living while religious organizations and the legal systems may contribute mainly to the legitimization and maintenance of basic values. Corrective institutions by and large focus on the integration need to assimilate deviants into the larger system. Educational organizations contribute centrally to human adaptation to the environment with its ever-changing values, knowledge and technological bases. Labor unions contribute to the adaptation need and also to the integration of disparate elements into more unified and manageable labor groups. Health organizations serve constructively on remedial, preventive and terminal levels.

A society has not only the collective concerns discussed above to satisfy, it has as a prerequisite concern the need to satisfy the individual needs and wants of its citizenry through the execution of the master functions. These needs and wants have been best explained by psychologists and exploited by marketers.

The Central Role of Government

It is the job of federal, state, county and city government agencies to oversee the entire societal operation, level by level, and to provide aid to smoldering and/or smoking friction points. So far it has succeeded in coordinating the greatest mesh in the world. Not with descriptive plans detailing how-to-do-it operations on a step-by-step basis, but mainly with a set of principles and laws that maximized human freedoms, that expected the best of man, that fundamentally endowed him with intrinsic dignity and stubbornly maintains this definition.

Recognizing that all men were created equal enlarged the pool from which great men rose through universal education, to lead an eager nation. The profit system, recognizing the legitimacy of self-interest, energized a large percentage to actualize their potentials. Checks and balances in government limited power and a wise leadership succeeded in distributing the income produced widely. A free press and pluralistic religious convictions monitored and rationalized and explained this grand experiment.

Rather than only receive criticism for its human short-run bureaucratic bungling, the government should also be appreciated for its superior macro-managerial successes over the long run. It exists to serve its citizenry by creating opportunities and by maintaining human freedoms and dignity. These are not easy tasks given the individualistic freedoms enjoyed by all in the most heterogeneous population ever assembled under one sovereignty.

And despite the nearly overwhelming proscriptive interdicting for more than two hundred years, the market economy with competition as its central feature remains the world's most admired way to orchestrate man's daily behavior. Hopefully in time, this descriptive model will enable it better to filter out unnecessary proscriptive meddling so as to emphasize more strongly the prescriptive format established by our founding fathers.

REFERENCES

"Bringing Stanford Back Strong" (*San Francisco Chronicle*, June 23, 1996, p. 3.)

Hampden-Turner, Charles, *Maps of the Mind* (New York: Macmillan Publishing Company, 1981, p. 8).

Parsons, Talcott, "An Outline of the Social System," in *Theories of Society*. Editors: Talcott Parsons, Edward Shils, Kaspar D. Naegle, Jesse R. Pitts (New York: The Free Press of Glencoe, 1961).

Statistical Abstract of the United States: 1995, 115th Edition (Washington, D.C.: U.S. Bureau of the Census, 1995).

Will, George, "The Tyranny of Nonchalance—Whatever" (*San Francisco Chronicle*, December 23, 1996, p. A19).

CHAPTER 9

The Metamorphosis of Macro I Into the Maccordion Format

It is the purpose here to develop the remaining elements of the societally integrated format to be temporarily called Macro I or Mac for short. In the previous chapter a list of the essential functions was presented that a society needs to have well discharged for its successful continuity. Now what more is needed besides the central functions and how do all the parts relate?

A Synoptic Overview of Mac

Reference to Figure 1 shows a wordy page with columns. Columns 1 and 5 represent the individualized human structure. They cradle between them columns 2, 3 and 4, shown in Figure 2, which represent the institutionalized superstructure that altogether does the work and produces the cornucopia of products, services and utilities from which each individual chooses that scale and style of living afforded by the income produced from his contributions to the process. Only columns 1, 3 and 5 are detailed in Figure 1.

This institutionalized superstructure is shown in Figure 2. It is the servant of man being shaped by the elements in Figure 1, on the left side by man's needs and on the right side by man's goals and aspirations. It is important, therefore, that a free society allow open expression of individual desires to shape directly the institutionalized superstructure and not presume to administer the shape or content of the products and services to satisfy those desires. At the same time it is also important that people be free to choose their own goals and change them at will from the total range of possible choices without coercive social, political, in-

Figure I
The Individualized Human Structure

COLUMN I	COLUMN III	COLUMN V
INDIVIDUALIZED HUMAN STRUCTURE 265 Million People +/- 67.5 Million Families +/- 96.4 Million Households +/-	FUNCTIONAL ACTIVITIES (+ or -)	INDIVIDUAL GOALS DIRECTIONAL: Affiliationism Materialism
Each Individual with PHYSIOLOGICAL NEEDS: Alimentary Excretory Protection Activity Recuperative Erotic Parental	Most individual personal and vocational activities are channeled into the group functions below: 1) Procreating/Nurturing 2) Providing Community & Fellowship 3) Socializing & Acculturating 4) Producing, Distributing, Consuming Goods & Services 5) Providing Orderly & Equitable Environment 6) Communicating 7) Transporting 8) Recreating & Playing 9) Teaching & Learning 10) Serving Health Needs 11) Engaging in Religious & Ceremonious Rites 12) Discovering New Knowledge & Techniques 13) Providing Welfare & Philanthropic Aid 14) Creating & Preserving Works of Art (Extrinsic/Intrinsic)	Estheticism Humanitarianism Intellectualism Spiritualism Hedonism Instrumentalism Eclecticism Nihilism Criminalism
+ PSYCHOLOGICAL & PSYCHOSOCIAL NEEDS: Safety Love & Belongingness Esteem Self-Actualization Desires to Know & Understand Esthetic (Maslow)		OPERATIONAL: (Materialistic) Making Money Saving Money Minimizing Taxes Prosuming Careful Buying Careful Consuming (Non-Materialistic) To seek enlightenment and deliver effectiveness in the pursuit of any of the Directional Goals listed above
+VALUES & INTERESTS: Power, Enlightenment, Wealth, Well-Being, Skill, Affection, Respect, Rectitude (Lasswell & Kaplan)		
All above have been expanded into countless WANTS & VELLEITIES & all of which combine to energize people to seek satisfactions both individually and through co-operation in group activities listed in Column III.		CONSTITUTIONAL: For the Individual: To seek satisfactions from those Inherited Family Values/Interests and those newly acquired For the Nation: "...to form a more perfect union, establish justice, secure domestic tranquility, provide for the common defense, promote the general welfare, etc."

Note: COLUMN II (omitted), COLUMN III (above) and COLUMN IV (omitted) form THE INSTITUTIONALIZED SUPERSTRUCTURE.

tellectual or religious interdiction. The resultant two-way squeeze by the people's needs on one side and by their goals on the other gives not only shape and meaning but also vitality to the institutionalized superstructure. It then becomes the powerful servant of its master, the collective people.

Before explaining the various components of the Maccordion Format, two concepts from the writings of economist John R. Commons during the first half of the twentieth century may be helpful in visualizing action across the format from left to right (Commons, pp. 21 & 43):

1. Commons defined institution as "collective action in control, liberation, and expansion of individual action" (p. 21).
2. He also suggested that "three types of transactions may be distinguished...These are the *rationing* transactions by the "policy-makers" of the organization...the *managerial* transactions between superiors and inferiors, mainly wage earners and salary earners in the production of wealth; the *bargaining* transactions...on the markets which transfer ownerships of corporeal property..." (p. 43).

Although the classification headings in figures 1 through 3 may appear to be static and boringly locked in place, they are all active participants in the fascinating dynamics of the entire society. Both individuals and institutions engage daily in the billions of transactions that Commons differentiated above as they strive to improve their relative positions both in the competitive and cooperative games of life. Some sense of this fantastic and ever-changing mosaic may be better appreciated if you engage in active role playing by tracking your own behavior across the columns. Your personal needs and wants as fine tuned by your goals and aspirations direct your daily behavior into the workplace and marketplace and deliver a lifetime of feedback experiences. Enjoy the trip and have fun en route!

The Human Structure

Column 1 of Figure 1 refers to a nation's entire population individually and collectively in almost countless groupings. From the 350 individuals counted in the first Virginia Colony census in 1610 to the 250,888 in 1700, population in the new country grew rapidly. It was estimated at 5,296,000 in 1800; 23,261,000 in 1850; 75,094,000 in 1890; and 151,683,000 in 1950. In 1980 total United States population was estimated at 226,500,000 and projections place it at 249,731,0900 for 1990 and 267,990,000 for the year 2,000 (*U.S. Bureau of the Census*, and *The World Almanac*, pp. 258–261).

Each individual is shown in column 1 of Figure 1 as possessing a unique combination of needs, values, interests, wants and velleities. Needs

Figure 2
The Institutionalized Superstructure

COLUMN I	COLUMN II	COLUMN III
The Needs & Values of all individuals in Column I combine with the Goals of individuals in Column V to energize the Institutional Superstructure to serve its organizational masters who in turn must cater to the individual. The Goals of individuals in Column V combine with the Needs, Values, Wants, Velleities, Interests of all individuals in Column I to direct the output of the institutionalized superstructure depicted in Columns II, III and IV.	CLASSIFICATION OF ORGANIZATIONS* Family & Other Households Trade, Business & Commercial Environmental & Agricultural Legal, Governmental, Public Administration, Military Engineering, Technological, Natural & Social Sciences Educational Cultural Social Welfare Health & Medical Public Affairs Fraternal, Ethnic & Nationality Religious Veteran, Hereditary & Patriotic Hobby & Avocational Athletic & Sports Labor Unions, Associations, Federations Chambers of Commerce, Trade & Tourism Greek & non-Greek Letter & Related Fan Clubs Subversive & Informal	FUNCTIONAL ACTIVITIES FOR SUSTAINING SOCIETY (+ or -) Most individual personal & vocational activities are channeled into one or more of these group functions: 1) Procreating & Nurturing 2) Providing Community & Fellowship 3) Socializing & Acculturating 4) Producing, Distributing, Consuming Goods & Services 5) Providing Orderly & Equitable Environment 6) Communicating 7) Transporting 8) Recreating & Playing 9) Teaching & Learning 10) Serving Health Needs 11) Engaging in Religious & Ceremonious Rites 12) Discovering New Knowledge & Techniques 13) Providing Welfare & Philanthropic Aid 14) Creating & Preserving Works of Art (Intrinsic and Extrinsic)

are recognized as physiological, psychological and psychosocial. Values may be identified as components of any acceptable value hierarchy, such as that shown. Interests represent those more specific areas to which an individual is attracted. These develop over time as a product of family background, abilities demonstrated along the maturation way, peer relationships, opportunities presented and rewards received.

Wants are seen as desires above the threshold of consciousness but below the threshold of implementing action. Velleities are considered to be latent desires in our unconscious but not yet part of our conscious awareness. Altogether this need-want-velleity-value-interest complex

Figure 2
The Institutionalized Superstructure

COLUMN IV	COLUMN V
ORGANIZATIONAL GOALS	INDIVIDUAL GOALS
Directional	Detail Omitted
Affiliationism	See Figure I
Estheticism	
Humanitarianism	Enhancement
Intellectualism	of Dignity &
Maintaining Order	Well-Being of
& Protectionism	the Individual
Materialism	
Spiritualism	Raising of Standards
Instrumentalism	of Living
Operational for Materialistic	Maintenance
Profit Seekers:	of Freedoms
Return on Investment	in Choosing
% Share of Market	from Widening
% Rate of Growth	Range of
% Rate of Investment	Life Styles
Developing New Markets	
Developing New Products	
Operational for Household	
Organizations:	
Making $ (Shorter Hours, Overtime,	
"Moonlighting," Saving $, Investing Wisely,	
Thrifty Buying, Careful Consuming)	
Operational for All Other	
Organizational Servicers:	
Operational Efficiency	
Operational Effectiveness	
in Delivering Services	
Constitutional	
As Stated in Originating Charters	
& Basic Documents	
Constitutional for Nation:	
Raising of Standards of Living for All	
by Addressing Emergent Problems	

alluded to in column 1, Figure 1, is meant to represent the "push" or drive that each person exerts individually and collectively through group association. Through its dynamic focusing, it helps to activate and direct the energy of each person and group to do what is necessary to satisfy the most demanding element or group of elements in the needs-thrusting complex, both collectively and individually.

The second part of the human structure is shown in column 5 of Figure 1. It consists of the individual's goal structure, implicit and explicit, and is classified under three headings: directional, operational and constitutional.

Positive Directional Goals

Directional goals are those listed in column 5. They have direction indicating distinctive paths or channels by which energy may be expended, experiences encountered and progress or retrogression recognized. They represent vectors without magnitude. Presumably most people wish to develop occupational careers in the directional channels of their dominant interests. Higher levels of ability supported by sustained attention should normally result in higher self-actualization of one's basic interests.

Affiiliationism points to the most basic bonding liaison centering on the nuclear family. Its original meaning issues from the root word, *filius* or son, and meant to adopt or take into a family as a son. It centers on mankind's most fundamental group, the family and its procreating, nurturing and socializing functions. Neglect and or cavalier treatment of these functions obviously imperils a society's future.

Materialism refers to concern with the making, consuming, possessing, giving, collecting and showing off of material or physical things and services. Estheticism refers to the doctrine that beauty is most basic and that other values or principles are ordered by beauty. Humanitarianism refers to concern for human welfare and regards the condition of mankind as paramount. Intellectualism is the doctrine that the faculty of knowing and understanding is important and that exercise of the intellect is man's highest calling. Spiritualism refers to special interest in metaphysical explanations and often the search for idealistic or religious values. Hedonism suggests that seeking pleasure is the dominant or chief end of life and that other values should be subordinated to it.

Not everybody feels clearly attracted to just one of the above directional dimensions. Many people feel equally divided between two or more. They may be seeking eclectic satisfactions and choose to build tandem (or even simultaneous) careers beginning with the best opportunity and then changing direction at various inflection points thereafter.

Another large contingent of people may be neutral or indifferent to any of the major directional choices listed and settle into the instrumentalism category. It is assumed that most poor immigrants are seeking mainly the opportunity and freedom to express themselves in any pragmatic direction, to hold steady jobs, to provide assured food and housing for their families and better educational opportunities for their children. They bring the work ethic without particular direction to the American workplace.

Others, with no compelling directional urge, may accept a beginning position in any one of the many organizations producing intermediate functional-type goods or services without any particular value orientation. After years of satisfactory service, they may only seek to progress along that organization's occupational ladder to greater prestige or financial reward. If any "occupational remorse" appears thereafter, there is always the opportunity to further one's education or training or adopt a worthy cause with a distinct value orientation and work for its advancement as an avocational hobby.

For those whose egos require domination, power or recognition above all else, any of the listed goal dimensions can be useful springboards to achieving the desired "bubble reputation." From this perspective, the listed individual goal dimensions may only be penultimate ends or operational means to satisfying one's most basic needs.

Negative Directional Goals

Another group of people may not be attracted to any of the more constructive directional dimensions and may be variously indifferent or even negative about the alleged value to society of any of them. These people range from being passively indifferent or even nihilistic about the general state of affairs to actively seeking reconstruction of society's established institutions. The passive contingent in the nihilism category may take a job in one of the major employing institutions but maintain a scoffing or unsupporting attitude, side with its critics or detractors, and be variously disruptive. The more actively oriented in this reconstructionist group may actually mount disruptive campaigns to criticize the existing institutional structures or to replace them with substitutes of their own. Because of its affluence and relatively open opportunities, the United States has so far experienced only sporadic incidents of demonstrated revolt. But discontented groups remain covertly active in many regions of the world such as in the Near East, the Balkans, Africa and sections of the former Soviet empire. Indeed, in many of these areas, the covert hostility has mushroomed into violent and persisting rebellion.

A last group that should be mentioned as a category in the classification of directional dimensions may be labeled as outright criminalism. It refers to those who have developed deep and abiding distrust of society's normative structure and seek to enhance their own welfare by breaking society's rules and laws. Some, if raised in conditions of broken families, poverty, pervasive political corruption and/or extensive crime, may see the criminal life as the only viable way to escape what they see as a vicious circle. But others, born to the benefits of affluence, may be attracted to a life of crime because of the excitement it generates and the pleasures of defying or outwitting authority.

When organized into groups pursuing goals generally considered undesirable, they have achieved such identifications as the *Cosa Nostra*, *Mafia*, "the Family" and in general, "the underworld."

Operational Goals

Operational goals refer to those goals that are usually more specific, short-term and measurable. They help the individual to progress along chosen directional dimensions and to some extent achieve one's mission or constitutional goals. If material welfare is important in one's value hierarchy, earning more money, saving 15 percent or more of one's income regularly, investing wisely, working legally to minimize one's income tax, being a prudent buyer and consumer and self-serving one's own needs when possible are all ways to maximize wealth. Doing so contributes to a healthy mental set, to progress along the materialism road and to the ultimate enhancement of the dignity and well-being of the individual.

Those pursuing the directional goal of esthetic development usually choose between active participation in one of the art forms or passive appreciation of the works of the masters or contemporary leaders in the designated art form. Operational goals might consist of reading two or more recommended books yearly or enrolling in a course of art appreciation or actively engaging in painting, sculpting, crafting and so forth or commencing art collection in a specific field because one wishes to be surrounded by the beauty of this expressive form (rather than simply showing off materialistic wealth, for example).

If one's predominant interest lies in humanitarian concerns, then besides working for agencies concerned with improving man's physical and mental welfare, one could establish operational goals like earning advanced academic degrees in branches of the subject, reading the latest research in the field, cultivating and supporting its leaders, organizing needed helping groups and so on.

Those with predominant interests in the intellectual or spiritual directional dimensions can seek to achieve advanced training, degrees and certifications in fields of special interest, develop related hobbies and avocational pursuits, join or help organize support groups in raising money for purposes deemed worthy.

If a person is hedonically inclined primarily to indulge in pleasures of the good life, that person could become a recognized and knowledgeable connoisseur in the consumption of those delights that intrigue him most. Gourmand or gourmet, one could spend a lifetime cultivating epicureanism and those fields named for the sophisticated satisfaction of man's other self-indulgent needs.

Those following the more general or less value-laden instrumental directive goal pattern may simply identify with the operational goals of the chosen organization and work to advance them, albeit in a less passionate manner.

Constitutional Goals

Most individuals remain singularly unaware of the role that constitutional goals or inherited value complexes play in their lives. Born into any cultural subset with varying values, they mostly accept their value inheritance with only minor equivocations because they have little choice to do otherwise. And then the institutionalized patterns of socialization by family, church, school and state combine to justify the original value stamp. The remaining objectives by which their energies and abilities can be measured lie in the directional and operational goals previously discussed.

Sequence of Activities in the Life Cycle

Altogether activation of the elements of the goal structure, column 5, Figure 1, represents the counter squeeze on the institutionalized superstructure, columns 2, 3 and 4 of Figure 2. It is exerted by individuals and groups to achieve the results or goal attainments desired from their activities. Their activities were initiated by some combination of need-goal alchemy in which the squeezing elements persuade and direct the gigantic institutionalized superstructure into a complex symphony of movements to satisfy its human masters. Central facets of the individual's plan of action over the life cycle revolve around school activities, curricular and extra-curricular, educational direction and achievement, work-job-career development, family-living style, avocational interests or hobbies, consumption attitudes, religious orientations and eventual retirement lifestyles.

After schooling most healthy individuals seek a job in a field of their choice to make their vocational contributions and in return receive the financial wherewithal to satisfy their abiding needs while moving their ways along one or more directional dimensions to achieve their various aspirations in life. The individual is free to concentrate on any one directional goal or any combination of them. The competition, however, to achieve success in any one direction increases with population growth. The days of the Renaissance Man who could achieve widespread social distinction in two or more fields are probably gone and most of us are pleased to settle for notable achievement in one field of endeavor. Still, the idea of the well-balanced, erudite, athletic and sensitive person-for-all seasons is a James Bond type that may never go completely out of style.

The Organizational Superstructure

The three column listings of Classification of Organizations, Functional Activities for Sustaining Society and Organizational Goals shown in Figure 2 as columns 2, 3 and 4 constitute the superstructure of institutionalized activity in this society. No originating mandate decreed which organizations should perform what function or for what purpose. The consequential design has evolved over two-hundred-plus years as the happy result of a free people freely choosing how to organize themselves, which activities to engage in, how specialized to become, how big to grow, how centralized or decentralized to operate and what goals to pursue.

If any organization failed to pay its way, its creditors usually insisted that its assets be liquidated and distributed *pro rata*. Since each organization, excepting governmental units, operated privately and independently, the failure of any one meant that the supply and demand for each would be self-correcting in the longer run. By limiting the federal (and lower) government's power to decide who should do what, a system of bribes and influence peddling was avoided. As much as anything else, abuse of this power has been a root cause of many other countries' inabilities to establish sound economies and to compound growth in constructive directions.

Of the estimated 1990 U.S. population of 240 million, about 116 million were considered to make up the active labor force. These individuals applied for positions in various organizations, were hired and then formed into groups of varying sizes to play different roles in accomplishing the work of each organization. Formal organizations in most areas of the United States must apply for recognition by the state or be appointed by the ruling authorities for permission to engage in the work of each function. The state issues charters or licenses to corporations, partnerships and single entrepreneurs to do business work, to educational institutions to engage in teaching activities, to religious groups to perform religious work, to hospitals and other health-care organizations to care for the sick and ailing. The family must apply for a marriage license to become an official organization recognized by the state. Even the individual must have a birth certificate to be an official member of a particular society.

Not all organizations need to be formally recognized to perform useful work. Most informal organizations are of a temporary nature such as casual cohabitation liaisons, baby-sitting clubs, study groups, poker and bridge clubs, dining-out groups, commuting co-ops and so forth. Even groups subversive in purpose may exist and engage in illegal activities from which they extract benefits to themselves though not necessarily to the society in which they operate.

Organizational Goals

We now have different organizations specifically chartered to engage in one or more of the fourteen listed group functions shown in column

3, Figure 2, and to contribute their value added in the form of products and services into society's marketplace for the consumption process.

Why do these organizations engage in these activities? What motivates them? The answers bring us to the third major concept of organizational goals, the purposes for which each organization executes its specialized functions. Altogether, the Structure-Function-Goal concept is the heart of the Functionalist model of society or as it is called here, Mac I. The concept applies equally well from the individual point of view to that of the largest organization. Any purposeful constituency serving within an organization or being served outside the organization can use the concept. Indeed, there is a whole galaxy of goals for every organization starting with the individual. The process of goal rationalization and goal attainment within nearly every organization deserves far more attention. More than an organization's compositional elements and functional activities, goal articulation and measurement remain a subjective, political, variable and altogether tricky subject.

Individuals, independent or union-organized workers, managers, stakeholders, competitors, suppliers, trade associations, consumers, government regulatory agencies, the supportive press and the critical press, may all have explicit goal expectations centering on any organization. Since most of these are not contractual or even written, there is a wide range of goal expectations from each constituency at each moment. Goal ambiguity can only be reduced through more attention to its composition and specificity. Useful classifications are a start. As on the individual level, three levels of goal differentiation are identified: operational, directional and constitutional.

Constitutional Goals for Organizations

Constitutional goals for most organizations may be inferred from originating charters usually issued by the various states. The application document usually asks petitioners to check which of many classifications they wish to operate in and also asks for a statement of organizational purpose.

In the beginning most governments, fearing the abuse of monopoly power, were very rigid and permitted corporations to be formed to engage in only one kind of business. Now they may be formed "for any lawful purpose." The United States Steel Company, for instance, was permitted to "exercise any and all powers which a copartnership or natural person could do and exercise and which now or hereafter may be authorized by law." Because of severe international competition and other unmanageable forces, U.S. Steel Corporation entered the petroleum and natural gas fields and changed its name to USX Corporation. Some restrictions remain, however, against most businesses engaging in banking, insurance or certain activities pertaining to public utilities.

Thus, businesses engage in business, church organizations in religious activities, schools in education, government agencies in governing and so forth. There is no law against cross-over patterns, however, as some religious interests establish corporations to engage in commercial activities for profit and some business organizations establish schools for various purposes. Quite likely, there are instances where an organization's secondary interests in a different field succeeded hugely and became that organization's primary interest. But usually an organization's primary mission can be found in its enabling charter to operate.

Directional Goals Aim to Fulfill Organizational Mission

Directional goals indicate also the general direction of an organization's orientation. Column 4 of Figure 2 lists such dimensional directions as affiliationism, estheticism, humanitarianism, intellectualism, maintaining order and protectionism, materialism, spiritualism—all of which are also listed under directional goals for individuals. The addition of *instrumentalism* completes the list. It is intended as a kind of miscellaneous category or perhaps a penultimate goal in which the important functions of maintaining order and health and camaraderie and a host of other activities can find redeeming purpose. This category is intended to encompass all facilitating and/or utilitarian functions that cannot easily identify an "ism" of their own. Hedonism perhaps should be listed only under directional goal choices for individuals as no organization would admit to pursuing it directly, even the aptly named Playboy Enterprises. The concepts of nihilistic and criminalistic behavior also should be restricted to alternative directional goals for the individual as no government would admit to licensing organizations to pursue such activities even though they may inadvertently have done so by providing legitimate "fronts" for other illegal activities.

Operational Goals for Organizations

Operational goals for organizations, as under individual goals, refer to those more specific, shorter-term and more measurable goals. Operational goals for a business organization pursuing the materialistic dimension of profit might specifically identify any combination or variations of the following:

- 15 percent return on investment for fiscal year's operation
- 20 percent share of defined market sales for fiscal year
- 5 new product or service introductions per year
- 5 new product or service ideas approved yearly for pilot testing or further research

- 100 new product or service concepts screened yearly
- 10 percent reduction each year in absenteeism, tardiness, rejected products, customer complaints, warranty costs, product liability suits
- 10 new accounts per sales territory yearly
- 20 percent fewer markdowns per year or season
- 20 percent less average inventory carried compared to last year
- 10 percent reduction in bad loans, employee theft, inventory shrinkage from all causes

Indeed, operational goals should be established and monitored for each department throughout the year. They should extend to every employee and group of employees and be integrated with incentives where appropriate.

Operational goals for a religious organization delivering spiritual satisfactions to its membership might include such items as:

- 10 percent increase in official conversions to the specific faith yearly
- 5 percent improved attendance generally or in selected ethnic groupings
- Specified percentage increase in dispensation of church's sacraments
- 10 percent increase in countable aid to international or local poverty or hardship problems
- Measurable increase in church-sponsored retreats, advances, meditations, vocations
- 10 percent growth in teen-age attendance
- Specified increase in financial contributions per fiscal year by various categories
- Specified increase in business advertising in church's weekly or monthly bulletin

Operational goals for a private university serving intellectual enrichment programs might include:

- Specified increase in number of new student applicants, number of arriving applicants
- Specified decline in student attrition by year, sex, age, major
- Specified increase in specific demographic characteristics sought as more athletes, more women, more ethnic minorities, more liberal-arts candidates, more international students
- Specified improvement in any nationally normed test for students in any field, all fields

- Specified increase in average SAT or ACT scores of entering freshmen
- Specified increase in number or percentage of graduates passing bar exams, professional certifications such as CPCU and CPA and other licensing exams
- Specified improvements in measurable terms of alumni support as in class reunions, annual giving, mentions in wills and trusts
- Specified improvement in faculty support for travel to attend yearly scholarly meetings, field by field, to engage in research, provide reading assistance, literature searchers
- Specified improvements in funds available for scholarships for needy students, for technology enhancements for information age on the Internet

The Triangulation Dynamic for the Organization

The most basic planning tool available to the management of any organization—from the very largest to the family household or individual—lies in the triangulation potentials of structural support, functional activity and operational goals. While all three are necessary to affect any progress along a chosen directional path, operational goals are the most crucial because they represent the starting point and because they require more thought and planning. Once realistic and measurable goals are specified in any organizational context, the mix of activities to accomplish them can be identified and the structural elements or power needed to support that chain of activities can be brought to bear.

For example, if a business organization specifies as a yearly operational goal a 10 percent reduction in inventory shrinkage, it can easily identify the possible sources of the losses, devise the means to appraise the more likely sources and then estimate the cost of the effort in new equipment, manpower surveillance or education. Priorities can be established for the possible sources of shrinkage, which might include faulty inventory-control procedures in the requisitioning, ordering, receiving, storing, shipping, accounting or counting of the inventoried parts or merchandise, actual breakage or theft by suppliers, customers, employees or unrelated persons. Functional deterrents in the form of new equipment, procedures or manpower can be considered in light of their structural or budgetary effects.

The Triangulation Dynamic for the Educational Organization

Or take the case of a university that establishes an operational goal of attracting an additional 10 percent of freshmen applications. What functional and structural elements are needed to complete the triangulation? On the functional side, presumably more physical input or a better qualitative effort would be needed. The qualitative input should be examined first. Are the admission office's personnel appropriately hospitable to visitors? Are the promotional documents, brochures, forms as well prepared, timely and helpful to prospective students as those of other colleges and universities? Are campus tours for high schoolers and other visitors well organized and enthusiastically executed? Do applicants receive accurate and timely responses to their inquiries? Are follow-up calls made to assure that the applicants have all the information they need?

If weaknesses are found in any on-going functional activity, efforts should be made to address them before considering additional programming. If additional programming activities are needed to meet competitive conditions, identify and rank them. Perhaps career counseling meetings could be scheduled at eligible high schools or receptions could be held at cooperative alumni homes or hotels in feeder cities. Perhaps a fresher or somehow different approach is needed in the style or design of the information packages. Public libraries in the U.S. Information Offices abroad (or especially in the United States!) may not carry your most recent catalogs.

When a program of action to achieve the 10 percent increase in student applications has been agreed on, attention can turn to the structural support or budgetary considerations. Financial constraints can help shape the quality and quantity of the total admissions effort. When funds are limited, priorities must be established in the functional programming. Thus, the budgetary support, functional programming and operational goals are linked together in the planning of any activity.

Even in cases where financial support to fund worthy improvements is lacking, imaginative leadership can induce a followership in playing the game of "chasing higher priorities." In one case familiar to the writer, a university president was successful in orchestrating a serious yearly review of project proposals and assigning them priority numbers for implementation when and if funding became available. Faculty and administrative personnel took this challenge seriously and submitted rewritten proposals yearly and even seemed pleased with feedback that their proposal was now ranked as 7, far better than its previous year's 10.

174 • The Maccordion Format

Figure 3
The Maccordion Format

COLUMN I	COLUMN II	COLUMN III
INDIVIDUALIZED HUMAN STRUCTURE	CLASSIFICATION OF ORGANIZATIONS*	FUNCTIONAL ACTIVITIES FOR SUSTAINING SOCIETY
265 Million People +/-		(+ or -)
67.5 Million People +/-	Family & Other	
96.4 Million Households +/-	Households	Most individual personal &
	Trade, Business &	vocational activities are
Each Individual with	Commercial	channeled into one or more
PHYSIOLOGICAL NEEDS	Environmental &	of these group functions:
Alimentary	Agricultural	
Excretory	Legal, Governmental,	1) Procreating & Nurturing
Protection	Public Administra-	2) Providing Community
Activity	tion, Military	& Fellowship
Recuperative	Engineering, Techno-	3) Socializing &
Erotic	logical, Social &	Acculturating
Parental +	Natural Sciences	4) Producint, Distrib-
	Educational	uting, Consuming
PSYCHOLOGICAL &	Cultlural	5) Providing Orderly &
PSYCHOSOCIAL NEEDS	Social Welfare	Equitable Environment
Safety	Health & Medical	6) Communicating
Love & Belongingness	Public Affairs	7) Transporting
Esteem	Fraternal, Ethnic &	8) Recreating & Playing
Self-Actualization	Nationality	9) Teaching & Playing
Desires to Know &	Religious	10) Serving Health Needs
Understand	Veteran, Hereditary &	11) Engaging in Religious &
Esthetic (Maslow) +	Patriotic	Ceremonious Rites
	Hobby & Avocational	12) Discovering New Know-
VALUES & INTERESTS	Athletic & Sports	ledge & Techniques
Power	Labor Unions, Associa-	13) Providing Welfare &
Enlightenment	tions, Federations	Philanthropic Aid
Wealth	Chambers of Commerce	14) Creating & Preserving
Well-Being	Trade & Tourism	Works of Art
Skill	Greek & non-Greek	
Affection	Letter & Related	(Extrinsic/Intrinsic)
Respect	Fan Clubs	
Rectitude	Subversive & Informal	
(Lasswell & Kaplan)		
	*Excepting for the first	
All Above Have Been	and last 2 items, all others	
Expanded into Countless	are taken from the Ency-	
Wants & Velleities & All	clopedia of Associations,	
of Which Combine to	Carolyn A. Fischer &	
Energize People to Seek	Carol A. Schwartz (Eds.),	
Satisfactions Both Individ-	Gale Research, Inc.,	
ually and Collectively	Detroit, MI, 1996.	
Through Group Activities		
Listed in Column III.		

TRIANGULATIO
GIVEN ANY 2 COORDINATE

Figure 3
The Maccordion Format

COLUMN IV

ORGANIZATIONAL
GOALS

DIRECTIONAL
   Affiliationism
   Estheticism
   Humanitarianism
   Intellectualism
   Maintaining Order
      & Protectionism
   Materialism
   Spiritualism
   Instrumentalism

OPERATIONAL
(For Materialistic Profit
  Seekers)
   Return on Investment
   % Share of Market
   % Rate of Growth
   Developing New Markets
   Developing New Products

OPERATIONAL
(For Household Organizations)
   Making $ (Shorter Hours,
     Overtime, "Moonlighting,"
     Saving $, Investing $ &
     Time Wisely, Thrifty Buying,
     Careful Consuming)
(For All Other Organizational
  Servicers)
   Operational Efficiency
   Operational Effectiveness
     in Delivering Services

CONSTITUTIONAL
(For Formal Organizations)
   As stated in Originating
   Charters & Basic Documents
(For Nation)
   Raising of Standards of Living
   for All by Addressing Emergent
   Problems & Opportunities

COLUMN V

INDIVIDUAL
GOALS

DIRECTIONAL
   Affiliationism
   Estheticism
   Humanitarianism
   Intellectualism
   Materialism
   Spiritualism
   Hedonism
   Eclecticism
   Instrumentalism
   Nihilism
   Criminalism

OPERATIONAL
(Materialistic)
   Making Money
   Saving Money
   Minimizing Taxes
   Prosuming
(Not Predominantly
  Materialistic)
   To seek satisfactions
   and deliver effective-
   ness in pursuit of any
   of directional goals
   listed above

CONSTITUTIONAL
   To seek satisfactions
   from those Inherited
   Family Values &
   Interests + those
   since acquired

Universality of the Triangulation Dynamic: Maccordion Success

The triangulation process described could operate at all levels in the institutionalized superstructure and also in the human structure. Unfortunately, it does not. Better organized businesses perhaps use the technique by other names. Some government units occasionally use the method. Some socialist countries have tried in their five year plans to achieve specified operational goals that in hindsight were deemed unrealistic. No doubt in many cases they provided ample budgetary support to well-detailed and thought-out functional plans but in most cases the goals were not met. Why not? Probably because the human structure's needs and goals were out of synchronization with the government-mandated institutionalized superstructure. Only when the people's needs and aspirations are directly connected to the organizational structure does the macro system work. The people must not only be involved but also motivated.

Perhaps an illustrative metaphor will explain better. Figure 3 combines the columns of figures 1 and 2. Imagine columns 1 and 5, the human structure, to be the two sides of an accordion and columns 2, 3 and 4, the institutionalized superstructure, to be the folded bellows. The keyboard on the right frame, society's individualized goal structure or column 5, plays the melody. The grip for operating the bellows and keys for full chords and bass notes, human needs and values, is on the left side, column 1. Only when the human structure's needs and goals squeeze the institutional bellows, columns 2, 3 and 4, does the accordion come alive and make great music. When a dictatorial government or self-appointed leader gives orders to the players and instruments, the music is strained, weak or uninspired. But when the human structure and organizational superstructure are well-coordinated and the music played is a direct projection of the needs, goals and aspirations of the players, then the music's sound can become sublime. Macro I or Mac has metamorphasized into the *Maccordion Format*.

Recognizing Deontological Dimensions in the Maccordion Format

Lest the dynamics of the Maccordion at work seem too mechanistic or automatic, let it be more appreciated that the whole spectrum of inquiry and study into human behavior can provide insight into the endless combinations of matches and mixes and yeas and nays that contribute to the Maccordion's music. For example, Amatai Etzioni contributes thusly (pp. xi–xii):

From the viewpoint of the particular deontological paradigm evolved here, the I/WE, individuals are not free-floating atoms within the society and the economy, nor do they relate to one another mainly on the basis of their personal attributes; their relations are shaped to a significant extent by their place in various social structures, which are forms their collectivities acquired. (Individuals may change these over time, but at any one point in time are largely subject to them.) These structures, in part, reflect shared values, and in part, power.

At issue is human nature: How wise are we and what is the role of morality, emotions, and social bonds in our personal and collective behavior? Also at issue is the extent to which free-standing individuals are the foundation of our society; or does the foundation consist of persons integrated into small groups and communities? Who is best able to maintain the mental equilibrium required to make free choices and to render effective decision-making, to combine an efficient and innovative economy with a viable and free society?

Perhaps neither the Maccordion Format nor the "I/WE" paradigm will ever completely portray an evolving society, but they do provide guideposts to help organize progress.

Although Good, It Could Be Better

But even in the United States, much of the triangulation potential is lost because operational goals are rarely articulated fully or carefully enough. Even though most groups are organized to conceptualize and implement their goals far better than individuals, too many department budgets are approved at last year's levels plus or minus 5 to 10 percent for inflationary effects. Too many organizations carry on as they have in the past with vague, unmeasurable goals. Too many managements operating without the full support of all their employees spend excessive time in housekeeping chores and contrived employee morale boosting. Too much time and effort are spent in crisis management.

Despite or perhaps because of the casual approach to explicit goal identification by individuals, the total system still works remarkably well. Most individuals retain their freedom to opt for their hidden, unrecognized or unverbalized goals whenever crunch time comes and they must choose between alternatives no longer postponable. They do this as consumer-citizens in our open-ended market system and when they vote in elections. In many cases they allow their feelings to guide their choices. Thus, do feelings or sentiments find important expression as implicit goals to combine with the explicit group and individual goals to help direct the Maccordion Format to help fulfill the American Dream.

On the Negative Side

Mac I or the Maccordion Format recognizes the existence of subversive organizations dealing in the various branches of organized crime. It is the job of Government to provide an overall environment orderly enough to permit the smooth execution of the other thirteen functions. When the operations of subversive organizations become sufficiently intrusive and damaging, Government must mount expensive deterrent campaigns. The cost of controlling organized and unorganized crime must be borne by all in the form of taxation. Unorganized crime by members of the Human Structure is a consequence of need frustration, obsession, greed and other imbalances in the people's need-value complex.

A second negative factor is noted by the +/– sign at the top of the list of functions, column 3. This is meant to suggest that not all functional behavior is positive or good for society. There are many tradeoffs in the execution of the master functions. Thus, negatively perceived air pollution is a consequence of the fuel consumption needed to provide the positively perceived transportation utility via millions of automobiles. The dilemma of abortion arises as a consequence of multiple social trends freewheeling in uncontrollable ways. But should procreation be abolished? There are negative social impacts associated with each of the master functions spinning off from the predominantly positive results that the execution of each provides. Overall, however, the Maccordion Format works better than any other system yet devised. It is truly a people's republic. It won't work well unless a majority of the people are fully involved in playing their right notes and rhythmically squeezing the box their way.

REFERENCES

Commons, John R., *The Economics of Collective Action* (New York: The Macmillan Company, 1950). Reprinted with the permission of Scribner, a Division of Simon & Schuster.

Etzioni, Amatai, *The Moral Dimension, Toward a New Economics* (New York: The Free Press, Division of Macmillan, 1988).

The World Almanac (New York: Newspaper Enterprise Association, 1986).

CHAPTER 10

Energizing the Maccordion Directly

Figure 3 presents the bare-bones outline of the Maccordion Format, or Mac for short. It is a comprehensive format purporting to show both actual and potential relationships of the major components of the U.S. society through the dynamic synthesis of a structure, function and goal arrangement. Although it is a busy page with triangles and brackets, it appears essentially static.

To make the model more dynamic, it is necessary to activate the arrangement: *structure* (human needs and values working through formal organizations) energized by *goal* aspirations *function* diversely to produce America, the bountiful. Or, in terms of the Maccordion metaphor: squeeze the box your way, gently or briskly in waltz time or in military time according to your taste and ability, and reap the benefits you earn.

Organizing the Organizations

Recall that no government mandate commanded that any group of people or organizations be required to perform any of the listed functions. It was more a matter of the government approving the charter applications of those requesting permission to operate in any of the listed functional areas. Initiative to form any organization to operate in any area lay with the people, with those entrepreneurs or free enterprisers who saw an opportunity to make a service contribution, a living, or a profit. Government agencies accept all applications that are complete and properly submitted regardless of whether the field might appear overcrowded. Anyone who wants the privilege or opportunity to operate as a

California corporation, for example, either profit or nonprofit, must carefully follow the requirements of the California Corporations Code as well as the rules set down by the Internal Revenue Service and the California Franchise Tax Board.

Business organizations officially may take the form of sole proprietorship, partnership or corporation as they are formally recognized by the state. California's simplified state law requires that the Articles of Incorporation contain less information than do most states. All of the requirements are set forth in Corporations Code 202, which provides that the Articles of Incorporation shall set forth the name and purpose of the corporation "...to engage in any lawful act or activity for which a corporation may be organized under the General Corporation Law of California other than the banking business, the trust company business or the practice of a profession permitted to be incorporated by the California Corporations Code" (Smith, p. 263).

Business organizations in California chartered under the Corporations Code or the Business and Professions Code normally seek profit and pay federal and state taxes on that profit. Business organizations have as their intrinsic function item 4 on the list of Group Functions shown in Figure 2 as Producing, Distributing and Consuming Goods and Services. Thus, all manufacturing, mining, farming, fishing, wholesaling and retailing enterprises fit under that heading as well as a host of other titles or specialized sub-functions in many wide-ranging industries such as various middlemen, dealers, brokers, buying agents, auctioneers, merchandisers, purchasing agents, exporters and importers, drop shippers, bankers, salesmen and functional representatives. Perhaps a little imagination is needed to encircle the group as it is very pervasive throughout the economy with something over six million business establishments employing over 92 million workers in 1991 *(Information Please Almanac,* p. 73).

Nonprofit Organizations

Most other organizations shown in Figure 2, column 2 under "classification of organizations," qualify for nonprofit corporate status under such codes as the 1980 California Corporation Code, Sections 5000–9927. Thereunder, nonprofit corporations are divided into three subgroups: 1) public-benefit corporations founded for scientific, literary, educational or charitable purposes; 2) religious corporations; and 3) mutual-benefit corporations such as trade associations, automobile clubs, tennis clubs. Special types of public-benefit corporations include chambers of commerce, boards of trade, mechanics institutes, producer or consumer cooperative corporations, medical or legal service corporations and humane societies formed by twenty or more persons for the prevention of cruelty to animals and children.

The term "nonprofit" as applied to corporations has a very special meaning. It is not to be interpreted literally as the law specifically permits "for profit" activity not necessary to accomplish the nonprofit purposes and still permits tax exemption (Mancuso, pp. 16–17). All California nonprofit corporations must be officially recognized as such by the California Secretary of State. This is accomplished by filing appropriate Articles of Incorporation with the Secretary of State's office in Sacramento.

Thus it is clear that the state government in California (and in other states as well) has seen fit to establish different and often more lenient rules for those engaged in religious, charitable, scientific, educational or artistic activities as opposed to those engaged solely or mainly for profit. A properly organized nonprofit corporation pays no or reduced taxes, and in many cases the people who contribute to the corporation qualify for tax deductions. However, there is a requirement that, when the nonprofit corporation breaks up, all monies will be distributed to similar nonprofit groups to insure that the people who manage the corporation cannot use the nonprofit form to provide windfall benefits to themselves.

Perceiving Employable Matches From the Pool of Mixed Talent

All of the organizations shown in Figure 3, column 2, are composed of individuals with varying need-value complexes as summarily shown in Figure 3, column 1. The total pool of widely varying human qualities assimilated from all corners of the earth and representing nearly all cultural orientations contribute to a full range of individual directional goal aspirations as briefly listed in Figure 3, column 5. It is the organization's job to select from this vast pool those individuals with characteristics they believe can most successfully adapt to or blend into the organization's present and desired future cultures. It is the individual's job to select an organization whose smooth functioning needs the special or most highly rewarded qualities that they believe they possess.

This two-way matching process results in the best allocation of human resources yet devised to benefit both the individual and the organization, and ultimately the society at large. The individual has the opportunity to maximize any one skill or to optimize his complex of abilities, interests and skills in a chosen vocational track. The organization has the opportunity to pick and choose from the rich talent pool available those individuals deemed to possess the most needed qualities for its present and prospective needs. Society benefits through the eventual production and general availability of goods and services competitively priced.

Adjust, Adapt or Leave...

After the matching process has been completed, the ordering specifics of job assignment, training and tracking the progress of each individual employee become the tasks of the organization's management. And the tasks of adapting, doing and contributing to organizational welfare become the challenges of each individual hired. The joint results achieved are mostly harmonious and successful even though the ever-vigilant press chronicles in large print the stories of massive layoffs, "downsizing," and other perceived maladjustments. A country-wide unemployment rate below 6 percent (considered by most economists to reflect a reasonably healthy economy) means that some 94 percent are tolerably well-positioned, productive, and positively contributing those special skills so desired by their organizational sponsors.

In every organization, however, there is some percentage of employees who variously do not fit in well or are in some way "out of sync" with their management's expectations. These employees usually know who they are as most managements do not hide their disapproval. They are usually given the time and training and warnings to adapt or else. Quite often, they may seek new positions in other organizations. Management, on the other hand, must be careful to apply the "due process" criterion to every employee in every way lest the red flag of unfair treatment cloud the dismissal issue. Many organizations from businesses to hospitals to government agencies and school districts now employ human-resource specialists in a variety of human pathologies to help sort out and administer to the needs of disaffected employees.

And thus does the Maccordion make music with a minimum of discordant notes given the magnitude of the fantastically complex job of matching and mixing human characteristics in the biggest and broadest assimilation ever attempted. While other countries are resorting to "ethnic cleansing" to homogenize the perceived sources of their human problems, the managerial insight of organizations operating in the United States within the little understood but largely beneficent Maccordion system has so far succeeded in melding the most heterogeneous lot of people ever assembled into the most efficient and effective production system so far developed.

But Wait...Perhaps?

While all may appear manageable and controllable under present circumstances, powder kegs of potential danger may be accumulating in unsuspected ways. For instance, sales of the antidepressant, Prozac, grew 37 percent in 1994 and 24 percent in 1995. The manufacturer of the prescription drug, Eli Lilly, has estimated that more than 21 million people worldwide have been prescribed the drug since its introduction in 1988.

Primary-care physicians "are finding that there's a lot of efficiency to be gained by treating depression effectively," according to William Glazer, associate clinical professor of psychiatry at Yale University School of Medicine (Burton, p. B3).

What might be behind all of this doctor-prescribed antidepressant drug consumption? Perhaps the advances in medical research can safely lead us to an improved state of equilibrium where we can easily and with no or mild side effects reduce the tensions of high-pressured work with its demanding deadline and quota schedules. Perhaps. Knowledgeable experts confirm positive probability expectations. But perhaps also this mood-altering panacea has a limit not yet perceived. And what about the increasing consumption of powerful and addictive illegal drugs? Have the pressures of modern living accelerated to the point where an increasing percentage of the population can safely indulge? Where are the limits? What are the long-range consequences?

These are risks that indulging individuals and groups in society have chosen to bear. Perhaps they are winnable risks and the consumption of these palliatives will one day be universal. And, if not, man will simply have to take a step or two back, regroup, and try other tactics to cope. "Twas ever thus."

Groping Our Way to Organizational Leadership

Given our inabilities to understand, let alone measure, the strength of the subjective need/value surpluses and deficits in our characters (Figure 3, column 1), we have to permit or encourage unrequited needs/values to surface and guide our directional aspirations. If and when this occurs, we gradually develop vocational commitment in a direction presumed to provide gratification to the initiating needs/values deficits. It is presumed without evidence that man naturally works for balance in his needs/values matrix. This, of course, may be partly or totally wrong as some people conceivably might prefer various imbalances and work to achieve or maintain them. This preference may be more acceptable now as we have moved into the computer age with its increasingly impersonal communications. Additionally, the emphasis on occupational specialization continues encouraging youth to emphasize their strengths and ignore their weaknesses.

If followed at all, this approach to career selection is felt intuitively rather than calculated rationally. The noise, clamor and confusion of today's world must confound most youth who rarely know for certain what career their talents are best suited for or even what they're really interested in. But still, they must choose and hope they've guessed right.

Eventually, most of us must enter the work force, with or without that educational preparation deemed appropriate for our profile of needs, values, abilities, goals and aspirations all hidden behind a nervous ego and uncertain personality. With our credentials listed on resumes, we reach out to those organizations serving the societal functions for which we've received some training. Years of ensuing experience confirm or deny the accuracy of our choices. Those who fail to achieve their levels of aspiration make the best of it and settle in or leave the organization and try again. Those who chose right and whose values were proved well matched to organizational purpose and culture presumably climb the managerial ranks of their chosen vehicles to become their leaders.

It is the leadership of most organizations serving society's functional activities that provides the dynamism, growth and direction to the overall model design or format. It is hoped that the societal overview provided by the Maccordion Format may serve as a general guideline for aspiring youth to match their values, interests and abilities with existing directional challenges in ways that will enhance both their individual careers and the overall welfare of all people served thereby.

Executing the Functions

The entire society exists to serve the individual's needs and wants (on a reciprocal basis of course). Individuals are created for society by the biological union of man and woman traditionally organized as a chartered or married family. Furthermore, the nuclear family is also charged with the nurturing and care-of-children function. Households are established (95.7 million in 1992) primarily for this purpose but they also serve as residential consumption centers for its members as they use their incomes to create personalized styles and scales of living from the marketed goods and services produced by all other organizations.

Figure 4 shows a rough alignment from left to right of major organizational types matched to both major societal functions performed and major directional goals. This matching process is admittedly a crude approximation and over-simplification of the complexities involved but it can serve to show the broad outlines of the system that has served us so well. It shows that affiliationism is the directional goal of the family unit and this conjures up thoughts of secondary social friendships and alliances derived from social, economic, religious and other sources.

Several of the other master functions also have major organizational types specifically created to deliver their utilities, benefits or satisfactions to the population at large. Thus, business organizations dominate in the production, distribution and consumption of goods and services; different government levels from national defense to local fire and police departments participate in providing the safe and orderly environments needed by all for stability, continuity and growth; the courts and justice systems work to assure equitable treatment for all; certain controlled-profit corporations called public utilities provide gas and electricity service, public communication and transportation facilities; schools of all kinds facilitate the teaching and learning functions; hospitals, clinics, and rehabilitation establishments provide diverse healthcare services; religious organizations build elaborate houses of worship and utilitarian schools while fraternal organizations erect halls and temples for their shared activities.

Directional Goals for Achievement

The directional goals for these matched pairs of organizational-functional relationships are shown variously as materialism or profit for business, intellectualism or learning for schools, humanitarianism for healthcare operations, spiritualism for religious activities and affiliationism again for fraternal, ethnic and nationality organizations. Where no clear "ism" can be identified as a directional goal for a major "inging" function, the term *instrumentalism* is used to indicate a facilitating role in maintaining viable conditions for man's pursuit of his more ultimate goals. Thus, government activities, public-utility services, environmental cleanups, and participation in amateur sports are shown as being mainly instrumental to providing conditions, collective or individual, conducive to permitting better execution of clearer or more compelling directional goals.

Those following the more general instrumental directive goal patterns may simply identify with the operational goals of the chosen organization and work to advance them, albeit with perhaps less passion than if they strongly identified with any of the other directional goals. As the organizational superstructure has become more complicated and specialized, it encourages youth to seek out and prepare for more specialized occupational careers. As they do so in increasing numbers, the educational establishment is pressured into following suit with ever more specialized curricula in ever narrower fields. A major consequence is that youth increasingly loses sight of "the big picture" and society's need for dedicated leaders in all directions other than just instrumentalism and materialism.

Several other basic functions may not have a single organizational type dedicated to serving them but may be jointly served by two or more organizational entities. The socializing function refers to the processes of training certain values into the consciousness of youth to make them better citizens. These culturally nurtured values are intended to assure that youth will grow up responsibly to obey the laws, pay their taxes, vote for representative government, and fight to defend their country if needed. Acculturating refers more to the process of absorbing new cultural traits, as in immigrants becoming Americanized. This function differs in that in most cases immigrants already possess an appreciation of their citizenship duties to their former countries and on entering the United States must accept an overlay of somewhat new or varying responsibilities owed to their newly adopted homeland. Parents, grandparents, schools, government and religious organizations, even businesses contribute to the socialization and acculturation processes.

The Powerful Facilitating Functions

Communicating and transporting are linking-pin connective functions facilitating maintenance of old and development of new product and service combinations from the totality of parts in the matrix of time, space, matter and energy. All organizations need both to unify, maintain and improve their productive outputs. Many business, engineering, military and technological organizations work independently and jointly to maintain and develop the existing and future technological infrastructures in communicating and transporting industries. Together, they provide the means to accelerate productivity in all the other functions. The content communicated and the distances traveled by all of us in all of our activities may not change much but the ever-improving technologies by which both are accomplished contribute greatly to increasing efficiency over time.

Recreating and playing are also discharged by several organizational structures whose primary responsibilities lie elsewhere. Certain business establishments and government park and recreation agencies exist to service these activities directly with facilities such as golf courses, tennis and swimming clubs, bowling alleys, horseback-riding stables, various playing fields and gymnasia in most communities. Religious groups, schools, businesses, fraternal and social organizations also contribute indirectly by organizing recreational activities for their memberships, students, employees and customers.

Improving the Status Quo

The role of providing dynamic improvement to the functioning of all activities lies with discovering new knowledge and in applying it to develop new techniques of operation. These are functions of investigative research.

Research has been classified into three levels: basic, applied and development. According to the *National Science Foundation*, basic or pure research seeks an understanding of the laws of nature without regard for specific utilitarian value. Thus, government is a large sponsor of such research as in *NASA* space probes and satellite missions. University and other private research laboratories also participate with much lower budgeted support. Applied research is carried out with practical and usually, but not necessarily, specific objectives in mind. Much applied research seeks detailed information regarding a specific situation for which the general laws are known from basic research. But increasing our understanding of natural laws, although important, is not the primary objective. Many organizational types participate at this level: business, government, scientific, engineering and technical laboratories both public and private, university research bureaus and various medical laboratories.

Development research has a more pragmatic objective in its definition as the systematic use of scientific knowledge directed toward the production of useful materials, devices, systems, methods, or processes. Business organizations perform most of the research and development while universities, underwritten by government financial support, conduct most of the basic research.

Providing welfare to the needy through charitable contributions and philanthropic aid is another function performed by a variety of organizational types from the family to business, government, cultural, social welfare, religious and fraternal groups. The concept of providing charitable aid dates back to earliest times but our more recent understanding of foundations and philanthropy stems from 1601 when the *Statute of Charitable Uses* was enacted in England identifying charitable purposes. Forms of assistance range from providing basic food, shelter, clothing and medical attention to needy individuals to providing financial grants to religious, educational, and various other service groups assisting in scientific research, health, the arts, to various recreation needs and special causes such as wildlife preservation. There are more than thirty-five thousand grant-making foundations in the United States, all of which stay busy processing requests for philanthropic aid.

Creating and Preserving Works of Art

Creating and preserving works of art are enduring functions that have emerged naturally from man's pride in his accomplishments and his striving to do better. The need to be creative, to do things differently, to reach for new combinations, to achieve more efficient, more exotic or more surprising results are all manifestations of this urge to create, to grow, to live more fully. Like plant life, creative people must grow or atrophy. Recognizing that this need is strong and deep in man's nature and that encouraging its expression leads to a richer and more integrated society, the normative organizations such as parents, schools, churches, foundations and certain government agencies under insightful leadership provide nurturing programs for youth interested in artistic expression and appreciation. Only a few succeed, of course, because the invention of new ideas and creative expression can only be encouraged, not produced to order. And even for the successful, there is an uneven future, much hard work, frustration and little financial security. More financial rewards lie in servicing the art "appreciators" peripherally with reproductive technology, landscaping design, interior decoration and pop-art product differentiations. Preserving worthy art and artifacts is more organizable than encouraging its creation in the first place.

For this preserving function there are many devoted organizations, from governmental archives and libraries to foundation-supported museums to religiously sponsored collections to education-allied art collections to business-endowed art collections of all descriptions. Most are fixed in permanent locations but some travel with yearly exhibition schedules.

Professional athletics proudly present their halls of fame. Wineries are prone to collect and display historically significant wine-making artifacts. Banks collect and display rare coins. Tourist cities like to preserve and display for new visitors the paraphernalia that contributed to their original reputations. A cosmetic manufacturer and distributor collected and had reproduced fancy perfume and fragrance dispensers that attracted many hobbyist collectors. Old automobiles, dolls, clothing, jewelry, glassware and hundreds of other products that have created a nostalgic memory of good times past have been assembled in museums and other locations for the enjoyment and education of interested devotees.

The Bonding Art of Music

Perhaps the art medium most universally enjoyed is music. Whether in popular form of contemporary music, classical, or something in between, nearly everybody relates positively to the rhythm, beat or many moods of music. It serves as a second language to everybody's first language and acts as an important cultural bridge not only between our rapidly integrating societies and continents but also to that valuable local or neighborly sociability that makes the daily grind more tolerable. It provides the peaks of contrast and relief that most people need to relieve the monotony and boredom of repetitive and uninspiring activity.

A huge multi-faceted industry has been developed for the various stages of producing and reproducing, delivering and reinterpreting music in all its manifestations. Overall, it generates an emotional togetherness connecting people in ways far beyond the more rational content of verbal expression, media discourse and other artistic expression. It bonds us.

Just Blowing in the Wind

After this brief overview of the major components of the Maccordion Format, the question still must be asked: what makes it work so well? What is the magic that enables the push and pull of energized people to produce such a grand symphony of sound or such an overflowing cornucopia of material abundance? Why does it work so well in the United States, for instance, and not so well in other more or less populated countries where ethnic diversity is less pronounced or where natural resources may be more abundant in relation to less population press?

The answer, my friends, is blowing in the wind. Well, almost and certainly in just as elusive a fashion. Just as adjacent high and low pressure systems in weather terminology compete to create winds of varying strength, different men and groups use human energy to compete against themselves and other elements in nature. The key word is "competition," from the Latin *competitio*, a competing rivalry.

Competition is perhaps the most pervasive behavior characteristic on earth while being the least understood and appreciated. It modulates the interactive balance of nature's air, water, soil and weather ecosystems. It initiated the animal rivalries for territoriality and dominance. Man's survival and success on earth followed his winning perennial struggles against nature and its extreme weather conditions and diseases, against competing ferocious and predatory animals, against other fighting human tribes.

The universality of competition was sweepingly summarized by Walton H. Hamilton (p. 142):

> It is manifest in a struggle between germ cells for a chance at life; plants, for sunlight and growth; bats and beavers and elephants, for food and mates; and kind against kind and like against unlike, for a foothold on the earth. It is evident in the strivings that attend the round of every day activities; one against another, bakers contend to provide wholesome bread; undertakers, to give peaceful rest to the dead; salesmen, to break down resistances; scholars, to surprise truth and make contributions to knowledge; and uplifters, to do good. It appears in social order in which men have lived; in the conflicts of tribes for unhappy hunting grounds; of holy men, for the glory of saying the most prayers; of barons for castles on the Rhine; of merchant adventurers, for the spoils of the East; and of capitalists, to bag the largest profits and to establish the biggest and best foundations.

Early Organized Competitions

While perhaps not perceived as such by early man, competition was the innate means to survival. Kill or be killed, dominate your neighbors or they will dominate you. Act and react aggressively in most encounters. Establish yourself high in the local "pecking order" by whatever means possible so as to enjoy favorable treatment at the feeding trough, to secure the best shelter and breeding spots, to attract the more comely of the young maidens. To the victor go the spoils!

So common and normal were the realities of competitive striving that it had to be perceived as the essence of life itself. What else was there besides the many Gods to be appeased? Since it was important for the food gatherers to be able to run fast enough to capture animals, the idea of competitive foot races for practice and improvement was a natural preparation. And so foot races were probably a major form of physical activity for the young men of every village in earliest times. Indeed, the first Olympic Games was reported to be held in 776 B.C. in conjunction with a religious festival. According to one source (*Oxford English Dictionary*, p. 781), there was only one event, the stade, but others were added over the ensuing decades. The stade was a competitive running event covering the length of a stadium, about 600 Greek feet. Competitive wrestling and the pentathlon were introduced in 708 B.C. The latter was an all-round competition consisting of five events: the long jump, javelin throw, discus throw, foot race and wrestling. This same source speculated that it was generally accepted that the Games were probably at least five hundred years old before 776 B.C. (p. 197).

Competition Cannot Be Totally Suppressed

Discontinued in 393 A.D. by the Roman emperor Theodosus I, the Olympic Games were only reestablished in 1896 by Baron Pierre de Coubertin of France. But the precedent was an old one and the concept of amateurish competitive games grew in popularity in all countries. Many now compete for the privilege of hosting the quadrennial event despite the huge risks involved not only monetarily but in controlling terroristic activities. The Greek citizens in Athens in 1997 were ecstatic over winning the international competition to host the Olympic Games in 2004 and see the event return to its birthplace.

As we enter the twenty-first century, the dynamics of professional sports have captured the imaginations of sports fans all over the world and it has burgeoned into another big-business enterprise, which in turn has spawned widespread ancillary activities such as hours-long tailgate parties before and after games, special tourism events, licensed clothing insignias and memorabilia of the stars, autograph collecting, popular sports magazines and gambling among others.

Building on the records achieved in all endeavors and noted in the mass media, the *Guiness Book of Records* is now published yearly to contain such competitive trivia as the locations of the world's largest wine cellar, sports stadium, hotel, the most lethal manmade chemical, the highest tensile strength, the least dense solids, the hottest flame, the fastest turtle, the heaviest twins, the oldest automobile driver and the tallest house of cards built without adhesives. Everything, even competition, can be used excessively. Like many other impulses and obsessions, competition feeds on itself. Individuals and organizations compete against themselves and nature to exceed the previous best record, not necessarily because it is meaningful or useful but just because it is there and presents a goal or takes a measure of ability to test with either repressed or extra energy.

All of the political posturing and legal wrangling emphasized in the daily press as so important to society's welfare may be necessary to keep the path of progress on track but it is the discharge of that restless competitive energy that provides the powerful thrust. To some extent our society has succeeded in pointing this relentless force in constructive directions and capitalized more than any other society in history by harnessing competition to public welfare and preventing it from aimlessly just blowing in the wind.

REFERENCES

Burton, Thomas M., "Medicine: Lilly Sales Rise As Use of Prozac Keeps Growing" (*The Wall Street Journal*, January 31, 1996).

Hamilton, Walton H., "Competition," *Encyclopedia of the Social Sciences*, volume 4. Editor-in-chief: Edwin R.A. Seligman (New York: The Macmillan Company, 1931).

Information Please Almanac (Boston: Houghton Mifflin Company, 1994).

Mancuso, Anthony, *The California Non-Profit Corporation Handbook* (Berkeley, California: Nolo Press, 1984). Reprinted with permission from the publisher.

Oxford English Dictionary, Volume X, 2nd Edition, Moulovum (Oxford: Clarendon Press, 1989).

Smith, J. B., editor. *Business Law in California* (San Francisco: General Publications, 1984).

Statistical Abstract of the United States: 1984 (Washington, D.C.: U.S. Bureau of the Census, 1984).

Figure 4
Matching Organizations to Functions and Goals

Classification of Organizations	Major Functions	Directional Goals
Family and Other Households	Procreating Nurturing Socializing	Affiliationism
Trade, Business, Commercial	Producing, Distributing, Consuming Goods and Services	Materialism
Environmental	Providing Orderly Environment	Estheticism or Instrumentalism
Agricultural	Producing , Distributing, Consuming Goods and Services	Materialism
Legal, Governmental, Public Administration, Military	Providing Orderly and Equitable Environment	Instrumentalism
Engineering, Technological, Natural and Social Sciences	Various	Materialism and/or Instrumentalism
Educational	Teaching and Learning	Intellectualism, Instrumentalism
Cultural	Various	Various
Social Welfare	Providing Welfare and Orderly Environment	Humanitarianism
Health and Medical	Serving Health Needs	Humanitarianism Instrumentalism
Public Affairs	Communicating and Various Others	Affiliationism and Instrumentalism
Fraternal, Ethnic and Nationality	Providing Community and Fellowship	Affiliationism
Religious	Engaging in Religious and Ceremonial Rites	Spiritualism

Figure 4
Matching Organizations to Functions and Goals

Classification of Organizations	Major Functions	Directional Goals
Veteran, Hereditary and Patriotic	Providing Community and Fellowship	Affiliationism
Hobby and Avocational	Recreating and Playing	Affiliationism Instrumentalism
Athletic and Sports, Amateur and Professional	Recreating and Playing	Instrumentalism Materialism
Labor Unions, Associations, and Federations	Producing, Distributing and Consuming Goods and Services	Materialism Instrumentalism
Chambers of Commerce	Communicating and Providing Orderly Environment	Materialism Instrumentalism
Trade and Tourism	Producing, Distributing and Consuming Goods and Services	Materialism Instrumentalism
Greek and Non-Greek Letter and Related	Providing Community and Fellowship	Affiliationism
Fan Clubs	Providing Community and Fellowship	Affiliationism
Subversive	Various	Criminalism
Informal	Various	Instrumentalism

CHAPTER 11

Energizing the Maccordion Indirectly

In the previous chapter you read about how the Maccordion Format was energized directly through the primary connections of major organizational efforts to discharge those master functions for which they were originally chartered.

Those organizations delivered their various products and services to the public at large as efficiently and effectively as they could. They compete and cooperate in multifarious ways in order to make a profit or otherwise earn the respect of their particular public by contributing to the affiliation, materialistic, esthetic, humanitarian, intellectual, spiritual or instrumental goals of people, which in turn contribute to satisfying the initiating needs and wants of the public, both individually and collectively. They provide the power for the major musical chords played by the Maccordion, which delivers the dominant melodies to which we dance in our styles and scales of living.

This country was primed by a youthful, energetic and aggressive approach to life and its leaders in all organizational adaptations could not resist the frequent opportunities available to reach beyond their original mandates to capitalize on adjacent or distant challenges. After all, it was a new country, a free country, and there were no laws and few restrictions against it. In some ways branching out beyond an organization's original definition was just the logical outcome of dynamic competition and the continuous search for innovation and better ways to accomplish your particular mission. Who wanted to stop progress?

An Inflection Point in the Historical Continuum

Being a relatively new country there weren't the centuries-old customs and traditions, unwritten codes and truces defining territories, quotas and restrictive agreements. Most of these barriers to change were established under the historic mindset in which the size of the collective pie was forever fixed, as in a zero-sum game. Rather, the United States from its beginning chose a wide-open and wide-eyed approach to growth, to freedom, to life. Circumstances favored it.

A new Constitution had been written in which government was mandated to do the minimum. Adam Smith's insightful concept of the market and competition as regulator was a most timely contribution in 1776. The beginning of the industrial revolution in England a few years earlier could be adopted and extended. Agriculture was still basic and dominant but there might be growth in other directions as well. And westward there was that vast expanse of territory to be settled with its visible stands of trees, herds of wild animals, great lakes and rivers and invisible but potential discoveries to be made in mining useful and precious metals. Opportunities abounded. And, protected on both sides by great oceans against easy invasions, the nation consolidated itself, grew bigger and stronger. With the arrival of the twentieth century, the United States became the dominant factor in the two world wars against aggressors in Europe and Asia and emerged to become arguably the political leader of the industrialized world.

The Hidden Magic

Was this leadership role won by virtue of the Maccordion's success in directly serving the needs of its people or might more be involved? It is hypothesized here that a strong supportive role was played by the indirect or secondary contributions of individuals and formal organizations both large and small in exercising their freedom and initiative to find weak spots in the nation's overall performance and, where feasible, doing something about it.

Whereas the full, half and quarter notes were played in true pitch on the Maccordion directly by the major organizations executing the master functions for which they were chartered, the instrument's overall harmony included many quicker eighth and sixteenth notes with accenting off-pitch sharps and flats designed to make the overall melody more intriguing, more compelling, more complete. These sharps and flats were played by the many organizations that contributed beyond their primary roles by participating in secondary activities or indirect roles.

The symphony of society's holistic interactions will remain unfinished as long as people and the organizations they support continue to find constructive new applications serving both the general public and their own proximate ends. This process combined with the benign oversight of government, an effective market system, and an educated public using the democratic voting process, will continue to improve the harmony and quality of life in our collective society.

Find a Need and Fill It
—Before Somebody Else Does!

None of the formal organizations listed in Figure 2, column 2, is formally restricted from participation beyond the function named in their originating charters. Indeed, most organizations could directly participate in all functions listed excepting that of human procreation. However, most organizations find their resources strained in the normal execution of their central functions and tend to restrict their involvements elsewhere to token activities. Still, many do contribute substantially to areas beyond their central focus when they find that the benefits exceed the costs. Government, for instance, has a hard time restricting its involvements to areas specifically identified in the Constitution. It is now actively involved in at least one segment of all functions listed.

Educational institutions, especially at the college and university levels, contribute substantially to the recreating and playing function with their entertaining theater and athletic competitions in football, basketball and other sporting events. Many colleges and universities maintain and operate museums and engage in religious rites as well as providing unparalleled mating grounds for youth. A case could be made that educational institutions in the aggregate, like government, make significant contributions to each of the listed functions. Religious organizations too get involved in the functional matrix well beyond their central mission as they frequently operate hospitals, schools and retirement centers, and make a major contribution across America in providing community and fellowship.

An interesting challenge would be to check out each major organizational type as to its involvement in all other functions beyond its central mission. Only by a thorough analysis of the pros and cons of these cross-over activities can we begin to appreciate the benefits of integrational togetherness in the American society. There are no formulas to predict or decide just how much functional integration is beneficial overall or whether strict adherence to functional specialization might produce superior social benefits. It's another freedom-for-all, as our Constitution mandated.

Figure 5 features the family unit in the organizational superstructure participating directly in its primary functions (solid lines) and indirectly with all other functions (dotted lines). Since the whole soci-

Two Special Cases Illustrated

Figure 5
Family Household Units Executing Primary and Secondary Functions

Column II
Classification of Organizations

Family & Other Households

Trade, Business & Commercial
Environmental & Agricultural
Legal, Governmental, Public Administration, Military
Engineering, Technological, Natural and Social Sciences
Educational
Cultural
Social Welfare
Health & Medical
Public Affairs
Fraternal, Ethnic & Nationality
Religious
Veteran, Hereditary & Patriotic
Hobby and Avocational
Labor Unions, Associations, Federations
Chambers of Commerce
Trade & Tourism
Greek & non-Greek Letter & Related
Fan Clubs
Subversive & Informal

Column III
Functional Activities for Sustaining Society
(+ or -)

1) Procreating/Nurturing
2) Providing Community & Fellowship
3) Socializing and Acculturating
4) Producing, Distributing, Consuming Goods and Services
5) Providing Orderly & Equitable Government
6) Communicating
7) Transporting
8) Recreating and Playing
9) Teaching and Learning
10) Serving Health Needs
11) Engaging in Religious and Ceremonious Rites
12) Discovering New Knowledge and Techniques
13) Providing Welfare and Philanthropic Aid
14) Creating and Preserving Works of Art

(Extrinsic and Intrinsic)

Figure 6
Business Organizations Executing Primary and Secondary Functions

Column II

Classification of Organizations

Family and Other Households

Trade, Business and Commercial

Environmental & Agricultural
Legal, Governmental, Public Administration, Military
Engineering, Technological, Natural and Social Sciences
Educational
Cultural
Social Welfare
Health & Medical
Public Affairs
Fraternal, Ethnic & Nationality
Religious
Veteran, Hereditary & Patriotic
Hobby and Avocational
Labor Unions, Associations, Federations
Chambers of Commerce
Trade & Tourism
Greek & non-Greek Letter & Related
Fan Clubs
Subversive & Informal

Column III

Functional Activities for Sustaining Society
(+ or -)

1) Procreating/Nurturing
2) Providing Community & Fellowship
3) Socializing and Acculturating
4) Producing, Distributing, Consuming Goods and Services
5) Providing Orderly & Equitable Government
6) Communicating
7) Transporting
8) Recreating and Playing
9) Teaching and Learning
10) Serving Health Needs
11) Engaging in Religious and Ceremonious Rites
12) Discovering New Knowledge and Techniques
13) Providing Welfare and Philanthropic Aid
14) Creating and Preserving Works of Art

(Extrinsic and Intrinsic)

ety exists for the sake of the individual, it is only to be expected that the individual would be able to participate in or benefit from all functions in any of his roles as producer or consumer or supportive participant. In a similar fashion, Figure 6 shows the business organization with a solid line between it and its primary function and dotted lines running between it and all other functions indicating secondary involvements in those activities. Similar figures could be drawn for all other organizations, individually or collectively, showing their primary and secondary functional connections. The family was chosen because it is the nuclear organization from which all human activity springs. The business organization was chosen because 1) it is the most pervasive and involves all individuals either as producer or consumer; 2) it is perceived by many as a powerful "workhorse" capable of doing more; and 3) it already participates actively and increasingly in most of the other functions.

Although figures 5 and 6 show connecting lines between the family and business organizations to all other functions, not every family or business entity needs to participate actively at each level or activity. The illustrations are meant to suggest that all options are available and that only some families and business firms engage in each of the other functions on a secondary or indirect level and perhaps only tangentially.

How the Family Regularly Participates

The family unit in this representation may consist of an individual living alone or in combination with others of the same or different sexes. If no children are involved, the primary function may be to establish community and share fellowship. When children are involved, the functional connection broadens to include procreation and nurturing. Both are depicted with solid lines.

The family participates in the socializing and acculturating function (a dotted line) by recognizing and honoring the cultural norms of society and by passing them along to any children as the expected behavior of participating and responsible citizens. One or more family members usually has a full-time job for an organization directly engaged in producing products or services for the market since a majority of the labor force are thus employed. All individuals are consumers of the products and services produced by the business organization although not everybody may buy, consume or even know of some of the products or services available.

The family unit or some of its members assist different levels of government in maintaining order first of all by honoring both the spirit and letter of all laws. Additional positive contributions can come in a wide variety of ways: by participating in various neighborhood safety watches, by banding together in sundry clean-up campaigns, by volunteering to serve at local elections, by acting as neighborhood safety patrols at highway intersections for school children, by serving in political campaigns, by voting, by being good neighbors and in a thousand similar ways.

By necessity all of us must participate in some level of communicating and being transported here and there. For use of the facilitating technologies, we pay our utility bills and transport cost. Many now contribute to their favorite interests via the Internet's chat sites. Others may cooperate in local transporting through car-pooling arrangements.

Even workaholics must relax occasionally and seek recreation outlets or risk eventual breakdowns. Some family members offer leadership skills or presence to neighborhood Pop Warner or Babe Ruth leagues. Many maintain active athletic skills in tennis, swimming, hiking, golf, skiing and so forth throughout their lifetimes. Whether active or passive in recreation and playing, most of us follow favorite professional or college athletic teams either in person or via television and the newspapers.

Teaching and learning are lifelong activities for most people on informal levels at least and sometimes formally as well. Much learning is absorbed indirectly through entertainment, at the workplace and through recreational or work-associated travel. Most family members require and/or receive medical attention at various points throughout life. Most today actually begin their official lives in hospitals, receive various shots at young ages, submit to physical examinations periodically for various purposes, and undergo operations and surgical repair when needed. Many individuals in every community voluntarily serve various health-service organizations for companionship, as an expression of compassion or good citizenship. Some family members engage in religious activities on the worshiping level and beyond in fellowship and providing welfare and philanthropic aid to the needy.

How the Family Occasionally Participates

Discovering knowledge new to the world's received fund of documented knowledge is largely restricted to scientists and scholars well advanced in their fields. But many talented individual tinkerers have assembled and patented useful devices by combining various components in new ways. Most families in their lifetimes have directly experienced the need to provide care and welfare to other family members or neighbors not capable of subsisting on their own. The universality of this human condition was less conspicuous in previous centuries when most families lived on farms. Now that this woeful condition has become so painfully visible on our big-city streets, we seem helpless to cope with it under existing laws and freedoms. Nevertheless, many still contribute time and money to food banks and homeless shelters for those wishing to partake.

Not many individuals can claim the fame associated with being the creator of an acknowledged masterpiece in any art form. But many try and do succeed in modest fashion. Many more are successful in the preservation and display of reproduced masterpieces in their homes and offices. Many collections of art works and limited reproductions exist as educational, avocational and vanity supports to their owners. Large industries have grown to service the photographic market that is supported by participation in most homes.

Given the higher levels of material abundance now available to millions of individuals and families today, we have the opportunity to become Renaissance Individuals in the consumption arts if no longer in the skills of production in several fields as was the Renaissance Man of the middle ages. Or as a perceptive psychologist (Allport, p. 194) has written:

> Assuming that the major fields of activity open to all normal people are the economic, the educational, the recreational, the political, the religious, and the domestic, we might assent that a healthy ego should find true participation in all of them. Or allowing one blind spot to the bachelor, the constitutional hater of sports or politics and the agnostic, there is still need for a balanced participation in, say, five fields.

The Indirect Role of Business

What should the business organization do for society beyond delivering its economic product or service at competitive prices? Absolutely nothing, say the Philistinian-oriented businessmen in the following fantasized soliloquy:

> Business is the only organization in society that has to compete vigorously in the marketplace for survival. Government does not protect us or subsidize us at all like they do the schools and hospitals. We have to pay income taxes on hard-earned profit while most of the others are exempt. They even double tax our earnings at the company level and then again at the stockholder level. The bureaucratic red tape we have to put up with can drive you crazy. It's up to all the other organizations in society to do their jobs as well as business does and then government can use its tax income to pick up the pieces or fix what's left. You don't see government having to pick up the pieces for business. We do our jobs or else! We provide steady work for most of the people, pay confiscatory taxes, and then they expect us to help out all the lame ducks in society. Give us a break! Government is just plain greedy and getting worse. Free enterprise is the only way to develop an economically progressive society in the democratic tradition. John Locke and Adam Smith legitimized this concept hundreds of years ago. Leave us alone!

Not so fast, say the more altruistic or perhaps more troublesome Bohemians arguing for a larger contributory role from the business establishment:

Business uses government protection for patents and copyrights and then charges monopolistic prices to make unholy profits to pay scandalous salaries and perks to those in power while it forces its workers to get unionized to squeeze out a living wage. Why should business be allowed so much freedom when it overworks and underpays its workers, irresponsibly indulges its inner circle, and simply screws the rest of us with its redundant and mediocre whiz-bangs and poisonous advertising? The free enterprise, maximum-profit philosophy is an anachronism. Times have changed, large companies stifle competition. Business exists by the permission of society, and its objective goal should be to serve society rather than its own subjective interests. Business uses social capital and should be expected to pay the full social costs for it. We need better balance in society for our undernourished school systems, underfunded welfare programs and old people squeaking by on miserly pensions. Let's share the wealth and not allow all those would-be merchant princes to prance and preen at our expense.

The Shareholder Versus Stakeholder Controversy

Both sides above have their arguments of course and exaggerate them to make points for each side. While we sift through their arguments, let's look around. The United States is not the only country to have embraced some degree of capitalism since World War II. Both Germany and Japan were reorganized somewhat along capitalist lines after that event and Great Britain under Prime Minister Margaret Thatcher initiated the privatization of many of the British industries that had been government owned and directed.

While the operational dynamics in the four cultures have many differences and existing comparative measurements leave much to be desired, a few contrasts are possible. The United States and Great Britain clearly lean more to shareholder capitalism that embraces the first position above, that of maximum profits first for company growth and shareholder benefit. Contributions to other worthwhile social causes will receive secondary consideration. Japan and Germany, on the other hand, tend to implement the stakeholder philosophy that means more balanced consideration to all stakeholders including employees, suppliers, customers, and the community at large. How have their countries fared under these different degrees of capitalism in the past thirty or forty years?

According to *The Economist* magazine (pp. 23–25), stakeholder capitalism experienced higher rates of growth in investment, productivity, research and development, and lower rates of unemployment in the years after World War II until about 1975. However, shareholder capitalism in the United States and Great Britain has closed several of those gaps since and the United States has forged ahead in manufacturing productivity, and especially so until the end of the century with its improving productivity rate compared to Japan's and Germany's domestic problems.

Widely varying special considerations cloud these comparisons. Both Japan and Germany and also Great Britain had substantial economic and infrastructure replacement to make following World War II devastations. The United States entered a boom period also but probably of lesser intensity in housing and manufacturing as all others had to make up for lost production during the war. Companies in both Germany and Japan had retained stronger loyalties to employees while companies in the United States regarded the customer as their chief endowment objective. With both manufacturing and distribution companies competing fiercely at each level and concentrating on quality, service and price to their customers, a substantially superior benefit has accumulated to customers in the United States as demonstrated in the wide assortments of goods and services generally available to them at competitive prices.

Evidence from Germany and Japan (*The Economist*, p. 25) suggests that the concept of lifetime or career employment in larger companies in those countries has been diluted or transferred downward to "core" employees only in order to give their managements more flexibility in adapting to the always fickle ebbs and flows of supply and demand in the marketplace. Fierce rivalry in international markets has caused the pendulum of competition to swing toward the shareholder interpretation.

The Evolving Social Responsibility of the Business Organization

In none of these leading industrialized countries was there an explicit formula or statement specifying what, where, or how much of a company's profit, sales or investment should go to serving social needs beyond the master function 4: Producing, Distributing and Consuming Goods and Services. Indeed, the phrase, "social responsibility" has defied consensus definition with quantitative parameters. Generally, it means behavior that leads to socially constructive results.

As a practical matter, it means whatever its supporters or detractors want it to mean depending on the argumentative context. A company need only operate in a legal manner obeying all the relevant laws while appropriately recognizing the strong customs and expectations of its culture. "Appropriate" may be stretched or shrunk to fit one's perception of current needs. This places a large responsibility on the company leadership to identify and implement that degree of social responsibility deemed most beneficial to both company and the society being served. In the United States the larger companies with longer histories, deeper resources and more assured futures are those most affected. Newer and smaller companies, say those with assets below a hundred million dollars or sales below a billion dollars, are little affected if at all and can rely on direct selling efforts and perhaps a little advertising to lead their marketing efforts.

The Entry of Public Relations As a Marketing Sales Tool

When any business organization first commences operations, its owners work long and hard to make sure that sales income exceeds all costs of maintaining and operating the business, whether it be in manufacturing, retailing or other service enterprise. The failure rate for new ventures has always been high and only a small percentage succeeds in the first generation to grow beyond its founding family. With years of continued success, these may become sizable corporations with lives in potential perpetuity and its leadership assumed by successive career managers increasingly unrelated to the founders. That first successful originating thrust was usually a single-minded focus on doing whatever was necessary to make a profit. This meant watching every penny, practicing conservation in every direction, working long hours, and certainly not giving money or goods away "willy nilly" to nonbusiness causes.

While the early days of each industry in the 1800s varied as the Industrial Revolution advanced, doing whatever it took to be successful meant taking large risks and capitalizing on every opportunity that presented itself or could be engineered by fair means or foul. In every group of operators from the laboring level to managers to professionals of all descriptions, there is always a small percentage of capable but more opportunistic and ruthless individuals. Some of these more reckless adventurers at the entrepreneurial level succeeded hugely when the stakes were high and the public's guard was down. There was rapid growth in certain industries such as the railroads, lumber, oil, banking, retailing, mining and others for the able and aggressively bold. Being in the right place at the right time with the right readiness to succeed resulted in quick fortunes for a few. Ethics were situational and coverups were perhaps more easily possible then than now.

The "Robber Baron" Era

But not all exploitations or coverups escaped public notice for long. Moral outrage was ignited later when a few journalists recounted some of the more questionable tactics and exploits of such as John D. Rockefeller, Jay Gould, Cornelius Vanderbilt, James Fisk and others. The term "robber barons" was successfully applied as an unsavory polarizing or demonizing device. Being placed on the defensive may have encouraged a few of these successful tycoons and their compatriots to consider public opinion more carefully.

One of the first successful books on this subject published *in 1923* was titled *Crystallizing Public Opinion* by Edward L. Bernays. He headed an organization trying to do just that for corporate clients who had become a bit more apprehensive. And gradually thereafter the subject came to receive more attention at top management levels as the press became more pervasive and influential. Public opinion and the press had to be managed or at least reckoned with. Thus gradually the concept of social responsibility came to confront that of social antagonism and move the collective business attitude more toward social indifference in the middle of the spectrum.

The Growth of Public Relations to Counter the "Honey-Combed Deception"

The means to influence public opinion soon came to be called public relations that was defined broadly as "a planned program of nonadvertising communication to influence understanding, acceptance, and cooperation by persons outside the managerial group" (*Marketing Handbook*, p. 19.1). Since the influencee is more readily persuaded to accept the positions of the influencer when credible good faith has been established and when the suitable *quid pro quo* is involved, the practice of more sophisticated public relations soon became well established, especially among the larger, more politically oriented companies. Not-so-sophisticated practices have always been with us under such names as "payola," "greasing the palm," "baksheesh" and "consideration lures" among others.

We need not be so squeamish about this practice or its seemingly backdoor entry into the marketplace in the United States. Reciprocity goes by a wide variety of names in other cultures where it is far more easily accepted. Perhaps there was something noble in the moral and largely religious posturing of our European predecessors who desired to establish a new society in the United States free from the excessive self-interest that had permeated the leaderships of the countries from which they came. Nevertheless, the reluctance to accept this reality has become a major stumbling block for American business firms in dealing with their foreign counterparts in many countries where commercial exchanges combined with leadership payoffs are routine.

The "Darker Side" of Man's Nature and Its Expression

There have been at least three major forces in human cultures that leaders throughout history have always resorted to when confronted with unwanted opposition: 1) sheer physical power to overcome the opponent; 2) deceptive trickery; and 3) clever combinations of both. Our collective distaste for these realities led us in the early years of our nationhood to accept the first reluctantly as an inevitable means to become free but to reject the second as somehow unworthy, somehow undignified in the equation of equality for all. We are still uncomfortable with the universality of deception as an innate human characteristic but it is still with us in many disguised and not-so-hidden forms. It has been the persistence of this characteristic combined with a perceived excessive interest in profit seeking that has led many scholars (and the hidden moralist in most of us) to castigate or malign the business institution in spite of its successes in delivering unparalleled standards of living to Americans. For example, the thinking in the following quotation written in 1895 (Ward, pp. 83–84) still surrounds and limits pride in the businessman's accomplishments:

> The law of mind as it operates in society as an aid to competition and in the interest of the individual is essentially immoral. It rests primarily on the principle of deception. It is an extension to other human beings of the method applied to the animal world by which the latter was subjected to man. This method was that of the ambush and the snare. Its ruling principle was cunning. Its object was to deceive, circumvent, ensnare, and capture. Low animal cunning was succeeded by more refined kinds of cunning. The more important of these go by the names of business shrewdness, strategy, and diplomacy, none of which differ from ordinary cunning in anything but the degree of adroitness by which the victim is outwitted. In this way social life is completely honeycombed with deception.

But man because of his perversity has always had to live with ambiguities, contradictions, and double or multiple standards that had to be confronted and dealt with. The business organization faces perhaps more of these than most other types of organizations. In the pursuit of growth most company managements must give serious consideration to any concept capable of increasing the sale of its products or services or otherwise enhancing its future prospects. Therefore, it was only a matter of time until a few duplicitous managers experimented with the notion of a "dubious little social investment" here and there to see if any favorable result might follow.

Successful results would mean that the scale and frequency of such tactics would probably increase and spread throughout an industry by copiers trying to "level the playing field." The control of these transgressions lies with government agencies under its mandate to maintain an orderly and equitable environment. A vigilant press provides watchdog oversight and negative public relations for those transgressors regularly featured. While business as an institution bears the brunt of this kind of immoral behavior, all other institutions share in the embarrassment when its leaders also engage in questionable conduct. Unfortunately in recent years, this spotlight has been turned on the highest offices in government, education, religion and should be a matter of grave concern to all responsible and law-abiding citizens.

Partners in Commercial Corruption

The beneficiaries of commercial bribery are often government officials passing judgment on the conditions and terms of international imports and exports. Built into these judgments too often are individuals stationed at interception points who have traditionally balanced their discretion with unearned emoluments under many headings. These bribes or *nuetzliche Ausgaben*, "useful expenditures" in German, have been institutionalized in so many countries in the world that they are very difficult to eliminate.

There is an organization founded in 1993 by a former director of the World Bank, Peter Eigen, however, which is applying visibility pressure to reduce the size of the problem. Called Transparency International and operating out of Berlin, Eigen has established branches in many countries to work on minimizing the corruption that harms economic development in poorer countries. So entrenched is the bribery duplicity that only a third of the 27 member-governments in the OECD committee forbid outright domestic tax deduction for foreign bribes paid by their nationals. Permitting such bribes to be counted for tax deduction purposes as legitimate expenses of doing business (as of October 1996) are Belgium, Luxembourg, France, Sweden, Greece and Germany. Not permitting this practice are the United States, Canada, Britain and Japan.

For comparative purposes, corruption rankings in 1996 for fifty-four countries based on the level of corruption in a country as perceived by employees of multinational firms and institutions listed Nigeria, Pakistan, Kenya, Bangladesh and China in that order as the worst in this regard and New Zealand, Denmark, Sweden, Finland and Canada in that order as the cleanest. New Zealand's rank was fifty-four while the United States was ranked forty (*The Wall Street Journal*, p. 6). Clearly, international commerce has a long way to go in providing that "level playing field" for its players.

Current Status on the Social Responsibility of Business

When compared to the social participation of business organizations in the societies of Germany, Japan and Great Britain, we can now speculate that business organizations in the United States started at a lower level of social involvement. Our government had established no level of extra-social participation contrary to practices in other countries where permission to practice in any field had been originally laced with onerous conditions mandated by a king, duke or emperor to take popular pressures away from the ruling head of state.

Involvement by the larger business organizations in the non-business functions of society since World War II has been substantial but little noticed. It was only in the middle of the Great Depression of the 1930s that the Internal Revenue Service allowed a charitable deduction for corporate gifts. The timing was poor as most business organizations were struggling to stay solvent. The business contributions to the World War II effort have been well documented. Its quick adaptation to turning out the necessary armaments for the military was a primary factor in winning the war.

Then in 1982 more changes in the tax law increased the charitable deduction of corporations from 5 to 10 percent of net income. With the advent of these incentives to participate, the larger business corporations headed by leaderships with higher levels of social awareness started to get involved. Direct corporate giving or company contribution programs that are administered within the corporation must be distinguished from company-sponsored foundations. Direct-giving programs are based solely on corporate funds and tend to rise and fall with corporate profits. Company-sponsored foundation contributions may not be as subject to the ups and downs of industry profit cycles. In years of large profits, some corporations may use their foundations to set aside funds that can be used to support their charitable giving programs in years when corporate income is lower.

A private foundation has been defined as "...a nongovernmental, nonprofit organization, with its own funds and program managed by its own trustees and directors, that was established to maintain or aid educational, social, charitable, religious or other activities serving the common welfare primarily by making grants to other nonprofit organizations" (*Corporate Foundation Profiles,* 1994).

According to figures supplied by the American Association of Fund Raising counsel, private foundations, corporations, individuals, charitable organizations and agencies gave an estimated 129.88 billion dollars in 1994, an increase of 3.6 percent over 1993. Of the total, corporations contributed 6.11 billion or 4.7 percent of all philanthropy in 1994. But corporate giving has been relatively flat at around the $6 billion level since 1989. According to this same source (*Annual Register of Grant Support: A Directory of Funding Sources*, 1996, p.vii), there are more than 35,000 grant-making foundations in the United States, 1,800 being company-sponsored foundations.

Uncle Sam Needs a Santa Claus

Whether the above information suggests a good, mediocre or poor performance by the business community in recognizing its social responsibility depends on one's personal orientation and expectations as to what system of social funding is preferable. No consensus is apparent at this time but it does appear that the size and rates of increase in overall social spending have become national issues commanding center-stage attention. Political rhetoric centering on the unhealthy size of the national debt suggests that recent social welfare, educational, Medicare, social security and other programs are unbalanced between benefits extended, corrective improvements made, and costs incurred and deferred to future generations. Implicit in the debate is the notion that Uncle Sam would appreciate some help from Santa Claus.

If and when the community at large or its political leadership decides that the business community should play a bigger role, it will mean that its larger contributions must be shared by some combination of stockholder and consumer sacrifice or by either alone. Will the people prefer to let the government through tax collections dominate the direction of social funding or will they prefer to delegate a bigger portion to the larger business organizations through its direct and foundation support or will they prefer to allow the present multiple sourcing system to continue? Unfortunately, the existing system permits national yearly deficits to accumulate and gives Congress the right to raise the debt ceiling at will, thus postponing the day of reckoning. While the ratio of national debt to gross domestic product is less than in some other countries, the cost of yearly interest on the debt is an embarrassment on several fronts and distorts the American economic profile severely. The requisite foundation accounting and information services are now in place and the data are available yearly to reflect any changes that may occur.

Current Business Popularity Criteria

The collective and current sentiment among leaders in the business community does not appear to rank community and environmental responsibility as a top criterion in identifying the most respected corporations in the nation. Indeed, in the 14th annual corporate survey conducted by *Fortune* magazine, more than eleven thousand executives including outside directors and financial analysts were asked to rate on a scale of zero to ten the ten largest companies by revenue in their respective industries according to eight criteria. The respondents were also asked to rank the criteria involved. From most important to least important, they collectively selected 1) quality of management; 2) quality of product or service; 3) ability to attract, develop, and keep talented people; 4) value as a long-term investment; 5) use of corporate assets; 6) financial soundness; 7) innovativeness; 8) community and environmental responsibility (Fisher, pp. 90–98).

The corporate names receiving the highest scores were mostly the larger leaders dominating each industry, such as Coca-Cola, Procter and Gamble, Rubbermaid, Johnson and Johnson, Intel, Merck, Microsoft, Mirage Resorts, Hewlett-Packard and Motorola. Considerable volatility is possible as evidenced by Merck's rise from twenty-four the previous year when the whole medical industry was under political siege. Prior to 1994, Merck had been rated number one for seven consecutive years, a remarkable feat. The same volatility presumably could alter the perceived value of the eight judging criteria if the issue of social responsibility rises in national importance and receives commensurate media coverage. Perhaps in time the three airlines rated among the least popular can rise in the rankings if that turbulent industry can get its difficult act together.

Popularity contests such as the *Fortune* survey have both short-run and long-run implications. In the short run they may suggest that the popular or winning companies are being managed well according to the currently dominant characteristics. For top-level ratings in the long run, however, company managements might need to be well regarded in each of the eight measures. Balance in the long run would mitigate against the fads and fashions of current popularity. The three companies rating highest in the community and environmental responsibility criterion in the 1996 survey were Levi Strauss, Johnson and Johnson and Minnesota Mining and Manufacturing. Of these, only Johnson and Johnson rated in the top ten overall for 1996.

Some Illustrations of Company Social Responsibility in Action

The implicit but unwritten policy in the United States concerning social responsibility seems to be to encourage volunteerism among its citizenry and organizational entities to give all they (comfortably) can to social causes of their choice and then let government and the general tax base take care of any problems that remain. Whenever either political party suggests the possibility of cutting personal income tax rates (a popular vote-getting strategy), moral suasion rises rapidly (along with blind faith and hope) to increase charitable donations to make up for potential decreases in tax income. Nobody denies that continuity in support is vital to all social, nonprofit agencies, but most of us are emotionally removed from their day-to-day struggles and fail to sense their angst.

Given this rationale, individuals and organizational contributions will normally be directed to those agencies most preferred or to those most capable of making a reciprocal or return contribution back to the giver. Most corporate contributions are made to agencies closely related to corporate activities or in communities where the parent company or its subsidiaries operate. Most managements are more receptive to social spending when they can see reciprocal benefits in which both giver and taker benefit, or "win-win" relationships.

Thus, the Merck Company Foundation representing that large pharmaceutical company is reported to have:

> ...Long directed its efforts to the enhancement of education in medicine and science at the college and university level. These efforts are effective, but it must be recognized that a majority of students are ill-prepared and uninterested in the sciences before they reach college. Indeed, the decline of education in science in U.S. schools threatens the quality and quantity of research-based innovation on which the American standard of living and way of life depend. Therefore, the Foundation is now making a limited number of grants aimed at stimulating an interest in science at the elementary and secondary level. Another important goal of our contributions program is to continue to support health and social services and civic and cultural activities in the communities where we operate. This helps ensure that our towns and cities can continue to offer employees and neighbors an environment with opportunities for a full and productive life *(Corporate Giving Directory,* p. 493).

The Dayton-Hudson Company based in Minneapolis–St. Paul, Minnesota, has been a leader in the establishment and growth of companies that give 5 percent of their pretax profits for community betterment. As of 1985 there were seventy-one corporate members of the Five Percent Club in the Minneapolis–St. Paul area and sixty-four corporate members in the Baltimore area; in addition there were 107 members of the Two Percent Club in the Kansas City area, fifty in the San Francisco area, and 145 in the Seattle area (Lydenberg, p. 21).

Community-Action Programs

Business groups have launched a wide variety of innovative involvements in the broader community since World War II. Many, such as General Mills and Clorox, have encouraged with strong incentives their employees to become actively involved in community affairs. Many businesses in every community in the nation have become involved with

Junior Achievement programs in high schools where students can gain actual experience in setting up and operating their own businesses under the direction of corporate executives who provide leadership and direction.

Responding to sharper national scrutiny, most businesses have improved their employment ratios for women and minorities. Most cooperate actively with community leaders and local and state chambers of commerce in supporting yearly United Fund crusades, countless community fund-raising drives to support youth clubs, assorted ethnic holidays, church-related soup kitchens, blood drives, local arts programs such as the symphony, opera, theater and assorted fund-raising activities for local causes deemed worthwhile. Many businesses offer to match their employee gifts to charities and continuing education programs on a one-to-one basis, and in some cases, on a two-to-one basis.

Most corporate foundation support is aimed at generating progress through research in science and medicine, in a wide variety of educational initiatives including teaching and research scholarships, capital building grants, awards to needy and worthy students and teachers, and to cultivating appreciation of the various art forms.

Passive Giving Versus Giving With Concerned Follow-Up

A recent Conference Board study surveying 463 companies in the United States found that companies taking a more businesslike approach to charity reported better results from their investments in a better public image, increased employee loyalty and improved business ties. More companies are providing free equipment with hands-on follow-up if needed. Monitoring results through feedback reports, on-the-job counseling and diverse follow-up techniques can result in what the Conference Board calls "strategic philanthropy" or "financially sound goodwill" ("Giving and Getting Something Back," p. 81). Just giving grants of money alone without accompanying or follow-up attention does not work as well. The desire for effectiveness in philanthropic giving may be emerging as an encouraging improvement to the total system.

Whether or Not Competition Is Male and Cooperation Female, Both Are Needed

Analysis beyond the few illustrations identified here and in the previous chapter will reveal that the business organization, and especially the largest two or three thousand business organizations, have made substantial contributions to every master function shown in Figure 2. With the Maccordion configuration in mind, the large amounts of an individual's time spent with television, newspapers, magazines and now the Internet can become an instructive daily lesson in how beautifully society operates with innovative illustrations daily of how all major organizations contribute to public welfare beyond their primary functions. Most of this has been accomplished without strong persuasion from either the federal government or the public at large. More attention to these innovative cross-purposed initiatives by the press and media and less to the usual emphases on crime, sex and violence would be major improvements in themselves.

To end this section on a positive note, if the business organizations were to receive a significant challenge to increase their involvement in the other functions of society, the results could well be spectacular. Whether called on to perform more or not, it's a comforting thought to know that large sources of reserve strength are available.

REFERENCES

Allport, Gordon W., *Personality and Social Encounter* (Boston, Massachusetts: The Beacon Press, 1960). Reprinted by permission of Beacon Press, Boston.

Annual Register of Grant Support: A Directory of Funding Sources, 29th Edition (New Providence, New Jersey: R.R. Bowker, 1996).

Bernays, Edward L., *Crystallizing Public Opinion* (New York: Boni and Liveright, 1923).

"Capitalism/Stakeholder Capitalism: Effect of Economic Productivity" (*The Economist*, February 10, 1996).

Corporate Foundation Profiles, 8th Edition. Editor: Francine Jones (New York: The Foundation Center, 1994.)

Corporate Giving Directory, 13th Edition. Editor: Susan E. Elnicki (Rockville, Maryland: The Taft Group, 1992).

Fisher, Anne B., "Corporate Reputations" (*Fortune*, March 18, 1996, pp. 90–98). Reprinted with permission of Time, Inc.

Lydenberg, Steven D., Alice Tepper Marlin, Sean O'Brien Strub, and the Council on Economic Priorities, *Rating America's Corporate Conscience* (New York: Addison-Wesley Publishing Company, 1986).

Marketing Handbook (New York: The Ronald Press Company, 1965).

"Review and Outlook: Commercial Corruption" (*The Wall Street Journal*, January 2, 1997, p. 6).

Schwartz, Nelson and Tim Smart, "Giving and Getting Something Back" (*Business Week*, August 28, 1995, p. 81).

Ward, L. F., "The Psychologic Basis of Social Economics," *Annals of the American Academy*, Volume III (Philadelphia: American Academy of Political and Social Science, 1895).

CHAPTER 12

The Important and Pervasive Role of Competition

Competition has been viewed variously as a capitalist renegade, an elusive abstraction, a necessary reality, a faulty hypothesis, a tool of the devil, a fiction by more socialized states and a fantasy of the courts. It may be all of these and more. Let us briefly examine whether or not and how it affects each of the fourteen master functions.

Competition in the Procreating and Nurturing Functions

Competition in the mating game plays an important part even before procreating activity or the birth of children. Both young men and women very early develop better-than-life versions of their idealized mates. The 36-20-35 silhouette of young women and the "hunk" characteristics of young men are quite clear to today's youth by virtue of endless profiling in the movies and mass media. Classified "relationships" advertising today succinctly state the desired mating specifications sought by the person placing the advertisement. More discreet and higher-priced mating services are provided by computer matching, taped interviewing and even genetic analyses.

Before most women entered the work force around 1960, competition among some groups of high-school girls was keen to see who would be the first married. Even today among some more independent male groups there is competition to win the race by being the last corralled. No doubt competition was a driving factor in population growth as couples contested for the most children, the most males, the most help on the farm. Perhaps it even affected the no contraceptive doctrine of some religions in their competitions to grow bigger. Even some countries attempt to attract "desirable" immigrants with favorable characteristics from other countries to stabilize or grow their economies or societies faster or in different directions.

For the nurturing of youth function, competition emerges in the early awareness by children that they are frequently compared to others in their age group. The response that pleases parents most is for them to win the comparisons, to run faster, to smile more cutely or do whatever it takes to make those important adults appreciate you, love you, cuddle you, spoil you. Then there is the famous notion of sibling rivalry amongst youth in the sharing of toys and seeking of parental attention. All of this before entering school and competing thereafter against classmates in the classroom, at recess time and on the playing fields.

Competition in Providing Community and Fellowship

The United States was remarkable from its beginning with a high degree of cultural diversity. All of the organizational types shown in Figure 3, column 2, both competed and cooperated actively in making new arrivals from wherever feel welcome. Affiliationism was the theme used to create bonds among the diverse values, traditions and customs, religious preferences, food preparations and taboos, languages and racial distinctions of the great majority of economically poor and otherwise harassed immigrants. The need to affiliate with those sharing common old-world characteristics was initially strong as the likelihood of assimilating harmoniously or quickly with suspicious looking strangers was small, even though they might be geographic neighbors. Thus, small groups of Swedes or Czechs who settled in Minnesota or Wisconsin were anxious to share experiences with kinfolk or fellow countrymen located elsewhere in the vast United States and also with those left behind in the old countries.

The church was a central unifying instrument in bringing together those with similar faiths. Many ethnic- and nationality-oriented organizations sprang up to help service the fears and aspirations of ethnic minorities all over the country. Newsletters, bulletins and newspapers to do this became common. A wide variety of voluntary and self-help cooperatives and associations sprang up to help the newcomers adjust. Community leaders such as a grocer or saloon keeper or priest frequently served as useful go-betweens in locating jobs and housing for the new arrivals. Their headquarters also served as central meeting places for a wide variety of other cooperative efforts. Mutual-aid societies were founded to aid families through crises such as sickness, accidents and death. Building and loan societies blossomed for many ethnic groups. Low-cost boarding houses were common.

Regional ethnic associations developed in the competitive efforts to preserve old-world loyalties against the growing affection for the new homeland. Voluntary associations grew among professional doctors, lawyers, dentists and teachers with similar ethnic backgrounds. Labor union affiliations grew with initially strong ethnic orientations.

In all of these efforts cooperation was more important than competition until the self-help organizations began overlapping and then modest forms of competition took over for membership support. By the third generation most immigrant families have become reasonably well assimilated or homogenized into the American melting pot and the role of the voluntary associations declined.

Community and Fellowship Today

Immigration continues, of course, and the newcomers' needs continue to be serviced by the usual family connections, church affiliations, fraternal, ethnic and nationality organizations and by those agencies of government, business, education and health that are organized to do so, either for profit or service.

For the well-assimilated great majority, however, the emphasis has evolved gradually from face-to-face socializing at church events, family dinners and reunions, social club meetings, school benefits and other small-town gatherings to somewhat more passive or indirect activities centered first on movie entertainment and now television in the home. Spectator sports and popular music festivals can command large audiences. Browsing on the Internet and communicating directly but no longer face-to-face have become the newest socializing fads. It has the potential to bring together for fast interaction thousands of widely separated people all focused on single topics. With or without personal computer partnerships, these more passive forms of socializing promise to change our lifestyles significantly. Competition is already fierce among Internet suppliers, Web sites and content providers all scrambling for preferred locations and exposure.

Socializing and Acculturating

A number of well-regarded social analysts such as Erik Erikson, Hans Kohn and Thomas C. Hartshorn among others have discussed in depth the potential and reality of an American identity crisis born out of the tens of millions of immigrants coming into the United States and experiencing the emigration, immigration and then Americanization syndrome. What is an American? What might the distillation of the widest range of human characteristics ever assembled produce in its evolving synthesis? Would the more harmonious and positive elements dominate or would the nasty and negative characteristics fuse into a discordant future?

Clearly, the tasks of integrating such a diverse population into a workable unity was a major challenge to the framers of the Constitution. As discussed previously, they did an admirable job by sticking to basics and minimizing the role of government. According to one noted scholar on the subject (Gleason, p. 31), "The United States defined itself as a nation by commitment to the principles of liberty, equality, and government on the basis of consent, and the nationality of its people derived from their identification with those principles."

Strongly supporting the eventual success of this simple but brilliant collective insight was the great abundance of opportunity to grow in any direction, to become, to move westward and discover or develop your destiny. The clear presence of growth opportunities for the able and aggressive and their quick successes fed the strengthening of a more open futuristic orientation as opposed to a regressive or backward orientation and more closed and bickering attitude.

Children continued to be reared according to the traditional family values brought over from the old country as their parents embraced new opportunities. But then the children were put in school and assimilation began in earnest. Both on the playground before and after school and in the classroom, socialization took place and the effects were taken home to influence others. In classrooms in 1892 and thereafter all students began the day with a recitation of the *Pledge of Allegiance to the United States of America*, or the singing of a patriotic song. Students were taught the basic tenets of the U.S. Constitution, the history of the United States and often that of their home states. The natural surge of competition and youthful enthusiasm in their extracurricular events usually induced group, school, town and state loyalties.

Acculturation as socialization for adults is accomplished mainly by living in the United States and partaking of its benefits. To become a citizen requires good moral character, the abilities to read, write and speak the English language and pass a test demonstrating a basic understanding of U.S. history and government.

The Role of Competition in Producing, Distributing and Consuming Goods and Services

As succinctly conceptualized by (Hamilton, p. 142), the evolved competitive structure in the United States

> consists of two pairs of institutions: private property and contract; profit making and freedom of trade. The usages of private property determine who is to hold and to control the various resources of society; the usages of contract, how persons, instruments and materials are to be brought together in the productive process. Together property and contract supply the mechanics of

competition. The lure of profit draws individuals and corporations into industry and impels them to produce and market goods. The openness of an industry to all who care to take its chances prevents monopoly and limits money making to reasonable gains. The bait of profit is beacon and guide; the freedom of trade is brake and governor. Together they direct industry, keep it orderly and adjust it to a changing social order.

Aye, the bait of profit. That is what motivates such a vigorous display of energy in the daily discharge of millions of commercial transactions at all levels, each carefully consummated to the last penny. The prices of most goods change daily in reaction to the myriad of supply and demand factors worldwide. At each operational level in the tens of thousands of businesses functioning daily, concerned managers are diligently micro-managing their enterprises with the latest in electronic-data information systems so that today's sales and other measures will at least equal or exceed that same day a year earlier. Other frames might be weekly, monthly, seasonal or three-year and five-year moving averages of individual organization or industry-wide sales or production measures.

The "Creative Destruction" of the Successful Entrepreneur

One of the still unsung benefits of a relatively free society is a higher level of entrepreneurial innovation and initiative that affects all of the functions variously but is especially prevalent in the production and distribution of the wide variety of goods and services composing our scales and styles of living. Economist Joseph A. Schumpeter (pp. 217–223) acknowledged the earlier (mid-1700s) recognition of the entrepreneur by Irish-French economist Richard Cantillon who "...had a clear conception of the function of the entrepreneur...with particular care for the case of the farmer." In his *Theory of Economic Development*, Schumpeter was among the first to appreciate and credit the entrepreneur as a major deterrent to Marx's insistence that the controlling heavy-hand of the bourgeoisie class would eventually force the working proletarian class into a revolution that would overthrow the ruling bourgeoisie. Schumpeter viewed the entrepreneur and the introduction of his newer concepts into the marketplace as instruments of "creative destruction" by which he meant that capitalism contained forces that incessantly revolutionize the economic structure from within, modifying the previous structure and evolving new combinations of competition and cooperation. Of course, this "incessant" influence operates unevenly thus leaving time and space for occasional strongholds of economic power to control for a time.

That Old Devil Monopoly

The concentration of power in the production or sales of any necessary consumption item can lead to monopolistic control and price fixing at noncompetitive levels and unreasonable gains for those so cornering the market. To oversee and moderate this possibility in the public interest, the United States government formed watchdog patrols called the Antitrust Division within the Department of Justice and the Federal Trade Commission. Their very presence has had a positive salutary effect on maintaining meaningful competition even though they are regularly criticized in the political press for over-managing here and under-managing there. That they have managed to avoid front-page condemnation since World War II attests to their effectiveness overall.

Efforts to stifle or eliminate competition are rarely completely successful despite the many attempts to do so. From conditions of pure competition (as when farmers merely dumped their crops on the market at the prevailing price), various industries have at one time or another been subject to competition in the forms of price, quality of goods or services, extent and effectiveness of support services, research and development contributing to product innovations, advertising, salesmanship and merchandising. When competition appears to be neutralized in one form, it breaks out in another. The American consumer is the beneficiary of this cycling and recycling of competition as the American marketplace presents the widest assortment of goods and services to be found anywhere in the world. And at relatively low prices.

The twenty-first century will see the accelerating spread of American know-how and innovative resourcefulness to those receptive countries genuinely interested in improving the welfare of their citizens. Countless joint commercial ventures, partnerships and trading agreements are already in place following that American corporate leadership that was earned in the trenches of competitive rivalry. Heartening results are already evident in China and the Far East as well as in South America and Central Europe.

That Old Devil Government

In different ways, perhaps, but with the same stifling effects produced by monopoly control, excessive government control can limit a country's freedom to exercise competitive advantages and gain economic benefits for its people. This was persuasively documented recently on release of the *1997 Index of Economic Freedom*, a comprehensive guide to growth in 150 countries from Albania to Zimbabwe. Published for two years by the libertarian Heritage Foundation, it was joined by *The Wall Street Journal* in publishing this third edition the purpose of which is to track international progress toward freer economies. To do this, ten key areas are evaluated: trade policy, taxation, government intervention, monetary policy, capital flows and foreign investment, banking policy, wage and price controls, property rights, regulation and black market activity. In each of these areas, more than fifty independent economic criteria were used to develop a snapshot of the level of economic freedom in each country.

Several key findings emerged:
1. Countries with the highest levels of economic freedom also have the highest living standards.
2. Countries with the lowest levels of economic freedom also have the lowest living standards.
3. As countries become more affluent, they tend to add extensive welfare and other social programs that were considered not affordable previously, Germany and France being notable examples thus impeding growth and depressing living standards.
4. Though the Index did not measure political freedom, its editors think there is a crucial link between it and economic freedom and that it's no accident that the world's biggest offenders of human rights show up near the bottom of the Index of Economic Freedom.

Ranking as most free in descending order were Hong Kong, Singapore, Bahrain, New Zealand, Switzerland and the United States (tied), the United Kingdom and Taiwan. Ranking as most oppressed in descending order were Cuba, Laos and North Korea (tied for worst), Iraq, and then Iran, Libya, Somalia and Vietnam all tied at third from the bottom. The results of serious studies such as this if published yearly and distributed widely may in time penetrate into those countries most oppressed and work to diminish the role of dictators and excessive government.

The Role of Competition in Providing an Orderly and Equitable Environment

As stated in the *Preamble* of the U.S. Constitution:
We the people of the United States in Order to form a more perfect Union, establish Justice, insure Domestic Tranquillity, provide for the common defense, promote the general Welfare, and secure the Blessings of Liberty to ourselves and our Posterity, do ordain and establish this Constitution for the United States of America.

To secure the Blessings of Liberty means that responsible freedom can be permitted to operate freely but that acts of irresponsible freedom must be controlled. Partly because of some men's innate aggressiveness and both planned and opportunistic tendencies to capitalize personally to the maximum on every perceived opportunity, this apparently benign role of government to maintain both orderly and equitable order has mushroomed beyond belief to the point where in 1992 over three million people were employed by the federal government plus another 1.6 million in the active and reserve military plus additional millions at the state, county and local levels (*Statistical Abstract of the United States*, pp. 346–358). Obviously, opportunity and growth have large social costs in a relatively free but vigorously competitive environment.

While many complain about the size of government, its intrusion into private lives and especially about the confusion of partially overlapping and conflicting laws in various domains, it should be remembered that no new law goes on the books without ample evidence of specific abuse followed by vigorous debate. Nevertheless, any system can get overloaded in time. Perhaps we should now reconsider the old Principle of Orderliness wherein for each new law enacted, an obsolete one must be discarded?

Competition in Providing Communicating and Transporting Service

Partly nationalized and partly privatized in various ways because of the huge capital investment outlays needed and the potential for overlapping waste in resources thereby, the competition displayed in various branches of these quite diverse industries varies widely but still requires continual monitoring by government and industry watchdogs.

The contemporary swing between competition and near monopoly in the communications industry has favored increasing competition in recent years. First, the federal courts broke up the long-distance telephone monopoly held by American Telephone and Telegraph Company in 1984. After years of negotiation and bickering among lobbyists, lawyers and regulators, the federal government in 1996 passed a law that will allow open competition between AT&T, Sprint, MCI and the seven former regional monopolies served by the "Baby Bells."

Another ten or twenty years might see a substantial revision of the telephone industry as mergers and new liaisons are being formed in all directions to capitalize on these new opportunities. Increasingly also, other countries are being served by joint-venture partnerships of the leading companies including besides the older telephone companies, cellular wireless operators and such cable-television network names as TIC, Compacts, Ox and Time-Warner.

The arrival of the World Wide Web on the Internet dealt a severe blow to such proprietary network stars as General Electric's Genie, AT&T's Interchange, News Corp's Delphi, Apple's EWorld and the IBM–Sears Roebuck's Prodigy, which initiated the online boom in the early 1980s. Opportunity to profit hugely and grow internationally now creates an exciting future for the whole communications industry and the high-tech electronic supporting companies.

Competition remains vigorous also among the major entities in transportation with only the railroads giving up on the passenger market and forcing the federal government into subsidizing the Amtrac extension. The airline passenger market remains one of the most competitive with staggering industry losses during the decade of the 1980s despite near-record-setting passenger-miles flown yearly.

The economics and politics of subsidized urban public transportation continue to plague most metropolitan areas as the very high capital investment involved prohibits meaningful competition. America's continuing love affair with the automobile complicates the urban transportation scene creating another modern dilemma. Sooner or later it is likely that automobile access to the downtown urban centers of most major cities will have to be sharply restricted.

Competition Where It Is Keenest

In none of the master functions is the spirit of competition more evident than in competitive sports at both amateur and professional levels. A subclassification under the general title of "playing and recreation," it is perhaps as important today is it was in the gladiator days of Greece and Rome. No longer do we watch duels to the death of the least-adept gladiator or watch human sacrifices mauled and tortured before being devoured by animals. Nevertheless, the animation and partisanship demonstrated in schoolyard games to major playoff competitions in football, basketball, baseball, hockey, golf and tennis in the United States must rival their ancient predecessors in the coliseums. Similar enthusiasm is shown in other countries for their most popular athletic contests. The revival of the international Olympics is now a featured world-class series of events.

A major reason why audience participation at sporting events is so attractive to so many is that it stimulates the emotional component of our personalities and provides the excitement that allows emotion to dominate the rational mindset for a few hours. Both early parental and school discipline worked for over a decade on most of us to encourage rational expression to dominate our emotional selves. But at a sporting event we can reverse the pattern and allow our emotions to vent fully. As suggested in an earlier chapter, this exchange of outlook and attitude provides a kind of needed perspective or change of pace to relieve the monotony of remaining in one mood-mode too long. What is emotion?

> According to biologist E. O. Wilson (pp. 112–113), emotion
> ...is the modification of neural activity that animates and focuses mental activity. It is created by physiological activity that selects certain streams of information over others, shifting the

body and mind to higher or lower degrees of activity, agitating the circuits that create scenarios, and selecting ones that end in certain ways. The winning scenarios are those that match goals preprogrammed by instinct and the satisfactions of prior experience.

Another reason competitive sports are so compelling lies in their being a miniaturized model of life itself. Unlike the set scenarios of a drama, opera or movie, the plot is open-ended and the conclusion is only revealed as the game and season progress. Correspondingly, the action is compressed into several hours or months each year unlike the long, drawn-out dramas of real life. The interest of the more loyal fans increases as the three- or four-month season progresses and reaches a fever pitch just before a champion is crowned. And then come the playoffs between champions in rival leagues. These can attract the attention of the less devoted partisans, the leadership element from most of the other institutional organizations, the political and even the religious elite. Jammed stadium attendances are assured. The prices climb. Scalpers go to work. The press gets excited. Television stations bid outrageous sums for the privilege of monopolizing coverage.

Finally the Super Game Day approaches. The players are the best (and in our secret dreams they may be acting out our fantasies or those of our heroes). They can be counted on to go all out when so much attention is focused on them. The rules are definite and clear to both sides. The referees or judges are carefully selected from those considered best by their performances during the previous league play. The radio, television and newspaper hype has grown heavier as game time arrives. The coaches and reserves are totally involved and contributing as best they can.

The Peaking of Spectator Excitement

The game begins. Both sides have their chances. Partisan fans can root or groan as intensely as they wish. They are usually surrounded by sympathetic supporters amidst a noisy crowd. There is a beginning. There will be an ending. In the meantime there will be hopeful ebbs and fretful tides as the fortunes of "our" team rise and fall. The sharp surprises and sudden disappointments en route keep the crowd on edge. As emotional levels rise, tension grows as time runs out and the score is tied. Last minute heroics are especially savored. A kind of tribal togetherness grows rapidly with friends and loyalists from school, city, state or country. Remaining seconds seem longer than minutes. Last minute do-or-die huddles or conferences are held. Long-practiced tactics are called on to carry the day.

It happens! We win! It worked! What a run or catch or hit or play! Unbelievable! Our son or daughter! What great kids! Time stands still.

Worries and concerns of the work week are forgotten. Life is great. Let the celebrations begin. We're ready. We deserved it. A toast to us! And to those pawns on the field. Our heroes. I can't wait to read what the sportswriters will say about this one tomorrow. We were underdogs but we showed 'em.

Competition to decide the champion under ideal conditions in just a few hours. To win, to share the spotlight of attention, to go into the record books, to be somebody that matters, that others will admire. Life in a nutshell. Why is it that cooperation has been glorified and competition condemned in so much literature? Who has it backward? What's the difference! We won, period. What time is it?

The Nonrole of Competition in Education

Decades of analysis by our nation's best minds have failed to produce arguments persuasive enough to generate action sufficient enough to reverse the decline in public education. Many causes of the measurable erosion have been discussed and massaged at length. Many well-intentioned initiatives have been attempted. Nevertheless, primary and secondary public education in the United States continues to suffer from a confusing combination of neglect, ineptitude and paralysis. Considered too important to be administered by amateurs without credentials or by profit-seeking entities, it has been treated like a national treasure and enshrined in a protective but opaque bubble to preserve its integrity.

But what integrity? The earlier perception of using the three Rs mainly as rigorous "training" for character development imperceptibly gave way to "education" in various subject matters as ends in themselves. The collective posture of youth reflected this change in emphasis as youthful values changed variously to embrace more aggressive peer values. These more aggressive peer values have gradually eroded the respect commanded by teachers at all levels to the point where classroom discipline has become the dominant challenge. Little wonder that most measures of literacy and numeracy have declined.

The Educational Vacuum May Now Be Leaking!

Operating in a near vacuum, education at most levels goes through its motions with a minimum of fuss and feathers. So long as a tolerable peace enshrouded the effort, all was accepted. The people had delegated to its governmental administrators monopolistic powers to service their children, their most cherished possessions. Our constitutional thinkers thought that surely our near-total concern for the welfare of our children was ample insurance to assure good results and therefore the element of competition so necessary in all other fields would be redundant or messy or confusing.

And so the setup was richly endowed by the state to provide appropriate education at all levels for their precious offspring with what was widely regarded as a network of ideal conditions: modern and well-maintained physical facilities neighborhood by neighborhood, educationally qualified teachers from closely monitored normal schools who were protected with tenure from any potential administrative abuse over freedom of speech issues, school-supplied books and other learning equipment, safe and well-supervised playing fields and facilities of various types. Cost, efficiency or effectiveness were not a concern. These were *our* children. Given this near perfect support system, what could possibly be wrong or perhaps missing? For two hundred years this system was operative. Only in the past several decades has this question even been asked.

Constructive National Concern and the Goals 2000 Program

Established in 1990 during President George Bush's administration, a Goals 2000 program was initiated to attack what was considered lacking in American education. Eight goals were established (*The National Education Goals Report*, pp. 2–3):

Goal 1: By the year 2000, all children in American will start school ready to learn;

Goal 2: By the year 2000, the high school graduation rate will increase to at least 90 percent;

Goal 3: By the year 2000, all students will leave grades 4, 8 and 12 having demonstrated competency over challenging subject matter including English, mathematics, science, foreign languages, civics and government, arts, history, and geography, and every school in America will ensure that all students learn to use their minds well, so they may be prepared for responsible citizenship, further learning, and productive employment in our Nation's modern economy;

Goal 4: By the year 2000, the Nation's teaching force will have access to programs for the continued improvement of their professional skills and the opportunity to acquire the knowledge and skills needed to instruct and prepare all American students for the next century;

Goal 5: By the year 2000, United States students will be first in the world in mathematics and science achievement;

Goal 6: By the year 2000, every adult American will be literate and will possess the knowledge and skills necessary to compete in a global economy and exercise the rights and responsibilities of citizenship;

Goal 7: By the year 2000, every school in the United States will be free of drugs, violence, and the unauthorized presence of firearms and alcohol and will offer a disciplined environment conducive to learning;

Goal 8: By the year 2000, every school will promote partnerships that will increase parental involvement and participation in promoting the social, emotional, and academic growth of children.

The 1996 U.S. scorecard on results achieved so far indicates that national performance has improved in five areas and declined in eight of the twenty-five core indicators selected to measure progress (p. 35). The bad news is a realization that making any progress in a movement so large and entrenched as education is a much longer program than any ten-year period. The good news is that a start has been made full of good intentions, that comparative international statistics are being collected and that the program likely will be continued into the future with perhaps a more modest or realistic redefinition of operational goals.

Another Simple Hypothesis to Explain Education's Weaknesses

The hypothesis advanced here is that it has been the absence of diverse forms of competition that has resulted in generations of mediocre to poor performance in our public schools. It is not hard to understand why this may be so. Youth is so naturally boisterous, uninhibited and rambunctious, teachers universally feel they must work hard to stifle their excessive exuberance. Maintaining order is never easy in any contemporary classroom but it is the first requisite to real learning. Since any form of competition usually tends to create more excitement and is hard to control, it is not a popular direction for teachers to advocate.

But perhaps the biggest contributor to weakness in education lies in the degradation of grades over the past several generations. Even though there was no or little competition among educational units as such, there had been vigorous competition among the students themselves to attain those eagerly sought As and Bs that had been necessary for admission into the more prestigious colleges and universities. Not appreciating the power of grade-seeking competition to motivate students to work harder to achieve more and earn the higher grades, teachers at all levels softened their grading postures by granting far more As and Bs and fewer Cs, Ds and failure grades. Some universities even eliminated the C grade.

To further dilute the grading systems, students have been allowed in many schools, colleges and universities to rate their instructors in yearly published manuals thus reversing at least partly the role of who judges whom in the educational process. Predictably, many dedicated and quality-oriented teachers who persevered with traditional grading standards suffered from this practice while those instructors with more lenient grading practices benefitted. In time, other wards of the state such as jailed prisoners may also introduce this practice to engineer "more humane treatment" from their keepers.

Still another factor contributing to the dilemma in education lies in the not widely perceived imbalance among those social pressures directing the development of youth. Youthful peer pressure, always a factor, had been relatively well controlled when a majority of concerned mothers were not working full time, when the student-teacher ratios were lower, when the grading system had more integrity, when most families had two parents monitoring the daily behavior of their children, when more extended families were involved, when more discipline existed all around. Under today's social conditions and the fragmented authority of its formerly controlling elements, youthful peer pressure has become dominant. It has a persistent and cumulative and damaging impact! More mature parental pressure, teacher pressure and various social pressures need a reconstituted and stronger mix to better balance the ever-present peer pressure of youth.

Fortunately, there are positive indications that the standards and conditions prevailing in the past may be on the cutting edge of constructive change. The Goals 2000 panel is beginning to get some experience and perspective. Private schools, home schools and state-supported charter schools are increasingly experimenting with new combinations in educational formats and techniques. The visibility accorded to future demonstrated successes may force some improvements in more progressive school districts. Thus might competition enter the vacuum and revitalize this most important function.

The Role of Competition in Serving Health Needs

Pharmaceutical companies have always competed vigorously through their research labs and marketing networks to create and deliver new products and services to the public. As in education, however, the traditional health establishment of hospitals and clinics served by the professional corps of medical doctors, dentists, nurses and various technicians and practitioners relied more on standardized state-mandated policies and procedures to serve its needful public. Operating in the volatile inflationary environment of the past several decades without cost-containment standards resulted in runaway increases in the cost of healthcare.

Although President Bill Clinton's bold attempt to restructure the nation's health plan met with political defeat, its considerable momentum was sufficient to derail the comfortably entrenched previous system that had become so obviously expensive that even its supporters agreed that change was overdue. The major changes introduced were the ideas that competition could be used to help contain rising health costs, that large health-maintenance organizations could usefully serve multiple roles by reducing fraud and excessive paperwork, by increasing competition amongst the insurance providers and pharmaceutical and other suppliers while also establishing new standards for various treatments and length of stays in hospitals.

As the new health-servicing structure emerges over the next decade, the aging population's physical health is generally good. Only two major enemies remain, one from within, one from without. The enemy within is not so much a physical health problem as it is one in the range from psychoneurosis to psychopathology and the human acting out of various antisocial impulses that in the aggregate fill our courtrooms and jails. The enemy without refers to the amazing adaptability of micro-organisms to become immune to science's anti-viral serums and treatments. We have mastered all the big beasties that challenged us from their jungle lairs but the "leetle beasties" have a strong instinct to survive by adapting and feasting on us. Perhaps the rapid increase of interest and research in the biotechnology sector will provide us with weapons to counter their bodily invasions.

Once again competition was invoked to increase both efficiency and effectiveness in a master function after alternative controls had failed.

Competition and Religion

When polytheism reigned, competition for the minds of men must have been substantial. After Moses established the principle of worshiping only one God, competition for the minds of men may have switched somewhat from a more combative posture to one emphasizing love, cooperation and harmony within a group.

Nevertheless, elements of competition are still practiced between various religious and brotherhood groups as each seeks to gain or hold the allegiance of incumbent members. Missionary and evangelical initiatives are still widely practiced but receive little attention from the reporting press as the emphases on violence and sensationalism dominate.

Competition in Research

The competition to discover new knowledge or to develop and apply new techniques to existing products or services has a different character than that most commonly found in the marketplace where daily statistics can be maintained on the changing status of replacement products. The intensity of competition generated by competitors known to be competing against each other grows as the results applied approach the payoff point. In pure or basic research, the investigator usually operates alone or in isolation with a few compatriots whether in a university, government agency, foundation or business laboratory. There are no guarantees in basic research that anything useful or marketable will be discovered and so any pressure generated to "produce or else" must come from the researcher or his or her superiors.

In applied research and product development, however, the pressure to produce or devise the product adaptation, supplement or idea that creates a significant improvement or modification of the former product grows in relation to the competitive dynamics perceived. The pressure can be intense to the degree that the leadership or management is counting on "your" innovation to keep up or jump ahead of competitors.

Researchers respond differently to these pressures. Some enjoy the stimulation, the excitement, the chase. Others may not. Fraud or various forms of deception may be employed as a means of competing more favorably. Copyright and patent laws were designed to protect the property rights of those who register significant product ideas and intellectual originations.

The United States continues to benefit hugely with its predominantly open systems and well-endowed research facilities emphasizing product development more than basic and applied research. Together, they attract thousands of well-educated domestic and ambitious foreign scientists, engineers and intellectuals in all fields yearly. Problems remain, however, in the international protection of property rights.

Competition in Providing Welfare and Philanthropy

Compassion for the unfortunate plight of others is the key word here, not competition or even cooperation. Estimates on the aggregate need for welfare are more than ambiguous. Definitions for poverty levels change periodically with inflation and relative circumstances. Politicians debate the effects of welfare payments affecting the willingness of workers to seek jobs. Fraud, avarice and greed combine with drugs, homelessness, despair, illegal immigration and assorted other afflictions to compound the difficulties of measuring or serving the needy. But aside from the worthiness of the individual case, help for the helpless should be readily available to assist kindred members of the human race.

Still, the citizenry at large does accept this responsibility somewhat and contributes substantially to the alleviation if not the elimination of poverty. According to *The Annual Register of Grant Support for 1996*, an estimated 129.88 billion dollars were given to various service organizations in 1994, of which some 105.09 billion came from individuals. Religion was the largest recipient with 58.87 billion followed by education with 16.71 billion. The United Way is reported to have raised an estimated 3.047 billion dollars in 1993. Most of this help was dedicated to the operational needs of the recipient organizations that then help the needy.

A Dilemma That Need Not Be

The political thrust "to end welfare as we know it" is recognition that simple handouts only compound the problem. Without that competitive headstart that comes from a healthy early family life and solid education, it is only natural for many to give up and take the easy road, or worse to give up on being a dignified person. After all, if competition is the name of the game and there are winners, then there must be losers too. To expect losers to act like it doesn't matter is not realistic. Why should they hide their true feelings? Why not fight back and at least make the winners feel guilty while taking their handouts? Isn't this a demonstration akin to the fighting spirit that motivates competitive behavior?

Recent history provides a clear lesson for this dilemma. If there is no acceptable work in the competitive marketplace for the unemployed, then society or its government must make work for them or continue the dole system with its deplorable results. Making work was initiated in the New Deal in the 1930s when the unemployment rate was several times higher. While most of the unemployed at that time were put to work on simple muscle-type jobs, those with special training or interests were directed into work outside the economic framework in such areas as writing, painting and helping in schools. The New Deal was terminated with the advent of World War II and relatively full employment. Perhaps it is time to consider implementation of New Deal II. There is no reason why a competitive marketplace should have a monopoly on employment. The noncompetitive marketplace can create jobs, provide work therapy for the needy, reduce both disguised and real unemployment, and make a substantial contribution to society at large. All it takes is insightful leadership with genuine compassion to support the political will to shame the naysayers into silence.

Clearly, the desperate needs of unhappy people are increasingly visible on city streets across the country. Given the existing individualistic collective value system at the beginning of the twenty-first century, their plight has become just another of the apparent dilemmas to be solved in the new millennium. It represents a challenge to which the role of competition as presently conceived can offer little of constructive value. However, an enlarged view of competition might suggest that it become an obligation of "winners" in the game of life to provide more to those considered not "losers" but "also-rans." Thus, a more progressive income tax can be justified so long as the proceeds are consigned to and administered to the needy.

The Role of Competition in Creating and Preserving Works of Art

Competition's role in creating works of art is somewhat similar to that described in searching for discoveries in basic research. It is a competition pitting one's current position, energies and talents against one's unknown potential in the effort to direct current fumbling and stumbling with visionary elements into something cohesive called creative expression, progress, or simply "art." It is reaching beyond one's present range of accomplishments to the frontiers of the undiscovered and organizing a new concept from disparate parts. It is at once all-consuming and frustrating but enormously satisfying when successful.

Creating is self-fulfillment via original expression. Originality is needed as art goes beyond accomplished manual skills and craftsmanship to suggest new combinations, new ideas, new discoveries. Absolute qualities in art elude us. We seem to be forever searching for new schools of expression. A new concept of artistic expression adds to the fund of existing communication and enriches all of us. It adds to the fund of existing linkages that may be innovatively connected for additional growth thereafter.

But not everybody can relate comfortably to new art achievements or new schools of art that paradoxically must be rated or judged by traditional standards and the existing set of rules that may or may not be applicable. Little wonder that the opinions of art critics range so widely and are masterpieces themselves in the synthetic art of obfuscation or double entendre. Many artistic landmarks were originally greeted with analytic rejections when first introduced. The ingredients that led to their later acceptance remain something of a mystery. Perhaps they represent premature answers to some of our disorderly questing? Anyway, when the time is ripe for us to appreciate an exquisite answer to a felt need, we can respond with enthusiasm.

More recognizable forms of competition occur amongst those organizations engaged in the preserving and displaying of works of art. Museums and art galleries have staffs that compete against each other in promoting their collections in the hope of attracting higher levels of attendance at their showings. Acquisitive collectors eagerly follow scheduled auctions and special events where latest competitive bid prices ratchet up the market value of acknowledged masterpieces and the works of promising young artists.

Is It Competition Overall or Underall?

Competition plays a vital role in nearly all of the master functions that society must have well executed for its orderly progression. Whether it's acknowledged competition overall that is the mainspring of progress in society or whether it remains an elusive, somewhat embarrassing element to be denied may not be important as long as its vigor persists. More importantly and in the execution of each master function, people will be people and reveal their dominant personal characteristics for leadership, for self-expression, for service to others, for personal gain. Competition *per se* can remain unrecognized as a hidden hero. The danger remains, however, that if the multiple beneficent values of competition are not sufficiently recognized and appreciated, there will continue to be a steady reduction of its vigor over time. Laws, rules, conventions, standards and tough love will continue to be modified in the names of fairness, honor, equity and even motherhood. An examination of each of the fourteen master functions would easily reveal how competition has been preferentially modified for special interests and with little thought to the longer-run welfare of society at large.

On the International Level

For years the World Economic Forum and the International Institute for Management Development (MID), both based in Switzerland, jointly published an annual *World Competitiveness Report*. After criticism that competitiveness between countries, unlike between companies, encouraged protectionism, the World Economic Forum modified its index. The Forum redefined competitiveness as "the ability of a country to achieve sustained high rates of growth in GDP (gross domestic product) per capita" *(The Economist,* p. 76). According to the same source, the MID's definition was more convoluted: "the ability of a country to create added value and thus increase national wealth by managing assets and processes, attractiveness and aggressiveness, globally and proximity, and by integrating these relationships into an economic and social model." The Forum uses 155 statistical measures plus subjective business opinion to form its ratings while the MID uses some 224 different indicators.

In its modified index, the Forum now attaches some two-thirds weight to just four categories as most important in promoting growth: 1) the openness of an economy to trade and investment; 2) the role of government (such as, public spending as a percentage of GDP and marginal tax rates); 3) the efficiency of the financial sector and the labor market (its flexibility); and 4) levels of achieved education and skills. The quality of management, infrastructure and technology, and the effectiveness of legal and political institutions complete the measures.

The United States was ranked first among countries rated by the MID in 1994, 1995 and 1996. The Forum ranked it number four in 1996, however, behind Singapore, Hong Kong and New Zealand. Competition or competitiveness may not be the right term for that total mix of complex ingredients that somehow combine best to produce overall conditions most conducive to optimize growth overall for any one country. Perhaps the more important consideration behind these comparisons lies in the fact that serious worldwide consideration is being given to such measures by leaders from all institutions in each country. It is encouraging to observe that continuing efforts to refine goals are being made at the highest levels so that the interaction of structure and function can best serve the people. And to note that, for lack of a better word, competitiveness is at the heart of it.

The Pervasiveness of Competition

As eloquently summarized by Walton H. Hamilton (p. 147),
...In any future ordering of human affairs, however backward, revolutionary or utopian, rivalry must have its place. Only in such a non-economy as heaven, where celestials are free from wants or there is a surfeit of all good things, can it be absent. The parties, the forms, the fashions, the rules, the intensity and the ends of struggle may change; but the norms of competition among persons, goods, industries, ideas, institutions and cultures must remain.

REFERENCES

Annual Register of Grant Support: A Directory of Funding Sources, 29th Edition (New York: R.R. Bowker's Database Publishing Group, 1996).

"The C-Word Strikes Back," (*The Economist*, June 1, 1996, p. 76).

Gleason, Philip, "American Identity and Americanization," in *Harvard Encyclopedia of American Ethnic Groups*. Editor: Stephen Thermstrom (Cambridge, Massachusetts and London, England: The Balkan Press of Harvard University Press, 1980, pp. 31–58).

Hamilton, Walton H. "Competition," *Encyclopedia of the Social Sciences*, volume 4. Editor-in-chief: Edwin R.A. Seligman; associate editor: Alvin Johnson (New York: The Macmillan Company, 1931).

The National Education Goals Report: Executive Summary (Washington, DC: U.S. Government Printing Office, 1996).

Schumpeter, Joseph A., *History of Economic Analysis* (New York: Oxford University Press, 1954).

Schumpeter, Joseph A., *Theory of Economic Development: An Inquiry into Profits, Capital, Credit, Interest and the Business Cycle*. Translator: R. Pie (Cambridge: Harvard University Press, 1934).

Statistical Abstract of the United States: 1994, 114th Edition (Washington, D.C.: U.S. Bureau of the Census, 1994, pp. 346–358).

Wilson, Edward O., *Consilience: The Unity of Knowledge* (New York: Alfred A. Knopf, 1998). Reprinted by permission of Alfred A. Knopf, a Division of Random House, Inc.

CHAPTER 13

Principles for the Maccordion

We have now completed our description of the Maccordion, a macro format of the total behavioral system operating in the United States and perhaps also to a lesser extent in other more or less democratic countries that also use combinations of competition and the discipline of the market to assist governmental overview and regulation. We have seen how the major components interrelate using the structure, function and goal paradigm. Through its direct competitive and indirect cooperative dynamics the needs and wants, goals and aspirations of its *proactive* people are met. Only the *conactive* or rebellious and indigent are not well served. Serious attention is needed to ameliorate their conditions and bring them and/or their children to the collective and bountiful table.

With this picture of the Maccordion in our minds, and the knowledge that it can be played both directly and indirectly, it might be helpful to apply some principles to it in order to 1) gain more understanding of its potential usefulness; 2) improve our individual abilities to use it conceptually and operationally in the important roles in our lives; and 3) figure out some ways to improve it.

Since the Maccordion Format embraces all people, organizations, activities and results in the total society, we can fall back on the use of selected generalizations called principles to help us gain the understanding and operational competence we seek. In later chapters we will attempt to apply selected principles to the structure, function and goal components of the Maccordion Format. But first, we must examine the concept of "principle" on which so much of the progress in our heritage has been built.

The Search for Truth and Principled Thought

Leaders in all periods of recorded history have relied on principles or universal truths for guidance. Just over two hundred years ago, the founding fathers of this nation assembled their leadership to address a question of national sovereignty. In the Declaration of Independence they wrote:

> We hold these truths to be self-evident: that all men are created equal; that they are endowed by their creator with certain inalienable rights; that among these are life, liberty, and the pursuit of happiness. That, to secure these rights, governments are instituted among men, deriving their just powers from the consent of the governed; that whenever any form of government becomes destructive of these ends, it is the right of the people to alter or abolish it, and to institute a new government, laying its foundation on such principles….

This declaration of principled thought dated July 4, 1776, on the way life ought to be ordered served as the justification for the Revolutionary War. Self-interest subsequently organized into economic interests compromised that thought and another war was fought over the alleged issue of whether some men were created more equal than others. Abraham Lincoln's persevering leadership in that Civil War was spearheaded by principled thought and action.

And the Beat Goes On…

One hundred years later an "emancipated" people grieved that they still were not being treated equally and behind the stirring leadership of Martin Luther King initiated a civil rights movement. The chief weapons of this movement were the principles enunciated in the Declaration of Independence and the Principle of Suffering the Truth. Gandhi had coined the word *Satyagrapha* to mean that pursuit of the truth does not permit violence being inflicted on one's opponent but that through patience and self-suffering the wayward can be led to see the truth. King insisted on nonviolent confrontations. He helped his cause by being adept at showmanship and rhetoric and staging first-class promotional confrontations.

Not everybody subscribes in words or especially in deeds to the logic in the *"We hold these truths to be self-evident"* statement. But enough do to permit a dissident movement that is supported by principled truth to improve its position through the creation and implementation of many affirmative-action programs. Other groups fighting for more equality include women, Native Indians, and gays among others. But just as a dog will not yield a prized bone readily, a vested majority of people have difficulty recognizing the rights of have-not groups. It takes the truth eloquently and persistently stated as principles to persuade them to recognize those with just claims.

What Is Truth?

Your dictionary states that truth is what accords with fact or reality. That which accords with *objective fact and reality*, not *subjective wishful thinking*. Organized societies long ago decided to honor and encourage the finding of truth as it not only explained perplexing natural phenomena better but it also served as a light or bellwether in settling human disputes short of physical combat or wars. But the search for truth in human affairs is not an easy one. Slanted perceptions of the full truth initiated by defensive posturing are common in everyday life.

Just as a water faucet controls the flow of water from full flow to complete stop, the individual too controls or directs his behavior from full good or constructive to complete bad or destructive with most behavior somewhere in between. However, the water system could have a monitoring flow chart hooked up to it which accurately measures the exact flow of water at any point or time. The human behavior system so far does not have an accurate monitoring system and we must rely on individual recollections of past events to reconstruct damaging incidents to life or property. Without credible witnesses or more reliable lie detectors to recall objectively just what happened, the judge and jury system is hard pressed. As a consequence, our courtrooms are clogged with disputation as we search for degrees of truth instead of the whole truth.

Stretching the Truth

Unadulterated truth is the common denominator for all of us. It is the universal base line from which springs nearly all attempts to relate one's legitimate position and claims. It is the squaring measure, the intellectual hitching post, the basic starting point for all objective systems of morality and law. It is also the proving ground for determining the legitimacy of all variations in thought and behavior.

Despite its venerated centrality in our culture, the near-universal game, even for those who wish to live by the truth, is to test its elasticity, that is, to stretch or shrink or squeeze truth to suit our currently perceived needs. This practice extends to practically all endeavors personal and collective and especially to such institutionally organized activities as politics and business. Political influence and pecuniary logic say that truth is what you want people to believe or what sells or what is not legally or provably false. Pseudo truths and "para-poetic hyperbole" extend from apparently innocent "little white lies" and "mere puffery" to well beyond the common borders of permissible deceit.

Even though such behavior is a near-universal practice at least in modest amounts, it would be improper to dignify this aberration with the halo of a principle—say, the Principle of Stretching the Truth. Since the term principle should be reserved for practices in pursuit of the truth, another term is needed to recognize those behavioral practices working in the opposite direction. The term advanced here is "dunciples" suggesting a precipitate of behavioral impropriety, or action taken with undue or unwise haste or an action taken without due deliberation or care. Thus our first "dunciple" then would be the "Dunciple of Stretching the Truth."

The "Dunciple" of Bullying the Truth

Persistent abuse in stretching the truth has led to another widespread practice here identified as the *Dunciple of Bullying the Truth*. This dunciple reaches beyond stretching the truth in daily behavior patterns to challenging the truth in confrontational showdowns and into courts of law. Denying the truth or selectively interpreting the truth as expressed in laws, regulations, contracts or even the conventional morality is used to maximize personal gain by a growing minority. In a few short generations we have witnessed the deterioration of binding accords from the handshake to printed and signed agreements to lawyer-written contracts to arbitration hearings to judge and jury verdicts to long, drawn-out suits and countersuits. Whether or not the most belligerent bully or the bully with the sharpest lawyer wins, all citizens must share the costs of a litigious society that so strains justice.

Since we seem to find it increasingly difficult to accept objective truth and abide by its conditions without prevarication, it is easy to understand that the application of positive principles (rather than negative dunciples) incorporating the distilled wisdom and truth of history has also become increasingly difficult to apply. However, the application of sound principles to difficult problems in the Maccordion Format would still appear to be a better approach to making music than simply applying trial-and-error methods or doing what appears pragmatically feasible in ever-changing and short-run contexts. The long history of truth as an end in itself is quite compelling.

The Persistence of Truth

Scholars through the ages have recorded their punchlines about the value of truth. A visit to any book of popular quotations will reveal such thoughts as the following:

"The truth is always the strongest argument."—Sophocles

"*Natura inest in mentibus nostris unsatiabilis.*" (Nature has planted in our minds an insatiable longing to see truth.)—Cicero

"The principle is more than half of the whole question." —Aristotle

"A truth is the highest thing that man may keep."—Chaucer

"To love truth for truth's sake is the principal part of human perfection in this world, and the seed-plot of all other virtues."—John Locke

"Certainly it is heaven on earth to have a man's mind…turn on the poles of truth."—Francis Bacon

"In the mountains of truth you never climb in vain."—F. F. Nietzsche

"Important principles may and must be flexible."—Abraham Lincoln

"The value of a principle is the number of things it will explain."—Ralph Waldo Emerson

"Truth is tough."—Oliver Wendell Holmes

"Truth is scattered far and wide in small portions among mankind, mingled in every system with the dross of error, grasped perfectly by no one, and only in some degree discovered by the careful comparison and collation of opposing systems."—W.E.H. Lecky

"The man who finds a truth lights a torch."—R. G. Ingersoll

"The best test of the truth is the power of the thought to get itself accepted in the competition of the market."—Mr. Justice O. W. Holmes

"The 'truths' that come down the ages are like a long stream of grasshoppers standing in a single file who jump over one another's backs. They continue without pause, always 'moving ahead,' until they arrive over and over again at the point they began. And where was that?"—Benjamin de Casseres

"It is my ambition to say in ten sentences what other men may say in whole books—what other men do not say in whole books."—F. W. Nietzsche

"Truth in spirit, not truth to the letter, is the true veracity."—R. L. Stevenson

"My way of joking is to tell the truth. It's the funniest joke in the world."—George Bernard Shaw

"Principles are not proved, they prove."—Legal Maxim

"Superstition, idolatry, and hypocrisy have ample wages, but truth goes a begging."—Martin Luther

"Truth means facts and their relations, which stand towards each other pretty much as subjects and predicates in logic."—John H. Newman

"It is the character of truth to need no proof but truth."—Jeremy Bentham

These sayings have been presented mainly to show that interest in discovering truth continues to the present for over 2000 years. Fresh generations, always faced with ever-more complex and changing organizational relationships, frequently find the handed-down truth and principles less useful and tend to deprecate their advice labeling them as bromides, homilies, slogans, aphorisms, proverbs, truisms, redundant tautologies, clichés, quick fixes and so on. But unless the best thinking of the past has been tried and found wanting, it deserves some attention. Perhaps even the word "principles" will in time join the rest with pejorative connotations and a new term will emerge as the best way to make sense out of increasingly complex and interrelated activity. Hopefully, it will not be "dunciples" or another hallucination heading the wrong way!

The Initiation and Evolution of Principles

Perhaps lured by the excitement of such remote events as surfing the waves in Hawaii or winning a big lottery, living within prescribed norms seems to trouble an increasing percentage of people in the United States. Before acceding to this idea, however, let's return to the past for a bit more grounding by comparing the evolution of religious principles with those of legal principles.

Both were designed to control or influence the earthly behavior of men. Before settled agriculture and the development of the city-states, the prevailing law was tribal and inter-tribal to some extent and enforced by tribal leadership. The following excerpts from H. G. Wells' classic, *The Outline of History* (pp. 94–95), provides some useful background:

> Certain very fundamental things may have been in man's minds long before the coming of speech. Chief among these must have been the fear of the Old Man of the tribe. The young of primitive squatting-place grew up under that fear. Objects associated with him were probably forbidden. Everyone was forbidden to touch his spear or to sit in his place, just as today little boys must not touch father's pipe or sit in his chair. He was probably the master of all women. The youths of the little community had to remember that. The idea of *something forbidden*, the idea of things being, as it is called, *tabu*, not to be touched, not to be looked at, may thus have got well into the human mind at a very early stage indeed. J.J. Atkinson in his *Primal Law*, an ingenious analysis of

these primitive tabus that are found among savage peoples all over the world, the tabus that make a man run and hide from his step-mother, traces them to such a fundamental cause as this.... And opposed to the Old Man, more human and kindlier, was the Mother, who helped and sheltered and advised.

Early tabus, reinforced by brutal physical force, made possible the social discipline needed for group survival and growth. More from H. G. Wells (pp. 101–103):

Out of all these factors, out of the Old Man tradition, out of the emotions that surround Women for men, Men for women, out of the desire to escape infection and uncleanness, out of the desire for power and success through magic, out of the sacrificial tradition of seed time, and out of a number of like beliefs and mental experiments and misconceptions, a complex something was growing up in the lives of men which was beginning to bind them together mentally and emotionally in a common life and action. This something we may call religion (Latin, *religare*, to bind). It was not a simple or logical something, it was a tangle of ideas about all sorts of "musts" and "must-nots."

In the earliest civilizations spirit worship or animism prevailed generally as so much was mysterious and unexplainable: life and death itself, the seasons, thunder, lightning, darkness, dreams, earthquakes, volcanoes, the stars, sun and moon, the animals, shadows. Each object of worship possessed a spirit that somehow communicated all sorts of commands to its followers: plant seeds in the full moon, sacrifice people at seed sowing time perhaps to appease the controlling spirits, cooperate in eating of the victims in order to share in the sacrificial benefits, excise body parts such as cutting off the nose, fingers, ears or teeth to propitiate the spirits. Conflicting and contradictory ideas abounded and were implemented without challenge.

Under these conditions of confused directions and frequently irrational or inexplicable behavior, it was to be expected that all sorts of leaders emerged: bold men, wise men, shrewd and cunning men; all with sizable egos, to serve as magicians, priests, chiefs and kings. The people needed direction and guidance. The need was so powerful it sustained those with occasional answers to perplexing questions.

The Slow but Persistent "Filtering" Process

As the questing for explanations persisted over the centuries, more consistent theories and connections were evolved. Answers to where the sun and stars went, why the seasons cycled, how plants grew gradually became more logical as communication improved and extreme answers were refined or discarded. The answers that were kept and used were the best because they conformed to reality, they best explained cause and effect relationships. They helped predict the cycle of events and removed some of the surrounding confusion.

Polytheism gradually replaced animism by the time of Hammurabi in Babylon. And then monotheism began its climb into religious sovereignty. Just as in the legal case of classifying hundreds of offenses against the community with their countless variations, the process of classifying and synthesizing the thousands of confusing commands, expectations and propitiations to and from the animistic and polytheistic gods required centuries of evolutionary simplifying.

The Procrustean Solution

The decalogue or ten commandments represented a monumental achievement in Procrustean simplification. The commandments themselves contained little that was new to the ancient world. Prohibition of other gods or images of gods parallels the stipulation of earlier treaties that the vassal commits breach of the covenant if he enters into relationships with other kings. Loyalty was important. Disrespect for parents, murder, theft, adultery, false accusations were all punishable in most earlier systems of tribal control.

Given the wide range of beliefs among the various tribes and religions, the new focus on moral behavior was remarkable. Take the *Golden Rule* for example. It may be found in one form or another in the scriptures of all the major religions (Browne, p. xv):

- Brahmanism: "This is the sum of duty: Do naught, unto others which would cause you pain if done to you." (*Mahabharata*, 5, 1517)
- Buddhism: "Hurt not others in ways that you yourself would find hurtful." (*Udana-Varga* 5, 23)
- Confucianism: "Is there one maxim which ought to be acted on throughout one's whole life? Surely it is the maxim of loving kindness: Do not unto others what you would not have them do unto you." (*Analects* 15, 23)
- Zoroastrianism: "That nature alone is good which refrains from doing onto another whatsoever is not good for itself."(*Dadistan-i-dinik*, 94, 5)
- Judaism: "What is hateful to you, do not to your fellow man. That is the entire law; all the rest is commentary." (*Talmud, Shabbat 31a*)
- Christianity: "All things whatsoever ye would that men should do to you, do ye even so to them: for this is the Law and the Prophets." (*Matthew 7, 12*)
- Islam: "No one of you is a believer until he desires for his brother that which he desires for himself." (*Sunnah*)

There are distinctions of phrasing in these eight quotations, but little differences in meaning, even though true believers in each of the faiths can make cases that their interpretation is superior. Paralleling or perhaps preceding the evolution of religious focusing on the verities came the behavior sanctions of the ruling elite designed to create some semblance of order in the communities they ruled.

The Evolution of Conforming Behavior and Legal Principles

It was in the city of Babylon, capital of Babylonia in southern Mesopotamia (now Iraq), known for its luxurious, even wicked styles of living, that our oldest set of behavior principles or laws was found. And it was under powerful and warlike King Hammurabi (2123–2081 B.C.) that the earliest set of laws or ordinances was carved on a large stone monument. Since he was the sixth king of the first *Amorite* dynasty of Babylon, it is logical to speculate that his predecessors and probably the Sumerians and others before them also contributed to the 282 laws designed to maintain order in Babylon.

Unearthed in 1901, we can now guess where the later Hebrews might first have encountered their law of "an eye for an eye" and other "equities" that were later attributed to Moses. The Code of Hammurabi, our first set of discovered laws to live by, was stern: all the heavier crimes were punishable by death. A few enactments for behavior receiving lesser punishments (Browne, pp. 17–23):

"If a son strike his father, his hands shall be hewn off."

"If any one strike the body of a man higher in rank than he, he shall receive sixty blows with an ox-whip in public."

"If a man violate the wife (betrothed or child wife) of another man, who has never known a man, and still lives in her father's house, and sleep with her and be surprised, this man shall be put to death, but the wife is blameless...."

Early Law and Early Religion Were Mutually Reinforcing

Some ten to twelve centuries later the ancient Greek philosophers developed sophisticated rationale for their substantive law and legal institutions. By the end of the first century B.C., all Greek *poleis* or city-states had become part of the Roman Empire. For centuries thereafter Roman law and Greek law lived and evolved side by side. Although the imperial Roman law came to dominate, it was heavily influenced by the Greek philosophical and legal thought.

And so we can only marvel while we speculate on the slow emergence of both religious thought and legal sanctions, each designed in its own way, to guide the behavior of humans along constructive channels. Each, consciously or not, helped to reinforce the prescriptions of the other. An obvious generalization might be that the number of laws grew empirically, that kings like Hammurabi at first identified specific transgressions and their specific punishments until literally thousand of crimes and punishments were identified and matched.

One can imagine that the system might have become too cumbersome to administer readily so that a classification system was invented separating the various offenses into major and minor (Class I, Class II, Class III and so forth) with the appropriate ranges of punishments for each. Feedback over the centuries from those being governed could have modified the punishments received for the crimes committed. Thus might these prescriptive behavior patterns and the thoughts supporting them gradually come to possess the sanctity of truth, especially as they were enforced and reinforced over the centuries.

The Accumulated Burden From the Past

While we have gratefully inherited all of the progress of the past, we only reluctantly have accepted some of the religious and legal rationale. The religious baggage from the past has been diluted variously by skeptical questioning from the scientific age. The legal baggage was passed along largely intact through the Middle Ages until the advent of the industrial revolution when the growth of technology and later the widespread adoption of the corporate form of business produced drastically larger scales of operation and new living arrangements. The industrial revolution sparked the movement to the cities where the factories were located near river or ocean ports. And the growth of large corporations increased their operating ranges and the complexity of their operations, all of which greatly increased the need for more and more law.

Now we are totally circumscribed by an elaborate network of laws and controls: family culture patterns, local laws, state laws, national laws and international laws. Indeed every major organizational or institutional type has a multi-volume code of operational etiquette. And not only are we being smothered by all of these restrictions, we must also recognize the elaborated sets of work rules that prescribe specifically and often in redundant detail just how each step of each job is to be accomplished. Beyond work rules but still within the individual organization are its policies to guide worker behavior not specifically addressed by work rules. Thus the combination of laws, specific work rules, organizational policies, the level and status of existing morality and law enforcement plus cultural mores and public opinion circumscribe the public domain in which each of us lives and works.

To function effectively in this society, it is desirable if not necessary to have been socialized into the existing morality, laws, mores and conventions that can explain the behavior that occurs. Because of its heritage, the United States is far more complex than most other countries. Indeed, foreign visitors may be fooled by the many apparent similarities in customs and conventions between their countries and the United States. The United States, through the process of cultural diffusion, is a growing and adapting synthesis of all other races and countries. Most Americans, born into a particular subset of cultural definition, never comprehend fully the rich diversity and pluralism of their nationality. Insightful principles, therefore, must accommodate the past and present while anticipating future adaptations.

The Revolt Against Overregulation

Given all the laws and controls surrounding us, it is no surprise that an increasing number seek the thrills that come with playing brinkmanship. And why not? If the ties that bind are too constrictive, let the fun begin say the bold. In their honor we have a "Dunciple of Brinkmanship": Whether to maximize wealth or to minimize costs, to taunt the enemy or to seduce the opposite sex, it is in human nature to flirt with the rewards/dangers of excessive reaching. The perceived dangers increase the adrenaline flow while stimulating the illusion of super-competence. It is a game we play to test ourselves against others, against nature and sometimes just in rebellion against the stifling present. Ah ha! But the ever-present caveat suggests we adopt safe margins for error in important stewardship functions while indulging this need in such trivial ways as gauging how many miles might be recorded on your auto's odometer before refueling. Prudence must not be totally lost!

And so it seems that many of us have thrown off or reduced the allegiance to inherited religions, excessive law and restrictions in general in the collective need to express some individualistic freedom. But as the waywardness increases, and a society becomes more contentious, the burden on the legal system increases in some compounding way to a point where it will someday become clear that costs exceed benefits and new methods of control or conflict resolution between us and the ties that bind must be found.

The Uncharted Balance Between Individualism and Conformity

There are no well-accepted norms by which a society knows for certain just where it is on the individualism/conformity scale. We don't even know the duration of such cycles if indeed they even exist outside our imaginations. But assuming they do exist, a case could be made that we are in the mid to latter stages of an individualism cycle that began sometime in the 1960s after World War II and was perhaps precipitated by the Vietnam War. Individualism has been defined as "the leading of one's life in one's own way without regard for others" and "the doctrine that the state exists for the individual and not the individual for the state." Conformity, on the other hand, is defined as behavior in agreement with generally accepted rules and customs, or accepting the tried and true traditions. Strangely, the rush to individualistic behavior during the 1960s came just a few years after President John F. Kennedy's ringing appeal for individuals "to ask not what your country can do for you; rather, ask what you can do for your country."

Fortunately, the pendulum swings both ways. After individualism has run its course, as it may already have, people will become amenable to adopting more centrist ways before overdoing the balance in the other direction toward excessive conformity. However, there is no clear indication of when or where the turnabout inflection point will be reached. Of course it will be reached when a majority of the people sense that our collective behavior needs reining in or needs loosening up and they make their feelings felt through the behavior of the institutions they serve and through their political representatives. But at present the evidence is ambiguous and a good case can be made to support either more individualism or a swing back to a more conservative posture.

A Scenario Describing the Road to Individualism

The current cycle of individualism that began in the decade of the 1960s had a number of initiating and reinforcing causes. The American society had been through one of its most severe depressions in the 1930s. With over 20 percent of its labor force unemployed and its industry and commerce in disarray, families were forced into creative and aggressive economizing and consolidating. Then came World War II and a different form of solidarity was invoked to marshal the necessary resources to win the war. Women had started going to college even before the war and were increasingly involved in the wartime defense effort. After the war young women went to colleges and universities in rapidly increasing numbers and later joined the swelling labor force to serve the burgeoning industrial and commercial markets to help crank out products and services for the war-starved but now flush citizenry.

The suburban housing concept became popular and soon most major cities were surrounded by three-bedroom, two-car garage homes and a large-scale baby boom that overcrowded the new suburban schools faster than they could be built. As the average student-teacher ratio increased all over the country, teachers soon reached their saturation levels as far as control and student discipline were concerned and rather quickly the young students enjoyed more freedom than they could constructively manage. The advantages of a counter-balancing control from the homes were also lost because of the increasingly large percentage of working women. The latch-key child phenomenon permitted more freedom for youth to indulge their fantasies.

And so they did by eroding the high schools in the late 1950s and then blasting the colleges in the 1960s. With control and discipline stretched beyond the breaking point in many cases, academics suffered badly almost everywhere even though the collective student grade-point averages climbed to the point where most were considered "good to excellent." The federal government was involved in putting a man on the moon before Russia did, coping with a missile threat from Cuba, and fighting the Korea and Vietnam containment struggles. The threat of conscription to military service to fight in unpopular struggles was a major cause for student rebellion during the 1960s. State and local governments were nearly helpless in coping with the energy and boundless spirit of alienated youth as they wreaked havoc on many college campuses across the country and caused many millions of dollars in damages. More importantly, their headstrong rebellion gave strong impetus to individualism's cause generally.

Individualism Extended

After the Vietnam fiasco inconclusively ended in the mid-1970s, all involved countries picked up the pieces of their collective lives and tried to restore more healthy conditions. But the basic trend in the United States toward increasing individualism continued. Emancipated women dispensed sexual favors more freely to willing men leading to increased venereal disease and higher divorce rates. Homosexual behavior chose this time to begin coming out of the closet. Men too often defaulted on their alimony and child-support payments. Sexual promiscuity became rampant. Drugs became more readily available and more widely consumed, even including students at the junior-high level as well as high school and college levels. Still in the closet is the story about drug consumption among working adults. Stories leaking from the increasing number of therapy sessions for addicts and their co-dependants are compounding.

The movies and television programming became more and more explicit in sexual displays and violent encounters. Crime rates increased in most urban centers even though police manpower was doubled. Styles in clothing and dress increasingly grew more casual. Why dress like the up-tight lawyer or businessman? Forget old-fashioned hair grooming and shoe polishing. The more tattered and torn the clothing, the better. Tinted hair gave way to the boldest primary colors. Tattoos and earrings for men and ubiquitous pierced body parts became fashionable among the more rebellious youth crying out for recognition in an impersonal age.

How, one may ask, does the leadership of a democratic country cope with the conspicuous and unconventional conduct of large elements of its population? Surely they must understand that these are the signs of incipient rebellion? As watch standers in the political parade of overseers, they can only smile grandly at the excesses they pretend to overlook, praise the better performances brought to their attention, condemn the more outrageous behavior, show toleration all round, and continue to execute, legislate and judge against the perceived excesses and otherwise act as though all was well. And continue to search harder than ever for principles to back up their rationale for unpopular positions they must take. Just bend and bend and bend some more....

Principles for All Seasons

Whatever the political climate or the level of social confusion, the potential of being guided by *principle* rather than *dunciple* will always be with us both in directing our interpersonal behavior and occupationally in the more complex organizational world. Leaders in all organizational contexts should work for a solid grounding in the principles most applicable to their situations and be able to illustrate them with contemporary examples that their followers can appreciate. On the interpersonal level, Plato set the stage when he suggested (*Dialogues*, p. I.711): "And this is the reason why every man should expend his chief thought and attention on the consideration of his first principles: are they or are they not rightly laid down?" Reflection on and personalization of *The Golden Rule* cited earlier presumably would be a good place in the beginning to focus this attention.

Assuming exemplary personal principled behavior (!), what additional principles would be desirable for sorting out the mumbo-jumbo of the organizational superstructure and the discharging of the fourteen master functions? What kind of principles might provide useful insight and oversight in the interpretation of the competitive dynamics and trends in any functional area?

The search for first principles has always intrigued philosophers and "deeper" thinkers in most fields. Philosophers seek the underlying or most basic source or cause. According to its Latin derivation, "principle" means a beginning or foundation. "Of first principles," Aristotle hypothesized, "we see some by induction, some by perception, some by a certain habituation" (*The Great Ideas, A Syntopicon*, p. 421.)

Philosophers ever since Aristotle have been interpreting and reinterpreting the major principles and propositions advanced by leading thinkers over the centuries. Indeed, the word "principles" acquired such a respectable connotation from all this attention that its reputation was adapted to works of far lesser merit. Today, use of the word has been broadened by marketing hucksters to include not only first causes but even the rudimentary rules and elementary concepts of a subject or how-to procedures for any occupation. Thus, today many textbooks in any field may carry the prefix "principles of." Not to worry, however, as this widespread borrowing of the term may make its general acceptance more palatable.

For the purposes of this work the term will mean a fundamental truth or assumption forming the basis for a chain of reasoning or a primary proposition professed as a guide to action or on which further reasoning is based. Clearly, it is important that the basic foundation block or *principle* be sound if the superstructure of ideas built on it is to be sustainable. Many organizations have failed because of faulty basic assumptions their leadership regarded as true principles.

The Role of Principles in Academia

As described earlier, it may be hypothesized that most academic disciplines from algebra to zoology may be analyzed into the following levels from the more general and abstract to the highly specific and concrete:

1. *Formats*: (Frames of Reference again!), comprehensive thought models or grand designs.
2. *Principles*: specific theories, concepts, organizing ideas setting a general direction.
3. *Current realities*: descriptive summaries of general to specific events in the fields, including anecdotal illustrations, topical examples.
4. *Techniques*: the how-to dimensions of skills in action.

Principles in this classification is placed below formats and above descriptions of current realities and techniques of performance. All levels are interrelated, of course, but may be singled out for special attention. The development of principles in every field is seen as the effort to distill significant insights from the myriad of experiential and operational data that are observed at the third and fourth levels. When recognized as principles, they can serve as important support systems or components of the frame of reference for that particular discipline.

When this classification of levels of knowledge is matched to their application areas in the real world, the following construct results:

Level of Knowledge	*Level of Application*
Formats	a) Societal organization into market-directed system (the Maccordion Format) or a budget-directed system (typical dictatorship)

	b) Ideological view of life
	c) Specific frames of reference for any subject or activity
Principles	a) Laws: descriptive and prescriptive
	b) Organizational policies
	c) Moral codes of approved behavior
Current Realities	a) "News" reporting based on current, recent or noteworthy events and illustrations
Techniques of Performance	a) Work rules and procedures devised for efficiency in creating and delivering useful products and services

How can one gauge the relative emphases placed on each of these levels in the hundreds of collegiate majors in the 2,100-plus four-year institutions of higher education in the United States? Most instructors tend to emphasize their most comfortable level, consciously or not. Multiple sections of an identically titled course in any college taught by multiple instructors using identical textbooks, reading materials and the same prescribed tests will be quite different courses depending on which of the four levels each instructor emphasized and which was relatively ignored.

Cheapening the Meaning of Principles

It matters little that the textbook may be titled *Principles of Whatever*, the content level may be completely or nearly devoid of any principle-derived content based on the definition of principle advanced in an earlier paragraph. Many of these textbooks contain exhaustive descriptive material and little else besides some recommended techniques of performance in that field.. Most students find the current realities and techniques levels quite comfortable intellectually and they can easily achieve good grades by doing the reading assignments. And, of course, there is a large amount of entertainment value in the racier anecdotal stories at the current realities level that many instructors use to spice up their lectures. It should also be acknowledged that the quantity approach to more reading (instead of rigorous analysis) has been instituted at some institutions.

Indeed, any instructor who dares to emphasize the formats and principles levels without serving up enough juicy anecdotal material is asking for a mediocre instructor rating when the students grade the instructor. The old student adage about giving the "prof" what he wants seems to have become a two-edged sword today when too many students and too many professors give each other what they want. As a consequence, undergraduate grade-point averages are at all time highs while qualifying scores for entry into graduate schools have been declining.

Technological Challenges to Use of Principles

The great increase in attention over the past few decades to probability methodologies as implemented by computer simulation has to some large extent muffled interest in the formulation and use of everyday behavioral principles in organizational life. But most operational situations requiring decision-making by most managers still are and probably always will be more amenable to principled rationale than probabilistic answers. Only so much can be quantified.

Qualitative synthesis and analysis of relevant contexts must be perceived and conceptualized before problematic situations can even be visualized. Problem definition must precede identification of possible alternative solutions. Ordinal classification must precede cardinal numbering and calculation. Techniques to develop perceptual and conceptual skills are in rudimentary states of development. To the present, education seems content to drown most students in oceans of fact while emphasizing analysis of ever smaller segments, more of which can be quantified.

The real-life usefulness of behavioral principles generally is manifested in laws and regulations of governance, the organizational policies of our major institutions, and the moral codes of behavior advanced by religious and other ideological groups. Specifically at the individual level, principles are useful in separating right from wrong, good from bad, the more desirable from the less desirable and all in the contexts of short-run to long-run benefits. For organizational guidance, perceptive principle selection becomes the fountainhead for initiating and sustaining the growth or stability desired.

The Partnership of Leadership and Principles

To the extent that one is content to be a "passive" worker or to engage only in routine or repetitive work, a limited appreciation of the employer's organizational context may be enough. Fairly specific work rules and procedures can be devised for most of the routine tasks in relatively closed-system operations where tight schedules and quality-control procedures dominate the production or servicing systems, whether in government, science, business, health, education or other activities.

As you move up the managerial ladder in any organizational context, however, and widen the scope of your responsibilities, it is desirable to understand more of the "cause-effect" and probabilistic arrangements of decisions that impact on the political, economic, and social systems of society more seriously than do the narrower system technical decisions. The higher the managerial level one achieves, the more important becomes the focus on conceptualizing and applying formats and principles and then continually reviewing and updating them in light of operational and directional goals sought.

REFERENCES

Browne, Lewis, *The World's Great Scriptures* (New York: The Macmillan Company, 1946). Reprinted with the permission of Scribner, a Division of Simon & Schuster.

The Great Ideas: A Syntopicon, volume II. Editor-in-chief: Robert Maynard Hutchins (Chicago: Encyclopaedia Britannica, 1952).

Plato, *Dialogues*, I.711.

Wells, H. G., *The Outline of History* (Garden City, New York: Garden City Publishing Company, 1920).

CHAPTER 14

Applying Principles to the Maccordion Format

In the previous chapter, a definition of principle was selected from the many available for our use in understanding, using and improving the Maccordion Format. Recall that the concept of principles chosen for this project had dual purposes as 1) a fundamental truth forming the basis for an extended chain of reasoning, and 2) a primary proposition professed as a guide to action. Thus, principles can be used to implement both the action and thought components of formats.

With this definition of principle, we can attempt to see how the Maccordion parts interrelate, analyze how they might operate differently and perhaps even better. Most of the principles to be used may have application value at several levels: 1) the individual; 2) the specific organization; 3) the generic class of which the organization is a member (i.e., hospitals or schools in general or industry trade associations); and 4) society as a whole.

To enrich application potentials further, many of the principles can have special relevance in different ways for various elements of the structure, function and goal components. A creative, brainstorming type of attitude is recommended in applying the principles for suitability in a wide range of applications. There are no right or wrong answers. Look for areas where improvement might be achieved through new combinations or in which you think waste might be lessened. In a dynamic society, few arrangements are permanent and most can stand improvement. Remember it takes a will to find a way!

Principle 1: Optimizing Output From Input Factors of Production

For a beginning we must put all of the major parts that we have to work with on the table. These include all the parts shown in Figure 3. Thus, Principle 1 is "optimizing output through coordinated use of the factors of production." As taken from basic economics, this principle states that there are four major productive factors generally classified as 1) property resources or land; 2) financial capital; 3) human resources or labor; and 4) the entrepreneurial ability and/or management that coordinates these inputs for the optimized results desired, organization by organization.

Physical resources include all natural resources, mineral deposits, forests, oceans and the land itself. Capital includes all manmade buildings, machinery, communication and transportation facilities and equipment. Labor includes all mental and physical abilities and energy available. Mainly physical in the beginning, the labor component has increasingly become mental, perhaps suggesting that the education of labor would be a better name for this factor of production. The entrepreneurial or managerial organizing factor arranges the input units so as best to achieve the results desired. Note that all of these factors of production have limited supplies except that of education. The growth and application of knowledge will expand exponentially the more it is used.

The term *optimizing* is a relative newcomer to economic jargon. Just a few decades ago managements were recorded in their annual reports as maximizing this and maximizing that as if no tradeoffs were needed. Since there is almost always a limited budget to support any organization's operations, it would be impossible to maximize all benefits to each of the various publics involved whether customers, employees, dealers and distributors in the distribution chain, or the community, while also at the same time maximizing company profit for itself and its stockholders. Some balancing tradeoffs would be required. Government appears to be the only exception being able in a short-run emergency to maximize expenditures in any direction without the need to balance its budget. Parenthetically, the dangers of so doing in nonemergency times have yet to be persuasively demonstrated but might be catastrophic.

On Rotational Recognition

Perhaps there is an unplanned and somewhat opportunistic rotational recognition in satisfying the various claimants for organizational attention. Anytime a major competitor makes available a new or superior product or service, the organization in question must match or exceed it as soon as possible or risk losing competitive position, market share or perceived prestige. When product or service quality is considered *inscru-*

table or the public accepts all such of its class as generic equals, then the organization can afford to spread its benefits more widely. In the case of the business corporation, when stockholders complain, management may liberalize dividend payments or try to raise the prices of outstanding shares on the stock market by buying back some ownership shares. Or when employees complain effectively, managements may recognize those complaints in more generous union contracts or salary increases. When labor unions become weaker, managements may seize the opportunity to increase their own remuneration through salary increases, stock options, or retirement benefits. At all times, however, most managements place highest priority on maintaining or increasing product superiority. After all, that is the lifeline that leads to the bottom line, profit or other measurements of institutional leadership.

What Is Product Superiority?

Product or service superiority, however, is normally a matter of perception in the eyes of the beholder rather than a verifiable reality. The word product as used hereafter is meant to include the term services. Many comparatively inferior products succeed in fooling some of the people most of the time through various combinations of advertising and merchandising. Definitions of "best product" can vary also. A large electronics company was credited many decades ago with initiating the intriguing concept of assembling a household appliance with all or most parts designed to last just over one year, the length of the product guarantee at the time. Not only could product obsolescence and necessary replacement be accelerated, costs of production of all component parts could be lowered by reducing their expected lifetime of service. Why encourage customers of their products to discard an appliance with only one part needing repair and a lifetime of potential service still available from the rest? Either improve the one defective part or lower the quality of the rest. Thus, the "best product" could be defined as that one delivering satisfactory or *satisficing* service in the short run perhaps but not in the long run.

One must wonder when passing a huge automobile junkyard about the investment to be lost in prompt recycling for base metals from all those automobile carcasses. And perhaps sympathize a bit more with the owner of the junkyard as he postpones recycling because he knows that there may be a small fortune rusting away in usable parts if customers with corresponding part needs would only show up.

The challenge to the management or leadership of all organizations, therefore, is to combine the resources available to it to produce some definition of the best products and /or services for its customers or clients. Similarly, the challenge to individuals is to do the best possible with the endowments or "factors" inherited and apply energy in selected directions. When both individuals and organizations deliver their services optimally, society at large will be the ultimate beneficiary with its enhanced largess available for all citizens.

What can we as individuals do to contribute to this process? Are we *maximizing* or *optimizing* or *satisficing* or merely *coasting* on the endowments granted to us? How about the contributions of our parents or the potentials of our children? What can the organizations that we are affiliated with do to improve their contributions? Constructive ideas implemented create compounding benefits over time.

Principle 2: Learning From Historical Perspective

If we can believe that the future will be a repetition of the past with only a few diverting technological whistles or bells to confuse us, why not focus more attention on the lessons from history? Perhaps the attention on historical events should concentrate more on cause and effect relationships or behavioral principles than on the personalities involved or the factual minutiae of key events. What did you learn in school from your history courses? Or better, what did you personalize as insight for future use, positively apply the concept thereof and benefit from?

There is a legion of wise sayings about the value of historical perspective such as:

> We shall never manage the present, or make sense of it, unless we have explained our past well enough to imagine our future (Walter Lippman).

> The eyes of man are not in his forehead, but in his hindhead (Ralph W. Emerson).

> History is a measure for the future through the rhythms and trends for societies and systems as they rise and fall (Kenneth Boulding).

To illustrate the concept of extracting principles from the historical continuum, consider the ten stages in the cycle of civilization that have been repeatedly observed: 1) bondage or loss of freedom; 2) spiritual faith; 3) courage; 4) freedom; 5) loss of freedom; 6) selfishness; 7) complacency; 8) apathy; 9) fear; and 10) dependency and return to bondage.

A national poll every few years or so asking different segments of people to place their country at one of the identified points in this described cycle of stages might be quite revealing, perhaps helpful. A follow-up question might inquire about recommended corrective measures to improve the national character in the direction of achieving or staying in the third, fourth or fifth stages. Which stage would you prefer and why? Where in the cycle would you place this country's position at this time and what would you recommend our leadership advocate for improvement? Need this merry-go-round circle forever?

Principle 3: Principle of Progress and Its Enabling Conditions

Unlike other animals, the human species has a compulsion to work, to organize the elements of nature so as to insure survival and even to establish comfort zones well above survival necessities.

The scales and styles of living enjoyed by a society and practiced by an individual are improvable to the extent that:

1. A pragmatic and enduring spirit supports the perfectibility of man collectively while permitting individual pursuit of happiness by encouraging innovations that creatively destroy older concepts and operational techniques and substitute the ever-emerging new knowledge and derivative applications.
2. Specialized institutions such as government, church, education, health and business deliver substantial proportions of their organizational missions to the people at reasonable cost.

On "Encouraging the Enabler"

While the driving force in this progressive thrust may be some inexplicable human compulsion, the enabling pull of power is transcendent knowledge. Growth at the frontiers of knowledge results in society's reception of enhanced power potential and ultimately more sophisticated technologies. Widespread and constructive use of all existing information in the public domain capitalizes on what exists. But the raw power of a new idea is spectacular.

The simple discovery that a whole entity can be analyzed into parts and the parts rearranged and recombined was powerful insight beyond imaginative use of all information already in the public domain. In the early 1900s it was discovered that there might be more than one type of blood and that if matching types were used in a human blood transfusion, the patient might be saved. Previously, it was a guessing game and old movies of frontier days sometimes show the deadly results of mismatched blood types. In a similar manner through continuing research, scientists have discovered much more about cholesterol, its component parts, and its effects on artery congestion and heart functioning. There is a "good" cholesterol and a "bad" cholesterol and pharmaceutical companies have developed drugs to lower the bad and raise the good. The whole brain has now been separated into the left side and the right side with different functional emphases for each. Research progresses in all areas and new breakthroughs continue. Artificial blood is now considered a distinct possibility to supplement and perhaps replace human-generated blood. Blood dialysis methodology may shortly be commonplace and contribute to cholesterol control and management. Capitalizing upon insight derived from analysis of the human genetic code may be our important contribution in the twenty-first century.

What works collectively for a society applies also to its constituent groups and begins with the individual whose welfare is the central theme of the entire design. At the same time the individual citizen must act promptly in enlightened self-interest to protect the integrity of those principles that have nourished him and preserved him from the onslaughts of special vested interests. What are those principles and in what ways might the individual citizen work harder to protect them?

Principle 4: Principle of Sustained Productivity Over Time

Productivity has been defined as a measure of efficiency between input factors and output results. Its positive benefits are enormous. Average productivity increases of 3 percent yearly over twenty years quantifies to more than a 60 percent increase that somehow compounds additionally and erratically because of quality improvements that are difficult to measure. It means that each succeeding generation can live that much more abundantly or at least allocate that much more in resources to living differently or better than the previous one.

Most often used to measure production results in the business community, it also can be usefully applied to government, health and education. Religion and the creative arts, perhaps, are the only major institutional areas mainly exempt from this measurement. But productivity can be more than a measure of efficiency. To maintain a healthy rate of sustained productivity, it is desirable to encourage different inputs working better, rather than the same inputs working harder. After all, it's results or effectiveness overall and in the long run that count.

People in the United States have been unknowing beneficiaries of this concept. Foreign visitors are often amazed by the paradox of how inefficient or casual we seem operationally at work but how effective our economy rates overall when compared to others. Immigrant workers contribute their zeal beneficially while the established citizenry in its labor role helps to engineer "more" by encouraging or at least permitting increasingly effective relationships among the historic factors of production. Studies are now forthcoming to measure the productivity of capital inputs (*The Economist*, p. 82) in which the United States has done far better than its international competitors. Perhaps eventually there will also be measures of the comparative productivity of managerial styles and natural-resource inputs with similar results.

Especially important is that vigorous competitive dynamic that helps to eliminate redundant and unnecessary activities that have outlived their original purposes and at the same time quickly gets new technology installed when it will aid efficiency or effectiveness. In comparing the effectiveness of different institutional organizations, what suggestions can you offer for crossover implementation? Why have these suggestions not been implemented to this date? What dispositions in the human character tend to impede quicker implementation of potential improvements? How might this be changed?

Principle 5: Principle of Systemic Circularity

Very few systems are totally open or totally closed. A perfect vacuum would be an example of a totally closed system in which no captured elements could escape nor any external elements be admitted. Because of our liberal immigration policy over the generations, progressive outlook and *absorbing* frontier, the United States has been a great beneficiary from its policies of supporting technical, social and political systems that are far more open than closed.

The shape of any system is dependent on its response to the following common characteristics of open systems (adapted from Katz and Kahn, pp. 19–26):

1. *The importation of energy* from the external environment and
2. *The transformation of this energy* into products/services resulting in
3. *The exportation* of some products/services into the environment and thereby contributing to
4. *The cyclic character of systems* and their repetitive cycles of events which prevents
5. *Natural entropy* from degenerating the system by generating negentropy. All the process above is accomplished through
6. *Information input, negative feedback and the coding process* to help sustain
7. *The steady state and dynamic homeostasis equilibrium* as organizations nevertheless seek continuing
8. *Differentiation and elaboration* and ever more specialization resulting in continuing need for
9. *Integration and coordination* by which the social organization achieves functional unification of tasks and roles through such devices as priority setting, prescribed routines, the timing and synchronizing of functions, and the scheduling and sequencing of events all of which are designed to achieve organizational goals in a particular way despite the (9 added in 2nd Edition, 1978, p. 30)
10. *Principle of equifinality*, which suggests that a system can reach the same final state from differing initial conditions and by a variety of paths. There is rarely one way only.

The main difference between open and closed systems is positive implementation of item 6: information input, negative feedback and the coding process. The coding process refers to methods that might be used to block reception of information deemed negative and thereby block subsequent analysis that could lead to progress.

Individuals also may be arrayed over a spectrum from relatively open to relatively closed regarding their receptivity to new ideas, new adventures, new encounters, new challenges. One's position along this spectrum is a consequence of all previous input factors and living experiences but can be moved either way with concerted effort.

With the open-to-closed system concept in mind, review the organizations with which you are familiar starting with yourself, friends, family, your employing organization and or others you have known. Are your friends more open or more closed than you think they are? Discuss with them which of you is more open to change or challenge. Which of your friends do you seek out for excitement? For consolation? What might be the advantages of a totally open or totally closed system to the individual or organization?

Principle 6: Principle of Selecting the Clear Looking Glass

Accurate diagnosis and correct remedy of large and small problems depend on seeing the problem in its proper context. Contextual frames of reference may range from the panoramic *eagle's-eye view* to the micro *beaver's-eye view*. For local operational defects amenable to trouble-shooting, the proper context might include a view just large enough to see connectedness of the part or process and its before-and-after relationships.

For larger problems in a micro setting to the largest macro dilemmas, the correct context must usually include comprehensive overviews of the basic supra- and infra-structural elements, the more dynamic functional interrelationships and the alternative directional path(s) of the whole design(s). Structural and directional orientations nearly always require the larger panoramic frame of reference for accurate problem definition. Government and international organizational problems frequently have need of these broad contexts. An organization such as the United Nations is particularly plagued by difficulties in defining its problems well. Might the old phrase that "a problem well defined is half solved" refer more specifically to defining the problem in its proper setting?

Problem Finding and Problem Solving

Ability to select the contextual format or lens that fits the problem or even finding deliberational time to think about it are continuing challenges to action-oriented operators who are usually measured by production results within prescribed time limits. This perceived time pressure encourages many problem solvers to jump on whatever clues are immediately evident, regardless of their superficiality, make a quick assumption or two and start building a complicated solution pattern that ultimately collapses either before or after application. Either way, both time and resources are wasted because the involved thinkers and their supporting managements did not appreciate that problem finding in the complex organization is more difficult than problem solving.

Reflect back on recent events in your own life for problems that you addressed prematurely or without getting to the root of the problem. Better yet, think about situations where your athletic coach or boss acted prematurely. Be assured also that not all problems lend themselves to clear definition or simple answers. Dilemmas are problems of super complexity with symptoms overlapping into ambiguous jurisdictions. Identify some in your own life and in that of your affiliated organizations.

It is usually in hindsight that we appreciate that our difficulties with a vexatious problem were in choosing the clear looking glass. Situational contexts are frequently deceptive because they're usually loaded with obvious clues to begin the problem-solving process. Only occasionally does the operational challenge require one to choose the correct lens as a first step.

Problems not immediately suggesting a relevant frame of reference are relatively rare, such as the following:

1. What is the order in the following numerical sequence: 8549176320?
2. Riddle of the Sphinx who asked, "What creature is it that walks on four legs in the morning, two legs at noontime and three legs in the evening?"

Principle 7: Principle of Double-Barreled Thinking

Focused thinking, as differentiated from its equally valuable counterpart, speculative or free-association thinking, requires the matching and mixing of complex abstract theories and concrete realities into interdependent cause and effect and probabilistic networks.

Emerging from these networks are guideline principles of thought that become ordered into policies that ultimately become translated into both individual and organizational plans and action. Distilled from the complexities of language in thought and action, from the findings in semantics, pragmatics and syntactics, useful bridges have emerged that facilitate man's thinking. Foremost among these are equilibrium and functionalist models or formats to assist in organizing thought. The former assumes a counterbalancing arrangement around an equilibrium point where conventional manipulations may be made on either side of the centerpiece for various purposes. The latter functional model becomes more useful when specific equilibria data or concepts do not exist but patterns are desired for directional guidance.

All thought is connected but the links are obscure to most of us most of the time. Thus we may settle for predominantly equilibrium-model thinking or functionalist-model thinking, whichever happens to dominate in our occupational specialty, and use the principles derivative from each mode of thinking.

The clear challenge for man is to develop greater facility in using each model as appropriate and then to develop the disposition and ability to switch back and forth for greater analysis and synthesis of thought. Like breathing in and breathing out, one can continuously alternate one's thinking focus between equilibrium and functionalist models. With the great shortage in such talented individuals, the next best approach is to form teams combining specialists in each mode of thinking and let them collaborate on troublesome problems or futuristic research.

In which mode of thought are you more comfortable? Have you ever in your schooling been challenged by the need for both types of thinking on the same problem? What did you do? Survey your friends and acquaintances as to whether they are mainly analytic or synthetic thinkers, equilibrium- or functionalist-oriented. What were their college majors? What other factors contributed to their thinking mindsets?

Principle 8: Principle of Anticipatory Holistic Thinking (Or Smelling a Rat)

Recognizing Machiavellianism, planning and negotiating should anticipate all possible relationships among collaborators and competitors, especially those between new associates and differing cultures. Not all operators in all cultures abide consistently by legalistic, moralistic, or altruistic codes of behavior though they may persuasively pretend to do so.

Managers trained only in normative or approved modes of thinking and sensing are handicapped when dealing with others not so limited. Full-circle thinking, which includes worst-case scenarios and sets up fall-back defenses against nefarious schemes, is needed. This includes not only relationships between people but also applies to designs of systems and equipment of all sorts.

Attorneys knowledgeable in deceptive practices guard important contracts against potential damages. Design engineers develop burglar-proof and tamper-proof machines and systems. Needed also are front-line organizational negotiators and planners with full-circle mindsets capable of 360-degree thinking on all matters such as developed by double agents or counter intelligence specialists.

Full-Circle Thinking

The following diagram illustrates the idea of full-circle thinking with degrees of approved and disapproved behavior above and below the center line. It refers to negotiations, exchanges, agreements and contracts between individuals, organizations of all types and inter-governmental agreements and treaties:

Diagram 5
Full-Circle Thinking

Behavior Zones		Characteristic Tactics Employed
Altruistic	Approved	Socially Responsible
Moralistic	Behavior	Enlightened Self-Interest
Legalistic		"Tough" Bargaining
One-Sided		Sharp Trading
Unprincipled	Disapproved	Misrepresentations
Felonious	Behavior	Clever Deceptions
		Fraud and Larceny

The implications of this principle affect nearly all facets of individual behavior and every organizational operation. The conflicts between self-interest, organizational interest and social interest are ever present, never predictable, and potentially very damaging. Recent revelations about alleged moral problems in governmental leadership positions, corruptive influences in the Civil Investigation Administration (CIA), Federal Bureau of Investigation (FBI), certain brokerage and banking operations both in the United States and elsewhere provide ample evidence that deception everywhere is alive and well. Even religious organizations have an increasing range and frequency of such problems. Cheating in schools and pilfering in stores suggest that this form of behavior may be more widespread than ever.

Beyond corruption within and between organizations, there is the ever-present threat of undercover terrorist bombings and other crimes contrary to public interest. The only answer to subversive activity of all types is to be alert and vigilantly maintain variable and unpredictable double checking at every stage of every operation. Whatever the cost, it is necessary to provide minimum levels of order and equity for the delivery of the satisfactions produced by all institutions in society. Never a popular political topic for general discussion, note the increase in private and commercial means of surveillance, detection and deterrence of antisocial behavior. Even religious organizations find it necessary to keep their houses of worship locked most of the time.

Lead a discussion group on the topic of whether higher degrees of individualism or conventionalism in society leads to indiscriminate or reckless behavior. Which do you think encourages it more? What counter forces might be organized to combat any perceived drift to immoral from amoral and morally approved behavior?

Principle 9: Principle of Emotional Involvement

Before actually experiencing any social event, most of us have learned to maintain a healthy doubt or skepticism that our first-hand enjoyments will be all they're cracked up to be by the hype merchants and critics. The personal *judgment* that rates each event/experience is a combination of intellect, imagination and emotion that focuses our subjective faculties on the object in view whether an art form, business deal, sporting event, tourist attraction or sex encounter.

This *dynamic assessment* is variously colored by the positive or negative balances of our physical and psychological well-being at the time. Our body rhythms have their up and down cycles, which affect our expectations and cause some surprising changes of mind as "it was better than I expected."

Expectations play a large role in the assessments, especially with highly organized people. We tend to be impressed mainly by peak emotional experiences and especially when the event proves far better or worse than expected. When physical needs are compelling and reinforced by strong psychological motivation, when the right people share in the event, when external pressures do not intrude, then we may say that *the time is ripe* for a peak experience. Later recall of such an event may be described as "I was really moved," or "I was deeply touched" or "I actually cried."

Emotional Versus Rational Impacts

Objective facts may reinforce the memorable experience but the key ingredient is emotional impact. Since the quantity and quality of memorable experience are the essence of life itself, the role of the emotions in filtering these events is crucial. As the late poet John Ciardi put it (p.20): "The difference between knowing and feeling is the same as the difference between sound waves and music, or between a glass of water and an ocean. Nothing really happens to the data of things until they have been taken into the emotion of perception."

This principle, too, has widespread relevance in our lives at all levels. For the manager in any organization, try to involve all employees with the emotional consequences of the team's operational game plan, the goals and frustrations of quotas, the dynamics of competition, the "game" of meeting or beating group targets such that your employees too may get emotionally involved and enjoy the participative flavor of successes and defeats.

On the individual level,

If the aim of life be joy, give free reign to emotional feelings whether at work or play;

If the aim of life be accumulation of things, deny the relevance of time-wasting emotions, and focus on operational effectiveness;

If the aim of life be variously mixed, switch mindsets smoothly for each of the important roles you play;

If you wish a happy marriage, share fully on both emotional and rational planes with your partner;

If you are a parent, share appropriately by relating to your child's stage of development.

Reflect back on experiences or events that you recall most vividly and try to identify the emotions that you felt. What kind of emotional experiences have the potential to bring tears to your eyes? On which level (emotional or rational) are you more comfortable? What can you do to improve the other?

Principle 10: Principle of Dichotomous Behavior

The twin goals of efficiency and effectiveness for most types of organizations require that we organize our relevant time, space, matter and energy dimensions with the best in systems and schedules to improve productivity or other goals sought. To do so completely, however, reduces man to repetitive routines that when fully implemented could ultimately deny him the pleasures of spontaneous or deviant behavior.

Spontaneity is that precious quality of life that permits or urges you to do something eccentric or wayward just because you feel like it at the time even though it may interrupt the continuity of your scheduled program. It is a function of trusting your instincts, of surprising yourself, of laughing at nothing or of doing the absurd to contrast your well-organized routine against its opposite and so maintain a balance. These unscheduled surprises help make the humdrum of the repetitive activity more tolerable.

On Seeking a Balance

Coffee breaks, timeouts and fresh-air sessions are scheduled as built-in techniques (or "the pause that refreshes") to relieve the tension of long stretches of routine concentration. Weekend retreats, vacations partially disguised as conventions at fancy resort destinations and other changes of pace may be available to some more privileged employees or managers but probably not to all. But all of these may not be sufficient or right for some souls who need to be in charge of their own breaks.

Might the opposite be true also? In a pleasure-dominated environment might a major pattern of hedonistic indulgence become relieved by occasional attention to constructive work? Many wealthy individuals have tired of endless carousing and returned to purposeful activity. Do you know any people who appeared to be happily retired but were not and returned to work? Do you think most social organizations that seem to be engaged in endless recruiting of volunteer help can provide satisfying jobs for those they recruit? Considering our major organizational types, which do you think does the best job of providing constructive and/or satisfying retirement jobs for senior citizens? What more might be done? There is an enormous potential here for increasing overall productivity in the nation and also for improving the quality of life for the well-functioning elderly.

And so it seems that humans require dichotomous behavior for healthy living. As psychologist Donald Snygg has written (*Goals* . . . , p. 342), we have alternating needs

> ...for activity and for relaxation, for security and for new experience, for self-assertion and for self-abasement, for imitativeness and for creative self-expression, for work and for leisure, for beauty and for practicability, for protection and for independence, for emotional security and for excitement, for superiority, for dominance, for status, for possession of children, for recognition, for achievement, for affection, for value, for ownership, for knowledge, for power, for prestige, for "value in general."

Principle 11: Principle of Maximizing (or "More With Lessing")

Given the historic conditions of scarcity relative to the insatiable needs and wants of people, the individual and organizational way of coping has been to maximize benefits available from nature and the production process while at the same time minimizing the cost of all input factors of production.

Or as textbook writers Katz and Kahn (p. 107) put it:

> The organization seeks to acquire more of the resources which will furnish energy for its activities to use these energies more efficiently in its productive output, and to improve the ratio of return to the organization for energy invested in its output. It is the principle behind the attempt to create favorable social con-

ditions for the organization in the external environment. It can be seen in the staff activities of research, planning and development by which the organization controls the future as well as the present. Also when it attempts to rationalize the past as in annual reports.

Perhaps Buckminster Fuller said it best: "More with Lessing."

Principle 12: Principle of Law of Entropy

The Second Law of Thermodynamics or the Law of Entropy states that thermodynamic degradation is irrevocable over time. The term was taken from physics where it refers to the theoretical measure of energy, such as steam, which cannot be transformed into mechanical work in a thermodynamic system. Applying it more generally as a form of degradation or erosion in general systems, entropy refers to the natural loss of information over time in such phenomena as a burned log that cannot be unburned or sand castles at the beach losing their shapes or ice sculptures melting in a warm room. To designate the opposite of entropy, the term negentropy was coined to mean the restoration of energy in some eroded systems. Since many situations call for a balance or equilibrium or homeostasis for their continuing functionality, the term fills a void.

All living systems suffer from depletion of resources that require renewal for continued operation. Capital equipment, tools, buildings all deteriorate and wear out and require replacement. Employees serve their time and move on or retire. Contracts, patents and copyrights expire. There are depletion and depreciation schedules and replacement reserves for most anticipated events. For those not anticipated losses or erosions there are contingency reserves.

In recent decades concern has been expressed about global warming trends and continuing pollution in many directions suggesting deterioration of the earth's environmental support systems for its six-plus billion people. Nature must have limits also and at some point suffer entropic deterioration. What can be done to arrest these conditions? What can you or the organizations you support do? Unlike the limited life of most earthly inventions, the corporation was granted life in perpetuity assuming it succeeds in well managing its affairs. Are these corporations doing enough to assure that their perpetuity will be there? Which organizational entity should assume leadership in this matter? Is it doing enough at this time?

Principle 13: Principle of Credibility Through Measurement (Or Principle of Show Me)

The products of physical science and engineering technologies have dominated contemporary living patterns because they have well-established rules of conservation that don't change over time. Their basic units of measurement are static. An inch is an inch now and tomorrow. An erg is an erg, a minute is 60 seconds, 90 degrees equals one quadrant, 6 feet equals a fathom and so on. Largely because of this, they have been able to build one technical success on another in an ever-compounding fashion.

The social sciences, fine arts, religion, government, business and other fields have yet to establish an acceptable unit to measure human behavior and it may be inherently impossible to do so. Consequently, they must all deal in secondary units such as dollars and units of product and these are not capable of as much mathematical induction and deduction.

To gain the acceptance of an idea outside of the quantifiable arena it is usually necessary to qualify it or somehow establish a consistent relationship between the idea and some fixed references or counterparts. In this technologically dominated age, authority can only be sustained with the support of objectively measured facts. The beliefs and opinions of the elite in matters of faith and opinion count only with the faithful and true believers. Provable fact and rules of evidence are more persuasive in practical matters.

To compensate for the lack of convincing superiority, many organizations rely on brand names, money-back guarantees, famous-person endorsements, and on-going public opinion polls and repetitive advertising to build customer and client loyalty. To prove his worth, the individual in society must show earned degrees from credible universities and have respected references on his resume. At least in competitive athletics there are quantitative records of past performances that the accomplished athlete may point to and capitalize on. The numbers validate his accomplishments.

In what other ways do individuals and organizations such as governments, religions, health-maintenance organizations, schools and businesses seek to establish credibility? What more could each do, both on the individual and organizational levels?

REFERENCES

Ciardi, John, "Manner of Speaking" (*Saturday Review*, September 24, 1966).

"America's Power Plants," *The Economist*, June 8, 1996, p.

Goals of Economic Life. Editor: Alfred Dudley Ward, J. M. Clark and others (New York: Harper, 1953).

Katz, Daniel and Kahn, Robert L., *The Social Psychology of Organizations* (New York: John Wiley and Sons, 1966). Reprinted by permission of John Wiley & Sons, Inc.

CHAPTER 15

More "Principling" on the Maccordion

Before resuming our exercises in applying selected principles to the Maccordion Format, it might be helpful to go back to a few earlier concepts of management and some principles introduced at the beginning of the twentieth century by an insufficiently appreciated French mining engineer, Henri Fayol. As the Managing Director of a mining and metallurgical company from 1888 to 1918, he presented his ideas in a book *(Administration Industrielle et Generale)*, which was translated in 1949 and given the title *General and Industrial Management*. Substitution of the term "management" for his use of "administration" was a source of dispute as it was argued that he was concerned only with industrial organizations. However, in his own preface he claims that

> the meaning which I have given to the word *administration* and which has been generally adopted, broadens considerably the field of administrative science. It embraces not only the public service but enterprises of every size and description, of every form and every purpose.

Since Fayol also studied the problems of state public services and lectured at the *Ecole Superior de la Guerre*, it is clear that his intention was to develop a general theory or concept for all types of organizations, thus providing a useful construct to apply to the Maccordion Format.

Universal Commandments for All Organizations

One of the first to appreciate and write about the powerful role of management in organizing and directing the factors of production that Alfred Marshall, the English economist had first consolidated, Fayol considered the following managerial activities as being universal to all organizations (p. xv):

1. To forecast and plan: "examining the future and drawing up the plan of action."
2. To organize: "building up the structure, material and human support of the undertaking."
3. To command: "maintaining activity among the personnel."
4. To coordinate: "binding together, unifying and harmonizing all activity and effort."
5. To control: "seeing that everything occurs in conformity with established rule and expressed command."

Following this list of functional requirements common to all organizations, Fayol identified his General Principles of Management as guidelines to be followed for their good execution (Fayol, pp. 19–42):

1. Division of work: specialization promotes expertise for greater efficiency.
2. Authority: the right for management to give orders and be judged by their effectiveness.
3. Discipline: considered essential for smooth operations and that good leadership will promote good followership.
4. Unity of command: orders to each worker should come from one boss to reduce conflict and promote unity.
5. Unity of direction: a single plan should guide each group of workers as multiple organizational goals confuse workers.
6. Subordination of individual interests to general interest as organizational goals are paramount and should not be compromised.
7. Remuneration: an important motivator even if no perfect system exists.
8. Centralization: an essential and natural consequence of large-scale organizations.
9. Scalar chain (line of authority): top to bottom for unity of direction but lateral communication permissible when open and known by management.

10. Order: material order is needed to minimize lost time and redundant handling of materials and the social order needed for teamwork can be achieved through organization and selection.
11. Equity: "a combination of kindliness and justice" should pervade.
12. Stability of tenure for personnel: needed to promote unity and reduce hiring and training expenses.
13. Initiative: encouraging widespread initiative brings zeal and energy to the job even if sometimes the "personal vanity" of managers must suffer.
14. *Esprit de corps*: teamwork is essential and management must encourage, coordinate and reward as appropriate without arousing latent jealousies.

Fayol on Principles

"This code of principles," Fayol wrote (pp. 41–42) "…is indispensable. Be it a case of commerce, industry, politics, religion, war, or philanthropy, in every concern there is a management function to be performed and for its performance there must be principles, that is to say acknowledged truths regarded as proven on which they rely."

Fayol then goes on to explain why these principles had to be added to the laws of the Decalogue and the Commandments of the Church (p. 42):

The explanation is this: the higher laws of religious or moral order envisage the individual only, or else interests which are not of this world, whereas management principles aim at the success of associations of individuals and the satisfying of economic interests. Given that the aim is different, it is not surprising that the means are not the same. There is no identity, so there is no contradiction. Without principles one is in darkness and chaos; interest, experience and proportion are still very handicapped, even with the best principles. The principle is the lighthouse fixing the bearings but it can only serve those who already know the way into port.

Fayol believed that planning for the future was so important that in 1916 he argued for a national plan for France to be produced by the government. Interestingly, the communist countries that have tried national plans since have not been able to make them work effectively. Which of his precepts might not have been followed or perhaps were poorly executed or overdone in the failed national plans?

Social Order and Social Control

Another scholar who has made fundamental contributions to our understanding of social organizations is sociologist Amatai Etzioni. One of his earlier concepts centered on the idea of variable compliance patterns among workers in widely varying organizational types and what managements could do to gain the level of compliance sought for their particular organizations. Through complicated control structures and bureaucratic routines, most organizations establish mazes of expected behavior patterns that employees are expected to honor. There are the hierarchy of authority, job descriptions, divisions of labor and clear-cut rewards and penalties by which each employee learns what is expected of him. There is also the degree of commitment and loyalty that each employee brings to the job. He argued that the more employees are committed, the less formal control mechanisms are needed.

Three Kinds of Power

Etzioni then identified three kinds of power: coercive, remunerative or utilitarian, and normative or identive. Coercive power rests on the application of physical force and is most suitable for organizations like penitentiaries, concentration camps and custodial mental wards. Remunerative or utilitarian power refers to the lure of financial reward to encourage compliance and is commonly the dominant control used in business. Normative or identive power uses such symbols as love, prestige or faith in a belief system to gain compliance from its membership. Religions, universities and voluntary associations rely on its influence.

Many variations can exist within the same class of organizations. Labor unions, Etzioni suggests, may use all three methods: underworld unions controlled by gangsters can rely on coercion and scare tactics; business unions can rely on wage increases and improved working conditions central to the remunerative method; while political unions might opt for ideological methods based on working class causes. Most organizations over time try to use all three influences to gain worker compliance to organizational objectives but usually emphasize one of the three. Emphases will usually differ at various hierarchical levels, with normative power more often used in the upper echelons and threats to remunerative punishments and/or coercive blandishments used at lower levels.

Etzioni then formed a matrix with different kinds of power on the vertical axis and different kinds of worker involvement on the horizontal axis (Pugh, Hickson and Hinings, pp. 30–35):

Diagram 6
The Power Matrix

Kinds of Power	Kinds of Organizational Involvement		
	Alienative	Calculative	Moral
Coercive	1	2	3
Remunerative	4	5	6
Normative	7	8	9

The Continuum of Organizational Morale

Employee commitment in any organization may range theoretically and in most cases practically from total spontaneous cooperation at the positive end through various stages of declining involvement to the worst possible conditions of malingering, promoting discord and even committing sabotage. Most organizations work with intermediate patterns of collective employee morale and most could stand considerable improvement.

Considering, however, that most employees bring their total bag of anxieties, frustrations, and fears along with their abilities, hopes and aspirations with them to the job, perhaps it is too much to hope for a cooperative seventh heaven. Managements must recruit and hire their new employees from the widest heterogeneous assortment of applicants and meld them into the collective working body, establish conditions and policies for the working environment and solve innumerable problems along the way. The matrix above includes the range of possible strategies to gain a higher degree of compliance to serve organizational goals.

Alienative involvement is at the extreme negative pole and suggests dysfunctional possibilities that warrant close observation. Convicts and prisoners of war are frequently alienated to the point of insurrection and coercive measures may be the only control possible. Those members of the organization possessing predominantly calculative involvement in the group affairs may tend to assess each situation from their personal viewpoint and lean mildly to the positive or negative side on various issues. This is the general condition for business relationships. Moral involvement in the organization's affairs suggests the likelihood of a more positive and cooperative posture in trying to achieve the organization's goals. Religious organizations, fraternal associations and hobby-related groups tend to benefit from this orientation.

Etzioni suggests that the most common forms of compliance found in organizations are the 1, 5 and 9 positions in the matrix. The pairs thus associated are coercive power and alienative behavior, remunerative power and calculative involvement, and normative power begetting moral involvement. Alternative emphases and combinations are always under experimentation and some succeed with some employees in most organizations. The format may be useful to all managers as a conceptual model within which to perceive how existing realities emerged from the past and work out new arrangements for possible improvements in the future.

Many other management specialists, analysts and scholars have made important contributions to knowledge now in the public domain about the role of organizations in society and about how they might be better managed. The basic purpose of this work, however, is to present the Maccordion overall format for the economy and society of the United States. For this reason we now return to the presentation of a few more general principles by which to deepen our understanding of the Maccordion Format. Partially stated before, but not as a principle, we return to a classification of goals that guides the whole concept.

Principle 14: Principle of Goal-Seeking and Goal-Measuring Behavior

Since means imply ends for rational man and his organizational means need guidance, goal statements provide it in different but complementary ways:

Constitutional goals at the individual level refer to enduring values acquired from a combination of family, religion and cultural inputs. Organizationally mandated constitutional goals are usually specified in originating charters. They are quite broad, rarely changed and usually have long-run implications.

Directional goals refer to unmeasurable and more general objectives that guide the entire structure-function design in the intended direction. As social vectors, they represent direction without magnitude.

Operational goals refer to specific, local, shorter-term and especially, measurable objectives.

A coherent, well-integrated set of goals is needed for every organization that wishes to perform well for multiple constituents. Indeed, the very process of setting and rethinking goals affects every facet of structure and function. Nevertheless, the higher managements of most organizations have resisted, perhaps unconsciously in some cases, facing directly the need of setting clear and measurable goals to which they themselves would be accountable. They have instituted goals and quotas in great detail at all subordinate levels but so far have successfully defended their own territories from the same discipline.

The Gap Between Achievement and Management Rewards

Peter Drucker, a long-time recognized guru of business management in the United States and proponent of business by objectives, sees the problem of building the new definition of management accountability into the American institutional structure as a major challenge (Drucker, p. 247):

> We need what a political scientist would call a constitution—provisions that spell out, as does the German company law, the duties and responsibilities of management and that clarify the respective rights of other groups, especially the shareholders.

Without managerial accountability by external audit experts, there is no real accountability and *good intentions* rather than *results achieved* frequently prevail to the detriment of all concerned. If business organizations that are the most competitive of all organizational types and have the most to gain refuse to implement workable accountability systems for their leadership roles, where do we turn?

Missing: The Original Check for Balance

Unfortunately, shareholders were effectively disenfranchised many decades ago, thus eliminating the built-in check and balance system and for which no replacement has been forthcoming. Organizational leadership does not have to campaign on its record as legislators do. Only retirement and provable corruption are causes to replace most executives in upper management echelons.

Do you see any forces at work in society that might combine to encourage major organizations to institute more accountability for leadership roles? Should the federal government devise a plan like Germany did to accomplish this? Until this major step is taken and widely implemented by the leaderships in all major organizations, the largest potential benefits accruing from the yearly compounding of higher achievements will be unfulfilled.

Might coalitions of activated retirement-fund or mutual-fund managements cooperate to apply positive pressure in this direction? The ninety-seven-billion-dollar California Public Employees' Retirement System has mounted a vigorous shareholder activism program and announced in 1996 its intentions to continue its corporate-governance program in Japan, the United Kingdom, France and Germany (*San Francisco Chronicle*, p. C2).

No doubt in time new and more broadly based alliances will be organized to formulate and promote more definite guidelines and/or parameters not only for the managerial accountability now lacking in many major organizations, but also to help structure more rational beneficiary participation among the various stakeholder claimants to organizational success: society at large, regional and local communities, employees, customers and clients, and stockholders. The prevailing concept of taking and giving "whatever the traffic will bear or accept" may face increasing modifications toward whatever levels in the future are perceived as "better balanced."

Principle 15: Principle of Distributed Effort

Learning (and many other activities) is more effective when the effort is evenly distributed over time rather than concentrated into intensive bursts of cram sessions. Given similar intellectual capacity, a student who crams may score as high on a given exam as the student who grinds it out on a regular study schedule. The difference in the two methods is that of "long-term effectiveness" in personalizing the knowledge and developing good work habits versus the deceptive "short-run efficiency" of minimizing one's involvement. The greater retentive value from the steady study of the former may be contrasted to the diploma orientation of the latter.

Crash programs such as sales blitzes and overtime production runs are common in most fields as means to elicit greater efforts to achieve operational goals that appear out of reach. Meeting deadlines and staying on schedule are important in the day-to-day operations. But the professional is the person who disciplines himself/herself to the rigors of daily effort while ALSO retaining the possibility but not the necessity of cramming. This is analogous to such historically based bromides as, "Don't put off until tomorrow what you can do today," and "You can't fatten the pig the day before the fair."

Principle 16: Principle of Concentrated Effort

The benefits of specializing for occupational success, departmentalizing an awkward organization, segmenting a heterogeneous market, cramming for an important meeting or test or even rushing the beau of your choice are widely acknowledged. Hyped-up situations encourage the flow of adrenaline and the super concentration necessary for winning results. Many facets of time, space, matter and energy are amenable to the persuasive heat of a concentrated or forced-draft approach.

Principle 17: Principle of Balanced Effort or Optimizing Tradeoffs

Elegantly conceptualized by Hegel in dialectical form as confronting thesis with its antithesis to produce a synthesis, managers and especially leaders must first find the proper frame of reference for their problematic situations. They must then perceive the correct existing and probable future situational tensions between and among a myriad of often polarized, usually ambiguous and generally confusing conditions before developing strategies and tactics that lean appropriately against current excesses and/or in the desired directions.

These paired dichotomies along or around which the tensions exist include the concepts of stability versus change, competition versus cooperation, unity versus diversity, convergence versus divergence, centralization versus decentralization, objectivity versus subjectivity, quantity versus quality, maximizing versus minimizing, mechanistic versus humanistic, fact versus value, means versus ends.

Evidence usually exists or can be found that current positions between one or more of these pairs of conditions are unsustainable at current levels and that one or more of the above polarized dimensions has been overextended. Personnel in some organizations may have experienced too much change too fast such that inefficiencies have begun to creep into production or delivery systems. Workers in another organization may collectively feel bored because there's too much stability or not enough change or excitement in their environment. Their reaction may be to slow down or get bored or start complaining. Finding, monitoring and maintaining the "right" balance between and among each pair of these guideline dichotomies is management's chief job.

Minimizing and maximizing are puristic and simplistic approaches not generally suitable for steady or long-run application in complex situations but are possible approaches for short-run catch-up situations along single dimensions. To maximize or minimize any specifics means to jeopardize or even destroy the sensitive balance of interdependent variables that altogether must be optimized for most successful or effective results. Overlooked too often in our pursuit of perfection in "hot" directions is the unifying concept of balance, homeostasis, equilibrium. Optimizing may be best achieved by maintaining all key variables within satisficing ranges.

Suboptimizing Versus Over-Optimizing

The countervailing principles of distributed effort and concentrated effort must still be used but combined effectively in ways that net a yield of the best short-run or long-term results for the time period specified.

An example on the individual level would be the contrast between workaholics under-playing and playboys under-working, both to their long-run detriment but short-run satisfaction. Each needs to introduce some of the other's overindulgence to create a better long-run balance.

An example on the collective level would be the contrast between *Gemeinschaft* and *Gesellschaft*: the social bonds of kinship, guild, community have lessened throughout the world as the rational, impersonal bonds of contract and exchange trading have taken over. Continuing specialization of function leads away from balanced self-sufficiency to physical, psychological, social and economic dependencies, each of which needs some form of relief or counterbalance to reestablish a more comfortable state of equilibrium.

Consider several pairs of the above identified dichotomies in relation to troublesome situations in which you are now involved. Has the balance overshifted in one direction or the other such that harmonious working relationships are strained? Might your department or team or family be overemphasizing some aspect of functioning such that a switch in the opposite direction might reinvigorate team spirit?

Principle 18: Principle of Successful Positioning

Whether one is aggressively seeking growth opportunities, positively avoiding involvement in any situation, seeking to marry the boss's son or daughter, or more characteristically, handling problems/opportunities as a hired hand, proper positioning among the major elements in the relevant environment is important.

There are two basic approaches, one tactical, one strategic or structural. The former involves becoming a competent situational opportunist capable of capitalizing on emergent opportunities by developing the ability to be in the right place at the right time with the right readiness to succeed. The latter involves becoming a structural fundamentalist capable of defending one's position or one's organization against expected and unexpected challenges.

Situational opportunism suggests sharp antennae and risk taking; structural fundamentalism suggests prudence and long-range planning. Both postures can be successful depending on the operational context and the apparent confidence of the operator. Both capabilities can be developed through habitually studying and relating one's personal and social experiences to relevant principles. Why be one dimensional when with thought and practice you can become two dimensional? You can improve your "good luck" and minimize your "bad luck" by personalizing this principle. Which way do you now lean? Analyze the current important contextual situations in your life in light of this principle and consider alternative behavior modes.

Principle 19: Principle of Insightful Understanding

Most of us "know" quite a lot but often fail to apply this knowledge usefully when the opportunity comes to apply that bit of knowledge in our lives. When this occurs it is clear that we do not "own" this special insight, that we have not yet "personalized" its meaning sufficiently to act on it. There is little value in the mere statement of a principle or any knowledge until it has been 1) thoroughly explained; 2) carefully illustrated; and 3) successfully and repeatedly applied in practice.

Thinking people can expect a deepening of insight over the years as ever fuller measures of understanding are appreciated. One's increasing ability to understand why events happen and reactions develop as they do is a combination of experiential and intellectual growth. It may continue even with no additional knowledge input simply by one's continuous mulling over pieces in the existing knowledge domain and putting two and two together in ever newer combinations. Some call it growing wisdom. As such, it is one of life's more satisfying pleasures.

Principle 20: Principle of Managerial Facilitation

Based on the principle of social facilitation, this principle states that action similar to the action of other members of a group is relatively easy, while contrary action is difficult even in routine or mundane matters. When the work environment becomes emotionally charged, contrary action becomes more difficult still. Managers and other group leaders should never underestimate the extent or potential of employee disaffection, for once a hard-to-detect critical mass of discontent has coalesced, formerly docile groups can become aroused and take on some psychological characteristics of the mob.

No matter how petty, all nonwork-related annoyances can easily be joined with real work-related grievances to fuel worker crusades that management too often labels "illogical" or "without merit." If unmitigated, this posturing can turn into a series of vicious actions leading to still further divisiveness, perpetuating and even institutionalizing the initial differences, however trivial.

Not sufficiently appreciated is the idea that worker cooperation is more readily forthcoming when an earned truce exists between and among all hierarchical levels. Without it, there are only various degrees of an armed truce, perfunctory performance and a correspondingly bigger need for management to increase productivity through ever larger doses of capital investment, research and organizational innovation.

Management's Biggest Mistake

Employees seek mainly that human respect accorded to partners in a common endeavor. Certainly there are stars on the team that command more attention and higher salaries, but the coaches, players and fans know that every player has a role to play and is important for overall success. To get caught up in the excessively structured logistical minutiae of officialdom to the point of denying employees the attention every person needs is management's biggest mistake. Specialized quality control can never replace positive worker involvement. The best kind of built-in quality control lies in the linkages of togetherness among employees. Sullen or bickering teams seldom win championships.

The growing size of many organizations usually leads to increasing specialization among workers to raise organizational efficiency but may prove to be partially self-defeating insofar as specialization increases the need for more or different kinds of integration and/or cooperation. Unless the important but intangible and unmeasurable need for increased integration is seen and properly addressed, worker morale will continue to decline. This is a roundabout way of stating that division of labor and integration are reciprocal principles that need dual recognition at the same time. But because the managerial thrust for greater efficiency is so strong, it frequently is implemented first and the need for greater integration is only addressed if at all when negative symptoms later become visible.

Thus, a case could be made that the larger the organization and the more specialized have become the work routines, the more time, effort and money management should spend to ameliorate matters that to all external appearances might be considered petty details. Reflect back on working conditions in organizations that you were involved with for illustrations of petty grievances becoming magnified into awkward confrontations with apparently dumbfounded management. How can this sensitivity to overall morale be communicated or taught?

Principle 21: Principle of Inflection-Point Myopia or Principle of "Contagious Means-itis"

Because experts in most fields must work with facts such as the quantity and quality of scarce resources to serve man's inexhaustible needs, most of their projections are understandably conservative if not pessimistic. However, this overemphasis on facts is why their predictions are often wrong. They are based on static conditions and miss the temporary buoyancy of group spirit rising to face a serious challenge. They are underestimating man's frequently observed but unpredictable ability to respond to incentives when under pressure or when positively motivated.

And when the collective adrenalin of a larger group flows freely, great odds can be overcome against sizeable obstacles.

This inflection-point shortsightedness is at least partially due to the lack of comprehensive overviews such as the Maccordion Format herein presented and the ever-creeping paralysis of increased specialization. Together, they frequently result in confusion between or even the transposing of means and ends such that the end becomes lost in fierce pursuit of the means. Untrained or sometimes naive observers interpret this intense activity favorably and adopt the same means as personal ends. Psychologists have a name for this stubborn adherence to prescribed means to achieve obsolete goals: goal displacement. Review incidents in your own life for illustrations of "means-itis."

Principle 22: Principle of the "Wow!" in Communication Design

The challenge to communicate the design of products and services is perhaps even larger than the challenge to communicate thoughts with words (Hench, pp. 27–28):

> That's the whole problem—to give form an identity, to make it say what you want it to say. Because there is a visual language. You have to distill a subject to its essence, to the point where you've eliminated contradictions and as many ambiguities as possible. That's something Walt Disney taught us. The first look, the big look, the "long shot" they call it in motion pictures, has got to be marvelous. You've got to feel Wow! Now the medium shot, you're getting closer, you're walking into it. It's got to substantiate that first impression, it can't contradict that. Then we come down to intimate details, something we can see or take hold of. They've got to reinforce all the others. You've got to still say Wow! The real secret of all three Disney parks is that attention to detail that substantiates those other first impressions. It's visual literacy.

Can you apply this concept to other products or services with which you are familiar? For example, Marshall McLuhan claimed that newspapers in Great Britain and the United States have long used the mosaic layout formula so as to dramatize the discontinuity and variety of news in daily life (Fabun, p. 6). How do you think that browsing on the Internet differs from browsing through a newspaper or magazine?

Principle 23: Principle of Perceptive Perception

Just as some people can discern differently colored patterns in a static color maze, others can perceive movement in a dynamic mosaic while others cannot. It is the gifted eye that can trace the pattern and rhythm of specific forces in a complex movement. A talented musician listening to a polyphonic piece can continue it in his imagination if the players suddenly stop. In a similar fashion, some talented and/or highly trained people have better "luck" in projecting curves and tracing the motions of parabola on ellipse in political and economic trends even to the stock market.

Is it intuition or something different that enables some people to project more accurately? How can people with these talents be identified? If it is a function associated with creative minds, is it trainable?

Principle 24: Principle of Innovative Association

Leaders and entrepreneurs of all kinds frequently achieve their positions by associating new combinations of input factors for competitive advantage. Intellectual leaders, however, are the diggers of thought association, as this quotation suggests (Rand, pp. 942-3):

> Reason is the faculty that perceives, identifies and integrates the material provided by his senses.... All thinking is a process of identification and integration. Man perceives a blob of color; by integrating the evidence of his sight and his touch, he learns to identify it as a solid object; he learns to identify the object as a table; he learns that the table is make of wood; he learns that the wood consists of cells, that the cells consist of molecules, that the molecules consist of atoms. All through this process, the work of his mind consists of answers to a single question: *What* is it?"

Intellectuals on the thought level succeed by researching into unexplored frontier areas to find new ideas, to verify assumed hypotheses, to develop interconnections and links among previously unconnected ideas. Applied intellectual thinkers then take these new pieces of the grand puzzle and relate them to their own intellectual specialties. Then eclectic browsers try to synthesize the multiple pieces into formats such as the Maccordion.

Innovators and inventors on the practical or applied level succeed by relating previously unrelated elements. One good description of innovation quoting E. G. Barnett (Fabun, p. 7) suggests that

> when innovation takes place, there is an intimate linkage or fusion of two or more elements that have not been previously joined in just this fashion, so that the result is a qualitatively distinct whole.... If we may use a biological analogy, an innovation is like a genetic cross or hybrid; it is totally different from either of its parents, but it resembles both of them in some respects. New products emerge in the economic realm through this process:

Let "A" be:

A^{n1}—a ball when rolling touches only a small part of its surface to the surface it rolls on;

A^{n2}—when a ball is enclosed in a socket, it can still roll but its movements can be controlled;

B^{n1}—when a dry surface is exposed to a wet medium, it will pick up a thin layer of the wet medium;

B^{n2}—when a wet surface is pressed against a dry surface, a portion of the wet will transfer to the dry;

If we combine $A^{n1} + A^{n2}$ with $B^{n1} + B^{n2}$ we get something new. What is it?

Can you identify other combinations of disparate parts joining together to form new thought or product or service? What are they? If you know other people more capable in this dimension, attempt to guess how or why or under what circumstances they seem able to generate these associations.

Principle 25: Principle of Sweating the Small Stuff

Leaders are often chosen because they appear to have that intangible called "vision." But unless they have proved their worth in the trenches of their callings, their leadership tenures may prove short lived as this quotation suggests (from advertisement for United Technologies as appeared in *The Wall Street Journal*, June 9, 1983, p. 28):

> Your true value to society comes when someone says, "Let me see your work." Your glib tongue may open a door or two and your artful use of the right fork may win an approving nod, but the real test of your work can be measured by the care you give to the job in front of you: a budget to plan; a solo to play; a report to draft; a leaky sink that needs fixing. Next time you write a memo, make sure you get all the facts straight. Pay attention to those details. *Sweat* the small stuff.

Again, we see the beneficial contrast and synergistic effects of polarized opposite characteristics as the tandem needed for realization of larger potentials on both individual and collective levels. Once more, it underscores the need for holistic modeling such as in the Maccordion Format that encompasses both kinds of abilities.

On which level of application do you feel more comfortable, that is, on being dependably good at "sweating" the small stuff at one extreme or looking good on the "impression" front while being just average or "so-so" to poor on details or results achieved? How can you improve in what you think is your weaker characteristic?

Principle 26: Principle of Getting Repotted

To be or not to be…repotted. That is the question too infrequently asked or acted on by managers and executives in overly comfortable work routines. The first step in a career plan is to get potted, that is, to have achieved that level of success that permits one a "breather," the opportunity to coast on previous accomplishments.

Despite allegations that ability automatically rises to its level of incompetence, much evidence points to many competent individuals becoming so "indispensable" in troublesome jobs that they are encouraged to stay put. Not just in staff jobs, these spots are not only in the management of office forces, purchasing, credit, traffic, but they are, in fact, everywhere.

By allowing ourselves to become potbound we lose the incentive, the momentum and in time the know-how to compete vigorously in fresh environments. To grow or not to grow in timely fashion according to our tastes and potentials is the real question. To do so requires being planted or replanted in environments that permit, encourage, even demand growth.

Thus, challenge becomes the primary ingredient in motivating and harnessing man's abilities. Walter Lippman is credited with the witticism that "…businessmen desire only as much competition as they cannot eliminate." Individuals too desire only as much challenge as they can comfortably handle. Society instituted antitrust legislation to ensure meaningful competition among business firms while business relies on incentives and promotions to challenge individual performance. So-called professionals are supposed to supply their own motivation.

To become successfully potted is not enough for the ambitious achiever, This person will aggressively manage his or her career through successive pottings and repottings until the fruit borne become conspicuous. Indeed, when another's potential has been achieved relatively more than most with commensurate ability, potbounded underachievers can only raise uneasy toasts to the successful "overachiever."

What sparks the desire for achievement? Is it competitiveness alone? Or perhaps competitiveness coupled with ability? Or ability that can't stand seeing opportunities go awasting? Or the search for adventure? Boredom? The restless but energized mind….

Principle 27: Principle of Relabeling the Spade

A recurring theme through all of recorded thought and history centers on the wisdom of calling a fig a fig or a spade a spade. From Aristophanes and Erasmus such frank discourse has been debated through the centuries between blunt truth and shifty guile. Tell men what they wish to hear if you want to be successful say the clever. Nay, say the candid confronters, the truth will out eventually so say it now and the sharper the better.

The debate is with us still and we are surrounded mainly by fanciful sugar-coated nostrums only occasionally relieved by fact-based messages as commercial interests continually put their best feet forward as depicted in arguable polarization by an unknown writer:

> But, really, there never has been too much mystery about human motivations in dealing with material objects. The basic motivations were described a long time ago in just four words—lust, sloth, greed and pride. These words describe rather well the reasons why people do things, and men have known them for thousands of years. In the advertising community these words are frowned on. They have a bad connotation, so they must be changed. Lust becomes the desire to be sexually attractive; it is her birthright. Sloth becomes the desire for leisure—for rest and recreation—and certainly all of us are entitled to that. Greed becomes the desire to enjoy the good things of this world. Why were they put here if not for us to enjoy? Pride, of course, becomes the desire for social status.

We have no way to measure the degree of relative deception over the centuries but with the rising levels of public education and media saturation, a case could be made that it may be less now than previously. Or it may only have changed in character to become more sophisticated to fit changing times and situations. And so the battle for patronage, for supremacy, for glory continues. *Caveat emptor* and may the devil take the hindmost seem to be the more persevering of all peace time battle cries. *En garde?*

Principle 28: Principle of Egregious Greed

The degree of control exercised *on the individual*, the organization and the society depends to a large extent on the collectively felt need in society for regulation of its different members. A society that perceives itself as relatively affluent will tend to be more casual and deliberative in imposing desirable controls while tolerating conspicuous inequities. A society perceiving itself to be struggling at survival levels will tend to be more strict and unilateral in imposing controls, however trivial or ineffective. The degree of control exercised *by the individual* and the organization on themselves will depend on the character of the individual and the character of the organization's leadership.

Just as some individual behavior is suspect, not all organizational behavior is good or healthy for society at large. Our forefathers had witnessed many earlier instances of the abuse of centralized power and took pains to design a comprehensive governing system with multiple checks and balances to control despotism in government. For other areas they relied on the concepts of social and public service, the power of the Golden Rule, professional ethics and competition in the marketplace. The emergence of a large middle class and the generally positive health of the society and economy at large attest to the wisdom of their original positions and subsequent governance.

However, in the more than two hundred years since our Constitution was written, the vigorous competitive dynamics and growth in all directions have stretched and altered the original frame of reference such that numerous situations were created in which the federal government followed by state and local governments found it necessary to intervene to "level the playing fields," or correct worsening imbalances in the public interest. Much of the discourse in public debate centers on the lobbying pros and cons of divisive issues focusing on special interests seeking to have emergent law bent favorably in their directions. The vast majority of these debates are being argued vigorously in open debate. A few, however, have so far escaped the scrutiny of such healthy open debate.

Reaching for the Brass Ring

One involves the runaway remuneration for top-level corporate executives who have either direct or indirect control over setting their own income levels. As in most occupational environments, most top-level executives are responsible if not modest individuals. However, in every group there are always a few more aggressive and bold operators who take unusual risks and reach aggressively for the brass ring. They capitalize personally on situational opportunities to feather their own nests well beyond the averages in their peer group and sometimes reach for the very top. They like being record setters. This competitive dynamic has also been observed in non-profit organizations as well, notably in church, charitable and educational institutions where the professional ethic and service to social groups are supposed to control.

Those passed over raise their eyebrows and wait for some cry of public outrage but the American public has been relatively well treated during the twentieth century and is quite content and tolerant. Even those investing in financial securities rarely read the detailed prospectuses or annual reports where some mention of executive salaries might be noted, but rarely their total remuneration aggregates. When little negative publicity occurs, they grow restless and uneasy in their secondary positions. Note that they are usually highly competitive and effective individuals or they wouldn't have achieved their eminent positions in the first place. And after all, if they've sacrificed their lives for this effort they can easily believe that they deserve to be "co-kings of the hill" or at least active in trying to replace the maverick(s) who displaced them.

A few indirect suggestions to friendlier members of the board of directors for the organization can start the catch-up-ball rolling to equalize the total incomes of those falling back. Actual salary levels may be kept in line but bonuses, stock options, insurance schemes and more generous retirement allowances can easily and more discreetly make up the difference. And who can quarrel with the decision since its total impact on total revenue or profit is such an insignificant amount statistically? Anyway, it'll probably be several months or years before some snooping reporter discovers it, if ever.

Note that it is not competition *per se* that is the root cause of this situation. Rather, it was the removal of the original check and balance power of the individual stockholder to have a significant collective voice through their boards of directors that permitted the unchallenged power grab. There may still be remedial hope, however, as the story has begun to attract more attention. The May 22, 1995, issue of *Forbes* magazine told the whole story on its cover with a few headlines: "800 Chief Executive Paychecks: Median Take $1.3 Million, Up 1%" followed by the main headline: "Pigging It Up: Corporate Managements Who Seduce Their Directors Into Submission." It should be acknowledged, however, that most corporate leaders who benefit far beyond their lavish living styles do invest their large surpluses somewhere in the world and often in their home countries, thus aiding the capital investment cycle.

Other Runaways...

A related question of overall fairness concerns the excessively generous severance payment to senior executives of an organization in the event of an unfriendly merger. Why should the top echelon be allowed to use its power and position to shelter its futures without equivalent protection for those in lower tiers? To see these plans being put in place in the midst of widespread layoffs and organizational downsizing suggests a willful arrogance that needs check and balance control.

A similar escalation in the salaries of professional athletes has taken place in the past twenty years. Having caught the fancy of a bored public seeking temporary excitement, franchise owners found they could raise admission prices yearly with no reduction of attendance. Throw in competitively increasing television revenues and merchandise endorsements, and the free-for-all began as the players' representatives (often lawyers) were smart enough to play the game to the hilt for the players (and their own) benefit. Fortunately, a little sanity has been restored and the professional leagues have resorted to overall franchise salary caps, which may in time put some ceiling on runaway salaries. No such income-containment caps appear in sight at this time for the corporate world.

The problem, of course, is various combinations of greed, lust and pride that seek power, money, recognition or whatever else is in short supply. Most of us are also afflicted with the same desires but lack the abilities and leverage to implement our aspirations. But we can unite to prevent others with those capabilities from using us to achieve their personal ends, especially if and when it so distorts "the equity balance" we seek.

Principle 29: Principle of Rotational Scapegoating

Depending on the degree of frustration with the status quo in society and the subsequent combativeness it produces, there is a need to reduce the tension generated by conflicting parties. The most common venting device is that of deflecting the heat elsewhere. Thus, business blames government and the unions blame business. The federal government has variously pointed to "big business," to various of its branches as the overly liberal or restrictive courts, the inconsistent or prejudicial law enforcement, to the lax military, or to the pandering press and even slack education. Only the organized churches and the general public have been spared.

Managements of our major institutions are about equally inept in defending the quality of their product when challenged abruptly "to shape up," or "play fair" or "to lay their cards on the table." Industry after industry has been challenged for some form of alleged surreptitious behavior against the public interest in recent decades: alcohol, asbestos, silicone implants and recently tobacco. Usually the press comes to the rescue in the inner pages and in fine print with their broader perspectives and deeper insights to diffuse the issues somewhat or at least correct overstatements "for the record."

Until the next round, that is, when the very same press initiates the new focus of heated attention on the front page and in bold letters. Negativity sells. Unfortunately, over time the public becomes accustomed to new and often lower levels of public morality as competition continues to be a two-edged sword.

In this way a free press not only supports itself by creating excitement, it also helps society to educate itself, helps to pass the ball of responsibility around, helps to reinforce major tenets of the social contract and helps to engineer progress by spotlighting and ultimately identifying and pursuing major abuses. On balance, the *fourth estate* has earned its spurs.

Principle 30: Principle of Selecting Best Qualified Leadership

Since organizational performance must rank next to our freedoms as a means to improve our standards and styles of living, it follows that selecting the best qualified persons for those top leadership roles is most important if that potential of organizational leverage is to be achieved. To be eligible for consideration to the higher leadership ranks of any large organization usually means that the candidate (male or female) possesses a winning combination composed of most but rarely all of the following characteristics:

1. Has "good" physical appearance with regular features. The taller the better if male. Wears clothing well, stays trim and is habitually and appropriately well-groomed.
2. Is highly competitive by nature but can alternate comfortably or graciously between "hard ball" or "soft ball" conditions as situations change.
3. Usually appears organized, calm and collected but can "rev up" emotionally and be persuasively articulate under pressure. Has proven work ethic, is results-oriented and has demonstrated adherence to basic principles.
4. Has comfortable marriage with healthy children, no hidden family scandal or buried skeletons. Silver-spoon heritage a decided plus. Has become involved in local community affairs.
5. Is technically competent in appropriate field with verifiable degrees or certificates for proof. Is generally aware of important national and international current realities and where the employing organization integrates into the bigger picture. Has or can quickly develop foreign language capabilities if needed.
6. Is generally well-liked among peers and relates easily with wide range of associates both above and below candidate's current level. Upper-scale facilitators desirable: golf, sailing, skiing or tennis.
7. Can alternate occasional "winning smile" with that sterner "commanding presence" as appropriate. Displays acceptable manners socially in dependable fashion. Commands respect.
8. Quick witted and jovial enough for playful repartee normally but can switch gears readily to write and/or deliver an inspiring or appropriately toned speech when needed to diverse audiences. Has occasional knack for "old boy" or "just between us girls" self-deprecatory stories.
9. Is normally considered by members of both sexes to be an honest and healthy extroverted and self-confident person with few "hangups."
10. Has achievement record to prove competence in previous positions where candidate was well regarded. Appears to have made no serious enemies, despite climbing over others.

Can you add more desirable characteristics for the ideal leadership candidate? Were you ever encouraged to develop some of these traits? Or do some of them just evolve in the normal course of events? Develop a rating scale for these characteristics and get some perspective on yourself and your associates by informally and confidentially playing "the success game."

These characteristics are listed in no particular order as each would receive a different ranking depending on current conditions and the organization involved. Outgoing management or the new leadership selection committee has the important task of matching the perceived talents and profiles of the candidates to the agreed-on specifications for the position(s).

Back-Room Politics

Because the matching of available talent to specifications sought is so important to the immediate and near-term success of the organization, "head-hunting" specialty firms have become central in the several-year-long process. Nevertheless, final selection decisions rest with the incumbent management of the hiring organization where variable degrees of subjectivity play an important role. The professional matchmakers can't divulge their many fascinating stories because of privileged and confidentiality arrangements. Conflict of interest stories must abound because not all departing leaders want their successors to look too much better than they have. Even though selection committees frequently bypass the judgment of the outgoing members, their influences may still be substantial. Well-respected departing leaders are frequently asked to accept honorary or emeritus part-time roles where their experience and mentorship potentials can be helpful.

Principle 31: Principle of Accountability

This principle requires that one deliver consistently in behavior and performance according to the accepted rules of conduct and measurable standards in effect both operationally in specific and applied fields as well as generally in meeting societal norms.

What goes in and gets mixed with other input ingredients going around in any operating system should result in products or services that are perceived to be somewhere in the acceptable range of predicted output expectations. This concept has almost universal application from education and government to health and business as well as in personal behavior among family and friends. When outputs differ substantially from expected and well-established norms, the deviant outputs are usually scrutinized carefully for unusual characteristics to explain, and then justify or condemn the deviation.

To measure efficiency or effectiveness over time in most fields of endeavor, ever more refined measures of input are tracked by ever more sophisticated techniques to measure ever more complex outputs. This process, fueled by the competitive rivalries currently existing in every segment throughout society, is variously dynamic and therefore somewhat unstable. This instability creates conditions for opportunistic adventurers to test the accountability of any existing system. By altering pre-existing conditions, even though only slightly in the short run, the drive for increased productivity or personal satisfaction changes the former accountability standards and permits the introduction or justification for deviant or exemplary performance.

Challenges to the generally accepted accountability norms occur daily in every sphere of activity. Both the frequency and seriousness of these challenges vary according to the society's relative position on the poorly perceived conformity-individualism spectrum. Given relatively open markets, a high level of competition and a period of accelerating individualism, it should not be surprising that existing standards have been challenged both more often and more seriously than in the recent past. The consequences are manifest: courts clogged with litigation, jails full, the divorce rate higher than ever, school grades highly inflated, rampant drug abuse. Clearly, the decline in the application of the principle of accountability has contributed to these worsening conditions. Hopefully, the full societal context as afforded by the Maccordion Format will provide clearer overall perspective and contribute to more recognition of the important role of accountability in the warp and woof of the societal fabric.

Principle 32: "Imperative of the Now" Principle

As suggested by James Michener (p. 343), this principle means "that an artist is obligated to wrestle with the problems of society as they arise—in his day—in the understandings of his own particular time." Surely, what applies to the artist in his work must apply to each of us in whatever career or vocation we earn our living. But look around! In most academic fields the emphasis is on the past, on the evolutionary development of current practices. In most industries and most governments, in most bureaucracies of all sorts, most behavior is carried out in traditional ways following obsolete patterns in many cases. Only in those leading institutions in each field are there leaders who see clearly enough and act strongly enough to cut the cake of custom and defy it with new breakthrough practices. It is hoped that holistic insight provided by *The Maccordion Format* will enable more leaders to act more decisively and more quickly while also energizing more followers to adopt more quickly, but also selectively, the recommendations of their leaders.

Principle 33: Principle of Focusing on Fundamentals

Whatever your occupational area or aspirational goals, identify their basic elements of structure and function and work to improve your understanding and skill in managing them. While maintaining an eagle's eye view of the superficial contemporary events and fads, try not to become overly absorbed in their daily rhythms. Our era of specialization and communication in all directions has created a potpourri of trivia around every activity to the point where we now have experts in every dimension thereof. Education with its increasing focus on passing tests at the expense of historical perspective and substantive content contributes to this wayward bias.

Social progress in the long run is achieved by increasing productivity through managerial and technological innovations initiated and engineered by basic thinkers and doers. Most of the daily excitement generated thereafter by the mass media is stirred by political and economic posturing interpreting man's quixotic behavior. Don't allow yourself to be seduced by the pervasiveness and triviality of this second-hand jostling and sparring for attention and position to claim a bigger share of the spoils. Instead, be a contributor to the enlargement process and observe the endless squalling with a wry smile.

Principle 34: Principle of Using the Biggest Mac

Persuaded that a balanced diet is desirable, many of us go out of our way to ingest appropriate doses of vitamins, minerals, protein, carbohydrates and selected fats to ensure good physical health. Some extend their concern to regular exercise.

We are not as aware of the need for balanced structure, community and meaning in our daily lives for good mental health as suggested by Alvin Toffler in *The Third Wave* (pp. 373–374). Nor are we aware of the need for an all-encompassing frame of reference to provide perspective and balance among these important elements.

Structure: (the "what") refers to the fixed points of reference that help organize daily life.
Shifting work/leisure patterns result in less organized behavior for many and uncomfortable periods of aimlessness for some. Women in the labor force outside the home and corporate juggling of capital/labor inputs have contributed elements of instability.

Community: (the "who") refers to the reciprocal sharing/caring that each of us needs for psychic togetherness. Many today feel lonely, cut off from the security and psychological warmth of family and close friends. Vicarious and indirect substitutes replace personal contact.

Meaning: (the "why") refers to satisfactions derived from contributing to worthwhile causes, productive work and the sense of progress or improving conditions in directions considered important to the individual. Increasing specialization in work/career/leisure plus lack of broadening perspectives have reduced the significance/meaning/fun derived from many activities thereby decreasing the level of intensity devoted to those activities.

The enlightened individual "...will seek to understand the manner in which the life of all is affected by the way he and his fellow workers are making a living. He will develop all the meaning there is in his work and go on to see to it that it has more and better meaning" (Hutchins, p. 16).

Escaping Reality

Frivolous substitutes abound to provide artificial satisfactions for basic deficiencies in structure, community and meaning: drugs, alcohol, television, pornography, overeating and under eating and exaggerated attention in many cases to pets, commercial sports and travel. The computer and its affiliated instrumentation promise to deliver us soon to paradise!

Blind optimism leads most to think they can juggle their intangible human needs effectively but life histories in retrospect reveal gross miscalculations. Better perspectives for the longer run are needed in addition to occupational training for the short run. Indeed, proper balance between short- and long-run perspectives is a life-long challenge. Just as a young child stumbles and loses his or her balance when unaware of objects in the immediate area, so too do our organizations and institutions also lose their balance and direction when they don't see everything in their larger environments.

In Conclusion

The Maccordion Format was designed to provide that holistic perspective now lacking in order:

1. To enable better comprehension of the interactive complexity of modern life and thereby make it more meaningful.
2. To help young individuals to identify just where their interests, talents and energies might best be focused for career participation in the continuing real-life drama.
3. To enable people to control and better direct their destinies and those of the organizations they support and thereby not become unknowing slaves to a demanding system they only partially understand.

Consult your Maccordion daily as you read or watch the current news-delivery system for the broader perspectives that can improve your judgment. As a life-long hobby, develop and refine new *principles* of your own that fit the environments in your life and are generally applicable. Be alert for incipient *dunciples* too and write them down with the disdain they deserve. Uphold the truth in all dimensions. Use the Maccordion Format to stretch your horizons, to transcend the orthodoxies of your vocational focus, to integrate the known components of the physical and supernatural worlds, to unify your visions of life in its entirety.

Play your Maccordion daily and become active in fixing whatever discordant notes you sense through seeing or hearing or touching or....

Refer to your Maccordion daily as you make those decisions large and small that affect the quality of life and the legacy you would like to leave to your successors.

REFERENCES

Barnett, E. G., *Innovation: The Basis of Cultural Change* (New York: McGraw-Hill Paperbacks, 1953) as quoted in Fabun, Don, *The Dynamics of Change* (Englewood Cliffs, New Jersey: Prentice-Hall, 1967).

"Calpers Goes Abroad" (*San Francisco Chronicle*, March 20, 1996, p. C2).

Drucker, Peter, *Managing for the Future* (New York: Truman Talley Books/Dutton, Penguin Books, 1992).

Fabun, Donald, *The Dynamics of Change* (Englewood Cliffs, New Jersey: Prentice-Hall, 1967).

Fayol, Henri, *General and Industrial Management* (London: Sir Isaac Pitman and Sons, Ltd., 1949). Translated by Constance Storrs with a foreword by L. Urwick, from the original *Administration Industrielle et Generale*, published by S.R.L. Dunod, 1916.

Hench, John, Senior Vice-President, WED Enterprises, collaborating with Walt Disney, in Daren Cure, "A Talk with John Hench," (*Disney News*, Winter 1982–1983).

Hutchins, Robert M., *The Great Conversation*, Volume I in the *Great Books of the Western World* (Chicago: Encyclopaedia Britannica, 1952).

Michener, James, *The Novel* (New York: Random House, 1991). Reprinted by permission of Random House, Inc.

Pugh, D. S., Hickson, D .J. Hinings, C. R., *Writers on Organization* (Harmondsworth, Middlesex, England, Great Britain: Penguin Books, 1971).

Rand, Ayn, *Atlas Shrugged* (New York: Signet Classic by The New American Library, 1957).

Toffler, Alvin, *The Third Wave* (New York: Bantam Books, 1981).

INDEX

A

Abraham 66
Academic American Encyclopedia 74
Academy in Athens 68
Achievement, means to 109
Addictions 293
Adler, Mortimer Jerome 7, 107
Adorno, Theodor 128
Aeschylus 62
Aesthetic Dimension, The 130
Affiiliationism 164
After Virtue 123
Against Method 124
Age of Pericles 61-62
    Antigone by Sophocles 62
    building of the Parthenon 62
    Delian League 62
    first production of Oedipus Rex 62
    history of Herodotus 62
    Medea by Euripides 62
    medicine of Hippocrates 62
    Phidias's statue of Athena Parthenos 62
    philosophy of Anaxagoras 62
    poetry of Pindar 62
    sculpture of Myron 62
    Thirty Years Peace 62
AIDS 25
Alice's Adventures in Wonderland 36
Allport, Gordon W. 202
America
    list of deficiencies xi-xii
America at Century's End 27
American Association of Fund Raising 209
American Hawaii Cruises 64
American Heritage Dictionary of the English Language 17
American Heritage Illustrated Encyclopedic Dictionary 17
American Reference Books Annual (ARBA) 23
American Telephone and Telegraph Company 222
American universities 30
Amtrac 223
Anatomy of the Soul, The 127
Anaxagoras 62
Animal worship 61. *See also* Zoolatry
Annual Register of Grant Support 210, 230
Anticipating the future, quotations on 135-136
Antigone 62
Apollonian 76
Apple's EWorld 222
Aquinas, St. Thomas 9, 69, 70, 127
Archimedes 77
Aristotle ix-x, 2, 18, 46, 69-70, 73, 119, 239, 248
    Politics 70, 119
Arrow, Kenneth 79
Art 130
Art
    competition in 232
    preserving works of 187-188
Artificial intelligence 97
As You Like It 97
Association of ideas 41
AT&T 222
Atkinson, J.J. 240
Augustine 9

B

Bacon, Francis 9, 18, 239
Bad as I wanna be 155
Barnett, E.G. 282
Bayes, Thomas 79, 96
Bayesian inference 96
Being and reality, quotations on 124-125
Being and Time 125
Bell, Clive 130
Benham, Martin 18
Bennett, William J. 27
Bentham, Jeremy 130, 240
Bernays, Edward L. 206
Bernoulli, Daniel and Jacob 79
Bernstein, Peter L. 78-79
Beyond Good and Evil 128
Blocks of institutions 48
Bok, Derek xi
Boredom 26
Bork, Robert 27
Boulding, Kenneth 256
Brahmanism 242
Braque 30
Browne 242
Buddhism 242
Bush, George 226
Business
    community-action programs 212-213
    destruction of the entrepreneur 219
    indirect role of 202-203
    monopoly 220
    popularity criteria 210-211
    social responsibility 204-205, 209-212
Business Organizations
    Executing Primary and Secondary Functions 199

C

Caesar, Augustus 103
Caesar, Julius 102, 103
Calder, Alexander 18
Calendar 101-104
    as frame of reference 102-103

Christian era 102
Gregorian calendar 102
Julian calendar 102
Muslim era 102
Olympiads of Greece 102
Roman era 102
days of the week 104
Greenwich Mean Time 104
naming of the months 103-104
restructuring of the months 103
reconstructing the calendar 103
Roman Republican calendar 103
California Corporations Code 180
California Franchise Tax Board 180
Campbell, Joseph 59
Cannon, W.B. 94
Cantillon, Richard 219
Capitalism 203-204
Cardano, Girolamo 79
Cardinal Richlieu 146
Cardinal virtues 69
Carey, Art 27
Carnap, Rudolf 121
Carter, Stephen L. 136
Chafe, William 33
Chain of Knowledge 108
Charity giving 213
Chaucer 18, 239
Check for balance 275-276
Childs, John 3
Christianity 242
Chronicle of Higher Education, The 32
Ciardi, John 264
Cicero 119, 238
Circle of Learning 107-108
Civil Investigation Administration (CIA) 263
Civil War 236
Classification systems 74-79
benefits of 75
deductive future 78-79
from inductive to basic deductive tools 77-78
Middle Ages 77
Renaissance 77
problem with 75
theoretical 75
Clinton, Bill 228
Clorox 212
Coca-Cola 211
Code of Hammurabi 65-66, 243
Cold War 154

Colgate University Catalog 12
Columbia Encyclopedia, The 102
Commons, John R. 132, 161
Compacts 222
Competition 189, 189-191
and religion 229
in education 225-227
Goals 2000 Program 226-227
weaknesses 227-228
in research 229-230
on the international level 233-234
pervasiveness of 234
role of 215-234
socializing and acculturating 217-218
destruction of the entrepreneur 219
government 220-221
in creating and preserving works of art 232
in orderly and equitable environment 221-222
in producing, distributing and consuming goods 218
in providing communicating and transporting service 222-223
in providing welfare and philanthropy 230-231
in serving health needs 228-229
monopoly 220
procreating and nurturing 215-216
providing community and fellowship 216-217
spectator excitement 224-225
Computer
networking 24-25
spreadsheets 15
Comte, Auguste 9, 114, 125
Concluding Unscientific Postscript 123
Conforming behavior and legal principles 243
Confucianism 242
Consequences, ends and goals, quotations on 132-133
Consilience: The Unity of Knowledge 28
Constitutional goals 274
Continuum of organizational morale 273-274
Copernicus, Nicolaus 102
Corporate Foundation Profiles 209

Corporate Giving Directory 212
Corruption, within organizations 263
Creativity, imagination and intuition, quotations 128-129
Critique of Pure Reason 128
Critique of the Gotha Program 120
Crystallizing Public Opinion 206
Cultural common denominators 49-50
Cultural gap 5-6
Culture 52-54

D
Dahrendorf 82
Dali, Salvador 18
Dayton-Hudson Company 212
de Casseres, Benjamin 239
de Fermat, Pierre 79
de Laplace, Marquis Pierre Simon 79
De Legibus 119
de Mere, Chevalier 79
de Moivre, Abraham 79
De Motu 119
de Spinoza, Benedict 69
De-valuing of America 27
Decision making
problem-centered researching 87-89
Democracy and Education 2, 8
Dennett, Daniel C. 129
Derber, Charles 27
Descartes, Rene 9, 124
Dewey, John 2-3, 8,-9, 112, 134
Dialogues 248
Dichotomies, conceptual 76-77
Dictionaries
American Heritage Dictionary of the English Language 17
American Heritage Illustrated Encyclopedic Dictionary 17
Dictionary of Philosophical Quotations, A 118
Oxford English Dictionary 17
Van Nostrand's Scientific Encyclopedia 17
Diderot 23
Dionysian 76
Directional goals 274
Disney, Walt 281
Drucker, Peter 275
Duke University 33
Dumbing Down: Essays on the Strip-Mining of American Culture 27

Dunciples 238, 245, 248
Durkheim 82

E

Early Greek philosophers 118-119
Eclecticism 70
Ecole Superior de la Guerre 269
Economist, The 136, 204, 233, 258
Education 1-5, 10-13, 33, 83, 147-149
   analysis and synthesis 83
   basics 3
   career paths 148
   competition in 225-227
   context in perspective 1-2
   costs of assisted social problems 27-28
   dawn of a new academic era 32-33
   discipline 26-27
   extensive 12
   failure of short-term fixes 28-31
      commentary about 29-31
   focus on specialization 84
   general
      major purposes of 17
   how learners learn 148
   how teachers learn 150-151
   jumblaya x-xi
   liberal 4-5, 11
      arguments for and against 4-5
   performance ix
   relationship between general and special 10
   use of x
   vocational 6
      arguments for and against 6
   voucher system 148
   weaknesses 227-228
Education and learning, quotations on 133-135
Education content ix-x
Eigen, Peter 208
800 Chief Executive Paychecks 287
Elbow Room: The Varieties of Free Will Worth Wanting 129
Eliot 30
Emerson, Ralph Waldo 239, 256
Encyclopaedia Britannica 23, 63, 73, 103, 105, 107, 109
Encyclopaedia Britannica, Macropaedia 102

Encyclopedia Americana 65, 67, 74, 102
Encyclopedia of Judaism 67
Encyclopedias. *See also* Dictionaries
   Encyclopaedia Britannica 23, 63, 73, 103, 105, 107, 109
   Encyclopedia Americana 65, 67, 74, 102
   Encyclopedia of American Agricultural History 23
   Encyclopedia of Electric Circuits 23
   Encyclopedia of Electrochemistry of the Elements 23
   Encyclopedia of Judaism 67
   Guide to Subject Encyclopedias and Dictionaries 23
   Harvard Encyclopedia of American Ethnic Groups 23
   Illustrated Encyclopedia of Aviation, The 23
   International Wildlife Encyclopedia, The 23
   Kirk-Othmer Encyclopedia of Chemical Technology 23
   Modern Encyclopedia of Russian and Soviet History, The 23
   New Encyclopedia of Sports 23

End of Philosophy, The 126
Enlightenment 30
Erikson, Erik 217
Essay Concerning Human Understanding, An 134
Essential Comte, The 126
Ethical Idealism: An Inquiry into the Nature and Function of Ideals 133
Ethics 132
Etzioni, Amatai 135, 176, 272
Euripides 2, 62
Evolution 31
Exodus, The 66, 67
Experience and Education 135
Explosion of ideas 104-105

F

Family Household Units Executing Primary and Secondary Functions 198
Family unit 200-202
Fayol, Henri 269-271
Federal Bureau of Investigation (FBI) 263
Feyerabend, Paul 124

Fichte, J.G. 133
Fisk, James 206
Five Percent Club 212
Forbes 143, 287
Forbes 500 listing 143
Formats vii, xii, 35-36, 55-71, 117-118. *See also* Models of society
   addressing dilemmas 45
   building blocks for 117-118
      Scientific Age 117-118
   business 144-145
   computer 37
   definition of vii, 35
   descriptive 141, 155
   early premonitions of 110-114
   educational 147-148
      U.S. Constitution 147
   emerging
      the balky struggle 101
   ever-bearing 79-80, 80
   functional requisites 155-156
   in history 55-71
      Canaanites 66
      from cave pictographs to early language 56
      from cuneiform to the alphabet 56-57
      from language to myth and magic 58-59
      Greeks 61-62
      Hawaiian 64
      mythology 59-60, 60-61
      original uses of languages 58
      Romans 62-63
      use of vowels 57-58
   master functions 156
   prescriptive 141-143, 156
   proscriptive 141, 151-152
   religious 145-147
      Edict of Nantes 146
      landing of the Mayflower 146
      management of 146-147
      role of 146
      U.S. Constitution 146
Formatting, from the simple to the complex 44-45
Fortune 211
Foucault, Michel 124
Foundations of Arithmetic, The 124
Frames of reference 36-37, 42, 55-56
   common 39
   in market research 97

objective 141-142
organizational 40-41
personal 37-39
subjective 141-142
Frege, Gottlob 123
French Louvre 65
Freud 7, 31
Full-circle thinking 263-264
Functional requirements,
  universal 270-271
*Fundamental Principles of the
  Metaphysic of Morals* 122
Funkhouser, Ray 136

G

Galileo 36, 79
Galton, Francis 79
Gandhi 236
Gates, Melinda French 33
Gauss, Carl Friedrick 79
Gay Science, The 121, 125, 128, 133
Gemeinschaft 76
General and Industrial Management 269
General Corporation Law of California 180
General Electric's Genie 222
General Mills 212
Genesis 66
Gesellschaft 76
Gestalt 76
Giddings, Franklin Henry 46
Glazer, William 183
Gleason, Philip 218
Goal displacement 281
Goals . . . 266
Goals 2000 Program 226-227
Golden Rule 242-243, 248
  other versions of 242-243
Goodman, Nelson 112, 130
Gould, Jay 206
Government 220-221
  central role of 157-158
Government and law,
  quotations on 119
Graham, Martha 30
Graunt, John 79
Great Books of the Western World, The 7, 107
Great Conversation, The 7, 10
Great Depression 209
Great Ideas, A Syntopicon, The 248
Great Ideas of the Western World, The 105
Greenwich Mean Time 104
Gregorian calendar 103
Gropius 30

Guide to Subject Encyclopedias and Dictionaries 23
Guiness Book of Records 190
Gutenberg, Johann 105

H

Hamilton, Walton H. 189, 218, 234
Hammurabi, King 65-66, 243
  Code of 65-66, 243
Hampden-Turner, Charles 62, 151
Hartshorn, Thomas C. 217
Harvard University xi
Hegel, Gorg Wilhelm Friedrich xiii, 69, 76, 113, 277
Heidegger, Martin 125, 126
Held, Virginia 113
Hench, John 281
Herodotus 62, 73
Hesiod 58, 62
  Theogeny 58
  Works and Days 58
Hewlett-Packard 211
Higher education xii-xiv, 29-31, 250
  blueprint for xii-xiii
Hippocrates 62
Hobbes, Thomas 119, 122, 132
Holmes, Justice O.W. 239
Holmes, Oliver Weldell 239
Homer 58
  Illiad 58
  Odyssey 58
Homosexual behavior 247
Honderich, Ted 123
Human ecology 51-53
Hume, David 111, 127
Hutchins, Robert Maynard 6-7, 107
  Great Books of the Western World 7
  Great Conversation, The 7
  Syntopicon 7

I

IBM–Sears Roebuck's Prodigy 222
Ideal model 75-76
Individualism
  extended 247-248
  road to 246-247
Individualism and conformity
  balance between 245-246
Individualized human structure 159
Information Please Almanac 180
Ingersoll, R.G. 239

Institutionalized superstructure 159
Institutio Oratoria 134
Intel 211
Internal Revenue Service 180, 209
International Institute for Management Development 233
Introduction to the Principles of Morals and Legislation, Collected Works 131
Isaac 66
Islam 242

J

Jacob 66
James, William 91
Jefferson, Thomas 1
Jesus Christ 102
Jewish history 66
John R. Commons, Legal Foundations of Capitalism 132
Johnson and Johnson 211
Joyce 30
Judaism 242
Julian calendar 102
Junior Achievement programs 213

K

Kant, Immanuel 111, 122, 128
Katz, Daniel and Kahn, Robert L. 259, 266, 268
Kenny, Anthony 126
Kierkegaard, Soren 123, 131
King Louis XIV 146
King, Martin Luther 236
Knight, Frank 79
Knowledge, compounding of 23-24
Kohn, Hans 217

L

Language 64
  as commercial product 97
Laws and principles, quotations on 130-132
Laws 65, 153
  Code of Hammurabi 65-66
  of Moses 66
  Ten Commandments 67
le Petit, Denys 102
Leadership positions,
  characteristics of 289
Lecky, W.E.H. 239
Leibnitz, Gottfried Wilhelm 129

Index • 299

Leinberger, Paul 27
Levi Strauss 211
Leviathan, English Works 119, 122, 132
Lewis, David 114
Liber de Ludo Aleae 79
Liberal education 4-5
   principle of depth 11
   principle of diversity 11
Life Without Father 27
Lilly, Eli 182
Lincoln, Abraham 236, 239
Lippman, Walter 47, 256, 284
Llewellyn, Emma C. and Audrey Hawthorn 50
Lobbying 153
Locke, John 9, 111, 134, 202, 239
Luther, Martin 239
Lydenberg, Steven D. 212

M

Mac I. *See* Maccordion Format
Maccordion Format xii-xiii, 159-178, 195-198
   applying principles to 253-268, 269-271
      emotional versus rational impacts 264-265
      encouraging the enabler 257-258
      gap between achievement and management rewards 275
      problem finding and problem solving 260-261
      product superiority 255-256
      reaching for the brass ring 286-287
      rotational recognition 254-255
      seeking a balance 265-266
      suboptimizing versus over-optimizing 278
      Universal Commandments for all organizations 270-271
   competition 189-191
   definition of xii
   designed to 293
   implementation of 179-191
      adaptation of 182
      executing the functions 184-185
      facilitating functions 186
      goals for achievement 185-186
      improving the status quo 186-187
      music 188
      nonprofit organizations 180-181
      organizational leadership 183-184
      organizing the organizations 179-180
      perceiving employable matches 181
      preserving works of art 187-188
   indirectly energizing 195-198
      business 202-203
      family unit 200-202
      filling a need 197
      hidden magic 196-197
      historical continuum 196
      special cases 198
   metamorphosis of Macro I into 159-178
      activities in the life cycle 167
      constitutional goals 167
      directional goals 170
      human structure 161-163
      negative directional goals 165
      operational goals 166, 170-172
      organizational goals 169, 169-170
      organizational superstructure 168
      positive directional goals 164-165
      synoptic overview 159-161
      triangulation dynamic 172
   principles of 235-252, 248-249
      accountability 290-291
      anticipatory holistic thinking 262
      balanced effort or optimizing tradeoffs 277
      cheapening the meaning 250-251
      communication design 281
      concentrated effort 276-277
      credibility through measurement 267-268
      dichotomous behavior 265
      distributed effort 276
      double-barreled thinking 261-262
      egregious greed 285-286
      emotional involvement 264
      evolution 240-241
      filtering process 241-242
      focusing on fundamentals 292
      getting repotted 284
      goal-seeking and goal-measuring behavior 274-275
      imperative of the now 291
      in academia 249-250
      inflection-point myopia 280-281
      innovative association 282-283
      insightful understanding 279
      Law of Entropy 267
      learning from historical perspective 256-257
      managerial facilitation 279
      maximizing 266-267
      optimizing output 254
      partnership of leadership 251
      perceptive perception 281-282
      progress and its enabling conditions 257
      relabeling the spade 284-285
      rotational scapegoating 288
      search for truth 236
      selecting best qualified leadership 288
      selecting the clear looking glass 260
      successful positioning 278-279
      sustained productivity over time 258-259
      sweating the small stuff 283
      systemic circularity 259-260
      technological challenges 251
      using the biggest mac 292-293
   purpose of xiv
   triangulation dynamic
      negative factors 178

what makes it work 188-189
Machiavelli, Nicolo 127
MacIntyre, Alasdair 122
MacIver, Robert M. 52
Man on His Nature 29
Management, mistakes by 280
Managerial activities, universal 270
Manifesto of the Communist Party 121
Man's nature
    commercial corruption 208
    the darker side 207-208
Marcuse, Herbert 130
Marketing Handbook 206
Markowitz, Harry 79
Marshall, Alfred 270
Marx, Karl 76, 90, 97, 120-121, 139, 219
Materialism 164
Mathematical symbols 78
Maxim, Legal 239
MCI 222
McKeon, Richard 51
McKinney, John C. 75
McLuhan, Marshall 281
Medea 62
Menzies, Kenneth 82
Merck Company 211-212
Merrill, Francis E. and H. Wentworth Eldredge 52
MGB (Master of Great Books) degree 7
Michener, James 291
Micklethwait, John and Adrian Woodridge 9
Microsoft 211
Middle East 5
Mill, John Stuart 10, 126
Mimima Moralia 129
Minnesota Mining and Manufacturing 211
Mirage Resorts 211
Models and systems, quotations on 120-121
Models of society vii-viii, 13-14, 45-48. *See also* Formats
    comprehensive descriptive integrating 149-150
    comprehensive, development of 81-83
    course-project assignment vii-viii
    definition of 91
    early organizing concepts 46-47
    equilibrium models, business use of 92-93
    functionalist models 94, 169
        business use of 96-97
        government use of 98
    holistic 13-15
    mathematical models 91
    Parsons, Talcott 13-14
        four-function paradigm 13
    proto mathematical models 91
    questionnaire 143-144
    search for basic 73-74
    speculative models 91
Mohammed 102
Money, Murder and the American Dream 27
Moral Dimension, Toward a New Economics, The 135
Morality and justice, quotations on 122-123
Mores 47
Moses 66
Motorola 211
Murdock 49
Music 188
Myron 62
Mythology 59-60, 60-61, 63
    Greek 62
    in early recorded history
        predynastic Egyptians 61
        Sumerian religion 60
Mythology, An Illustrated Encyclopedia 60, 62

N

Nachlass 125
National debt 210
National Education Goals Report, The 226
National Science Foundation 186
New Deal 231
New Deal II 231
New Encyclopaedia Britannica, The 57
New Essays on Human Understanding, Philosophical Writings 129
New Individualists: The Generation After the Organization Man 27
New Propaedia, The 107
Newman, John H. 240
News Corp's Delphi 222
Newton, Sir Isaac 36
Nichomachean Ethics 119
Nietzsche 76
    Apollonian 76
    Dionysian 76
Nietzsche, F.F. 239
Nietzsche, F.W. 239
Nietzsche, Friedrich 121, 123-124, 128-129, 133
1997 Index of Economic Freedom 220
Nixon, Richard viii
Nonprofit organizations 180-181
Nowell-Smith, P.H. 131
Nuclear capability 22

O

Odysseus 58
Oedipus Rex 62
Of Mind and Other Matters 130
Old Testament 66
Olympic games 190, 223
Open systems, characteristics 259
Operational goals 274
Oresteia 62
Organization of thought 41-42
Organizations
    matching functions and goals 192-193
Ouspensky, P.D. 111, 126
Outline of History, The 240
Outline of Knowledge 107, 109
Overregulation 245
    dunciple of brinkmanship 245
Ox 222
Oxford English Dictionary, The 17, 78, 190
Oxford University 9

P

Parsons, Talcott 13-14, 81-83, 94, 157
Pascal, Blaise 79
Pentateuch 66, 67
Perception and art, quotations on 129-130
Perspective 17-23, 293-294
    compounding of knowledge 23-24
    contemporary adaptations of 18
    definition of 17-18
    in daily life 18-19
    individual 19-21
        inside the box 19-21
        outside the box 21-22
    why needed 22-23
Phidias 62
Philosophy of the Inductive Sciences, The 29
Picasso 18, 30

Pictor, Fabius 62
Pigging It Up 287
Pindar 62
Pitzer College Catalog 12
Plant ecology concepts 50
Plato 2, 7, 68, 69, 118, 248
   Apology 68
   Crito 68
   Euthyphio 68
   Protagoras 68
   The Republic 68
Pledge of Allegiance to the United States of America 218
Points of reference 55
Politics, back-room 290
Pompilius, Numa 103
Pope Gregory XIII 102
Popenoe, David 27
Population growth 104-105
Portable Nietzsche, The 123
Power and will, quotations on 127-128
Power
   matrix 273
   three kinds 272-273
Power/Knowledge 124
Primal Law 240
Prince, The 127
Principle of association 41
Problems of the Self 132
Process and Reality 128
Procrustean solution (a.k.a. Golden Rule) 242-243
Procter and Gamble 211
Professors' research 151
Profit, pursuit of 145
Propaedia, The 105, 156
   other features 108
Protagoras 118
Protestant Ethic and the Spirit of Capitalism, The 133
Public relations 205-206
   as a marketing tool 205
   honey-combed deception 206
   robber baron era 205-206
Pythagoras 77
Pythagoreans 73, 102
Pythagorian Principle 77

Q

Quetelet, Lambert Adolphe Jacques 79
Quine, Willard V.O. 112
Quintilian, Marcus Fabius Quintilianus 133

R

Rand, Ayn 282
Recorde, Robert 77
Regan, William 92
Religion 145-147
   and competition 229
Renaissance 30
Republic 118
Rescher, Nicholas 133
Research, compeition in 229-230
Revolutionary War 236
Robber baron era 205-206
Robotizing 42-44
   of students 43-44
   of workers 42-43
Rockefeller, John D. 206
Rodman, Dennis 154
Roman Republican calendar 103
Romulus and Remus 63
Rorty, Richard 112
Rostov, W.W. 92
Rousseau, Jean-Jacques 120, 122, 127
Rubbermaid 211
Rubin, Robert 135

S

San Francisco Chronicle 153, 276
Satyagrapha 236
Schumpeter, Joseph A. 81, 219
Science and technology, quotations on 125-127
Science of Knowledge 133
Scientific Age 117
Scottish Enlightenment period 23
Second Discourse 122
Sequential symbolism 14
Shakespeare, William 18, 97
Shaw, George Bernard 239
Sheedy, Charles E. 67
Sherrington, Charles 29
Shils, Edward 83
Slouching Towards Gomorrah 27
Smith, Adam 120, 144, 196, 202
Snygg, Donald 266
Social and technological change 25-26
   acceleration of 25-26
Social Contract, The 120, 128
Social order and social control 272
Social prerequisites 51
Social problems 25, 27-28

Society xi-xii
   collective ix
   contemporary vii
   objective x
   problems of xi-xii
Sociological Perspectives 121
Sociology 48-50
Socrates 68, 118
Socrates-Plato-Aristotle immersion 70-71
Sophocles 62, 238
Soren Kierkegaard's Papirer 131
Spinoza, Benedict 119
Spinoza, Benjamin 110
Sprint 222
St. John's [College], Annapolis, Maryland 11
Stages of Economic Growth 92
Stages of Retail Development 92
Stanford University xiv, 13
Star Wars 4
State of the Nation, The xi-xii
State University of New York at Binghamton 32
Statistical Abstract of the United States 153, 222
Statute of Charitable Uses 187
Stephen L. Carter, *Voices of Authority* 136
Stevenson, R.L. 239
Stonehenge 102
Stravinsky 30
Structure and function 94-95
Summa Theologiae 127
Sumner, William Graham and Albert Galloway Keller 47-48, 54
Swarthmore College Bulletin, The 11
Syntopicon to the Great Books of the Western World, The 7, 105-107
   objectives of 106-107
   use of models in 109-110
System managers viii
System of Logic, A 126

T

Tautologies 93-94
Taxonomy 74
Teachers, curriculum content 150-151
Technology, global concerns 5-6
Ten Commandments 67, 71, 151, 242
Tertium Organum 126
Textbooks 24-25
Thatcher, Margaret 203
Theodosus I 190

Theogeny 62
Theory of Economic Development 219
Third New Science, The 120
Third Wave, The 92, 292
Thomas, Lewis 43
Thornton, John 27
Through the Looking Glass 36
TIC 222
Time-Warner 222
Toffler, Alvin 89-90, 92, 292
Tonnies, Ferdinand
  Gemeinschaft 76
  Gesellschaft 76
Tonniesm, Ferdinand 76
Topical road maps 105-106
Tough love 26-27
Tractatus Theologico-Politicus 119
Transparency International 208
Treatise of Human Nature, A 127
Triangulation dynamic 172-176
  for the educational organization 173
  for the organization 172
  Maccordion success 176
Trinity College at Duke 33
Triumvirate
  of goals 95-96
  triangulating among components of 96
Trojan War 58
Truth 237-238
  definition of 237
  dunciple of bullying 238
  quotations on 238-240
  stretching 237-238
Truth and logic, quotations on 123-124
Tucker, Bruce 27
Two Percent Club 212
Typological classification 73
Typology 74. *See also* Classification systems
Tyranny of Nonchalance—Whatever, The 154

U

U.S. Census Bureau 26, 163
U.S. Constitution 144-147, 153, 196, 218
  Bill of Rights 143, 152
  First Amendment 146
  Preamble 221

U.S. District Courts 153
U.S. House of Representatives 143
U.S. Senate 143
U.S. Steel Corporation 170
United Fund crusades 213
United Nations 14
United States of Incompetence, The 27
United Technologies 283
Unity of Science, The 121
Universal commandments for all organizations 270-271
University of California at Los Angeles 12
University of Chicago 6, 107
University of Notre Dame 67
University of San Francisco vii
Upstairs-downstairs syndrome 86-87

V

Values
  America at Century's End 27
  De-valuing of America 27
  Dumbing Down: Essays on the Strip-Mining of American Culture 27
  importance of 27
  Life Without Father 27
  Money, Murder and the American Dream 27
  New Individualists: The Generation After the Organization Man 27
  Slouching Towards Gomorrah 27
  United States of Incompetence, The 27
Van Nostrand's Scientific Encyclopedia 17, 74
Vanderbilt, Cornelius 206
Vico, Giambattista 120
Vietnam War viii, 246-247
Vindication of the Rights of Men, Works, A 134
Violence for Equality: Inquiries in Political Philosophy 123
Virginia Colony 162
VNR Concise Encyclopedia of Mathematics 78
Vocational education 6
Voices of Authority 135, 136
Von Neumann 79

W

Wall Street Journal, The 208, 220, 283
Wanderer and His Shadow, The 125
Ward, L.F. 207
Washburn, Katherine 27
Wealth of Nations 121, 144
Weber, Max 82, 121, 133
Webster's Third New International Dictionary 3, 91
Welfare 230-231
Wells, H.G. 240, 241
Western influence 22
  technology 5
  thought 5
Whetstone of Witte, The 78
Whewell, William 29
White, Leslie A. 52, 53, 95
Whitehead, Alfred North x-xi, xii, 9, 69, 71, 128
Will, George xiv, 154
Will to Power, The 130
Williams, Bernard 132
Wilson, Edward O. 28, 31-32, 136, 223
Wisdom of the Body 94
Wolfe, Alan 27
Wollstonecraft, Mary 134
Woolley, Leonard 56, 57
Works, III 131
World Almanac and Book of Facts 104
World Almanac of 1986, The 143
World Almanac, The 2, 163
World Bank 208
World Competitiveness Report 233
World Economic Forum 233
World War II 154, 203-204, 209, 212, 220, 231, 246
  post-era 25
World Wide Web 222
Wright, Frank Lloyd 30
Wynar, Bohdan S. 23

Y

Yale University School of Medicine 183
Yarnell, Steven M. 97

Z

Zoolatry 61
Zoroastrianism 242

Give the Gift of
THE MACCORDION FORMAT
to Your Friends and Colleagues

CHECK YOUR LEADING BOOKSTORE OR ORDER HERE

❏ **YES**, I want_____ copies of *The Maccordion Format* at $29.95 each, plus $4 shipping per book (California residents please add $2.47 sales tax per book). Canadian orders must be accompanied by a postal money order in U.S. funds. Allow 15 days for delivery.

My check or money order for $_____ is enclosed.

Name _____

Organization_____

Address _____

City/State/Zip_____

Phone _____

Please make your check payable and return to:
Pandemic Formats
703 Woodwren Court
Walnut Creek, CA 94595

Call your credit card order to: 925-930-7419
wjrear@worldnet.att.net